J. C. Frémont.

MEMOIR

OF

THE LIFE AND PUBLIC SERVICES

OF

JOHN CHARLES FREMONT,

INCLUDING AN ACCOUNT OF HIS EXPLORATIONS, DISCOVERIES AND ADVENTURES ON FIVE SUCCESSIVE EXPEDITIONS ACROSS THE NORTH AMERICAN CONTINENT; VOLUMINOUS SELECTIONS FROM HIS PRIVATE AND PUBLIC CORRESPONDENCE; HIS DEFENCE BEFORE THE COURT MARTIAL, AND FULL REPORTS OF HIS PRINCIPAL SPEECHES IN THE SENATE OF THE UNITED STATES.

BY JOHN BIGELOW.

WITH SPIRITED ILLUSTRATIONS, AND AN ACCURATE PORTRAIT ON STEEL.

NEW YORK:
DERBY & JACKSON, 119 NASSAU ST.
H. W. DERBY & CO., CINCINNATI.
1856.

W. H. Tinson, Stereotyper.

To

ALEXANDER VON HUMBOLDT,

THIS MEMOIR OF ONE WHOSE

GENIUS HE WAS AMONG THE FIRST TO DISCOVER AND ACKNOWLEDGE,

IS RESPECTFULLY INSCRIBED BY

THE AUTHOR.

PREFACE.

The engrossing and universal interest recently awakened, in the subject of this memoir, by the presentation of his name as a candidate for the Presidency, is the author's apology for the faults of hasty preparation, which appear in the following pages. He felt, however, that the public were more concerned with the matter than the manner of his work, and would pardon almost anything in its execution more readily than delay. Under this impression he has aimed at but two results—fullness and accuracy. He has endeavored to lay before the reader every event in the life of Col. Fremont, and the substance of every letter, report, or speech of a public character that he has written or made, having a tendency to enlighten the country in regard to his qualifications for the highest honors of the Republic. The author is not conscious of having suppressed anything that ought to have been revealed, or of having stated a single fact which he did not believe to be susceptible of proof. To escape the suspicions, however, to which a biography of a presidential candidate is necessarily exposed, he has uniformly given official documents and contemporary evidence of the events he records, whenever it was practicable, that his readers may have as little trouble as possible in adjusting the measure of allowance to be made for the partialities of political or personal friendship. A glance at the following pages will satisfy the most cursory observer that it is no mere eulogy, but a faithful record of the life of Colonel Fremont, prepared, if not with skill and elegance, at least with diligence and a conscientious regard for truth. He regrets that the brief time allowed for its preparation, and the pressure of engrossing professional duties have prevented his making it less unworthy of its subject.

CONTENTS.

PAGE

CHAPTER VI.

CHAPTER VII.

CHAPTER VIII.

CHAPTER IX.

CHAPTER X.

PAGE

CHAPTER XI.

CHAPTER XII.

CHAPTER XIII.

CHAPTER XIV.

CHAPTER XV.

CHAPTER XVI.

THE LIFE

OF

JOHN CHARLES FREMONT.

CHAPTER I.

PARENTAGE, BIRTH AND EDUCATION.

In the social disruptions of the French Revolution, many broken fortunes were replanted in America, and in the words of Chateaubriand, then himself a wanderer in our country, "the names of settlements in the United States became a touching record of the wrecks of European homes." What seemed then only an adverse stroke of fortune to those upon whom it fell, proved the establishment of many prosperous families—the seed scattered by the storm bearing a hundred fold on the rich soil of the New World.

During this time, a passenger ship bound to one of the French West Indian possessions, was taken by an English man-of-war on the eve of reaching her destination. The passengers, with the ship, were carried prisoners into one of the English islands, where they experienced the usual rigid treatment of prisoners of war in that day. Among them was a young Frenchman of the name of Fremont, from the neighborhood of Lyons, who was on his way to join an aunt in St. Domingo.

During his protracted captivity, M. Fremont eked out the scanty prison allowance by basket-making—a common resource among the prisoners—in which his superior taste soon enabled him to excel. Some skill in painting, too, procured him occasional employment in decorating ceilings with the frescoes which are common in the dwellings of the wealthier families of the tropics.

After some years' detention, he was finally liberated or escaped (the latter, it is believed), and in his endeavors to find his way homeward, finally arrived at Norfolk, Virginia. Being entirely without resource for the farther prosecution of his homeward voyage, he gave lessons in his native language to the citizens of Norfolk. He was a man of superior accomplishments and high breeding, spoke English fluently, and was a welcome guest in the best society of the city and State. He here became acquainted with, and afterwards married, the future mother of John Charles Fremont, Anne Beverley, one of the daughters of Col. Thomas Whiting, of Gloucester county, an orphan, and one of the most beautiful women of her day in the State of Virginia. This Colonel Whiting's father was the brother of Catharine Whiting, who was a grand aunt of George Washington.* In her commenced the connection by marriage of the Whitings of Virginia with the most illustrious family of this, or perhaps of any country; a connection subsequently drawn still closer by repeated matrimonial alliances.†

* Sparks's Washington, vol. i., 548 ; ib. vol. v., 268 ; ib. vol. vi., 296.

† In a brief sketch of his family descent, which General Washington furnished at the request of Sir Isaac Heard, in 1792, he says :

Colonel Whiting, Mrs. Fremont's father, was one of the most wealthy and prominent men of his day in Virginia; he was a leading member of the House of Burgesses, and during the Revolution was President of the Naval Board at Williamsburgh (then the seat of government), officially the most exalted position, at that time, in the Colony.* Prior to the revolution he had been king's attorney.

"Lawrence Washington, his eldest son (of John Washington, the founder of the family in this country) married Mildred Warner, daughter of Colonel Augustine Warner, of Gloucester county, by whom he had two sons, John and Augustine, and one daughter, named Mildred. He died in 1697, and was interred in the family vault at Bridge's Creek.

"John Washington, the eldest son of Lawrence and Mildred, married Catharine Whiting (sister of Colonel Thomas Whiting, the grandfather of Mrs. Fremont the elder) of Gloucester county, where he settled, died, and was buried. He had two sons, Warner and Henry, and three daughters, Mildred, Elizabeth, and Catharine, all of whom are dead.

"Warner Washington married first Elizabeth Macon, daughter of Col. William Macon, of New Kent county, by whom he had one son, who is now living, and bears the name of Warner. His second wife was Hannah, youngest daughter of the Honorable William Fairfax, by whom he left two sons and five daughters as follows, namely: Mildred, Hannah, Catharine, Elizabeth, Louisa, Fairfax and Whiting. The three eldest of the daughters are married, Mildred to —— Throckmorton, Hannah to —— Whiting, and Catharine to —— Nelson. After his second marriage he removed from Gloucester, and settled in Frederick county, where he died in 1791.

"Warner Washington, his son, married —— Whiting, of Gloucester, by whom he has many sons and daughters." * * *—*Sparks's Washington*, vol. i., p. 548.

* In Henning's Statutes at Large, vol. ix., we find the following ordinance in relation to this commission:

"MAY, 1776.—INTERREGNUM.

"*An ordinance for establishing a Board of Commissioners, to superintend and direct the Naval affairs of this Colony.*

"*Whereas*, the Naval preparations of this Colony will be carried on

He was also a man of large wealth. He owned the whole of the land lying between North River and Ware River, in Gloucester county. His prominence as the president of the Naval Board exposed him specially to the depredations of the English on the coast, notwithstanding which, when he died, he left eight separate estates to his eight surviving children, and thirty negroes with each.* The principal residence of the family was at Elmington.

with greater expedition and success if proper persons are appointed, whose business it shall be particularly to superintend and direct the same,

"*Be it therefore ordained, by the delegates of Virginia now in General Convention, and it is hereby ordained by the authority of the same*, That Thomas Whiting, John Hutchings, Champion Travis, Thomas Newton, Junior, and George Webb, Esquires, be, and are hereby appointed and declared a Board of Commissioners," &c., &c.

* The following is a copy of Col. Whiting's will. The estate was largely increased before the division took place:

WILL OF THOMAS WHITING, GRANDFATHER OF COL. FREMONT.

"In the name of God. Amen. I, Thomas Whiting, of the Parish of Abingdon, in the County of Gloucester, do make this my last will and testament, as followeth——— *Imprimis*, I desire all my just debts to be paid. I give to my son, Thomas Whiting, the land purchased of Jos. Devenport and Edward Howe, lying in Abington Parish and County aforesaid, containing about six hundred acres, more or less, to him and his heirs. I do give unto my said son, Thomas, the houses and lots I possess in Glostertown, to him and his heirs. I give unto my two sons, Henry Whiting and Horatio Whiting, and their heirs, my two plantations, lying in the Parish and County aforesaid, called and known by the names, Hackney and Rumford, including the land purchased of Wm. Sawyer, and the land purchased of Robert Coleman's estate, jointly with Col. Warner Lewis—equally to be divided between them. It is my wish and desire, that my wife, Eliza Whiting, take her dower of my lands in those divided to my sons, Henry and Horatio, and not in the land divided to my son Thomas; but if she should, then I give my son Thomas, in case

Col. Whiting also enjoyed the notable distinction of having held the infant George Washington in his arms, when he was baptized, an incident which, though

my wife should take her dower in his lands as aforesaid, his choice either to take the lands devised to his brothers as aforesaid, or of the lands before devised to him; and if he should make choice of the Hackney and Rumford, and the other lands therewith devised, and then in such a case, I give the lands devised to Thomas, to the said Henry and Horatio, equally to be divided between them and their heirs: in either case my son Thomas to have my houses and lots and Glostertown, subject to my wife's dower. I give unto my son, Thomas Whiting, and his heirs, thirty slaves, and that he may have my coachman, Porter, in his part, and boy Dunmore. I give to my daughter, Sarah Whiting, fifteen slaves to her and her heirs, and that she may have Peg, Sall's daughter, and also Harriet, in her part. I give unto my daughter, Catharine Whiting, and her heirs, fifteen slaves, and that she may have Frank, and Patt, and her children, in her part. I give unto my daughter, Eliza T. Whiting, fifteen slaves, to her and her heirs, and that she may have in her part, mulatto Kate and her four children—Dinah, Molly, Will, and Dennis—and as my wife will have her dower in all my slaves, I desire that she may have in her part—that is, in her dower—three slaves, to wit: the cook Hannah, Abigail, Agatha, Bob, Barnaby, Ailee, and her child, Porter; Amarillis, Nelson, Egine, Rachel, Sue, Hannah's son Will, Isabel, Lawrane, and Augustie. I give unto my five youngest children, Henry, Horatio, Susanna, Jane, and Ann Whiting, all the rest of my slaves—that is, exclusive of those before devised—and my wife's dower, to them and their heirs, equally to be divided between them, and after my said wife's death. I also give unto my said five youngest children, herein mentioned, the slaves she may hold as her dower aforesaid, and their increase to them and their heirs, equally to be divided between them and their representatives; and it is my desire in the division and allotment of my said slaves, that regard may be had to the ages and sexes of them, so as to make them as nearly equal in value, as may be agreeable to the bequest aforesaid. I give to my son Thomas, my gun, sword, books, and Hector; also a mare and colt formerly given him. I do appoint my friends, Charles M. Thurston, guardian to my son Thomas, and daughter Eliza; and do give unto the said Charles M. Thurston full power to sell and dispose of any part of my said son's estate, real and personal, if he shall judge it for my said son's interest and advantage so to do. I give

trifling perhaps in itself, serves to show the kind of relations subsisting between the two families.

He was married three times and had fifteen children, eight of whom survived him. His last wife, Elizabeth Sewall, by whom he had three of them, including Anne Beverley, afterwards the mother of Colonel Fremont, survived him, and married Samuel Carey, by whom she had four children.* Mr. Carey managed the estate so

unto my grandson, Thomas Hubard and his heirs, all the lands I have in Petsworth Parish, in the county aforesaid. All the rest of my estate, not heretofore devised, I give to be equally divided among all my children, to wit: Thomas, Henry, Horatio, Sarah, Catharine, Eliza T., Susanna, Jane, and Ann Whiting. Lastly, I appoint my beloved wife, Eliza Whiting, Executrix, and my friends, Charles M. Thurston, John Page of Rosewell, and Warner Lewis, jun., Executors of this my last will, hereby revoking all wills heretofore by me made. In witness whereof, I have hereunto set my hand and seal the 15th day of October, Anno Domini 1780.

"THOMAS WHITING."

"Signed, sealed, published, and declared by the testator as and for his last will, in presence of us,

RICHARD CARY,
JOHANNA DUNLAP,
ROBERT INNIS."

* This intermarriage with the Carys, established another marital connexion between the Whiting and the Washington families, a daughter of Col. Carey having married a son of Lord Fairfax, whose cousin's daughter married George Washington's brother, Lawrence.

This connexion lends interest to the following extract from a letter written by Washington to George Wm. Fairfax in 1778.

* * * * * * * *

"Lord Fairfax, as I have been told, after having been bowed down to the grave and in a manner shaken hands with death, is perfectly restored and enjoys his usual good health and as much vigor as falls to the lot of ninety. Miss Fairfax was upon the point of marriage in December last, with a relation of mine, a Mr. Whiting; but her ill health delayed it at that time and what has since happened I am not informed. Your nieces in Alexandria are both married; the elder to Mr. Herbert, the younger

improvidently that the children by the first marriage were ultimately compelled to resort to the courts for an account and apportionment of the property.*

to Mr. Harvey Whiting, son of Frank in Berkeley. Mrs. Carey, her son Col. Carey, Mr. Nicholas, Mrs. Ambler and their respective families were all well about two months ago. Miss Carey is married to Thomas Nelson, second son to the Secretary. * * * *

—*Sparks's Washington, vol. v. p.* 268.

* Among the records of the Superior Court of Chancery held in Richmond, June 13th, 1810, there is a petition and decree on file (one of the fruits we presume of the litigation referred to in the text), directing that the slave of which the said father Thomas Whiting died possessed or to which he was entitled, and the increase of the females, be divided and allotted to the several parties according to their respective rights," by commissioners named in the decree. The award of the commissioners, in itself a sufficiently curious document, runs as follows:

"In pursuance of the above annexed decree. We the subscribers being commissioners named therein, have this day divided the slaves belonging to the estate of Thomas Whiting deceased, which were produced to us by Robert Cowne, his executor, in the following manner, viz.:

"To John Lowry and Susanna his wife the negroes contained in lot No. 1. viz: Bob $400, Coxen $400, Aggy and child Lucy $380, Augusta and children Billey, Harriet, Agnes and Edmond, $820. Old Betty—and the estimated value of negroes sold by said Lowry about six years ago $455.

"To John C. Pryor, ad'm. of Henry Whiting deceased, the negroes contained in lot No. 2, viz.: Peter $400, Barnaba $333, Henry $300, Jane and children, Mary and an infant 10 months old, $465. Lucy and children Betty, Cate, Mariah, and a male infant, $730, Sarah $150, Joe $60, and old Frank $5.

"To John Pryor and Ann his wife the negroes contained in lot No. 3, viz.: Phil $400, Black Peter $400, Peggy $300, Hannah* and children Stirling and Salley $580, Billey $250. Eugene $230, and the estimated value of a negro sold by said Pryor about about two years ago $224, and to Morgan Tomkies, who it appears is entitled to the interest of Charles Grymes and Jane his wife, the negroes contained in lot No. 4,

* The slave Hannah mentioned in the above list was afterwards Colonel Fremont's nurse.

viz.: Frank $400, Black Phil $400, Nelly $300. Venus and children, Kitty, Daniel, Charles and Phil $830, Daniel $250. Alice $150, and Gardner Frank $160—and for reasons appearing to us lot No 4 is to pay lot No. 3 $21 50, to lot No. 2, $12 50, and to lot No. 1, 50 cents. It also appears to us after the above allotment was made, that Joe, in lot No. 2, was appraised to $160 instead of $60, wherefore it is directed, that lot No. 2, shall pay to the other lots the sum of $15 cash.

"Given from under our hands this 16th day of July, 1810.

ROBERT WEST.
JOHN HUGHES.
WM. K. PERRIN."

The following entries are taken from a fragment of the Abington church records, which are deposited at the Gloucester Court-house. They appear to give most of the important marriages and deaths in the family, for more than half a century, and they also furnish interesting evidence of the solicitude of Col. Whiting, to have all his slaves baptized.

1732, Major Peter Whiting, was buried February 28.
1735, Mary, the daughter of Francis Whiting, and his wife was born 20th April, and baptized 6th of May.
1738, Ann, the daughter of Mr. Beverley Whiting, and his wife was born December 22, and baptized January 12.
1742, Sally, Merit, Tony, Patt, to Whiting, baptized June 27.
1742, Catey to Mr. Whiting, born January.
1743, November, Betty to Mr. Brodr. Whiting.
1743, November, Betty, to Mr. Whiting born.
1744, Rob. to Mr. Beverley Whiting, born February.
1744, Sept. Chevr, Dfty. to Whiting, were baptized.
1744, Eliz. daugh. of Thomas and Eliz. Whiting, born Nov. 29.
1746, Anne, daugh. of Thos. and Eliz. Whiting, born August 22.
1747, Aggy, to Mr. Thomas Whiting, born February 26.
1747, Francis Whiting was married to Mrs. Frances Perrin, Jan. 24.
1749, Mrs. Elizabeth Whiting, departed this life April 20.
1749, Richard, male slave, to Mr. Thomas Whiting, baptized Oct. 15.
1749, Diana, slave to Mr. Thos. Whiting, baptized January 28.
1750, Esther, slave to Mr. Thomas Whiting, about 8 years old, baptized Aprll 8.
1751, Phill. slave to Thos. Whiting, baptized January 26.
1753, Grace, slave to Mr. Thomas Whiting, baptized September 9.

1754, Henry, slave to Capt. Thomas Whiting, 2 months old, baptized September 15.

1754, Nelley, slave to Mr. Beverley Whiting, baptized Oct. 13.

1755, Mr. Beverley Whiting, departed this life.

(leaf torn,) Thos. Whiting baptized Sept 7—(uncertain).

1756, Joe, slave to Capt. Thomas Whiting, born May 26, and baptized August 1,

1756, Frank, slave to Mrs. Whiting, in town, baptized August 15.

1756, Beverley, son of John and Mary Whiting, baptized Oct. 18.

1757, Frank, slave to Capt. Thos. Whiting, born April 1, baptized May 8.

1757, Jerry, slave to Capt. Thos. Whiting, baptized Sept. 25.

1758, Amey, " " " " " February 8.

Francis, " " " " April 16.

1758, Johnny, slave to Mrs. Whiting, Gloucestertown, baptized May 28.

1758, Else, slave to Capt. Thos. Whiting, baptized August 27.

1758, Beverley, son of Thomas and Eliz. Whiting, born March 10.

1758, Hannah, Frankey, slaves to Capt. Thos. Whiting, baptized April 1.

1759, Beverley, son of Capt. Thos. Whiting, died Oct. 28.

1759, William, son of Capt. Thomas Whiting, died October and was buried 24.

1759, A negro child belonging to Mrs. Whiting, in Gloucester, died December 3.

1776, Mingo, slave to Mr. John Whiting, died December 8.

1776, Rosse, slave to Col. Thos. Whiting, baptized December 29.

Buster, slave to John Whiting, died December 26.

1777, Cattie, slave to Col. Thomas Whiting, baptized January 25.

1777, Bristol, slave to John Whiting, died January.

1760, Amos, slave to Capt. Thomas Whiting, 8 months old, baptized June 1.

1760, Phill, slave to Mrs. Eliza Whiting, in town, 10 months old, baptized June 1.

1760, Robert, slave to Capt. Thomas Whiting, baptized Sept. 7.

1760, Frederic, at Mrs. Whiting's in Glen Town, died the last of Oct. and was buried 2d of Nov.

1761, Ben and Ned, slaves to Mrs. Whiting, in Gloucestertown, baptized March 22.

1761, William, slave to Thos. Whiting, baptized April 19.

1761, John, slave to Capt. Thos. Whiting, baptized May 24.

1761, Frank, slave to Capt. Thos. Whiting, baptized Nov. 1.

Anne Beverley, Mr. Fremont's mother, was but six months old when her father died. When her step-mother died, she went to reside with her sister Catherine, the wife of a Mr. Lowrey, one of the oldest families in Virginia, and the proprietor of the whole of Back River. This change of home was one of the results of the angry litigation which had been going on between the children of Thomas Whiting and Mr. Cary, in consequence of their ineffectual efforts to get from him their respective shares of their father's estate, and which had made Mr. Cary's house an unpleasant home for all who were interested in a distribution of the property.

Anne being the youngest, was most defenceless in the hands of Mr. Cary, and instead of being an heiress she found herself at an early age, almost dispossessed of a large proportion of the ample heritage which had been left her. When she had reached the age seventeen, her sister, Mrs. Lowry,* desiring to provide for her against what in those days and in that circle was deemed the greatest of all calamities, poverty, arranged a marriage for her with Major Pryor, also of Gloucester county, who was very rich and very gouty, and sixty-two years of age; just forty-five years her senior.

Aside from the fatal disparity of years, Major Pryor, lacked refinement and sensibility, and was in every respect repulsive to the young creature, who was sacrificed to him. Anne resisted the importunities of her

* Mrs. Lowrey is still living, and although eighty-five years of age, is in the enjoyment of good health and unimpaired faculties. Her first husband was a Lieutenant Stevenson of the Continental army, and a relative of Andrew Stevenson minister to England in 1836.

sister as long as she could, but finally, overcome by a sense of her homeless and dependent condition, which were constantly pressed upon her consideration, the despairing orphan yielded to her venerable suitor, and became Mrs. Major Pryor. Marriage only increased her regret for the sacrifice to which she had submitted. She became melancholy; shunned the gay society and habits of life to which her husband was addicted, and thus dragged out twelve long years of wedded misery. By this time, as they were childless, both had become convinced that the happiness of neither would be promoted by continuing to live longer together, and they separated. As both had influential friends, the legislature of the State, which happened to be in session, promptly sanctioned their separation, by passing an act of divorce. Not long after both married again, Mrs. Pryor to Mr. Fremont, and Major Pryor, in the 76th year of his age, to his housekeeper. This connexion of course gave great dissatisfaction to the Whitings, who were one of the most aristocratic families in Virginia, and could not understand how any person who earned his bread, especially by teaching, could be a gentleman. But Mrs. Pryor having taken their advice once, as to her first marriage, the folly of which she had expiated by many long years of gilded wretchedness, determined in this instance to act for herself, and to give her heart with her hand, to one whom she esteemed worthy of both. She had some means, and he had talents, and both had courage, and they did not feel called upon at the expense of their own happiness to spare that family pride, which had not spared the gentle orphan twelve years before, when she was helpless and dependent.

After their marriage, in the gratification of an interest which Mr. Fremont in common with most cultivated Europeans felt in the American Indians, and which the remnants of his wife's fortune enabled him to indulge, they travelled for several years in the Southern States, where large tracts of country were still occupied by the aboriginal tribes.

The means of communication in that country then were very rude, and they travelled as was the custom of the day, when means permitted, with their own carriage, horses, and servants, stopping where convenience of towns and dwellings required, and not unfrequently passing the night in Indian villages or by a camp-fire. It was during one of these excursions that they chanced to pass the night at the inn in Nashville where occurred the personal encounter between Gen. Jackson and Col. Benton—well remembered in that country—the balls from whose pistols passed through the rooms in which they happened to be sitting. And it was during a temporary halt at Savannah, in Georgia, in the progress of the same expedition, on the 21st of January, 1813, that Mrs. Fremont gave birth to their eldest child and son, John Charles Fremont, the subject of this memoir, who, with his father's name, seems to have inherited also his nomadic instincts.

The second child, a daughter, was born in Tennessee, and the youngest, a son, in Virginia ; shortly after which, Mr. Fremont's preparations to return to France were defeated by his death, which occurred in the year 1818. At this time, an elder brother, Francis was in Norfolk, with his family. He had emigrated early from St. Domingo. The loss of his eldest son, a boy of sixteen, who was killed by the bursting of a gun at a fourth of July celebration in Norfolk, saddened the place to him, and he returned with his family to France. He had been anxious to take with him his brother's family, and made it a point with his widow to accompany him. Her decided refusal to leave her own country, occasioned an alienation between them also, and she was left to herself with the usual defenceless lot and narrow circumstances which are not the most uncommon heritage of widows and orphans.

Of the brother's family, which returned to France, we have no knowledge, except of the recent death of a daughter named Cornelia, in a convent in South America. The widow, with her young family now removed permanently to Charleston, South Carolina.

At an early age the eldest boy, with whose future fortunes we are more particularly concerned, entered the law office of John W. Mitchell, Esq., one of the prominent citizens of Charleston. Here he gave such evidence of intelligence and industry as greatly to interest Mr. Mitchell, who found pleasure in directing the capacity he seemed to possess, and devoted many of his leisure hours to young Fremont's instruction. The lad's vigorous application required more time than Mr. Mitchell had at his disposal, and, in prosecution of the plan he had formed for him, he placed him under the instruction of Dr. John Roberton, a Scotch gentleman, who had been educated at Edinburgh, and who had established himself as a teacher, principally of ancient languages, at Charleston.

A brief but interesting memorial of this part of young Fremont's life from Dr. Roberton himself, who, though bending under the weight of some seventy winters, still continues in the faithful exercise of his profession at Philadelphia, is preserved in the preface to an excellent interlinear translation of Xenophon's Anabasis which was published by him some six years ago. In the course of it he refers especially to the intellectual and personal habits of Fremont, while under his charge, and commends them to his pupils, to whom the book is dedicated, as pre-eminently worthy of imitation.

"For your further encouragement," he says, "I will here relate a very remarkable instance of patient diligence and indomitable perseverance:

"In the year 1827, after I had returned to Charleston from Scotland, and my classes were going on, a very respectable lawyer came to my school, I think some time in the month of October, with a youth apparently about sixteen, or perhaps not so much (14), of middle size, graceful in manners, rather slender, but well formed, and upon the whole what I should call handsome; of a keen, piercing eye, and a noble forehead, seemingly the very seat of genius. The gentleman stated that he found him given to study, that he had been about three weeks learning the Latin rudiments, and (hoping, I suppose, to turn the youth's attention from the law to the ministry) had resolved to place him under my care for the purpose of learning Greek, Latin, and Mathematics, sufficient to enter Charleston College. I very gladly received him, for I immediately perceived he was no common youth, as intelligence beamed in his dark eye, and shone brightly on his countenance, indicating great ability, and an assurance of his future progress. I at once put him in the highest class, just beginning to read Cæsar's Commentaries, and although at first inferior, his prodigious memory and enthusiastic

COL. FREMONT'S ENCAMPMENT, ACCOMPANIED BY HIS WIFE, MRS. JESSIE FREMONT, NEAR THE PRESENT SITE OF LECOMPTE, IN KANSAS.

application soon enabled him to surpass the best. He began Greek at the same time and read with some who had been long at it, in which he also soon excelled. In short, in the space of one year he had with the class, and at odd hours he had with myself, read four books of Cæsar, Cornelius Nepos, Sallust, six books of Virgil, nearly all Horace, and two books of Livy; and in Greek, all Græca Minora, about the half of the first volume of Græca Majora, and four books of Homer's Iliad. And whatever he read, he retained. It seemed to me, in fact, as if he learned by mere intuition. I was myself utterly astonished, and at the same time delighted with his progress. I have hinted that he was designed for the church, but when I contemplated his bold, fearless disposition, his powerful inventive genius, his admiration of warlike exploits, and his love of heroic and adventurous deeds, I did not think it likely he would be a minister of the Gospel. He had not, however, the least appearance of any vice whatever. On the contrary, he was always the very pattern of virtue and modesty. I could not help loving him, so much did he captivate me by his gentlemanly conduct and extraordinary progress. It was easy to see that he would one day raise himself to eminence. Whilst under my instruction, I discovered his early genius for poetic composition in the following manner. When the Greek class read the account that Herodotus gives of the battle of Marathon, the bravery of Miltiades and his ten thousand Grecks raised his patriotic feelings to enthusiasm, and drew from him expressions which I thought were embodied, in a few days afterward, in some well-written verses in a Charleston paper, on that far-famed, unequal but successful conflict against tyranny and oppression; and suspecting my talented scholar to be the author, I went to his desk, and asked him if he did not write them; and hesitating at first, rather blushingly, he confessed he did. I then said, 'I knew you could do such things, and I suppose you have some such pieces by you, which I should like to see. Do bring them to me.' He consented, and in a day or two brought me a number, which I read with pleasure and admiration at the strong marks of genius stamped on all, but here and there requiring, as I thought, a very slight amendment.

"I had hired a mathematician to teach both him and myself (for I could not then teach that science), and in this he also made such wonderful progress, that at the end of one year he entered the Junior Class in Charleston College triumphantly, while others who had been studying for years and more, were obliged to take the Sophomore Class. About the end of the year 1828 I left Charleston, but I heard that he highly distinguished himself, and graduated in 1830. After that he taught mathematics for some time. His career afterwards has been one of heroic adventure, of hair-breadth escapes by flood and field, and of scientific explorations, which have made him world-wide renowned. In a letter I received from him very lately, he expresses his gratitude to me in the following words: '*I am very far from either forgetting you or neglecting you, or in any way losing the old regard I had for you. There is no time to which I go back with more pleasure than that spent with you, for there was no time so thoroughly well spent, and of anything I may have learned, I remember nothing so well, and so distinctly, as what I acquired with you.*' Here I cannot help saying that the merit was almost all his own. It is true that I encouraged and cheered him on, but if the soil into which I put the seeds of learning had not been of the richest quality, they would never have sprung up to a hundred fold in the full ear. Such, my young friends, is but an imperfect sketch of my once beloved and favorite pupil, now a senator, and who may yet rise to be at the head of this great and growing Republic. My prayer is that he may ever be opposed to war, injustice and oppression of every kind, a blessing to his country and an example of every noble virtue to the whole world."

At the age of sixteen young Fremont was "confirmed" in the Protestant Episcopal Church, in which faith his mother, who was a Protestant, had educated her children, and in which faith all his own children have been baptized.* About this time he became acquainted

* Colonel Fremont's religion having become the subject of some discussion, it may not be improper to give in this connection the following certificate of the baptism of his children, from the rector of the Church of the Epiphany at Washington City, showing that they were all baptized in the Episcopal Church.

"WASHINGTON CITY, *July* 12, 1856.

"The following children of J. Charles and Jessie Benton Fremont have been baptized in the church of the parish of the Epiphany, Washington, D.C.—their baptisms being recorded in the register of said parish:

"1848, Aug. 15, Elizabeth McDowell Benton Fremont.

"1848, Aug. 15, Benton Fremont.

"1853, Dec. 28, John Charles Fremont.

"1855, Aug. 1, Francis Preston Fremont.

"As none were baptized in a house, *but all were brought to the church*, the order of the Protestant Episcopal Church for 'the Ministration of Public Baptism of Infants,' was that which was used.

"J. W. FRENCH,

"*Rector of the parish of the Epiphany, Washington, D. C.*

Among the sponsors of these children were Col. Benton, Kit Carson, Capt. Lee. U.S.N., Francis P. Blair and Col. Fremont himself.

with a young West Indian girl, whose raven hair and soft black eyes interfered sadly with his studies. He was absent for days together from the college, and repeatedly arraigned and reprimanded by the faculty, but to no purpose. Taking counsel of his heart, and not of his head, he set college rules at defiance. The faculty bore with him for a long time on account of his high standing in his studies, good scholarship, and abundant promise; but at length, irritated with his insubordination and bad example, for which no explanation was given, they expelled him from the college.

His application, though interrupted, had been vigorous while it lasted, and his acquirements, especially in mathematics, had been remarkable. After this abrupt and perhaps unfortunate termination of his collegiate career, he engaged in teaching mathematics, principally to senior classes in different schools, and also took charge of the "Apprentices' Library," an evening school under a board of directors, of which Dr. Joseph Johnston was president. But his career as an instructor was destined soon to be interrupted by a succession of domestic calamities which exerted an important influence upon his character. It was about this time that the death of his sister, then in her seventeenth year, occurred. His brother, who possessed an ardent and enthusiastic temperament and unusual ability, when but fifteen years of age, in consequence of an association with amateur players, had his taste turned to the stage, on which he imagined that fame and fortune are of easy acquisition. With these ideas, full of the generous impulses which belonged to his age and character, he suddenly, and without consulting his family, left his home to work out his fortune for himself.

His brief life gave little space for the employment of

energies which might have realized his youthful expectations. A few years after this an injury received at a riot in Buffalo permanently affected his health, and he returned to his mother and died in Charleston, when he was little more than twenty years old.

The death of his sister and the departure of his brother made a harsh inroad on the domestic quiet of his family, and gave a sudden check to the careless and unreflecting habits which had hitherto marked the conduct of the youthful Fremont.

He now awoke to the sober interests of life, as circumstances brought him into ruder contact with them, and he devoted himself to earnest labor, which, since then, has never been intermitted.

CHAPTER II.

CHOOSES HIS PROFESSION—MARRIES JESSIE BENTON.

In 1833, the sloop of war Natchez entered the port of Charleston to enforce Gen. Jackson's proclamation against the Nullifiers. Being thence ordered on a cruise to South America, Fremont, then just twenty years of age, obtained through the Secretary of the Navy, Mr. Poinsett, the post of teacher of mathematics, and made in her, in that capacity, a cruise of some two and a half years' duration. Shortly after his return to Charleston, he received from the college, which had once expelled him—Dr. Adams being still its President—the degrees of Bachelor and Master of Arts.

A law had in the meantime been enacted creating Professorships of Mathematics in the Navy, and Fremont was one of a few among many candidates who successfully passed a rigorous examination before a board convened for this purpose at Baltimore, and was appointed to the frigate Independence. But he had in the meantime decided to labor in a profession which offered a larger field to energy and promised greater rewards, and for which his studies had particularly qualified him. He made his first essay as surveyor and railroad engineer in an examination for an improvement of the railway line between Charleston and Augusta.*

About this time a corps of engineers was organized under the direction of Capt. G. W. Williams, of the United States Topographical Engineers (killed in the battle of Monterey), and Gen. W. G. McNeill, for the purpose of making a preliminary survey of a route for a railway line from Charleston to Cincinnati, and Fremont was appointed one of the assistant engineers, charged with the exploration of the mountain passes between South Carolina and Tennessee, where he remained until the work was suspended in the fall of 1837.

The parties engaged in this work occasionally stopped at the farm-houses scattered through the mountains, but more frequently lived in camp, being provided with tents and all the necessary equipage for a camp life, of which this was Fremont's first experience. It was a country well calculated to make such first impressions durable and attractive—rough and wild, and abounding in those natural beauties which make the summer in that region particularly delightful.

He remained here until the suspension of the work. Capt. Williams being then ordered to make a military reconnoissance of the mountainous country comprehending portions of the States of Georgia, North Carolina and Tennessee, occupied at this time by the Cherokee Indians, Fremont accompanied him as one of his assistants. This was a winter survey—made hurriedly, in

* In after years, when the result of a court-martial had deprived Fremont of his commission in the army, he was offered the presidency of this railroad, with a salary of $5,000.

anticipation of hostilities already threatening with the Indians—and the surveyors at times were occupied, with a guide only, in making rapid reconnoissances on horseback, and at other times in slower operations, with a party of eight or ten men, with pack mules to carry their tents and provisions; it being a forest country, sparsely occupied by Indian farms. At night they felled trees, and made large fires of hickory logs, around which the panther's cry was occasionally heard, and owls hooted from the hemlocks. This was the first experience of a winter's campaign to one destined to go to the verge of human endurance in similar scenes. From this work, in the spring, he went directly to the Upper Mississippi, whence he set out on an exploring expedition over the northwestern prairies, under the command of J. N. Nicollet.

M. Nicollet was a French gentleman of distinction, a member of the Academy of Sciences, eminently distinguished for varied and extraordinary ability and for his scientific attainments, "whose early death," says Humboldt in his *Aspects of Nature*, "deprived science of one of her brightest ornaments." As a geographer, our northwestern country had for him a peculiar interest. It had been the field in which the earlier French discoverers and Catholic missionaries had labored, and it had been one of his most cherished wishes to visit the scenes of their labors and to draw together the scattered materials of a history which he thought redounded to the honor of his countrymen. With these views, and in the interest of geography, he had recently made an extended journey around the sources of the Mississippi, the map and materials of which had been adopted by our government, and he had been commissioned to make an examination of our almost unexplored northwestern region in continuation of his own labors.

Mr. Poinsett, then Secretary of War, remembered Fremont as a suitable person to co-operate in his work, and procured for him the appointment of principal assistant, in which capacity he accompanied M. Nicollet. during the years '38, and '39, in two separate explorations of the greater part of the region lying between the Missouri and the Upper Rivers, and extending north to the British line. During his absence, in '38, Fremont was appointed by Mr. Van Buren a second-lieutenant in the corps of topographical engineers which had been re-organized by General Jackson, who provided that half of the corps should be taken from the civil service. Fremont was one of the first who profited by this provision. After the return of these expeditions, more than a year was occupied in the reduction of their materials, with a map and report in illustration of them; and during this time Fremont resided with M. Nicollet and Mr. Hassler, then the head of the coast survey. In the familiar society and conversations of these two remarkable men he enjoyed the rare opportunity of a daily association with science in her most attractive guise. They were not men who had worked laboriously up, branch by branch, to obtain an incomplete knowledge of science; their genius had spread out its fields distinctly before them, and they had surveyed them from an eminence. They had invented new forms for the easier expression of scientific results, and new instruments to extend and apply them.

The natural result of such an intercourse was to give him confidence in his resources, and to inspire him with those enlarged views which have distinguished his subsequent career, and secured for him flattering attentions from the most eminent philosophers of his age.

Among the friendly and social relations formed at this time, which, perhaps, more than any other, influenced his future life, by identifying him most directly with the interests of the West, was his intimacy with the family of Mr. Benton, then senator from Missouri in whose second daughter, Jessie, then only fifteen, he became deeply interested. His suit was favorably entertained by the daughter, but not so by her parents.

To the marriage of their daughter with an officer, both Mr. and Mrs. Benton were decidedly opposed. Mr. Benton, because, in his judgment, the army was not a profession, only a salary during lifetime, throwing the widow upon the War Department, to which Mrs. Benton added the farther objection of her daughter's extreme youth. Both had the highest personal regard for Mr. Fremont, whom they had known well during the two winters previous, and but for these reasons, the marriage would have been, what it afterwards became, one entirely agreeable to them in every respect.

During the summer of 1841, and while the poor young officer was struggling as best he might with the obstacles which his suit had encountered, he received a mysterious but inexorable order to make an examination of the river Des Moines, upon the banks of which the Sacs and Fox Indians still had their homes, Iowa being at that time a frontier country. He sat out to the discharge of this duty with such spirits as he could command, finished it, and returned to Washington, when shortly after his return, and on the 19th October, 1841, the impatient lovers were married.

CHAPTER III.

FIRST EXPLORING EXPEDITION—EXPLORES THE SOUTH PASS—PLANTS THE AMERICAN FLAG ON THE HIGHEST PEAK OF THE ROCKY MOUNTAINS—SPEECH OF SENATOR LINN.

THE knowledge already acquired by Fremont of our northwestern territories was sufficient to reveal to him the utter ignorance upon the whole subject which prevailed generally among his countrymen. He discovered that pretty much all that was known about them was made up of travellers' tales over their camp-fires about fabulous rivers and mountains and lakes, which never had any existence except in the imagination of these frontier *raconteurs* and their too credulous listeners. As late as 1846, one of the earlier editions of a general map of the United States for the year in the Congressional library at Washington, regarded and quoted as an authority on the Oregon question that year, even by the President himself, with entire confidence, represented the great Salt Lake as discharging itself by three great rivers into the Pacific ocean—from its southern extremities into the Gulf of California—from its western side through the Sierra Nevada range into the bay of San Francisco, and from its western extremity into the embouchure of the Columbia river.* In his

* Humboldt, in his *Aspects of Nature*, p. 50, says: "The physical and

various explorations Fremont had already not only disabused his mind of many such absurdities as this, upon which public curiosity had been fed, but he had also become strongly impressed both with the feasibility and the necessity of an overland communication of some kind between the Atlantic and Pacific States. This became a leading idea with him in his subsequent explorations, to which we are about to direct our readers' attention, and remained at all times and in all situations one of his favorite dreams.

It was in 1842 that his first extended plan of geographical survey was projected, comprehending in its design the whole of our western territories lying between the Missouri and the Pacific ocean. His first step was the exploration of the northwestern frontier of the State of Missouri, terminating eastwardly with the Wind River peak of the Rocky Mountains, upon the highest of which, 13,000 feet above the ocean, he succeeded in planting the American flag, and to which he has given his name. Mr. Benton informs us* that when Lieut. Fremont applied for this employment, Col. Abert, the chief of the topographical corps, gave him an order to go to the frontier, beyond the Mississippi. "That order," adds the historian, "did not come up to his views. After receiving it he carried it back, and got it altered, and the Rocky Mountains inserted as an object of his exploration, and the South Pass in those

geognostical views entertained respecting the western part of North America have been rectified, in many respects, by the adventurous journey of Major Long, the excellent writings of his companion, Edward James, and more especially by the comprehensive observations of Captain Fremont.'

* Benton's Thirty Years' View, vol. ii., p. 478.

mountains named as a particular point to be examined, and its position fixed by him. It was through this pass that the Oregon emigration crossed the mountains, and the exploration of Lieut. Fremont had the double effect of fixing an important point in the line of the emigrants' travel, and giving them encouragement from the apparent interest which the government took in their enterprise. At the same time, the government, that is, the executive administration, knew nothing about it. The design was conceived by the young lieutenant: the order for its execution was obtained, upon solicitation, from his immediate chief—importing, of course, as to be done by his order, but an order which had its conception elsewhere."

Mr. Fremont left Washington, with his instructions, on the second day of May, 1842; completed his arrangements at Choteau's trading-house, a few miles beyond the western boundary of the State of Missouri, and set out upon his expedition on the 10th of June.

He had collected in the neighborhood of St. Louis twenty-one men, principally Creole and Canadian *voyagéurs*, who had become familiar with prairie life in the service of the fur companies in the Indian country. Mr. Charles Preuss, a native of Germany, was his assistant in the topographical part of the survey. L. Maxwell, of Kaskaskia, had been engaged as hunter, and Christopher Carson (more familiarly known, for his exploits in the mountains, as Kit Carson) was his guide. The persons engaged in St. Louis were: Clément Lambert, J. B. L'Esperance, J. B. Lefevre, Benjamin Potra, Louis Gouin, J. B. Dumes, Basil Lajeunesse, François Tessier, Benjamin Cadotte, Joseph Clément, Daniel Simonds, Leonard Benoit, Michel Morly, Bap tiste Bernier, Honoré Ayot, François Latulippe, François Badeau, Louis Ménard, Joseph Ruelle, Moïse Chardonnais, Auguste Janisse, Raphael Proue.

In addition to these, Henry Brant, son of Colonel J. B. Brant, of St. Louis, a young man of nineteen years of age, and Randolph, a lively boy of twelve, son of the Hon. Thomas H. Benton, accompanied him. All were well armed and mounted, with the exception of eight men, who conducted as many carts, in which were packed the stores, with the baggage and instruments, and which were each drawn by two mules. A few loose horses, and four oxen, which had been added to the stock of provisions, completed the train. The day on which they set out happened to be Friday—a circumstance which his men did not fail to remember and recall during the hardships and vexations of the ensuing journey.

For a detailed account of the romantic incidents of this expedition, of its hazards, privations, and achievements; of its geographical and scientific results, which have received repeated acknowledgment from the most distinguished sources, the reader is referred to the official report, of which several editions have been published in addition to the one printed by Congress for the use of the government. We shall content ourselves with a few extracts which will best serve to illustrate some of the more striking points in Col. Fremont's character. His journey lay along the bed of Platte River, through what has since become famous as the South Pass, which he first explored; thence north, to the Wind River peak of the Rocky Mountains, which he first ascended, and to which he has given his name; and thence home by way of the Loup fork of the Platte River. When the party arrived on their way out, at Fort Laramie on the 12th of July, they found a bad state of feeling had grown up between the Cheyennes and Sioux Indians on the one hand, and the whites on the other, in consequence of an unfortunate engagement which had recently occurred, in which the Indians had lost eight or ten warriors. Some eight hundred Indian lodges were ascertained to be in motion against the whites, and great alarm had been inspired by the intelligence received of their movements. What followed, we have thought of sufficient interest to quote at length in Col. Fremont's own words:

"Thus it would appear that the country was swarming with scattered war-parties; and when I heard, during the day, the various contradictory and exaggerated rumors which were incessantly repeated to them, I was not surprised that so much alarm prevailed among my men. Carson, one of the best and most experienced mountaineers, fully supported the opinion given by Bridger of the dangerous state of the country, and openly expressed his conviction that we could not escape without some sharp encounters with the Indians. In addition to this, he made his will; and among the circumstances which were constantly occurring to increase their alarm, this was the most unfortunate; and I found that a number of my party had become so much intimidated that they had requested to be discharged at this place. I dined to-day at Fort Platte, which has been mentioned as the junction of Laramie River with the Nebraska. Here I heard a confirmation of the statements given above. The party of warriors, which had started a few days since on the trail of the emigrants, was expected back in fourteen days, to join the village with which their families and the old men had remained. The arrival of the latter was hourly expected, and some Indians had just come in who had left them on the Laramie fork, about twenty miles above. Mr. Bissonette, one of the traders belonging to Fort Platte, urged the propriety of taking with me an interpreter and two or three old men of the village; in which case, he thought there would be little or no hazard in encountering any of the war-parties. The principal danger was in being attacked before they should know who we were.

"They had a confused idea of the numbers and power of our people, and dreaded to bring upon themselves the military force of the United States. This gentleman, who spoke the language fluently, offered his services to accompany me so far as the Red Buttes. He was desirous to join the large party on its return, for purposes of trade, and it would suit his views, as well as my own, to go with us to the Buttes; beyond which point it would be impossible to prevail on the Sioux to venture, on account of their fear of the Crows. From Fort Laramie to the Red Buttes, by the ordinary road, is one hundred and thirty-five miles; and, though only on the threshold of danger, it seemed better to secure the services of an interpreter for the partial distance, than to have none at all.

"So far as frequent interruption from the Indians would allow, we occupied ourselves in making some astronomical calculations, and bringing up the general map to this stage of our journey; but the tent was generally occupied by a succession of our ceremonious visitors. Some came for presents, and others for information of our object in coming to the country; now and then, one would dart up to the tent on horseback, jerk off his trappings, and stand silently at the door, holding his horse by the halter, signifying his desire to trade. Occasionally a savage would stalk in with an invitation to a feast of honor, a dog feast, and deliberately sit down and wait quietly until I was ready to accompany him. I went to one; the women and children were sitting outside the lodge, and we took our seats on buffalo robes spread around. The dog was in a large pot over the fire, in the middle of the lodge, and immediately on our arrival was dished up in large wooden bowls, one of which was handed to each. The flesh appeared very glutinous, with something of the flavor and appearance of mutton. Feeling something move behind me, I looked round, and found that I had taken my seat among a litter of fat young puppies. Had I been nice in such matters, the prejudices of civilization might have interfered with my tranquillity; but fortunately, I am not of delicate nerves, and continued to empty my platter.

"The weather was cloudy at evening, with a moderate south wind, and the thermometer, at six o'clock, 85 degrees. I was disappointed in my hope of obtaining an observation of an occultation, which took place about midnight. The moon brought with her heavy banks of clouds, through which she scarcely made her appearance during the night.

"The morning of the 18th was cloudy and calm, the thermometer, at six o'clock, 64 degrees. About nine o'clock, with a moderate wind from the west, a storm of rain came on, accompanied by sharp thunder and lightning, which lasted about an hour. During the day the expected village arrived, consisting principally old men, women, and children. They had a considerable number of horses and large troops of dogs. Their lodges were pitched near the fort, and our camp was constantly crowded with Indians of all sizes, from morning until night; at which time some of the soldiers generally came to drive them all off to the village. My tent was the only place which they respected. Here only came the chiefs and men of distinction, and generally one of them remained to drive away the women and children. The numerous strange instruments, applied to still stranger uses, excited awe and admiration among them, and those which I used in talking with the sun and stars they looked upon with special reverence, as mysterious things of 'great medicine.' Of the three barometers which I had brought with me thus far successfully, I found that two were out of order, and spent the greater part of the 19th in repairing them—an operation of no small difficulty in the midst of the incessant interruptions to which I was subjected. We had the misfortune to break here a large thermometer graduated to show fifths of a degree, which

I used to ascertain the temperature of boiling water, and with which I had promised myself some interesting experiments in the mountains. We had but one remaining, on which the graduation extended sufficiently high; and this was too small for exact observations.

"During our stay here, the men had been engaged in making numerous repairs, arranging pack-saddles, and otherwise preparing for the chances of a rough road and mountain travel. All things of this nature being ready, I gathered them around me in the evening, and told them that 'I had determined to proceed the next day.' They were all well armed. I had engaged the service of Mr. Bissonette as interpreter, and had taken every means possible in the circumstances to ensure our safety. In the rumors we had heard, I believed that there was much exaggeration, and then they were men accustomed to this kind of life and to the country; and that these were the dangers of every day occurrence, and to be expected in the ordinary course of their service. They had heard of the unsettled condition of the country before leaving St. Louis, and therefore could not make it a reason for breaking their engagements. Still, I was unwilling to take with me, on a service of some certain danger, men on whom I could not rely; and as I had understood that there were some among them who were disposed to cowardice, and anxious to return, they had but to come forward at once, and state their desire, and they would be discharged with the amount due to them for the time they had served. To their honor be it said, there was but one among them who had the face to come forward and avail himself of the permission. I asked him some few questions, in order to expose him to the ridicule of the men, and let him go. The day after our departure, he engaged himself to one of the forts, and set off with a party to the Upper Missouri.

"I did not think that the situation of the country justified me in taking our young companions, Messrs. Brant and Benton, along with us. In case of misfortune, it would have been thought, at the least, an act of great imprudence; and, therefore, though reluctantly, I determined to leave them. Randolph had been the life of the camp, and the '*petit garçon*' was much regretted by the men, to whom his buoyant spirits had afforded great amusement. They all, however, agreed in the propriety of leaving him at the fort, because, as they said, he might cost the lives of some of the men in a fight with the Indians.

"*July* 21.—A portion of our baggage, with our field notes and observations, and several instruments, were left at the fort. One of the gentlemen, Mr. Galpin, took charge of a barometer, which he engaged to observe during my absence; and I entrusted to Randolph, by way of occupation, the regular winding up of two of my chronometers, which were among the instruments left. Our observations showed that the chronometer which I retained for the continuation of our voyage, had preserved its rate in a most satisfactory manner. As deduced from it, the longitude of Fort Laramie is 7 hours 01 minutes 21 seconds, and from lunar distance, 7 hours 01 minutes 29 seconds—giving for the adopted longitude 104 degrees 47 minutes 48 seconds. Comparing the barometical observation made during our stay here, with those of Dr. G. Engleman, at St. Louis, we find for the elevation of the fort above the Gulf of Mexico, 4,470 feet. The winter climate here is remarkably mild for the latitude; but rainy weather is frequent, and the place is celebrated for winds, of which the prevailing one is west. An east wind in summer, and a south wind in winter, are said to be always accompanied with rain.

"We were ready to depart; the tents were struck, the mules geared up, and our horses saddled, and we walked up to the fort to take the *stirrup-cup* with our friends in an excellent home-brewed preparation. While thus pleasantly engaged, seated in one of the little cool chambers, at the door of which a man had been stationed to prevent all intrusion from the Indians, a number of chiefs, several of them powerful, fine looking men, forced their way into the room in spite of all opposition. Handing me the following letter (in French), they took their seats in silence:

[TRANSLATION.]

"FORT PLATTE, *July* 1, 1842.

"'MR. FREMONT: The chiefs, having assembled in council, have just told me to warn you not to set out before the party of young men which is now out shall have returned. Furthermore, they tell me, that they are very sure they will fire upon you as soon as they meet you. They are expected back in seven or eight days. Excuse me for making these observations, but it seems my duty to warn you of danger. Moreover, the chiefs who prohibit your setting out before the return of the warriors are the bearers of this note.

"'I am your obedient servant,

"'JOSEPH BISSONETTE.

"'By L. B. CHARTRAIN.

"'*Names of some of the Chiefs.*—The Otter Hat, the Breaker of Arrows, the Black Night, the Bull's Tail.'

"After reading this, I mentioned its purport to my companions; and, seeing that all were fully possessed of its contents, one of the Indians rose up, and, having first shaken hands with me, spoke as follows:

"'You have come among us at a bad time. Some of our people have been killed, and our young men, who are gone to the mountains, are eager to avenge the blood of their relations, which has been shed by the whites. Our young men are bad, and if they meet you, they will believe that you are carrying goods and ammunition to their enemies, and will fire upon you. You have told us that this will make war. We know that our great father has many soldiers and big guns, and we are anxious to have our lives. We love the whites, and are desirous of peace. Thinking of all these things, we have determined to keep you here until our warriors return. We are glad to see you among us. Our father is rich, and we expected that you would have brought presents to us—horses, guns, and blankets. But we are glad to see you. We look upon your coming as the light which goes before the sun; for you will tell our great father that you have seen us, and that we are naked and poor, and have nothing to eat; and he will send us all these things.'

"He was followed by the others, to the same effect.

"The observations of the savage appeared reasonable; but I was aware that they had in view only the present object of detaining me, and were unwilling I should go further into the country. In reply, I asked them, through the interpretation of Mr. Boudeau, to select two or three of their number to accompany us until we should meet their people—they should spread their robes in my tent and eat at my table, and on our return I would give them presents in reward of their services. They declined, saying that there were no young men left in the village, and that they were too old to travel so many days on horseback, and preferred now to smoke their pipes in the lodge, and let the warriors go on the war path. Besides, they had no power over the young men, and were afraid to interfere with them. In my turn I addressed them:

"'You say that you love the whites: why have you killed so many already this spring? You say that you love the whites, and are full of many expressions of friendship to us; but you are not willing to undergo the fatigue of a few days' ride to save our lives. We do not believe what you have said, and will not listen to you. Whatever a chief among us tells his soldiers to do, is done. We are the soldiers of the great chief, your father. He has told us to come here and see this country, and all the Indians, his children. Why should we not go? Before we came, we heard that you had killed his people, and ceased to be his children; but we came among you peaceably, holding out our hands. Now we find that the stories we heard are not lies, and that you are no longer his friends and children. We have thrown away our bodies, and will not turn back. When you told us that your young men would kill us, you did not know that our hearts were strong, and you did not see the rifles which my young men carry in their hands. We are few, and you are many, and may kill us all; but there will be much crying in your villages, for many of your young men will stay behind, and forget to return with your warriors from the mountains. Do you think that our great chief will let his soldiers die, and forget to cover their graves? Before the snows melt again, his warriors will sweep away your villages as the fire does the prairie in the autumn. See! I have pulled down my *white houses*, and my people are ready: when the sun is ten paces higher, we shall be on the march. If you have anything to tell us, you will say it soon.'

"I broke up the conference, as I could do nothing with these people; and, being resolved to proceed, nothing was to be gained by delay. Accompanied by our hospitable friends, we returned to the camp. We had mounted our horses, and our parting salutations had been exchanged, when one of the chiefs (the Bull's Tail) arrived to tell me that they had determined to send a young man with us; and if I would point out the place of our evening camp, he should join us there. 'The young man is poor,' said he; 'he has no horse, and expects you to give him one.' I described to him the place where I intended to encamp, and, shaking hands, in a few minutes we were among the hills, and this last habitation of whites shut out from our view."

They were not disturbed farther by the Indians in the prosecution of their journey, but they encountered a more formidable enemy toward the close of the week, in the scarcity of provisions; a great drought and the grasshoppers having swept the country so, that not a blade of grass was to be seen, nor a buffalo to be found through the whole region. Some Sioux Indians whom they met, stated that their people were nearly starved to death; had abandoned their villages, and their receding tracks might be marked by the carcases of horses strewed along the road, of which they had eaten, or which had died of starvation. Bisonnette advised

Fremont to return. The latter called up his men, informed them of what he had heard, and with that inflexibility of purpose and faith in himself, which always seem in hours of greatest peril to have sustained him, avowed his fixed determination to proceed in the execution of the enterprise for which he had been commissioned, at the same time giving them to understand that, in view of the dangers to which they were exposed, it was optional with them to go with him or to return.

"Among them," says Fremont, "were some five or six whom I knew would remain. We had still ten days' provisions; and should no game be found, when this stock was expended, we had our horses and mules, which we could eat when other means of subsistence failed. But not a man flinched from the undertaking. 'We'll eat the mules,' said Basil Lajeunesse; and thereupon we shook hands with our interpreter and his Indians, and parted. With them I sent back one of my men, Dumés, whom the effects of an old wound in the leg rendered incapable of continuing the journey on foot, and his horse seemed on the point of giving out. Having resolved to disencumber ourselves immediately of everything not absolutely necessary to our future operations, I turned directly in toward the river, and encamped on the left bank, a little above the place where our council had been held, and where a thick grove of willows offered a suitable spot for the object I had in view." Mr. Fremont then proceeds as follows:

"The carts having been discharged, the covers and wheels were taken off, and, with the frames, carried into some low places among the willows, and concealed in the dense foliage in such a manner that the glitter of the iron work might not attract the observation of some straggling Indian. In the sand, which had been blown up into waves among the willows, a large hole was then dug, ten feet square, and six deep. In the meantime, all our effects had been spread out upon the ground, and whatever was designed to be carried along with us separated and laid aside, and the remaining part carried to the hole and carefully covered up. As much as possible, all traces of our proceedings were obliterated, and it wanted but a rain to render our *cache* safe beyond discovery. All the men were now set at work to arrange the pack-saddles and make up the packs.

"The day was very warm and calm, and the sky entirely clear, except where, as usual along the summits of the mountainous ridge opposite, the clouds had congregated in masses. Our lodge had been planted, and on account of the heat the ground pins had been taken out, and the lower part slightly raised. Near to it was standing the barometer, which swung in a tripod frame; and within the lodge, where a small fire had been built, Mr. Preuss was occupied in observing the temperature of boiling water. At this instant, and without any warning until it was within fifty yards, a violent gust of wind dashed down the lodge, burying under it Mr. Preuss and about a dozen men, who had attempted to keep it from being carried away. I succeeded in saving the barometer, which the lodge was carrying off with itself, but the thermometer was broken. We had no others of a high graduation, none of those which remained going higher than 130° Fahrenheit. Our astronomical observations gave to this place, which we named *Cache* camp, a longitude of 106° 38′ 26″, latitude 42° 50′ 53″."

The care with which Mr. Fremont records the preservation of this barometer lends interest to his subsequent account of its destruction and the ingenuity with which he repaired its loss. In crossing the New Fork of Green river about a week after the events last

FREMONT PLANTS THE AMERICAN FLAG ON THE HIGHEST PEAK OF THE ROCKY MOUNTAINS.

described, the current was very swift, and he accidentally broke it. It was the only barometer he had been able to preserve up to that point in his journey, and in recording the calamity in his journal, he adds:

"A great part of the interest of the journey for me was in the exploration of these mountains, of which so much had been said that was doubtful and contradictory; and now their snowy peaks rose majestically before me, and the only means of giving them authentically to science, the object of my anxious solicitude by night and day, was destroyed. We had brought this barometer in safety a thousand miles, and broke it almost among the snow of the mountains. The loss was felt by the whole camp—all had seen my anxiety, and aided me in preserving it. The height of these mountains, considered by the hunters and traders the highest in the whole range, had been a theme of constant discussion among them; and all had looked forward with pleasure to the moment when the instrument, which they believed to be true as the sun, should stand upon the summits, and decide their disputes. Their grief was only inferior to my own."

The skill and patience exhibited by him in repairing his loss illustrates one of the most characteristic and remarkable traits of Mr. Fremont's character—his fertility of resource and his habitual self-reliance. The incident cannot be better described than in his own words.

"As soon as the camp was formed," he says, "I set about endeavoring to repair my barometer. As I have already said, this was a standard cistern barometer, of Troughton's construction. The glass cistern had been broken about midway; but as the instrument had been kept in a proper position, no air had found its way into the tube, the end of which had always remained covered. I had with me a number of vials of tolerably thick glass, some of which were of the same diameter as the cistern, and I spent the day in slowly working on these, endeavoring to cut them of the requisite length; but, as my instrument was a very rough file, I invariably broke them. A groove was cut in one of the trees, where the barometer was placed during the night, to be out of the way of any possible danger, and in the morning I commenced again. Among the powder horns in the camp, I found one which was very transparent, so that its contents could be almost as plainly seen as through glass. This I boiled and stretched on a piece of wood to the requisite diameter, and scraped it very thin, in order to increase to the utmost its transparency. I then secured it firmly in its place on the instrument, with strong glue made from a buffalo, and filled it with mercury, properly heated. A piece of skin, which had covered one of the vials, furnished a good pocket, which was well secured with strong thread and glue, and then the brass cover was screwed to its place. The instrument was left some time to dry; and when I reversed it, a few hours after, I had the satisfaction to find it in perfect order; its indications being about the same as on the other side of the lake before it had been broken. Our success in this little incident diffused pleasure throughout the camp; and we immediately set about our preparations for ascending the mountains."

The great achievement of this expedition, however, and one of the greatest ever accomplished by any traveller in any age, all the circumstances considered, was the ascent of the Wind River peak of the Rocky Mountains, the highest peak of that vast chain, and one which was probably never trod before by any mortal foot. The simplicity of Mr. Fremont's account of this day's journey befits the sublimity of the events he records. His companions in the ascent were Mr. Preuss, Basil Lajeunesse, Clement Lambert, Janisse and Descoteaux. We can add nothing to the interest or impressiveness of the narrative.

"When we had secured strength for the day (15 Aug.) by a hearty breakfast, we covered what remained, which was enough for one meal, with rocks, in order that it might be safe from any marauding bird; and saddling our mules, turned our faces once more towards the peaks. This time we determined to proceed quietly and cautiously, deliberately resolved to accomplish our object if it were within the compass of human means. We were of opinion that a long defile which lay to the left of yesterday's route would lead us to the foot of the main peak. Our mules had been refreshed by the fine grass in the little ravine at the Island camp, and we intended to ride up the defile as far as possible, in order to husband our strength for the main ascent. Though this was a fine passage, still it was a defile of the most rugged mountains known, and we had many a rough and steep slippery place to cross before reaching the end. In this place the sun rarely shone; snow lay along the border of the small stream which flowed through it, and occasional icy passages made the footing of the mules very insecure, and the rocks and ground were moist with the trickling waters in this spring of mighty rivers. We soon had the satisfaction to find ourselves riding along the huge wall which forms the central summits of the chain. There at last it rose by our sides, a nearly perpendicular wall of granite, terminating 2,000 to 3,000 feet above our heads in a serrated line of broken, jagged cones. We rode on until we came almost immediately below the main peak, which I denominated the Snow Peak, as it exhibited more snow to the eye than any of the neighboring summits. Here were three small lakes of a green color, each of perhaps a thousand yards in diameter, and apparently very deep. These lay in a kind of chasm· and, according to the barometer, we had attained but a few hundred feet above the Island lake. The barometer here stood a 20·450, attached thermometer 70°.

"We managed to get our mules up to a little bench about a hundred feet above the lakes, and turned them loose to graze. During our rough ride to this place, they had exhibited a wonderful surefootedness. Parts of the defile were filled with angular, sharp fragments of rock, three or four and eight or ten feet cubic; and among these they had worked their way leaping from one narrow point to another, rarely making a false step, and giving us no occasion to dismount. Having divested ourselves of every unnecessary encumbrance, we commenced the ascent. This time, like experienced travellers, we did not press ourselves, but climbed leisurely, sitting down so soon as we found breath beginning to fail. At intervals we reached places where a number of springs gushed from the rocks, and about 1,800 feet above the lakes came to the snow line. From this point our progress was uninterrupted climbing. Hitherto I had worn a pair of thick moccasins, with soles of *parflêche*, but here I put on a light thin pair, which I had brought for the purpose, as now the use of our toes became necessary to a further advance. I availed myself of a sort of comb of the mountain, which stood against the wall like a buttress, and which the wind and the solar radiation, joined to the steepness of the smooth rock, had kept almost entirely free from snow. Up this I made my way rapidly. Our cautious method of advancing in the outset had spared my strength; and with the exception of a slight disposition to headache, I felt no remains of yesterday's illness. In a few minutes we reached a point where the buttress was overhanging, and there was no other way of surmounting the difficulty than by passing around one side of it, which was the face of a vertical precipice of several hundred feet.

"Putting hands and feet in the crevices between the blocks, I succeeded in getting over it, and, when I reached the top, found my companions in a small valley below. Descending to them, we continued climbing, and in a short time reached the crest.

I sprang upon the summit, and another step would have precipitated me into an immense snow-field five hundred feet below. To the edge of this field was a sheer icy precipice; and then, with a gradual fall, the field sloped off for about a mile, until it struck the foot of another lower ridge. I stood on a narrow crest, about three feet in width, with an inclination of about 20° N. 51° E. As soon as I had gratified the first feeling of curiosity, I descended, and each man ascended in his turn; for I would only allow one at a time to mount the unstable and precarious slab, which it seemed a breath would hurl into the abyss below. We mounted the barometer in the snow of the summit, and fixing a ramrod in a crevice, unfurled the national flag to wave in the breeze where never flag waved before. During our morning's ascent, we had met no sign of animal life, except the small sparrow-like bird already mentioned. A stillness the most profound and a terrible solitude forced themselves constantly on the mind as the great features of the place. Here, on the summit, where the stillness was absolute, unbroken by any sound, and the solitude complete, we thought ourselves beyond the region of animated life; but while we were sitting on the rock, a solitary bee (*bromus, the humble bee*) came winging his flight from the eastern valley, lit on the knee of one of the men.

"It was a strange place, the icy rock and the highest peak of the Rocky Mountains, for a lover of warm sunshine and flowers; and we pleased ourselves with the idea that he was the first of his species to cross the mountain barrier—a solitary pioneer to foretell the advance of civilization. I believe that a moment's thought would have made us let him continue his way unharmed; but we carried out the law of this country, where all animated nature seems at war; and seizing him immediately, put him in at least a fit place—in the leaves of a large book, among the flowers we had collected on our way. The barometer stood at 18·293, the attached thermometer at 44°; giving for the elevation of this summit 13,570 feet above the Gulf of Mexico, which may be called the highest flight of the bee. It is certainly the highest known flight of that insect.* From the description given by Mackenzie of the mountains where he crossed them, with that of a French officer still farther to the north, and Col.

* The encounter of Col. Fremont with this solitary pioneer of human civilization upon the summit of the highest peak of the Rocky Mountains, is a curious commentary upon the familiar lines which concludes Bryant's poem of the Prairies, and which will already have occurred to many of our readers upon the perusal of the affecting incident so gracefully recorded by Col. Fremont.

* * * * "The bee,
A colonist more adventurous than man,
With whom he came across the Eastern deep—
Fills the savannas with his murmurings,
And hides his sweets, as in the Golden Age,
Within the hollow oak. I listen long
To his domestic hum, and think I hear
The sound of that advancing multitude
Which soon shall fill these deserts. From the ground
Comes up the laugh of children, the soft voice
Of maidens, and the sweet and solemn hymn
Of Sabbath worshippers. The low of herds
Blends with the rustling of the heavy grain
Over the dark-brown furrows. All at once,
A fresher wind sweeps by, and breaks my dream,
And I am in the wilderness alone.

"Fremont, in the expedition which he made between the years 1842 and 1844, at the command of the United States government, discovered and measured barometrically the highest peak of the whole chain of the Rocky Mountains to the north-northwest of Spanish, James', Long's, and Laramie's Peaks. This snow-covered summit, which belongs to the group of the Wind River Mountains, bears the name of Fremont's Peak, on the great chart published under the direction of Colonel Abert, chief of the topographical department at Washington. This point is situated in the parallel of 43° 10′ north latitude, and 110° 7′ west longitude, and, therefore, nearly 5° 30′ north of Spanish Peak, which, according to direct measurement, is 13,568 feet, must, therefore, exceed by 2,072 feet that given by Long to James' Peak, which would appear, from its position, to be identical with Pike's Peak, as given in the map above referred to. The Wind River Mountains constitute the dividing ridge (*divortia aquarum*) between the two seas.

* * * * * * * *

"To the surprise of the adventurous travellers, the summit of Fremont's

Long's measurements to the south, joined to the opinion of the oldest traders of the country, it is presumed that this is the highest peak of the Rocky Mountains. The day was sunny and

Peak was found to be visited by bees. It is probable that these insects, like the butterflies which I found at far higher elevations in the chain of the Andes, and also within the limits of perpetual snows, had been involuntarily drawn thither by ascending currents of air. I have even seen large-winged lepidoptera, which had been carried far out to sea by land winds, drop on the ship's deck, at a considerable distance from the land, in the South Sea.

"Fremont's map and geographical researches embrace the immense tract of land extending from the confluence of Kansas River with the Missouri, to the cataracts of the Columbia, and the Missions of Santa Barbara, and the Pueblo de los Angelos, in New California, presenting a space amounting to 28 degrees of longitude (about 1360 miles) between the 34th and 45th parallels of north latitude. Four hundred points have been hypsometrically determined by barometrical measurements, and for the most part, astronomically; so that it has been rendered possible to delineate the profile above the sea's level, of a tract of land measuring 3,600 miles, with all its inflections, extending from the north of Kansas to Fort Vancouver, and to the coasts of the South Sea (almost 720 miles more than the distance from Madrid to Tobolsk), As I believe I was the first who attempted to represent, in geognostic profile, the configuration of Mexico and the Cordilleras of South America (for the half-perspective projections of the Siberian traveller, the Abbé Chappe*, were based on mere, and, for the most part, on very inaccurate estimates of the falls of rivers); it has afforded me special satisfaction to there find the graphical method of representing the earth's configuration in a vertical direction, that is, the elevation of solid over fluid parts, achieved on so vast a scale. In the mean latitudes of 37° to 43°, the Rocky Mountains present, besides the great snow-crowned summits, whose height may be compared to that of the Peak of Teneriffe, elevated plateaux of an extent scarcely to be met with in any other part of the world, and whose breadth from east to west is almost twice that of the Mexican highlands. From the range of the mountains which begin a little westward to Fort Laramie, to the further side of the Wahsatch Mountains, the elevation of the soil is uninterruptedly maintained from five to upwards of seven thousand feet above the sea level; nay, this elevated portion

* Chappe d'Auteroche: *Voyage en Sibérie, fait en* 1761. 4 vols., 4to., Paris, 1768.

bright, but a slight shining mist hung over the lower plains, which interfered with our view of the surrounding country. On one side we overlooked innumerable lakes and streams, the spring of the Colorado of the Gulf of California; and on the other was the Wind River valley, where were the heads of the Yellowstone branch of the Missouri; far to the north, we just could discover the snowy heads of the *Trois Têtons*, where were the source of the Missouri and Columbia rivers; and at the southern extremity of the ridge, the peaks were plainly visible, among which were some of the springs of the Nebraska or Platte River. Around us, the whole scene had one main striking feature, which was that of terrible convulsion. Parallel to its length, the ridge was split into chasms and fissures; between which rose the thin lofty walls, terminated with slender minarets and columns. According to the barometer, the little crest of the wall on which we stood was three thousand five hundred and seventy feet above that place, and two thousand seven hundred and eighty above the little lakes at the bottom, immediately at our feet. Our camp at the Two Hills (an astronomical station) bore south 3° east, which, with a bearing afterward obtained from a fixed position, enabled us to locate the peak. The bearing of the *Trois Têtons* was north 50° west, and the direction of the central ridge of the Wind River mountains south 39° east.

occupies the whole space between the true Rocky Mountains and the Californian snowy coast range from 34° to 45° north latitude. This district, which is a kind of broad longitudinal valley, like that of the Lake Titicaca, has been named the *Great Basin*, by Joseph Walker and Captain Fremont, travellers well acquainted with those western regions. It is a *terra incognita* of at least 8,000 geographical (or 128,000 English) square miles, and almost uninhabited, and full of salt lakes, the largest of which is 3,940 Parisian (or 4,200 English) feet above the level of the sea, and is connected with the narrow Lake Utah,* into which 'Rock River' (*Timpan Ogo*, in the Utah language) pours its copious stream."—*Humboldt's Aspects of Nature. Pp.* 32–3–4.

*Fremont: *Report of the Exploring Expedition*, pp. 154 and 273—276.

"The summit rock was gneiss, succeeded by sienitic gneiss. Sienite and feldspar succeeded in our descent to the snow line, where we found a feldspathic granite. I had remarked that the noise produced by the explosion of our pistols had the usual degree of loudness, but was not in the least prolonged, expiring almost instantaneously. Having now made what observations our means afforded, we proceeded to descend. We had accomplished an object of laudable ambition, and beyond the strict order of our instructions. We had climbed the loftiest peak of the Rocky Mountains, and looked down upon the snow a thousand feet below, and, standing where never human foot had stood before, felt the exultation of first explorers. It was about two o'clock when we left the summit; and when we reached the bottom, the sun had already sunk behind the wall and the day was drawing to a close. It would have been pleasant to have lingered here and on the summit longer; but we hurried away as rapidly as the ground would permit, for it was an object to regain our party as soon as possible, not knowing what accident the next hour might bring forth.

"We reached our deposit of provisions at nightfall. Here was not the inn which awaits the tired traveller on his return from Mont Blanc, or the orange groves of South America, with their refreshing juices and soft fragrant air; but we found our little *cache* of dried meat and coffee undisturbed. Though the moon was bright, the road was full of precipices, and the fatigue of the day had been great. We therefore abandoned the idea of rejoining our friends, and lay down on the rock, and in spite of the cold, slept soundly."

On the following day, the 17th of August, came the welcome order to turn their faces homeward, and on the 22d they reached the encampment of their party at Rock Independence. Here a little incident occurred which shows that amid the manifold trials and dangers through which Fremont had passed, he had not forgotten the protecting arm which had always been near to support and defend him. We quote again from his journal:

"23d.—Yesterday evening we reached our encampment at Rock Independence, where I took some astronomical observations. Here, not unmindful of the custom of early travellers and explorers in our country, I engraved on that rock of the Far West a symbol of the Christian faith. Among the thickly inscribed names, I made on the hard granite the impression of a large cross, which I covered with a black preparation of India rubber, well calculated to resist the influence of wind and rain. It stands amidst the names of many who have long since found their way to the grave, and for whom the huge rock is a giant tombstone.

"One George Weymouth was sent out to Maine by the Earl of Southampton, Lord Arundel, and others; and in the narrative of his discoveries, he says: 'The next day we ascended in our pinnace that part of the river which lies more to the westward, carrying with us a cross—a thing never omitted by any Christian traveller—which we erected at the ultimate end of our route.' This was in the year 1605: and in 1842 I obeyed the feeling of early travellers and left the impression of the cross deeply engraved on a vast rock, one thousand miles beyond the Mississippi, to which the discoverers have given the national name of Rock Independence."

With his brief but thrilling account of an attempt to visit Goat Island, in the Platte River, by which he was nearly losing many of the most important results of his expedition, as well as his life, we will close our extracts from his journal:

"August 24th.—We started before sunrise, intending to breakfast at Goat Island. Mr. Preuss accompanied me, and with us were five of our best men. Here appeared no scarcity of water, and we took on board, with various instruments and baggage, provisions for ten or twelve days. We paddled down the river rapidly, for our little craft was light as a duck on the water; and the sun had been some time risen, when we heard before us a hollow roar, which we supposed to be that of a fall, of which we had heard a vague rumor, but whose exact locality no one had been able to describe to us. We were approaching a ridge, through which the river passes by a place called 'canon' (pronounced *canyon*), a Spanish word, signifying a piece of artillery, the barrel of a gun, or any kind of tube; and which, in this country, has been adopted to describe the passage of a river between perpendicular rocks of great height, which frequently approach each other so closely overhead as to form a kind of tunnel over the stream, which foams along below, half choked up by fallen fragments.

"We passed three cataracts in succession, where perhaps one hundred feet of smooth water intervened; and finally with a shout of pleasure at our success, issued from our tunnel into open day beyond. We were so delighted with the performance of our boat, and so confident in her powers, that we would not have hesitated to leap a fall of ten feet with her. We put to shore for breakfast at some willows on the right bank, immediately below the mouth of the canon; for it was now 8 o'clock, and we had been working since daylight, and were all wet, fatigued and hungry.

"We re-embarked at 9 o'clock, and in about twenty minutes reached the next canon. Landing on a rocky shore at its commencement, we ascended the ridge to reconnoitre. Portage was out of the question. So far as we could see, the jagged rocks pointed out the course of the canon, on a wending line of seven or eight miles. It was simply a narrow, dark chasm in the rock; and here the perpendicular faces were much higher than in the previous pass, being at this end two to three hundred, and further down, as we afterwards ascertained, five hundred feet in vertical height. Our previous success had made us bold, and we determined again to run the canon. Everything was secured as firmly as possible; and having divested ourselves of the greater part of our clothing, we pushed into the stream. To save our chronometer from accident, Mr. Preuss took it and attempted to proceed along the shore on the masses of rock, which in places were piled up on either side; but, after he had walked about five minutes, everything like shore disappeared, and the vertical wall came squarely down into the water. He therefore waited until we came up. An ugly pass lay before us. We had made fast to the stern of the boat a strong rope about fifty feet long; and three of the men clambered along among the rocks, and with this rope let her down slowly through the pass. In several places high rocks lay scattered about in the channel; and in the narrows it required all our strength and skill to avoid staving the boat on the sharp points. In one of these, the boat proved a little too broad, and stuck fast for an instant, while the water flew over us; fortunately it was but for an instant, as our united strength forced her immediately through. The water swept overboard only a sextant and pair of saddle-bags. I caught the sextant as it passed by me, but the saddle-bags became the prey of the whirlpools. We reached the place where Mr. Preuss was standing, took him on board, and, with the aid of the boat, put the men with the rope on the succeeding pile of rocks. We found this passage much worse than the previous one, and our position was rather a bad one. To go back was impossible; before us the cataract was a sheet of foam; and shut up in the chasm by the rocks, which, in some places, seemed almost to meet overhead, the roar of water was deafening. We pushed off again; but, after making a little distance, the force of the current became too great for the men on shore, and two of them let go the rope. Lajeunesse, the third man, hung on, and was jerked headforemost into the river from a rock about twelve feet high; and down the boat shot like an arrow, Basil following us in the rapid current, and exerting all his strength to keep in mid-channel—his head only seen occasionally like a black spot in the white foam. How far he went, I do not exactly know; but we succeeded in turning the boat into an eddy below. ''*Cré Dieu*,' said Basil Lajeunesse, as he arrived immediately after us, '*Je crois bien que j'ai nagé un demi mile.*' He had owed his life to his skill as a swimmer, and I determined to take him and the two others on board, and trust to skill and fortune to reach the other end in safety. We placed ourselves on our knees, with the short paddles in our hands, the most skillful boatman being at the bow; and again we commenced our rapid descent.

"We cleared rock after rock, and shot past fall after fall, our little boat seeming to play with the cataract. We became flushed with success, and familiar with the danger; and, yielding to the excitement of the occasion, broke forth together into a Canadian boat song. Singing, or rather shouting, we dashed along; and were, I believe, in the midst of the chorus, when the boat struck a concealed rock immediately at the foot of a fall, which whirled her over in an instant. Three of my men could not swim, and my first feeling was to assist them, and save some of our effects; but a sharp concussion or two convinced me that I had not yet saved myself. A few strokes brought me into an eddy, and I landed on a pile of rocks on the left side. Looking around, I saw that Mr. Preuss had gained the shore on the same side, about twenty yards below; and a little climbing and swimming soon brought him to my side. On the opposite side, against the wall, lay the boat, bottom up; and Lambert was in the act of saving Descoteaux, whom he had grasped by the hair, and who could not swim; '*Lâche pas*,' said he, as I afterwards learned, '*lâche pas, cher frère*.' '*Crains pas*,' was the reply, '*Je m'en vais mourir avant que de te lâcher*.' Such was the reply of courage and generosity in the danger. For a hundred yards below the current was covered with floating books and boxes, bales and blankets, and scattered articles of clothing; and so strong and boiling was the stream, that even our heavy instruments, which were all in cases, kept on the surface, and the sextant, circle and the long black box of the telescope, were in view at once. For a moment I was somewhat disheartened. All our books, almost every record of the journey, our journals and registers of astronomical and barometrical observations, had been lost in a moment. But it was no time to indulge in regrets; and I immediately set about endeavoring to save something from the wreck. Making ourselves understood as well as possible by signs (for nothing could be heard in the roar of waters), we commenced our operations. Of everything on board, the only article that had been saved was my double-barreled gun, which Descoteaux had caught, and clung to with drowning tenacity. The men continued down the river on the left bank. Mr. Preuss and myself descended on the side we were on; and Lajeunesse, with a paddle in his hand, jumped on the boat alone, and continued down the canon. She was now light, and cleared every bad place with much less difficulty. In a short time he was joined by Lambert, and the search was continued for about a mile and a half, which was as far as the boat could proceed in the pass.

"Here the walls were about five hundred feet high, and the fragments of rocks from above had choked the river into a hollow pass, but one or two feet above the surface. Through this and the interstices of the rock, the water found its way. Favored beyond our expectations, all of our registers had been recovered, with the exception of one of my journals, which contained the notes and incidents of travel, and topographical descriptions, a number of scattered astronomical observations, principally meridian altitudes of the sun, and our barometrical register west of Laramie. Fortunately, our other journals contained duplicates of the most important barometrical observations which had been taken in the mountains. These, with a few scattered notes, were all that had been preserved of our meteorological observations. In addition to these, we saved the circle; and these, with a few blankets, constituted everything that had been rescued from the waters.

"The day was running rapidly away, and it was necessary to reach Goat Island, whither the party had preceded us, before night. In this uncertain country, the traveller is so much in the power of chance, that we became somewhat uneasy in regard to them. Should anything have occurred in the brief interval of our separation, to prevent our rejoining them, our situation would be rather a desperate one. We had not a morsel of provisions —our arms and ammunition were gone—and were entirely at the mercy of any straggling party of savages, and not a little in danger of starvation. We therefore set out at once in two parties. Mr. Preuss and myself on the left, and the men on the opposite side of the river. Climbing out of the canon, we found ourselves in a very broken country, where we were not yet able to recognize any locality. In the course of our descent through the canon, the rock, which at the upper end was of the decomposing granite, changed into a varied sandstone formation. The hills and points of the ridges were covered with fragments of a yellow sandstone, of which the strata were sometimes displayed in the broken ravines which interrupted our course, and made our walk extremely fatiguing. At one point of the canon the red argillaceous sandstone rose in a wall of five hundred feet, surmounted by a stratum of white sandstone; and in an opposite ravine a column of red sandstone rose, in form like a steeple, about one hundred and fifty feet high. The scenery was extremely picturesque, and notwithstanding our forlorn condition, we were frequently obliged to stop and admire it. Our progress was not very rapid. We had emerged from the water half naked, and, on arriving at the top of the precipice, I found myself with only one moccasin. The fragments of rock made walking painful, and I was frequently obliged to stop and pull out the thorns of the *cactus*, here the prevailing plant, and with which a few minutes' walk covered the bottom of my feet. From this ridge, the river emerged into a smiling prairie, and descending to the bank for water, we were joined by Benoist. The rest of the party were out of sight, having taken a more inland route. We crossed the river repeatedly—sometimes able to ford it, and sometimes swimming—climbed over the ridges of two more canons, and towards evening reached the cut, which we here named the Hot Spring gate. On our previous visit in July, we had not entered this pass, reserving it for our descent in the boat; and when we entered it this evening, Mr. Preuss was a few hundred feet in advance. Heated with the long march, he came suddenly upon a fine bold spring gushing from the rock, about ten feet above the river. Eager to enjoy the crystal water, he threw himself down for a hasty draught, and took a mouthful of water almost boiling hot. He said nothing to Benoist, who laid himself down to drink: but the steam from the water arrested his eagerness, and he escaped the hot draught. We had no ther mometer, to ascertain the temperature, but I could hold my hand in the water just long enough to count two seconds. There are eight or ten of these springs discharging themselves by streams large enough to be called runs. A loud hollow noise was heard from the rock, which I suppose to be produced by the fall of the water. The strata immediately where the issue is a fine white and calcareous sandstone, covered with an incrustation of common salt. Leaving this Thermopylæ of the West, in a short walk we reached the red ridge which has been described as lying just above Goat Island. Ascending this, we found some fresh tracks and a button, which showed that the other men had already arrived. A shout from the man who had first reached the top of the ridge, responded to from below, informed us that our friends were all on the island; and we were soon among them. We found some pieces of buffalo standing around the fire for us, and managed to get some dry clothes among the people. A sudden storm of rain drove us into the best shelter we could find, where we slept soundly, after one of the most fatiguing days I have ever experienced."

On the 17th of October, Colonel Fremont was at St. Louis, and on the 29th in Washington. His report was completed and in the hands of the War Department before the winter was over. It was called for by the Senate, and when reported, Dr. Linn, then one of the senators from the State of Missouri, accompanied a motion to print extra copies with some complimentary remarks, which we give as reported in the *Congressional Globe* of that date :

"In support of his motion," Mr. L. said, "that in the course of the last summer a very interesting expedition had been undertaken to the Rocky Mountains, ordered by Colonel Abert, chief of the Topographical Bureau, with the sanction of the Secretary of War, and executed by Lieut. Fremont of the Topographical Engineers. The object of the expedition was to examine and report upon the rivers and country between the frontiers of Missouri and the basis of the Rocky Mountains; and especially to examine the character, and ascertain the latitude and longitude of the South Pass, the great crossing place to these mountains on the way to the Oregon. All the objects of the expedition have been accomplished, and in a way to be beneficial to science and instructive to the general reader, as well as useful to the government.

"Supplied with the best astronomical and barometrical instruments, well qualified to use them, and accompanied by twenty-five *voyageurs*, enlisted for the purpose at St. Louis, and trained to all the hardships and dangers of the prairies and the mountains, Mr. Fremont left the mouth of the Kansas, on the frontiers of Missouri, on the 10th of June; and, in the almost incredibly short space of four months, returned to the same point, without an accident to a man, and with a vast mass of useful observations, and many hundred specimens in botany and geology.

"In executing his instructions, Mr. Fremont proceeded up the Kansas River far enough to ascertain its character, and then crossed over to the Great Platte, and pursued that river to its source in the mountains, where the Sweet Water (a head branch of the Platte), issues from the neighborhood of the South Pass. He reached this Pass on the 8th of August, and describes it as a wide and low depression of the mountains, where the ascent is as easy as that of the hill on which this Capitol stands, and where a plainly-beaten wagon road leads to the Oregon, through the valley of Lewis's River, a fork of the Columbia. He went through the pass, and saw the head waters of the Colorado, of the Gulf of California; and leaving the valleys to indulge a laudable curiosity, and to make some useful observations, and attended by four of his men, he climbed the loftiest peak of the Rocky Mountains, until then untrodden by any known human being; and, on the 15th of August, looked down upon ice and snow some thousand feet below, and traced in the distance the valleys of the rivers which, taking their rise in the same elevated ridge, flow in opposite directions to the Pacific Ocean and to the Mississippi. From that ultimate point he returned by the valley of the Great Platte, following the stream in its whole course, and solving all questions in relation to its navigability, and the character of the country through which it flows.

"Over the whole course of this extended route, barometrical observations were made by Mr. Fremont, to ascertain elevations both of the plains and of the mountains; astronomical observations were taken to ascertain latitudes and longitudes; the face of the country was marked as arable or sterile; the facility of travelling, and the practicability of routes noted; the grand features of nature described, and some presented in drawings; military positions indicated; and a large contribution to geology and botany was made in the varieties of plants, flowers, shrubs, trees, and grasses, and rocks and earths, which were enumerated. Drawings of some grand and striking points, and a map of the whole route, illustrate the report, and facilitate the understanding of its details. Eight carts drawn by two mules each accompanied the expedition; a fact which attests the facility of travelling in this vast region. Herds of buffaloes furnished subsistence to the men; a short, nutritious grass, sustained the horses and mules. Two boys (one of twelve years of age, the other of eighteen), besides the enlisted men, accompanied the expedition, and took their share of its hardships; which proves that boys, as well as men, are able to traverse the country to the Rocky Mountains.

"The result of all his observations Mr. Fremont had condensed into a brief report—enough to make a document of ninety or one hundred pages; and believing that this document would be of general enterest to the whole country, and beneficial to science, as well as useful to the government, I move the printing of the extra number which has been named.

"In making this motion, and in bringing this report to the notice of the Senate, I take a great pleasure in noticing the activity and importance of the Topographical Bureau. Under its skillful and vigilant head [Colonel Abert] numerous valuable and incessant surveys are made; and a mass of information collected of the highest importance to the country generally, as well as to the military branch of the public service. This report proves conclusively that the country, for several hundred miles from the frontier of Missouri, is exceedingly beautiful and fertile; alternate woodland and prairie, and certain portions well supplied with water. It also proves that the valley of the river Platte has a very rich soil, affording great facilities for emigrants to the west of the Rocky Mountains."

The London *Athenæum*, of March, 1844, commences a review of this report in the following complimentary terms, which we quote to show the impression it produced in the literary circles of the old world:

"The government of the United States did well when in furtherance of the resolution to survey the road across the Great Western Prairie and the Rocky Mountains to the Oregon territory, it selected Lieut. Fremont for the execution of the work. We have rarely met with a production so perfect in its kind as the unpretending pamphlet containing this report. The narrative, clear, full and lively, occupies only 76 pages, to which are appended 130 pages, filled with the results of botanical researches, of astronomical and meteorologiacal observations. What a contrast does this present to the voluminous emptiness and conceited rhodomontade so often brought forth by our costly expeditions. The country gone over by Lieut. Fremont is certainly not the most interesting in the world, nor is it quite new. Yet he is evidently not the man to travel 2,000 miles without observing much which is worthy of being recorded or to write a page which is likely to prove tedious in the reading. His points of view are so well chosen, his delineation has so much truth and spirit, and his general remarks are so accurate and comprehensive, that under his guidance we find the far west prairies nearly as fresh and tempting as the most favored Arcadian scenes, the hallowed groves of which were never trodden by the foot of squatting emigrant or fur trader."

CHAPTER IV.

SECOND EXPLORING EXPEDITION—KIT CARSON—MRS. FREMONT WITHHOLDS ORDERS FROM THE WAR DEPARTMENT—COLONEL BENTON'S ACCOUNT OF THE EXPEDITION—DISCOVERS THE INLAND SEA—PERILOUS VOYAGE TO ITS ISLANDS IN A LINEN BOAT—ARRIVES AT FORT VANCOUVER AND FULFILLS THE INSTRUCTIONS OF HIS GOVERNMENT.

The results of Col. Fremont's first expedition were so unexpected, and his success altogether so extraordinary, that his government took no time to deliberate upon the propriety of sending him again into a field of duty, where he made the department of the public service, with which he was connected, appear to so much advantage. He had scarcely seen his maps and report through the press, before he embarked on a second expedition, from the same point on the frontier, but with purposes even more comprehensive than those with which he set out in 1842.

He was instructed to connect the exploration with the surveys of the Pacific coast, by Captain Wilkes, who had commanded the South Sea Exploring Expedition, so as to give a connected survey of the interior of our continent. His party consisted principally of Creole and Canadian French and Americans, amounting in all to 39 men; among whom were several who accompanied him in his first expedition. Mr. Thomas Fitzpatrick, whom many years of hardship and exposure in the western territories, had rendered familiar with a portion of the country it was designed to explore, had been selected as his guide, and Mr. Charles Preuss, who had been his assistant in the previous journey, was again associated with him in the same capacity.

In compliance with directions from the War Department, Mr. Theodore Talbot, of Washington city, was attached to the party, with a view to advancement in his profession; and at St. Louis he was joined by Mr. Frederick Dwight, a gentleman of Springfield, Massachusetts, who availed himself of this escort, to visit the Sandwich Islands and China, by way of Fort Vancouver.

The men engaged for the service were: Alexis Ayot, François Badeau, Oliver Beaulieu, Baptiste Bernier, John A. Campbell, John G. Campbell, Manuel Chapman, Ransom Clark, Philibert Courteau, Michel Crélis, William Creuss, Clinton Deforest, Baptiste Derosier, Basil Lajeunesse, François Lajeunesse, Henry Lee, Louis Ménard, Louis Montreuil, Samuel Neal, Alexis Pera, François Pera, James Power, Raphael Proue, Oscar Sarpy, Baptiste Tabeau, Charles Taplin, Baptiste Tesson, Auguste Vasquez, Joseph Verrot, Patrick White, Tiery Wright, Louis Zindel, and Jacob Dodson, a free young colored man of Washington city, who volunteered to accompany the expedition. Two Delaware Indians were engaged to accompany the expedition as hunters. L. Maxwell, who had accompanied the expedition as one of the hunters in 1842, being on his way to Taos, in New Mexico, also joined him. He was subsequently joined by his invaluable friend, Kit Carson, whom he was so fortunate as to fall in with on the confines of New Mexico.*

The party was armed generally with Hall's carbines, which, with a brass 12-lb. howitzer, had been furnished to

* As Kit Carson figures somewhat extensively in the reports of Col. Fremont, to whom he proved of incalculable service in each of his several exploring expeditions, we submit the following sketch of his life gathered mainly from his own lips.

Christopher Carson was born in Kentucky in the year 1810 or 1811; his father having been one of the early settlers, and also a noted hunter and Indian fighter. In the year following Kit's birth the family moved to the territory of Missouri. On this frontier, bred to border life, he remained to the age of fifteen, when he joined a trading party to Santa Fe. Instead of returning, Kit found his way by various adventures south, through New Mexico to the Copper mines of Chihuahua, where he passed nine months as a teamster.

When about seventeen he made his first expedition as a trapper on the Rio Colorado of California. The enterprise was successful, though attended with considerable dangers, the Mexicans being even at that early day very jealous of American enterprise. He made good his return to Tao in New Mexico, and soon after joined a trapping party to the head waters of the Arkansas River, whence he went northward to the region of the Rocky Mountains which gives rise to the Mississippi and Columbia rivers, where he remained engaged in the trapping business eight years. He became noted throughout that region and on both sides of the Rocky Mountains, as a successful trapper, an unfailing shot, an unerring guide, and for bravery, sagacity, and steadiness in all circumstances. He was chosen to lead in almost all enterprises of unusual danger, and in all attacks on the Indians. At one time with a party of twelve, he tracked a band of near sixty Crows who had stolen some of the horses belonging to the trappers; cut loose the animals which were tied within ten feet of the strong fort of logs in which the Indians had taken shelter; attacked them and made good his retreat with the recovered horses, an Indian of another party who was with the trappers bringing away a Crow scalp as a trophy. In one combat with the Blackfeet Indians, Carson received a rifle ball which broke his left shoulder. Save this, he escaped the manifold dangers to which he was exposed without serious bodily injury.

Of course in so turbulent and unrestrained a life, where there were no

him from the United States Arsenal at St. Louis, agreeably to the orders of Col. S. W. Kearney, commanding the third military division. We are thus particular in mentioning this piece of ordnance for reasons which

laws and no prisons, there were not unfrequent personal rencontres amongst the trappers, nor could the most peaceably disposed always avoid them. On one occasion a Frenchman who ranked as a bully, and had whipped a good many Canadians, insulted the Americans by saying they were only fit to be whipped with switches. Carson resented this instantly by saying that he was the most trifling one among the Americans, and that the braggart had better begin with him. After exchanging a few more words, each went away and armed himself, Carson with a pistol, the Frenchman with a rifle, and both mounted for the fight. Riding up until the horses' heads nearly touched—both fired almost at the same instant. Carson was a little the quickest, however, and his ball passing through the Frenchman's head, made him jerk up his gun, and sent the ball, which was intended for Carson's heart, grazing by his left eye and singeing his hair. This is, he says, the only serious personal quarrel he ever had.

Col. Fremont owed his good fortune in procuring Carson's services to an accidental meeting on board the steamboat above St. Louis, neither having ever heard of the other before, as he was setting out on his first expedition. Carson remained with him until he recrossed the mountains. His courage, fidelity, and excellent character, so completely won the heart of his commander that in his second expedition he was glad to avail himself of Kit's services, on falling in with him as he chanced to do on the confines of New Mexico. Kit again left the party on its arrival this side of the mountains—not however, until Fremont had obtained a promise from him to join the third expedition in case one should be organized, a promise which he faithfully kept under circumstances calculated to test his devotion to his late commander. In the interim between the second and third expeditions, Carson had settled himself near Taos and had begun to farm, preparing to lead a quiet life, when he received a note from Fremont, written at Bent's Fort reminding him of his promise and telling him that he waited there for him. In four days from the receipt of this note, Carson joined the party, having sold house and farm for less than half the sum he had first expended on it, and put his family under the protection of a friend, the late Gov. Bent, until he should return from a certainly long and dangerous journey. This pro-

FREMONT'S DANGEROUS PASSAGE THROUGH A CAÑON IN THE PLATTE RIVER—PAGE 58.

will appear presently. Three men were especially detailed for its service, under the charge of Louis Zindel, a native of Germany, who had been nineteen years a non-commissioned officer of artillery in the Prussian army, and regularly instructed in the duties of his profession. The camp equipage and provisions were transported in twelve carts, drawn each by two mules; and a light covered wagon, mounted on good springs, had been provided for the safe carriage of instruments. These were: One refracting telescope, by Frauenhofer; one reflecting circle, by Gambey; two sextants, by Troughton; one pocket chronometer, No. 837, by Goffe, Falmouth; one pocket chronometer, No. 739, by Brockbank; one syphon barometer, by Bunten, Paris; one cistern barometer, by Frye & Shaw, New York; six thermometers, and a number of small compasses.

To make the exploration as useful as possible, Mr. Fremont determined to vary the route to the Rocky Mountains from that followed in the year 1842. The route was then up the valley of the Great Platte River to the South Pass, in north latitude 428; the route now determined on was up the valley of the Kansas River, to the head of the Arkansas River, and to some pass in the mountains, if any could be found, at its source.

By making this deviation from the former route, the problem of a new road to Oregon and California, in a

tection unfortunately proved insufficient, for at the infamous Taos massacre which soon ensued, Carson's brother-in-law was massacred, and Mrs. Carson only saved her life by flight, leaving her house to be pillaged by the Mexicans.

When Carson was in Washington in 1847, he received from President Polk the commission of lieutenant in the rifle regiment of which Col. Fremont was lieutenant colonel.

climate more genial, might be solved; and a better knowledge obtained of an important river, and the country it drained, while the great object of the expedition would find its point of commencement at the termination of the former, which was at that great gate in the ridge of the Rocky Mountains called the South Pass, and on the lofty peak of the mountain which overlooks it, deemed the highest peak in the ridge, and from the opposite sides of which four great rivers take their rise, and flow to the Pacific or the Mississippi.

The party started from the little town of Kansas on the 29th of May, 1843, and did not get back to the United States again until August of the following year. What they accomplished and what they endured could not be more forcibly described than it has been by Colonel Benton, who gives facts in regard to the course taken by our government towards this expedition which were never before revealed. We give what he says of this expedition therefore, entire.*

"'The government deserves credit for the zeal with which it has pursued geographical discovery.' Such is the remark which a leading paper made upon the discoveries of Fremont, on his return from his second expedition to the great West; and such is the remark which all writers will make upon all his discoveries who write history from public documents and outside views. With all such writers the expeditions of Fremont will be credited to the zeal of the government for the promotion of science, as if the government under which he acted had conceived and planned these expeditions, as Mr. Jefferson did that of Lewis and Clark, and then selected this young officer to carry into effect the instructions delivered to him. How far

* *Thirty Years' View*, vol. ii. chap. 134.

such history would be true in relation to the first expedition, which terminated in the Rocky Mountains, has been seen in the account which has been given of the origin of that undertaking, and which leaves the government innocent of its conception; and, therefore, not entitled to the credit of its authorship, but only to the merit of permitting it. In the second, and greater expedition, from which great political as well as scientific results have flowed, their merit is still less; for, while equally innocent of its conception, they were not equally passive to its performance—countermanding the expedition after it had begun—and lavishing censure upon the adventurous young explorer for his manner of undertaking it. The fact was, that his first expedition barely finished, Mr. Fremont sought and obtained orders for a second one, and was on the frontier of Missouri with his command when orders arrived at St. Louis to stop him, on the ground that he had made a military equipment which the peaceful nature of his geographical pursuit did not require! as if Indians did not kill and rob scientific men as well as others if not in a condition to defend themselves. The particular point of complaint was that he had taken a small mountain howitzer, in addition to his rifles; and which, he was informed, was charged to him, although it had been furnished upon a regular requisition on the commandant of the arsenal at St. Louis, approved by the commander of the military department (Colonel, afterward General Kearney). Mr. Fremont had left St. Louis, and was at the frontier, Mrs. Fremont being requested to examine the letters that came after him, and forward those which he ought to receive. She read the countermanding orders and detained them! and Fremont knew nothing of their existence, until after he had returned from one of the most marvellous and eventful expeditions of modern times—one to which the United States are indebted (among other things) for the present ownership of California, instead of seeing it a British possession. The writer of this View, who was then in St. Louis, approved of the course which his daughter had taken (for she had stopped the orders before he knew it); and he wrote a letter to the department condemning the recall, repulsing the reprimand which had been lavished upon Fremont, and demanding a court-martial for him when he should return. The Secretary of War was then Mr. James Madison Porter, of Pennsylvania; the chief of the topographical corps the same as now (Colonel Abert), himself an office man, surrounded by West Point officers, to whose pursuit of easy service, Fremont's adventurous expeditions was a reproach; and in conformity to whose opinions the secretary seemed to have acted. On Fremont's return, upwards of a year afterwards, Mr. William Wilkins, of Pennsylvania, was Secretary of War, and received the young explorer with all honor and friendship, and obtained for him the brevet of captain from President Tyler. And such is the inside view of this piece of history—very different from what documentary evidence would make it.

"To complete his survey across the continent, on the line of travel between the State of Missouri and the tide-water region of the Columbia, was Fremont's object in this expedition; and it was all that he had obtained orders for doing; but only a small part, and to his mind, an insignificant part, of what he proposed doing. People had been to the mouth of the Columbia before, and his ambition was not limited to making tracks where others had made them before him. There was a vast region beyond the Rocky Mountains—the whole western slope of our continent—of which but little was known; and of that little, nothing with the accuracy of science. All that vast region, more than seven hundred miles square—equal to a great kingdom in Europe—was an unknown land—a sealed book, which he longed to open, and to read. Leaving the frontier of Missouri in May, 1843, and often diverging from his route for the sake of expanding his field of observation, he had arrived in the tide-water region of Columbia in the month of November; and had then completed the whole service which his orders embraced. He might then have returned upon his tracks, or been brought home by sea, or hunted the most pleasant path for getting back; and if he had been a routine officer, satisfied with fulfilling an order, he would have done so. Not so the young explorer, who held his diploma from nature, and not from the United States Military Academy. He was at Fort Vancouver, guest of the hospitable Dr. McLaughlin, Governor of the British Hudson Bay Fur Company; and obtained from him all possible information upon his intended line of return—faithfully given, but which proved to be disastrously erroneous in its leading and governing feature. A southeast route to cross the great unknown region diagonally through its heart (making a line from the Lower Columbia to the Upper Colorado of the Gulf of California), was his line of return: twenty-five men (the same who had come with him from the United States) and a hundred horses, were his equipment; and the commencement of winter the time of starting—all without a guide, relying upon their guns for support; and, in the last resort, upon their horses—such as should give out! for one that could carry a man, or a pack, could not be spared for food.

"All the maps up to that time had shown this region traversed from east to west—from the base of the Rocky Mountains to the Bay of San Francisco—by a great river called the *Buena Ventura:* which may be translated, the *Good Chance.* Governor McLaughlin believed in the existence of this river, and made out a conjectural manuscript map to show its place and course. Fremont believed in it, and his plan was to reach it before the dead of winter, and then hybernate upon it. As a great river he knew that it must have some rich bottoms, covered with wood and grass, where the wild animals would collect and shelter, when the snows and freezing winds drove them from the plains: and with these animals to live on, and grass for the horses, and wood for fires, he expected to avoid suffering, if not to enjoy comfort, during his solitary sojourn in that remote and profound wilderness.

"He proceeded—soon encountered deep snows which impeded

progress upon the highlands—descended into a low country to the left (afterwards known to be the Great Basin, from which no water issues to any sea)—skirted an enormous chain of mountain on the right, luminous with glittering white snow—saw strange Indians, who mostly fled—found a desert—no Buena Ventura; and death from cold and famine staring him in the face. The failure to find the river, or tidings of it, and the possibility of its existence seeming to be forbid by the structure of the country, and hybernation in the inhospitable desert being impossible, and the question being that of life and death, some new plan of conduct became indispensable. His celestial observations told him that he was in the latitude of the Bay of San Francisco, and only seventy miles from it. But what miles! up and down that snowy mountain which the Indians told him no men could cross in the winter—which would have snow upon it as deep as the trees, and places where people would slip off, and fall half a mile at a time;—a fate which actually befell a mule, packed with the precious burden of botanical specimens, collected along a travel of two thousand miles. No reward could induce an Indian to become a guide in the perilous adventure of crossing this mountain. All recoiled and fled from the adventure. It was attempted without a guide—in the dead of winter—accomplished in forty days—the men and surviving horses—a woeful procession, crawling along one by one; skeleton men leading skeleton horses—and arriving at Sutter's Settlement in the beautiful valley of the Sacramento; and where a genial warmth, and budding flowers, and trees in foliage, and grassy ground, and flowing streams, and comfortable food, made a fairy contrast with the famine and freezing they had encountered, and the lofty Sierra Nevada which they had climbed. Here he rested and recruited; and from this point, and by way of Monterey, the first tidings were heard of the party since leaving Fort Vancouver.

"Another long progress to the south, skirting the western base of the Sierra Nevada, made him acquainted with the noble valley of the San Joaquin, counterpart to that of the Sacranento; when crossing through a gap, and turning to the left, he skirted the Great Basin; and by many deviations from the right line home, levied incessant contributions to science from expanded lands, not described before. In this eventful exploration, all the great features of the western slope of our continent were brought to light—the Great Salt Lake, the Utah Lake, the Little Salt Lake; at all which places, then deserts, the Mormons now are; the Sierra Nevada, then solitary in the snow, now crowded with Americans, digging gold from its flanks: the beautiful valleys of the Sacramento and San Joaquin, then alive with wild horses, elk, deer, and wild fowls, now smiling with American cultivation; the Great Basin itself, and its contents; the Three Parks; the approximation of the great rivers which, rising together in the central region of the Rocky Mountains, go off east and west, towards the rising and the setting sun—all these, and other strange features of a new region, more Asiatic than American, were brought to light and revealed to public view in the results of this exploration.

"Eleven months he was never out of sight of snow; and sometimes, freezing with cold, would look down upon a sunny valley, warm with genial heat;—sometimes panting with the summer's heat, would look up at the eternal snows which crowned the neighboring mountain. But it was not then that California was secured to the Union—to the greatest power of the New World—to which it of right belonged; but it was the first step towards the acquisition, and the one that led to it. The second expedition led to a third, just in time to snatch the golden California from the hands of the British, ready to clutch it. But of this hereafter. Fremont's second expedition was now over. He had left the United States a fugitive from his government, and returned with a name that went over Europe and America, and with discoveries bearing fruit which the civilized world is now enjoying."

Thrilling as this brief sketch by Col. Benton is, it conveys to the reader but an imperfect idea of the hardships of this awful journey, and of the heroism of the little band who endured them. Fremont set out from the town of Kansas, as we have already stated, on the 29th of May. On the 6th of September, and after travelling over 1,700 miles, he came in sight of the Salt Lake, the most important geographical result of his travels to that point. The description of his approach to this Inland Sea, as he then termed it, and his perilous voyage to an island with which it was gemmed in his linen boat, the first of any kind that ever ploughed that unexplored water, cannot be given to better advantage than in his own words. The night before they had encamped a few miles distant on what was known as Weber's Fork, a stream from 100 to 150 feet wide. He continued his narrative as follows:

" *September 6th.*—Leaving the encampment early, we again directed our course for the peninsular *butte* across a low shrubby plain, crossing in the way a slough-like creek, with miry banks, and wooded with thickets of thorn (*cratægus*) which were loaded with berries. This time we reached the butte without any difficulty, and, ascended to the summit, immediately at our feet beheld the object of our anxious search—the waters of the Inland Sea, stretching in still and solitary grandeur far beyond the limit of our vision. It was one of the great points of the exploration; and as we looked eagerly over the lake in the first emotions of excited pleasure, I am doubtful if the followers of Balboa felt more enthusiasm when, from the heights of the Andes, they saw for the first time the great western ocean. It was certainly a magnificent object, and a noble terminus to this part of our expedition; and to travellers so long shut up among mountain ranges, a sudden view over the expanse of silent waters had in it something sublime. Several large islands raised their high rocky peaks out of the waves; but whether or not they were timbered, was still left to our imagination, as the distance was too great to determine if the dark hues upon them were woodland or naked rock. During the day, the clouds had been gathering black over the mountains to the westward, and, while we were looking, a storm burst down with sudden fury upon the lake, and entirely hid the islands from our view. So far as we could see, along the shores there was not a solitary tree, and but little appearance of grass; and on Weber's Fork, a few miles below our last encampment, the timber was gathered into groves, and then disappeared entirely. As this appeared to be the nearest point to the lake where a suitable camp could be found, we directed our course to one of the groves, where we found a handsome encampment, with good grass and an abundance of rushes (*equisetum hyemale*). At sunset the thermometer was 55°; the evening clear and calm, with some cumuli.

"*September* 7.—The morning was calm and clear, with a temperature at sunrise of 39° 5'. The day was spent in active preparation for our intended voyage on the lake. On the edge of the stream a favorable spot was selected in a grove, and, felling the timber, we made a strong *corral*, or horse pen, for the animals, and a little fort for the people who were to remain. We were now probably in the country of the Utah Indians, though none reside upon the lake. The India-rubber boat was repaired with prepared cloth and gum, and filled with air, in readiness for the next day.

"The provisions which Carson had brought with him being now exhausted, and our stock reduced to a small quantity of roots, I determined to retain with me only a sufficient number of men for the execution of our design; and accordingly seven were sent back to Fort Hall, under the guidance of François Lajeunesse, who, having been for many years a trapper in the country, was considered an experienced mountaineer. Though they were provided with good horses, and the road was a remarkably plain one, of only four days' journey for a horseman, they became bewildered (as we afterwards learned), and losing their way, wandered about the country in parties of one or two, reaching the fort about a week afterwards Some straggled in of themselves, and the others were brought in by Indians who had picked them upon Snake River, about sixty miles below the fort, travelling along the emigrant road in full march for the Lower Columbia. The leader of this adventurous party was François.

"We formed now but a small family. With Mr. Preuss and myself, Carson, Bernier, and Basil Lajeunesse, had been selected for the boat expedition—the first ever attempted on this interior sea; and Badeau, with Derosier, and Jacob (the colored man), were to be left in charge of the camp. We were favored with most delightful weather. To-night there was a brilliant sunset of golden orange and green, which left the western sky clear and beautifully pure; but clouds in the east made me lose an occultation. The summer frogs were singing around us, and the evening was very pleasant, with a temperature of 66°—a night of a more southern autumn. For our supper we had *yampah*, the most agreeably flavored of the roots, seasoned by a small fat duck, which had come in the way of Jacob's rifle. Around our fire to-night were many speculations on what to-morrow would bring forth, and in our busy conjectures we fancied that we should find every one of the large islands a tangled wilderness of trees and shrubbery, teeming with game of every description that the neighboring region afforded, and which the foot of a white man or Indian had never violated. Frequently, during the day, clouds had rested on the summits of their lofty mountains, and we believed that we should find clear streams and springs of fresh water; and we indulged in anticipations of the luxurious repasts with which we were to indemnify ourselves for past privations. Neither, in our discussions, were the whirlpool and other mysterious dangers forgotten, which Indian and hunter's stories attributed to this unexplored lake.

"The men had discovered that, instead of being strongly sewed (like that of the preceding year, which had so triumphantly rode the canons of the Upper Great Platte), our present boat was only pasted together in a very insecure manner, the maker having been allowed so little time in the construction that he was obliged to crowd the labor of two months into several days. The insecurity of the boat was sensibly felt by us; and mingled with the enthusiasm and excitement that we all felt at the prospect of an undertaking which had never before, been accomplished, was a certain impression of danger, sufficient to give a serious character to our conversation. The momentary view which had been had of the lake the day before, its great extent and rugged islands, dimly seen amidst the waters in the obscurity of the sudden storm, were well calculated to heighten the idea of undefined danger with which the lake was generally associated.

"*September* 8.—A calm, clear day, with a sunrise temperature of 41°. In view of our present enterprise, a part of the equipment of the boat had been made to consist in three air-tight bags, about three feet long, and capable each of containing five gallons. These had been filled with water the night before, and were now placed in the boat, with our blankets and instruments, consisting of a sextant, telescope, spy-glass, thermometer, and barometer.

"We left the camp at sunrise, and had a very pleasant voyage down the river, in which there was generally eight or ten feet of water, deepening as we neared the mouth in the latter part of the day. In the course of the morning we discovered that two of the cylinders leaked so much as to require one man constantly at the bellows, to keep them sufficiently full of air to support the boat. Although we had made a very early start, we loitered so much on the way—stopping every now and then, and floating silently along, to get a shot at a goose or a duck—that it was late in the day when we reached the outlet. The river here divided into several branches, filled with fluvials, and so very shallow that it was with difficulty we could get the boat along, being obliged to get out and wade. We encamped on a low point among rushes and young willows, where there was a quantity of drift wood, which served for our fires. The evening was mild and clear; we made a pleasent bed of the young willows; and geese and ducks enough had been killed for an abundant supper at night, and for breakfast the next morning. The stillness of the night was enlivened by millions of water fowl Latitude (by observation) 41° 11′ 26″; and longitude 112° 11′ 30″.

"*September* 9.—The day was clear and calm; the thermometer at sunrise at 49°. As usual with the trappers on the eve of any enterprise, our people had made dreams, and theirs happened to be a bad one—one which always preceded evil—and consequently they looked very gloomy this morning; but we hurried through our breakfast, in order to make an early start, and have all the day before us for our adventure. The channel in a short distance became so shallow that our navigation was at an end, being merely a sheet of soft mud, with a few inches of water, and sometimes none at all, forming the low-water shore of the lake. All this place was absolutely covered with flocks of screaming plover. We took off our clothes, and, getting overboard, commenced dragging the boat—making, by this operation, a very curious trail, and a very disagreeable smell in stirring up the mud, as we sank above the knee at every step. The water here was still fresh, with only an insipid and disagreeable taste, probably derived from the bed of fetid mud. After proceeding in this way about a mile, we came to a small black ridge on the bottom, beyond which the water became suddenly salt, beginning gradually to deepen, and the bottom was sandy and firm. It was a remarkable division, separating the fresh waters of the rivers from the briny water of the lake, which was entirely *saturated* with common salt. Pushing our little vessel across the narrow boundary, we sprang on board, and at length were afloat on the waters of the unknown sea.

"We did not steer for the mountainous islands, but directed our course towards a lower one, which it had been decided we should first visit, the summit of which was formed like the crater at the upper end of Bear River valley. So long as we could touch the bottom with our paddles, we were very gay; but gradually, as the water deepened, we became more still in our frail bateau of gum cloth distended with air, and with pasted seams. Although the day was very calm, there was a considerable swell on the lake; and there were white patches of foam on the surface, which were slowly moving to the southward, indicating the set of a current in that direction, and recalling the recollection of the whirlpool stories. The water continued to deepen as we advanced; the lake becoming almost transparently clear, of an extremely beautiful bright-green color; and the spray, which was thrown into the boat and over our clothes, was directly converted into a crust of common salt, which covered also our hands and arms. 'Captain,' said Carson, who for some time had been looking suspiciously at some whitening appearances outside the nearest island, "what are those yonder?--won't you just take a look with the glass?" We ceased paddling for a moment, and found them to be the caps of the waves that were beginning to break under the force of a strong breeze that was coming up the lake.

"The form of the boat seemed to be an admirable one, and it rode on the waves like a water bird; but at the same time, it was slow in its progress. When we were little more than half way across the reach, two of the divisions between the cylinders gave way, and it required the constant use of the bellows to keep in a sufficient quantity of air. For a long time we scarcely seemed to approach our island, but gradually we worked across the rougher sea of the open channel, into the smoother water under the lee of the island; and began to discover that what we took for a long row of pelicans, ranged on the beach, were only low cliffs, whitened with salt by the spray of the waves; and about noon we reached the shore, the transparency of the water enabling us to see the bottom at a considerable depth.

"It was a handsome broad beach where we landed, behind

which the hill, into which the island was gathered, rose somewhat abruptly; and a point of rock at one end enclosed it in a sheltering way; and as there was an abundance of drift wood along the shore, it offered us a pleasant encampment. We did not suffer our fragile boat to touch the sharp rocks, but getting overboard, discharged the baggage, and lifting it gently out of the water, carried it to the upper part of the beach, which was composed of very small fragments of rock.

"Among the successive banks of the beach, formed by the action of the waves, our attention, as we approached the island, had been attracted by one 10 to 20 feet in breadth, of a dark-brown color. Being more closely examined, this was found to be composed, to the depth of seven or eight and twelve inches, entirely of the *larvæ* of insects, or, in common language, of the skins of worms, about the size of a grain of oats, which had been washed up by the waters of the lake.

"The cliffs and masses of rock along the shore were whitened by an incrustation of salt where the waves dashed up against them; and the evaporating water, which had been left in holes and hollows on the surface of the rocks, was covered with a crust of salt about one-eighth of an inch in thickness. It appeared strange that, in the midst of this grand reservoir, one of our greatest wants lately had been salt. Exposed to be more perfectly dried in the sun, this became very white and fine, having the usual flavor of very excellent common salt, without any foreign taste; but only a little was collected for present use, as there was in it a number of small black insects.

"Carrying with us the barometer, and other instruments, in the afternoon we ascended to the highest point of the island—a bare rocky peak, 800 feet above the lake. Standing on the summit, we enjoyed an extended view of the lake, enclosed in a basin of rugged mountains, which sometimes left marshy flats and extensive bottoms between them and the shore, and in other places came directly down into the water with bold and precipitous bluffs. Following with our glasses the irregular shores, we searched for some indications of a communication with other bodies of water, or the entrance of other rivers; but the distance was so great that we could make out nothing with certainty. To the southward, several peninsular mountains, 3,000 or 4,000 feet high, entered the lake, appearing, so far as the distance and our position enabled us to determine, to be connected by flats and low ridges with the mountains in the rear. These are probably the islands usually indicated on maps of this region as entirely detached from the shore. The season of our operations was when the waters were at their lowest stage. At the season of high waters in the spring, it is probable that the marshes and low grounds are overflowed, and the surface of the lake considerably greater. In several places the view was of unlimited extent—here and there a rocky islet appearing above the water at a great distance; and beyond, everything was vague and undefined. As we looked over the vast expanse of water spread out beneath us, and strained our eyes along the silent shores over which hung so much doubt and uncertainty, and which were so full of interest to us, I could hardly repress the almost irresistible desire to continue our exploration; but the lengthening snow on the mountains was a plain indication of the advancing season, and our frail linen boat appeared so insecure that I was unwilling to trust our lives to the uncertainties of the lake. I therefore unwillingly resolved to terminate our survey here, and remain satisfied for the present with what we had been able to add the unknown geography of the region. We felt pleasure also in remembering that we were the first who, in traditionary annals of the country, had visited the islands, and broken, with the cheerful sound of human voices, the long solitude of the place. From the point where we were standing, the ground fell off on every side to the water, giving us a perfect view of the island, which is twelve or thirteen miles in circumference, being simply a rocky hill, on which there is neither water nor trees of any kind; although the *Fremontia vermicu-*

laris, which was in great abundance, might easily be mistaken for timber at a distance. The plant seemed here to delight in a congenial air, growing in extraordinary luxuriance seven to eight feet high, and was very abundant on the upper parts of the island, where it was almost the only plant. This is eminently a saline shrub; its leaves have a very salt taste; and it luxuriates in saline soils, where it is usually a characteristic. It is widely diffused over all this country. A chenopodiaceous shrub, which is a new species of OBIONE (O. rigida, *Torr. & Frem.*), was equally characteristic of the lower parts of the island. These two are the striking plants on the island, and belong to a class of plants which form a prominent feature in the vegetation of this country. On the lower parts of the island, also, a prickly pear of very large size was frequent. On the shore, near the water, was a woolly species of *phaca;* and a new species of umbelliferous plant *(leptotæmia)* was scattered about in very considerable abundance. These constituted all the vegetation that now appeared upon the island.

"I accidentally left on the summit the brass cover to the object end of my spy-glass; and as it will probably remain there undisturbed by Indians, it will furnish matter of speculation to some future traveller. In our excursions about the island, we did not meet with any kind of animal; a magpie, and another larger bird, probably attracted by the smoke of our fire, paid us a visit from the shore, and were the only living things seen during our stay. The rock constituting the cliffs along the shore where we were encamped, is a talcous rock, or steatite, with brown spar.

"At sunset, the temperature was 70°. We had arrived just in time to obtain a meridian altitude of the sun, and other observations were obtained this evening, which place our camp in latitude 41°10′ 42″, and longitude 112° 21′ 05″ from Greenwich. From a discussion of the barometrical observations made during our stay on the shores of the lake, we have adopted 4,200 feet for its elevation above the gulf of Mexico.

In the first disappointment we felt from the dissipation of our dream of the fertile islands, I called this *Disappointment Island.*

"Out of the drift wood, we made ourselves pleasant little lodges, open to the water, and, after having kindled large fires to excite the wonder of any straggling savage on the lake shores, lay down, for the first time in a long journey, in perfect security; no one thinking about his arms. The evening was extremely bright and pleasant; but the wind rose during the night, and the waves began to break heavily on the shore, making our island tremble. I had not expected in our inland journey to hear the roar of an ocean surf; and the strangeness of our situation, and the excitement we felt in the associated interests of the place, made this one of the most interesting nights I remember during our long expedition.

"In the morning the surf was breaking heavily on the shore, and we were up early. The lake was dark and agitated, and we hurried through our scanty breakfast, and embarked—having first filled one of the buckets with water from the lake, of which it was intended to make salt. The sun had risen by the time we were ready to start; and it was blowing a strong gale of wind, almost directly off the shore, and raising a considerable sea, in which our boat strained very much. It roughened as we got away from the island, and it required all the efforts of the men to make any head against the wind and sea, the gale rising with the sun; and there was danger of being blown into one of the open reaches beyond the island. At the distance of half a mile from the beach, the depth of water was sixteen feet, with a clay bottom; but, as the working of the boat was very severe labor, and during the operation of rounding it was necessary to cease paddling, during which the boat lost considerable way, I was unwilling to discourage the men, and reluctantly gave up my intention of ascertaining the depth, and the character of the bed. There was a general shout in the boat when we found ourselves in one fathom, and we soon after landed on a low point of mud, immediately under the butte of the peninsula, where we unloaded the boat and carried the baggage about a quarter of a mile to firmer ground. We arrived just in time for meridian observation, and carried the barometer to the summit of the butte, which is 500 feet above the lake. Mr. Preuss set off on foot for the camp, which was about nine miles distant; Basil accompanying him to bring back horses for the boat and baggage.

"The rude-looking shelter we raised on the shore, our scattered baggage and boat lying on the beach, made quite a picture; and we called this the *Fisherman's Camp. Lynosiris graveolens,* and another new species of OBIONE (O confertifolia—*Torr. & Frem.*), were growing on the low grounds, with interspersed spots of an unwholesome salt grass, on a saline clay soil, with a few other plants.

"The horses arrived late in the afternoon, by which time the gale had increased to such a height that a man could scarcely stand before it; and we were obliged to pack our baggage hastily, as the rising water of the lake had already reached the point where we were halted. Looking back as we rode off, we found the place of recent encampment entirely covered. The low plain through which we rode to the camp was covered with a compact growth of shrubs of extraordinary size and luxuriance. The soil was sandy and saline; flat places, resembling the beds of ponds, that were bare of vegetation, and covered with a powdery white salt, being interspersed among the shrubs. Artemisia tridentata was very abundant, but the plants were principally saline; a large and vigorous chenopodiaceous shrub, five to eight feet high, being characteristic, with Fremontia vermicularis, and a shrubby plant which seems to be a new *salicornia.* We reached the camp in time to escape a thunder storm which blackened the sky, and were received with a discharge of the howitzer by the people, who, having been unable to see anything of us on the lake, had begun to feel some uneasiness."

On the 4th of November, Col. Fremont and his party reached Fort Vancouver, on the Columbia River, the appointed terminus of his journey. He remarks in his journal that it would have been very gratifying to have gone down to the Pacific, and solely in the interest and in the love of geography, to have seen the ocean on the western as well as on the eastern side of the continent, so as to give a satisfactory completeness to the geographical picture which had been formed in his mind; but the rainy season had now regularly set in, and the air was filled with fogs and rain, which left no beauty in any scenery, and obstructed observations. The object of his instructions had been entirely fulfilled in having connected his reconnoissance with the surveys of Captain Wilkes; and although it would have been agreeable and satisfactory to have completed there his astronomical observations, he did not feel that for such a reason he would be justified in waiting for favorable weather. He therefore signified his intention to his companions to set out for the east without an hour's unnecessary delay.

CHAPTER V.

SECOND EXPLORING EXPEDITION CONTINUED—SETS OUT FROM FORT VANCOUVER—INTERESTING INDIAN COUNCIL—SPEECH OF COL. FREMONT—JOURNEY THROUGH THE MOUNTAINS—INSANITY OF HIS MEN FROM PRIVATION AND COLD—PREUSS LOSES HIS WAY—ARRIVAL AT THE RANCHE OF CAPTAIN SUTTER.

IN two days, preparations for their return were completed, and on the 10th of November, his little party embarked on their homeward journey, in which he contemplated a circuit to the south and southeast, and the exploration of the Great Basin between the Rocky Mountains and the *Sierra Nevada*. Three principal objects were indicated, by report or by maps, as being on this route, the character or existence of which he wished to ascertain, and which he assumed as land marks, or leading points, on the projected line of return. The first of these points was the *Tlamath* Lake, on the table-land between the head of Fall River, which comes to the Columbia, and the Sacramento, which goes to the bay of San Francisco; and from which lake a river of the same name makes its way westwardly direct to the ocean. The position of this lake, on the line of inland communication between

Oregon and California; its proximity to the demarkation boundary of latitude 42°; its imputed double character of lake, or meadow, according to the season of the year; and the hostile and warlike character attributed to the Indians about it—all made it a desirable object to visit and examine. From this lake he intended to go about southeast, to a reported lake called Mary's, distant some days' journey in the Great Basin; and thence, still on southeast, to the reputed *Buenaventura* River, which has had a place in many maps, countenancing a belief in the existence of a great river flowing from the Rocky Mountains to the bay of San Francisco. From the Buenaventura his destination was that section of the Rocky Mountains which includes the heads of Arkansas River, and of the opposite waters of the California gulf; and thence down the Arkansas to Bent's fort, and home. This was his projected line of return—a great part of it absolutely new to geographical, botanical, and geological science—and the subject of endless rumors of lakes, rivers, deserts, and savages hardly above the condition of wild animals, all tending to inflame his curiosity and love of adventure to its highest pitch.

It was a serious enterprise, at the commencement of winter, to undertake the passage of such a region, and with a party consisting only of twenty-five persons, and they of many nations—American, French, German, Canadian, Indian, and colored—and most of them young, several of them being under twenty-one years of age. All knew that a strange country was to be explored, and dangers and hardships to be encountered; but no one blenched at the prospect. On the contrary, courage and confidence animated the whole party.

Cheerfulness, readiness, subordination, prompt obedience, characterized all; nor did any extremity of peril or privation, to which they were afterwards exposed, says Mr. Fremont, ever belie, or derogate from, the fine spirit of this brave and generous commencement.

He was not permitted to execute this plan precisely as he had marked it out; but we must refer to his official report, those who wish to know how he was forced by desert plains and mountain ranges, and deep snows, far to the south, and along the western base of the Sierra Nevada; where, indeed, a new and ample field of exploration opened itself before him. The reader will be able to form a tolerably satisfactory idea of the hardships endured by him and his heroical party during the eleven months that he was struggling for a passage over the mountains, by a few extracts from his journal for the months of January, February, and March, which are here submitted. No one can rise from the perusal of them without feeling that the powers of human endurance had never been so fully tested before.

"*January 28th.*—To-day we went through the pass with all the camp, and, after a hard day's journey of twelve miles, encamped on a high point where the snow had been blown off, and the exposed grass afforded a scanty pasture for the animals. Snow and broken country together made our travelling difficult. We were often compelled to make large circuits, and ascend the highest and most exposed ridges in order to avoid snow, which in other places was banked up to a great depth. * * *

"To-night we did not succeed in getting the howitzer into camp. This was the most laborious day we had yet passed through, the steep ascents and deep snow exhausting both men and animals. Our single chronometer had stopped during the day, and its error in time occasioned the loss of an eclipse of a satellite this evening. It had not preserved the rate with which we started from the Dalles, and this will account for the absence of longitudes along this interval of our journey.

"*January* 29*th*.—Several Indians appeared on the hillside, reconnoitring the camp, and were induced to come in; others came in during the afternoon; and in the evening we held a council. The Indians immediately made it clear that the waters on which we were, also belong to the Great Basin, in the edge of which we had been since the 17th of December; and it became evident that we had still the great ridge on the left to cross before we could reach the Pacific waters.

"We explained to the Indians that we were endeavoring to find a passage across the mountains into the country of the whites, whom we were going to see; and told them that we wished them to bring us a guide, to whom we would give presents of scarlet cloth, and other articles, which were shown to them. They looked at the reward we offered, and conferred with each other, but pointed to the snow on the mountains, and drew their hands across their neck and raised them above their heads, to show the depth: and signified that it was impossible for us to get through. They made signs that we must go to the southward, over a pass through a lower range, which they pointed out; there, they said, at the end of one day's travel we would find people who lived near a pass in the great mountain; and to that point they engaged to furnish us a guide. They appeared to have a confused idea, from report, of whites who lived on the other side of the mountain; and once, they told us, about two years ago, a party of twelve men like ourselves, had ascended their river, and crossed to the other waters. They pointed out to us where they had crossed; but then, they said, it was summer time; but now it would be impossible. * * *

"The Indians brought in during the evening an abundant supply of pine-nuts, which we traded from them. When roasted, their pleasant flavor made them an agreeable addition to our now scanty store of provisions which were reduced to a very low ebb. Our principal stock was in peas, which it is not necessary to say contain scarcely any nutriment. We had still a little flour left, some coffee, and a quantity of sugar, which I reserved as a defence against starvation.

* * * * * *

"The other division of the party did not come in to-night, but encamped in the upper meadow, and arrived the next morning. They had not succeeded in getting the howitzer beyond the place mentioned, and where it had been left by Mr. Preuss in obedience to my orders; and, in anticipation of the snow-banks and snow-fields still ahead, foreseeing the inevitable detention to which it would subject us, I reluctantly determined to leave it there for the time. It was of the kind invented by the French for the mountain part of their war in Algiers; and the distance it had come with us proved how well it was adapted to its purpose. We left it, to the great sorrow of the whole party, who were grieved to part with a companion which had made the whole distance from St. Louis, and commanded respect for us on some critical occasions, and which might be needed for the same purpose again.

"*January* 30.—Our guide, who was a young man, joined us this morning; and leaving our encampment late in the day, we descended the river. * * * *

"With our late start we made but ten miles, and encamped on the lower river bottom, where there was no snow, but a great deal of ice; and we cut piles of long grass to lay under our blankets, and fires were made of large dry willows, groves of which wooded the stream. * * * *

"*January* 31.—We took our way over a gently rising ground, the dividing ridge being tolerably low; and travelling easily along a broad trail, in twelve or fourteen miles reached the upper part of the pass; when it began to snow thickly, with very cold weather. The Indians had only the usual scanty covering, and appeared to suffer greatly from the cold. All left us, except our guide. Half hidden by the storm, the mountains looked dreary; and, as night began to approach, the guide showed great reluctance to go forward. I placed him between two rifles, for the way began to be difficult. Travelling a little further, we struck a ravine, which the Indian said would conduct us to the river; and as the poor fellow suffered greatly, shivering in the snow which fell upon his naked skin, I would not detain him any longer; and he ran off to the mountain, where he said there was a hut near by. He had kept the blue and scarlet cloths I had given him tightly rolled up, preferring rather to endure the cold than to get them wet. In the course of the afternoon, one of the men had his foot frost-bitten; and about dark we had the satisfaction to reach the bottoms of a stream timbered with large trees, among which we found a sheltered camp, with an abundance of such grass as the season afforded for the animals.

"We had scarcely lighted our fires, when the camp was crowded with nearly naked Indians; some of them were furnished with long nets in addition to bows, and appeared to have been out on the sage hills to hunt rabbits. These nets were perhaps thirty to forty feet long, kept upright in the ground by slight sticks at intervals, and were made from a kind of wild hemp, very much resembling in manufacture those common among the Indians of the Sacramento valley. They came among us without any fear, and scattered themselves about the fires, mainly occupied in gratifying their astonishment. I was struck by the singular appearance of a row of about a dozen, who were sitting on their haunches perched on a log near one of the fires, with their quick sharp eyes following every motion.

"We gathered together a few of the most intelligent of the Indians, and held this evening an interesting council. I explained to them my intentions. I told them that we had come from a very far country, having been travelling now nearly a year, and that we were desirous simply to go across the mountain into the country of the other whites. There were two who appeared particularly intelligent—one, a somewhat old man. He told me that, before the snow fell, it was six sleeps to the place where the whites lived, but that now it was impossible to cross the mountain on account of the deep snow; and showing us, as the others had done, that it was over our heads, he urged us strongly to follow the course of the river, which he said would conduct us to a lake in which there were many large fish. There, he said, were many people; there was no snow on the ground; and we might remain there until the spring.

"From their descriptions, we were enabled to judge that we had encamped on the upper waters of the Salmon Trout River. It is hardly necessary to say that our communication was only by signs, as we understood nothing of their language; but they spoke, notwithstanding, rapidly and vehemently, explaining what they considered the folly of our intentions, and urging us to go down to the lake. *Tah-ve*, a word signifying snow, we very soon learned to know, from its frequent repetition. I told him that the men and the horses were strong, and that we would break a road through the snow; and spreading before him our bales of scarlet cloth, and trinkets, showed him what we would give for a guide. It was necessary to obtain one, if possible, for I had determined here to attempt the passage of the mountain. Pulling a bunch of grass from the ground, after a short discussion among themselves, the old man made us comprehend, that if we could break through the snow, at the end of three days we would come down upon grass, which he showed us would be about six inches high, and where the ground was entirely free. So far, he said, he had been in hunting for elk; but beyond that (and he closed his eyes) he had seen nothing; but there was one among them who had been to the whites, and, going out of the lodge, he returned with a young man of very intelligent appearance. Here, said he, is a young man who has seen the whites with his own eyes; and he swore, first by the sky, and then by the ground, that what he said was true.

With a large present of goods, we prevailed upon this young man to be our guide, and he acquired among us the name Mélo —a word signifying friend, which they used very frequently. He was thinly clad, and nearly barefoot; his moccasins being about worn out. We gave him skins to make a new pair, and to enable him to perform his undertaking to us. The Indians remained in the camp during the night, and we kept the guide and two others to sleep in the lodge with us—Carson lying across the door, and having made them comprehend the use of our fire-arms. The snow, which had intermitted in the evening, commenced falling again in the course of the night, and it snowed steadily all day.

"In the morning I acquainted the men with my decision, and explained to them that necessity required us to make a great effort to clear the mountains. I reminded them of the beautiful valley of the Sacramento, with which they were familiar from the descriptions of Carson, who had been there some fifteen years ago, and who, in our late privations, had delighted us in speaking of its rich pastures and abounding game, and drew a vivid contrast between its summer climate, less than a hundred miles distant, and the falling snow around us. I informed them (and long experience had given them confidence in my observations and good instruments) that almost directly west, and only about seventy miles distant, was the great farming establishment of Captain Sutter—a gentleman who had formerly lived in Missouri, and, emigrating to this country, had become the possessor of a principality. I assured them that, from the heights of the mountains before us, we should doubtless see the valley of the Sacramento River, and with one effort place ourselves again in the midst of plenty. The people received this decision with the cheerful obedience which had always characterized them; and the day was immediately devoted to the preparations necessary to enable us to carry it into effect. Leggings, moccasins, clothing—all were put into the best state to resist the cold. Our guide was not neglected. Extremity of suffering might make him desert: we therefore did the best we could for him. Leggings, moccasins, some articles of clothing, and a large green blanket, in addition to the blue and scarlet cloth, were lavished upon him, and to his great and evident contentment. He arrayed himself in all his colors; and clad in green, blue, and scarlet, he made a gay-looking Indian; and with his various presents, was probably richer and better clothed than any of his tribe had ever been before.

"I have already said that our provisions were very low; we had neither tallow nor grease of any kind remaining, and the want of salt became one of our greatest privations. The poor dog, which had been found in the Bear River Valley, and which had been a *compagnon de voyage* ever since, had now become fat, and the mess to which it belonged requested permission to kill it. Leave was granted. Spread out on the snow, the meat looked very good; and it made a strengthening meal for the greater part of the camp. Indians brought in two or three rabbits during the day, which were purchased from them.

* * * * * *

"*February* 4.—I went ahead early with two or three men, each with a led horse, to break the road. We were obliged to abandon the hollow entirely, and work along the mountain side, which was very steep, and the snow covered with an icy crust. We cut a footing as we advanced, and trampled a road through for the animals; but occasionally one plunged outside the trail, and slid along the field to the bottom, a hundred yards below.

"Towards a pass which the guide indicated here, we attempted in the afternoon to force a road; but after a laborious plunging through two or three hundred yards, our best horses gave out, entirely refusing to make any further effort; and, for the time, we were brought to a stand. The guide informed us that we were entering the deep snow, and here began the difficulties of the mountain; and to him, and almost to all, our enterprise seemed hopeless. I returned a short distance back, to the break in the hollow, where I met Mr. Fitzpatrick.

"The camp had been all the day occupied in endeavoring to ascend the hill, but only the best horses had succeeded; the animals, generally, not having sufficient strength to bring themselves up without the packs; and all the line of road between this and the springs was strewed with camp stores and equipage, and horses floundering in snow.

"To night we had no shelter, but we made a large fire around the trunk of one of the huge pines; and covering the snow with small boughs on which we spread our blankets, soon made our selves comfortable. The night was very bright and clear, though the thermometer was only at 10°. A strong wind, which sprang up at sundown, made it intensely cold, and this was one of the bitterest nights during the journey.

"Two Indians joined our party here; and one of them, an old man, immediately began to harangue us, saying that ourselves and animals would perish in the snow; and that if we would go back, he would show us another and a better way across the mountain. He spoke in a very loud voice, and there was a singular repetition of phrases and arrangement of words, which rendered his speech striking, and not unmusical.

"We had now begun to understand some words, and, with the aid of signs, easily comprehended the old man's simple idea. 'Rock upon rock—rock upon rock—snow upon snow—snow upon snow,' said he; 'even if you get over the snow, you will not be able to get down from the mountains.' He made us the sign of precipices, and showed us how the feet of the horses would slip, and throw them off from the narrow trails which led along their sides. Our Chinook, who comprehended even more readily than ourselves, and believed our situation hopeless, covered his head with his blanket, and began to weep and lament. 'I wanted to see the whites,' said he; 'I came away from my own people to see the whites, and I wouldn't care to die among them; but here'—and he looked around in the cold night and gloomy forest, and drawing his blanket over his head, began again to lament.

"Seated around the tree, the fire illuminating the rocks and the tall boles of the pines round about, and the old Indian harangu ing, we presented a group of very serious faces.

"*February* 5.—The night had been too cold to sleep, and we were up very early. Our guide was standing by the fire, with all his finery on: and seeing him shiver in the cold I threw on his shoulders one of my blankets. We missed him a few minutes afterwards, and never saw him again. He had deserted. His bad faith and treachery were in perfect keeping with the estimate of Indian character, which a long intercourse with this people had gradually forced upon my mind. * * *

"*February* 23.—This was our most difficult day; we were forced off the ridges by the quantity of snow among the timber, and obliged to take to the mountain side, where occasionally rocks and a southern exposure afforded us a chance to scramble along. But these were steep, and slippery with snow and ice, and the tough evergreens of the mountains impeded our way, tore our skins, and exhausted our patience. Some of us had the misfortune to wear moccasins with *parflèche* soles, so slippery that we could not keep our feet, and generally crawled across the snow beds. Axes and mauls were necessary here to-day, to make a road through the snow. Going ahead with Carson to reconnoitre the road, we reached in the afternoon the river which made the outlet of the lake. Carson sprang over, clear across a place where the stream was compressed among the rocks, but the *parflèche* sole of my moccasin glanced from the icy rock, and precipitated me into the river. It was some few seconds before I could recover myself in the current, and Carson, thinking me hurt, jumped in after me, and we both had an icy bath. We tried to search awhile for my gun, which had been lost in the fall, but the cold drove us out; and making a large fire on the bank, after we had partially dried ourselves, we went back to meet the camp. We afterwards found that the gun had been slung under the ice which lined the banks of the creek.

"*February* 24.—We rose at three in the morning, for an astronomical observation, and obtained for the place a latitude of 38°

46′ 58″, longitude 120° 34′ 20″. The sky was clear an l pure, with a sharp wind from the northeast, and the thermometer two degrees below the freezing point. * * *

"Another horse was killed to-night, for food. *

"My favorite horse, Proveau, had become very weak, and was scarcely able to bring himself to the top. I left Jacob to bring him on, being obliged to press forward with the party, as there was no grass in the forest. We grew very anxious as the day advanced and no grass appeared, for the lives of our animals depended on finding it to-night. They were in just such a condition that grass and repose for the night enabled them to get on the next day.

"*February* 29.—We lay shut up in the narrow ravine, and gave the animals a necessary day; and men were sent back after the others. Derosier volunteered to bring up Proveau, to whom he knew I was greatly attached, as he had been my favorite horse on both expeditions. Carson and I climbed one of the nearest mountains; the forest land still extended ahead, and the valley appeared as far as ever. The pack horse was found near the camp, but Derosier did not get in. * *

"We began to be uneasy at Derosier's absence, fearing that he might have been bewildered in the woods. Charles Towns, who had not yet recovered his mind, went to swim in the river, as if it were summer, and the stream placid, when it was a cold mountain torrent foaming among rocks. We were happy to see Derosier appear in the evening. He came in, and, sitting down by the fire, began to tell us where he had been. He imagined that he had been gone several days, and thought we were still at the camp where he had left us; and we were pained to see that his mind was deranged. It appeared that he had been lost in the mountain, and hunger and fatigue, joined to weakness of body, and fear of perishing in the mountains had crazed him. The times were severe when stout men lost their minds from extremity of suffering—when horses died—and when mules and horses, ready to die of starvation, were killed for food. Yet there was no murmuring or hesitation.

"A short distance below our encampment the river mountains terminated in precipices, and, after a fatiguing march of only a few miles we encamped on a bench where were springs and an abundance of the freshest grass. In the meantime Mr. Preuss continued on down the river, and, unaware that we had encamped so early in the day, was lost. When night arrived, and he did not come in, we began to understand what had happened to him; but it was too late to make any search.

"*March* 3.—We followed Mr. Preuss's trail for a considerable distance along the river, until we reached a place where he had descended to the stream below and encamped. Here we shouted and fired guns, but received no answer; and we concluded that he had pushed on down the stream. I determined to keep out from the river, along which it was nearly impracticable to travel with animals, until it should form a valley.

"We repeated our shouts for Mr. Preuss; and this time we were gratified with an answer. The voice grew rapidly nearer, ascending from the river; but when we expected to see him emerge, it ceased entirely. We had called up some straggling Indian—the first we had met, although for two days back we had seen tracks—who, mistaking us for his fellows, had been only undeceived on getting close up. Ignorant of the character of the people, we had now an additional cause of uneasiness in regard to Mr. Preuss; he had no arms with him, and we began to think his chance doubtful.

"The mountains now were getting sensibly lower; but still there is no valley on the river, which presents steep and rocky banks; but here, several miles from the river, the country is smooth and grassy; the forest has no undergrowth; and in the open valleys or rivulets, or around spring heads, the low groves of live oak give the appearance of orchards in an old cultivated country. At one of these orchard grounds, we encamped about noon to make an effort for Mr. Preuss. One man took his way along a spur leading into the river, in hope to cross his trail; and another took our own back. Both were volunteers; and to the successful man was promised a pair of pistols—not as a reward, but as a token of gratitude for a service which would free us all from much anxiety.

"We had among our few animals a horse which was so much reduced, that with travelling, even the good grass could not save him; and, having nothing to eat, he was killed this afternoon. He was a good animal, and had made the journey round from Fort Hall. * * * * * *

"The absence of Mr. Preuss gave me great concern; and, for a large reward, Derosier volunteered to go back on the trail. I directed him to search along the river, travelling upward for the space of a day and a half, at which time I expected he would meet Mr. Fitzpatrick, whom I requested to aid in the search; at all events he was to go no further, but return to this camp, where a *cache* of provisions was made for him.

"Continuing the next day down the river, we discovered three squaws in a little bottom, and surrounded them before they could make their escape. They had large conical baskets which they were engaged in filling with a small leafy plant, (*erodium cicutarium*) just now beginning to bloom, and covering the ground like a sward of grass. They did not make any lamentations, but appeared very much impressed with our appearance, speaking to us only in a whisper, and offering us smaller baskets of the plant, which they signified to us was good to eat, making signs also that it was to be cooked by the fire. We drew out a little cold horse meat, and the squaws made signs to us that the men had gone out after deer, and that we could have some by waiting till they came in. We observed that the horses ate with great avidity the herb which they had been gathering; and here also for the first time, we saw Indians eat the common grass—one of the squaws pulling several tufts, and eating it with apparent relish. Seeing our surprise, she pointed to the horses; but we could not well understand what she meant, except, perhaps, that what was good for the one was good for the other.

* * * * * * * *

"Towards evening we heard a weak shout among the hills

behind, and had the pleasure to see Mr. Preuss descending towards the camp. Like ourselves, he had travelled to-day twenty-five miles, but had seen nothing of Derosier. Knowing, on the day he was lost, that I was determined to keep the river as much as possible, he had not thought it necessary to follow the trail very closely, but walked on, right and left, certain to find it somewhere along the river, searching places to obtain good views of the country. Towards sunset he climbed down towards the river to look for the camp; but, finding no trail, concluded that we were behind, and walked back until night came on, when, being very much fatigued, he collected drift wood and made a large fire among the rocks. The next day it became more serious, and he encamped again alone, thinking that we must have taken some other course. To go back would have been madness in his weak and starved condition, and onward towards the valley was his only hope, always in expectation of reaching it soon. His principal means of subsistence was a few roots, which the hunters call sweet onions, having very little taste, but a good deal of nutriment, growing generally in rocky ground, and requiring a good deal of labor to get, as he had only a pocket knife. Searching for these, he found a nest of big ants, which he let run on his hand, and stripped them off in his mouth; these had an agreeable acid taste. One of his greatest privations was the want of tobacco; and a pleasant smoke at evening would have been a relief which only a voyageur could appreciate. He tried the dried leaves of the live oak, knowing that those of other oaks were sometimes used as a substitute; but these were too thick, and would not do. On the 4th he made seven or eight miles, walking slowly along the river, avoiding as much as possible to climb the hills. In little pools he caught some of the smallest kind of frogs, which he swallowed, not so much in the gratification of hunger, as in the hope of obtaining some strength. Scattered along the river were old fire-places, where the Indians had roasted muscles and acorns; but though he searched diligently, he did not there succeed in finding either. He had collected fire-wood for the night, when he heard at some distance from the river the barking of what he thought were two dogs, and walked in that direction as quickly as he was able, hoping to find there some Indian hut, but met only two wolves; and, in his disappointment, the gloom of the forest was doubled.

"Travelling the next day feebly down the river, he found five or six Indians at the huts, of which we have spoken; some were painting themselves black, and others roasting acorns. Being only one man, they did not run off, but received him kindly, and gave him a welcome supply of roasted acorns. He gave them his pocket knife in return, and stretched out his hand to one of the Indians, who did not appear to comprehend the motion, but jumped back, as if he thought he was about to lay hold of him. They seemed afraid of him, not certain as to what he was.

"Travelling on he came to the place where we had found the squaws. Here he found our fire still burning, and the tracks of the horses. The sight gave him sudden hope and courage; and, following as fast as he could, joined us at evening.

"*March* 6.—We continued on our road, through the same surpassingly beautiful country, entirely unequalled for the pasturage of stock by anything we had ever seen. In a few hours we reached a large fork, the northern branch of the river, and equal in size to that which we had descended. Together they formed a beautiful stream, 60 to 100 yards wide, which at first, ignorant of the nature of the country through which that river ran, we took to be the Sacramento. * * * *

"We made an acorn meal at noon, and hurried on; the valley being gay with flowers, and some of the banks being absolutely golden with the California poppy (*eschscholtzia crocea.*) Here the grass was smooth and green, and the groves very open; the large oaks throwing a broad shade among sunny spots. Shortly afterwards we gave a shout at the appearance on a little bluff of a neatly built *adobe* house with glass windows. We rode up, but, to our disappointment, found only Indians. There was no appearance of cultivation, and we could see no cattle, and we supposed that the place had been abandoned. We now pressed on more eagerly than ever; the river swept round in a large bend to the right; the hill lowered down entirely; and, gradually entering a broad valley, we came unexpectedly into a large Indian village, where the people looked clean, and wore cotton shirts and various other articles of dress. They immediately crowded around us, and we had the inexpressible delight to find one who spoke a little indifferent Spanish, but who at first confounded us by saying there were no whites in the country; but just then a well-dressed Indian came up, and made his salutations in very well spoken Spanish. In answer to our inquiries, he informed us that we were upon the *Rio de los Americanos* (the river of the Americans), and that it joined the Sacramento River about ten miles below! Never did a name sound more sweetly. We felt ourselves among our countrymen; for the name of American, in these parts, is applied to the citizens of the United States. To our eager inquiries he answered, 'I am a *vaquero* (cow herd) in the service of Captain Sutter, and the people of this *rancheria* work for him.' Our evident satisfaction made him communicative; and he went on to say that Captain Sutter was a very rich man, and always glad to see his country people. We asked for his house. He answered that it was just over the hill before us; and offered, if we would wait a moment, to take his horse and conduct us to it. We readily accepted his civil offer. In a short distance we came in sight of the fort; and, passing on the way the house of a settler on the opposite side (a Mr. Sinclair), we forded the river; and in a few miles were met a short distance from the fort by Captain Sutter himself. He gave us a most frank and cordial reception—conducted us immediately to his residence—and under his hospitable roof we had a night of rest, enjoyment and refreshment, which none but ourselves could appreciate. But the party left in the mountains with Mr. Fitzpatrick were to be attended to; and the next morning, supplied with fresh horses and provisions, I hurried off to meet them. On the second day we met, a few miles below the forks of the Rio de los Americanos: and a more forlorn and pitiable sight than they presented, cannot well be imagined. They were all on foot—each man, weak and emaciated, leading a horse or mule as weak and emaciated as themselves. They had experienced great difficulty in descending the mountains, made slippery by rains and melting snows, and many horses fell over precipices, and were killed; and with some were lost the *packs* they carried. Among these was a mule with the plants, which we had collected since leaving Fort Hall, along a line of 2,000 miles travel. Out of sixty-seven horses and mules with which we commenced crossing the Sierra, only thirty-three reached the valley of the Sacramento, and they only in a condition to be led along.

"Mr. Fitzpatrick and his party, travelling more slowly, had been able to make some little exertion at hunting, and had killed a few deer. The scanty supply was a great relief to them; for several had been made sick by the strange and unwholesome food which the preservation of life had compelled them to use. We stopped and encamped as soon as we met; and a repast of good beef, excellent bread, and delicious salmon, which I had brought along, were the first relief from the sufferings of the Sierra, and their first introduction to the luxuries of the Sacramento. It required all our philosophy and forbearance to prevent plenty from becoming as hurtful to us now, as scarcity had been before."

CHAPTER VI.

SECOND EXPEDITION CONCLUDED—ENCAMPS AMONG THE DIGGER INDIANS—THEIR HABITS AND CHARACTER—MASSACRE OF TABEAU—RECOVERY OF HIS REMAINS—RETURN TO UTAH LAKE—ANALYSIS OF THE RESULTS OF THE EXPEDITION BY ITS COMMANDER.

After refreshing himself and men, and procuring such a stock of provisions as they required, Col. Fremont resumed his journey on the 24th of March. He proposed to avail himself of the pass at the head of the San Joaquin River, about 500 miles south of Sutter's place, and thence to cross the rim of the Great Basin, so as to reach the head of the Arkansas river on the opposite side of the mountains. In the course of this journey, he had the misfortune to lose one of his best men among the Digger Indians, on the Rio de los Angeles, under circumstances peculiarly distressing. His narrative first introduced this degraded race to the acquaintance of civilized men, which is a sufficient excuse for presenting it here again at length.

"*May* 5.—On account of our animals, it was necessary to remain to-day at this place. Indians crowded numerously around us in the morning; and we were obliged to keep arms in hand all day, to keep them out of the camp. They began to surround the horses, which, for the convenience of grass, we were guarding a little above, on the river. These were immediately driven in, and kept close to the camp.

"In the darkness of the night we had made a very bad encampment, our fires being commanded by a rocky bluff within fifty yards; but, notwithstanding, we had the river and small thickets of willows on the other side. Several times during the day the camp was insulted by the Indians; but, peace being our object, I kept simply on the defensive. Some of the Indians were on the bottoms, and others haranguing us from the bluffs; and they were scattered in every direction over the hills. Their language being probably a dialect of the *Utah*, with the aid of signs some of our people could comprehend them very well. They were the same people who had murdered the Mexicans; and towards us their disposition was evidently hostile, nor were we well disposed towards them. They were barefooted, and nearly naked: their hair gathered up into a knot behind; and with his bow, each man carried a quiver with thirty or forty arrows partially drawn out. Besides these, each held in his hand two or three arrows for instant service. Their arrows are barbed with a very clear translucent stone, a species of opal, nearly as hard as the diamond; and, shot from the long bow, are almost as effective as a gunshot. In these Indians, I was forcibly struck by an expression of countenance resembling that in a beast of prey; and all their actions are those of wild animals. Joined to the restless motion of the eye, there is a want of mind—an absence of thought—and an action wholly by impulse, strongly expressed, and which constantly recalls the similarity.

"A man who appeared to be a chief, with two or three others, forced himself into camp, bringing with him his arms, in spite of my orders to the contrary. When shown our weapons, he bored his ear with his fingers, and said he could not hear. 'Why,' said he, 'there are none of you.' Counting the people around the camp, and including in the number a mule which was being shod, he made out 22. 'So many,' said he, showing the number, 'and we—we are a great many;' and he pointed to the hills and mountains round about. 'If you have your arms,' said he, twanging his bow, 'we have these.' I had some difficulty in restraining the people, particularly Carson, who felt an insult of this kind as much as if it had been given by a more responsible being. 'Don't say that, old man,' said he; 'don't say that—your life's in danger'—speaking in good English; and probably the old man was nearer to his end than he will be before he meets it.

"Several animals had been necessarily left behind near the camp last night; and early in the morning, before the Indians made their appearance, several men were sent to bring them in. When I was beginning to be uneasy at their absence, they returned with information that they had been driven off from the trail by Indians; and, having followed the tracks in a short distance, they found the animals cut up and spread out upon bushes. In the evening I gave a fatigued horse to some of the Indians for a feast; and the village which carried him off refused to share with the others, who made loud complaints from the rocks of the partial distribution. Many of these Indians had long sticks, hooked at the end, which they used in hauling out lizards, and other small animals, from their holes. During the day they occasionally roasted and ate lizards at our fires. These belong to the people who are generally known under the name of *Diggers;* and to these I have more particularly had reference when occasionally speaking of a people whose sole occupation is to procure food sufficient to support existence. The formation here consists of fine yellow sandstone, alternating with a coarse conglomerate, in which the stones are from the size of ordinary gravel to six or eight inches in diameter. This is the formation which renders the surface of the country so rocky, and gives us now a road alternately of loose heavy sands and rolled stones, which cripple the animals in a most extraordinary manner.

"On the following morning we left the *Rio de los Angeles*, and continued our way through the same desolate and revolting country, where lizards were the only animal, and the tracks of the lizard eaters the principal sign of human beings. After twenty miles' march through a road of hills and heavy sands, we reached the most dreary river I have ever seen—a deep rapid stream, almost a torrent, passing swiftly by, and roaring against obstructions. The banks were wooded with willow, acacia, and a frequent plant of the country already mentioned (*Garrya elliptica*), growing in thickets, resembling willow, and bearing a small pink flower. Crossing it, we encamped on the left bank, where we found a very little grass. Our three remaining steers, being entirely given out, were killed here. By the boiling point, the elevation of the river here is 4,060 feet; and latitude, by observation, 36° 41′ 33″. The stream was running towards the southwest, and appeared to come from a snowy mountain in the north. It proved to be the *Rio Virgen*—a tributary to the Colorado. Indians appeared in bands upon the hills, but did not come into camp. For several days we continued our journey up the river, the bottoms of which were thickly overgrown with various kinds of brush; and the sandy soil was actually covered with the tracks of *Diggers*, who followed us stealthily, like a band of wolves; and we had no opportunity to leave behind, even for a few hours, the tired animals, in order that they might be brought into camp after a little repose, a horse or mule, left behind, was taken off in a moment. On the evening of the 8th, having travelled 28 miles up the river from our first encampment on it, we encamped at a little grass plat, where a spring of cool water issued from the bluff. On the opposite side was a grove of cottonwoods at the mouth of a fork, which here enters the river. On either side the valley is bounded by ranges of mountains, everywhere high, rocky and broken. The caravan road was lost and scattered in the sandy country, and we had been following an Indian trail up the river. The hunters the next day were sent out to reconnoitre, and in the meantime we moved about a mile farther up, where we found a good little patch of grass. There being only sufficient grass for the night, the horses were sent with a strong guard in charge of Tabeau to a neighboring hollow, where they might pasture during the day; and, to be ready in case the Indians should make any attempt on the animals, several of the best horses were picketed at the camp. In a few hours the hunters returned, having found a convenient ford in the river, and discovered the Spanish trail on the other side.

"I had been engaged in arranging plants; and, fatigued with the heat of the day, I fell asleep in the afternoon, and did not awake until sundown. Presently Carson came to me, and reported that Tabeau, who early in the day had left his post, and, without my knowledge, rode back to the camp we had left, in search of a lame mule, had not returned. While we were speaking, a smoke rose suddenly from the cottonwood grove below, which plainly told us what had befallen him; it was raised to inform the surrounding Indians that a blow had been struck, and to tell them to be on their guard. Carson with several men well mounted, was instantly sent down the river, but returned in the night without tidings of the missing man. They went to the camp we had left, but neither he nor the mule was there. Searching down the river, they found the tracks of a mule, evidently driven along by Indians, whose tracks were on each side of those made by the animal. After going several miles, they came to the mule itself, standing in some bushes, mortally wounded in the side by an arrow, and left to die, that it might be afterwards butchered for food. They also found, in another place, as they were hunting about on the ground for Tabeau's tracks, something that looked like a puddle of blood, but which the darkness prevented them from verifying. With these details they returned to our camp, and their report saddened all our hearts.

"*May* 10.—This morning as soon as there was light enough to follow tracks, I set out myself, with Mr. Fitzpatrick and several men, in search of Tabeau. We went to the spot where the appearance of puddled blood had been seen; and this, we saw at once, had been the place where he fell and died. Blood upon the leaves, and beaten down bushes, showed that he had got his wound about twenty paces from where he fell, and that he had struggled for his life. He had probably been shot through the lungs with an arrow. From the place where he lay and bled, it could be seen that he had been dragged to the river bank and thrown into it. No vestige of what had belonged to him could be found, except a fragment of his horse equipment. Horse, gun, clothes—all became the prey of these Arabs of the New World.

"Tabeau had been one of our best men, and his unhappy death spread a gloom over our party. Men, who have gone through such dangers and sufferings as we had seen, become like brothers, and feel each other's loss. To defend and avenge each other, is the deep feeling of all. We wished to avenge his death; but the condition of our horses, languishing for grass and repose, forbade an expedition into unknown mountains. We knew the tribe who had done the mischief—the same which had been insulting our camp. They knew what they deserved, and had the discretion to show themselves to us no more. The day before, they infested our camp; now, not one appeared; nor did we ever afterwards see but one who even belonged to the same tribe, and he at a distance."

On the 23d of May, Colonel Fremont reached Utah Lake. Having completed the immense circuit of twelve degrees diameter North and South, and ten degrees East and West, he found himself at the end of eight months on the same sheet of water which he had left the September previous, the Utah being the Southern limb of the Great Salt Lake of which remarkable sheet of water he had now seen and been able to fix the points both of its Northern and Southern extremities. During the eight preceding months he had travelled 3500 miles, and had a view of Oregon and of North California from the Rocky Mountains to the Pacific Ocean, and of the two principal streams which form bays or harbors on the coast of that sea. During the entire eight months he was never out of the sight of snow, and the point where they crossed the Sierra Nevada was was near 2,000 feet higher than the South Pass of the Rocky Mountains.

With one single quotation more to illustrate Mr. Fremont's faculty of generalization, we close our account of this expedition.

"Having completed this circuit, and being now about to turn the back upon the Pacific slope of our continent, and to recross the Rocky Mountains, it is natural to look back upon our footsteps, and take some brief view of the leading features and general structure of the country we had traversed. These are peculiar and striking, and differ essentially from the Atlantic side of our country. The mountains all are higher, more numerous, and more distinctly defined in their ranges and directions; and, what is so contrary to the natural order of such formations, one of these ranges, which is near the coast (the Sierra Nevada and the Coast Range), presents higher elevations and peaks than any which are to be found in the Rocky Mountains themselves. In our eight months' circuit, we were never out of sight of snow· and the Sierra Nevada, where we crossed it, was near 2,000 feet higher than the South Pass in the Rocky Mountains. In height, these mountains greatly exceed those of the Atlantic side, constantly presenting peaks which enter the region of eternal snow; and some of them volcanic, and in a frequent state of activity. They are seen at great distances, and guide the traveller in his courses.

"The course and elevation of these ranges give direction to the rivers and character to the coast. No great river does, or can take its rise below the Cascade and Sierra Nevada range; the distance to the sea is too short to admit of it. The rivers of the San Francisco bay, which are the largest after the Columbia, are local to that bay, and lateral to the coast, having their sources about on a line with the Dalles of the Columbia, and running each in a valley of its own, between Coast range and the Cascade and Sierra Nevada range. The Columbia is the only river which traverses the whole breadth of the country, breaking through all the ranges, and entering the sea. Drawing its waters from a section of ten degrees of latitude in the Rocky Mountains, which are collected into one stream by three main forks (Lewis's, Clark's, and the North Fork) near the centre of the Oregon valley, this great river thence proceeds by a single channel to the sea, while its three forks lead each to a pass in the mountains, which opens the way into the interior of the continent. This fact, in relation to the rivers of this region, gives an immense value to the Columbia. Its mouth is the only inlet and outlet to and from the sea; its three forks lead to the passes in the mountains; it is, therefore, the only line of communication between the Pacific and the interior of North America; and all operations of war or commerce, of national or social intercourse, must be conducted upon it. This gives it a value beyond estimation, and would involve irreparable injury if lost. In this unity and concentration of its waters, the Pacific side of our continent differs entirely from the Atlantic side, where the waters of the Alleghany Mountains are dispersed into many rivers, having their different entrances into the sea, and opening many lines of communication with the interior.

"The Pacific coast is equally different from that of the Atlantic. The coast of the Atlantic is low and open, indented with numerous bays, sounds, and river estuaries, accessible everywhere, and opening by many channels into the heart of the country. The Pacific coast, on the contrary, is high and compact, with few bays, and but one that opens into the heart of the country. The immediate coast is what the seamen call *iron bound.* A little within, it is skirted by two successive ranges of mountains, standing as ramparts between the sea and the interior country; and to get through which, there is but one gate, and that narrow and easily defended. This structure of the coast, backed by these two ranges of mountains, with its concentration and unity of waters, gives to the country an immense military strength, and will probably render Oregon the most impregnable country in the world.

"Differing so much from the Atlantic side of our continent, in coast, mountains, and rivers, the Pacific side differs from it in another most rare and singular feature—that of the Great interior Basin, of which I have so often spoken, and the whole form and character of which I was so anxious to ascertain. Its existence is vouched for by such of the American traders and hunters as have some knowledge of that region; the structure of the Sierra Nevada range of mountains requires it to be there; and my own observations confirm it. Mr. Joseph Walker, who is so well acquainted in those parts, informed me that, from the Great Salt Lake west, there was a succession of lakes and rivers which have no outlet to the sea, nor any connection with the Columbia, or with the Colorado of the Gulf of California. He described some of these lakes as being large, with numerous streams, and even considerable rivers, falling into them. In fact, all concur in the general report of these interior rivers and lakes; and, for want of understanding the force and power of evaporation, which so soon establishes an equilibrium between the loss and supply of waters, the fable of whirlpools and subterraneous outlets has gained belief, as the only imaginable way of carrying off the waters which have no visible discharge. The structure of the country would require this formation of interior lakes; for the waters which would collect between the Rocky Mountains and the Sierra Nevada, not being able to cross this formidable barrier, nor to get to the Columbia or the Colorado, must naturally collect into reservoirs, each of which would have its little system of streams and rivers to supply it. This would be the natural effect; and what I saw went to confirm it. The Great Salt Lake is a formation of this kind, and quite a large one; and having many streams, and one considerable river, four or five hundred miles long, falling into it. This lake and river I saw and examined myself; and also saw the Wah-satch and Bear River mountains which enclose the waters of the lake on the east, and constitute, in that quarter, the rim of the Great Basin. Afterwards, along the eastern base of the Sierra Nevada, where we travelled for forty-two days, I saw the line of lakes and rivers which lie at the foot of that Sierra; and which Sierra is the western rim of the Basin. In going down Lewis's Fork and the main Columbia, I crossed only inferior streams coming in from the left, such as could draw their water from a short distance only; and I often saw the mountains at their heads, white with snow; which, all accounts said, divided the waters of the *desert* from those of the Columbia, and which could be no other than the range of mountains which form the rim of the Basin on its northern side. And in returning from California along the Spanish trail, as far as the head of the Santa Clara Fork of the Rio Virgen, I crossed only small streams making their way south to the Colorado, or lost in sand—as the Mo-hah-ve; while to the left, lofty mountains, their summits white with snow, were often visible, and which must have turned water to the north as well as to the south, and thus constituted, on this part, the southern rim of the Basin. At the head of the Santa Clara Fork, and in the Vegas de Santa Clara, we crossed the ridge which parted the two systems of waters. We entered the Basin at that point, and have travelled in it ever since, having its southeastern rim (the Wah-satch Mountain) on the right, and crossing the streams which flow down into it. The existence of the Basin is, therefore, an established fact in my mind; its extent and contents are yet to be better ascertained. It cannot be less than four or five hundred miles each way, and must lie principally in the Alta California; the demarkation latitude of 42° probably cutting a segment from the north part of the rim. Of its interior, but little is known. It is called a *desert*, and, from what I saw of it, sterility may be its prominent characteristic; but where there is so much water, there must be some *oases*. The great river, and the great lake, reported, may not be equal to the report; but where there is so much snow, there must be streams; and where there is no outlet, there must be lakes to hold the accumulated waters, or sands to swallow them up. In this eastern part of the Basin, containing Sevier, Utah, and the Great Salt lakes, and the rivers and creeks falling into them, we know there is good soil and good grass, adapted to civilized settlements. In the western part, on Salmon Trout River, and some other streams, the same remark may be made.

"The contents of this Great Basin are yet to be examined. That it is peopled, we know; but miserably and sparsely. From all that I heard and saw, I should say that humanity here appeared in its lowest form, and in its most elementary state. Dispersed in single families; without fire-arms; eating seeds and insects; digging roots (and hence their name)—such is the condition of the greater part. Others are a degree higher, and live in communities upon some lake or river that supplies fish, and from whence they repulse the miserable *Digger*. The rabbit is the largest animal known in this desert; its flesh affords a little meat; and their bag-like covering is made of its skins. The wild sage is their only wood, and here it is of extraordinary size—sometimes a foot in diameter, and six or eight feet high. It serves for fuel, for building material, for shelter for the rabbits, and for some sort of covering for the feet and legs in cold weather. Such are the accounts of the inhabitants and productions of the Great Basin; and which, though imperfect, must have some foundation, and excite our desire to know the whole.

"The whole idea of such a desert, and such a people, is a novelty in our country, and excites Asiatic, not American ideas. Interior basins, with their own systems of lakes and rivers, and often sterile, are common enough in Asia; people still in the elementary state of families, living in deserts, with no other occupation than the mere animal search for food, may still be seen in that ancient quarter of the globe; but in America such things are new and strange, unknown and unsuspected, and discredited when related. But I flatter myself that what is discovered, though not enough to satisfy curiosity, is sufficient to excite it, and that subsequent explorations will complete what has been commenced.

"This account of the Great Basin, it will be remembered, belongs to the Alta California, and has no application to Oregon, whose capabilities may justify a separate remark. Referring to my journal for particular descriptions, and for sectional boundaries between good and bad districts, I can only say, in general and comparative terms, that, in that branch of agriculture which implies the cultivation of grains and staple crops, it would be inferior to the Atlantic States, though many parts are superior for wheat; while in the rearing of flocks and herds it would claim a high place. Its grazing capabilities are great; and even in the indigenous grass now there, an element of individual and national wealth may be found. In fact, the valuable grasses begin within one hundred and fifty miles of the Missouri frontier, and extend to the Pacific ocean. East of the Rocky mountains, it is the short curly grass, on which the buffalo delight to feed (whence its name of buffalo), and which is still good when dry and apparently dead. West of those mountains it is a larger growth, in clusters, and hence called bunch grass, and which has a second or fall growth. Plains and mountains both exhibit them; and I have seen good pasturage at an elevation of ten thousand feet. In this spontaneous product the trading or travelling caravans can find subsistence for their animals; and in military operations any number of cavalry may be moved, and any number of cattle may be driven; and thus men and horses be supported on long expeditions, and even in winter, in the sheltered situations.

"Commercially, the value of the Oregon country must be great, washed as it is by the north Pacific ocean—fronting Asia—producing many of the elements of commerce—mild and healthy in its climate—and becoming, as it naturally will, a thoroughfare for the East India and China trade."

The soundness of these inductions have all been since abundantly verified.

Immediately upon his return from this expedition, Fremont, who at that time held the rank of second lieutenant of topographical engineers, received the double brevet of captain in the army, upon the recommendation of General Scott, who made the colonel's services in the topographical corps the subject of a special report. This report, which is now on file in the War Department at Washington, consists of two parts: the first an argument that a double brevet, under the law, might be granted; and secondly, that, in consideration of "Fremont's" gallant and highly meritorious services "in the expeditions commanded by himself, the first to the Rocky Mountains, which terminated October 17, 1842, and the second beyond those mountains, which terminated July 31, 1843," they ought to be granted. This tribute from General Scott was the more flattering from the fact that, at that time, he had no personal acquaintance with Fremont, nor were his relations with Colonel Benton at all intimate. It was a spontaneous and officer-like acknowledgement of talents and services which had already conferred additional distinction upon their common profession.

CHAPTER VII.

THIRD EXPEDITION—FIRST VISIT TO MARIPOSAS—STRANGE PHASES OF INDIAN LIFE—FIGHT WITH HORSE-THIEF INDIANS—LOSES ALL HIS CATTLE IN THE SNOW—HOSTILE MESSAGE FROM GOVERNOR CASTRO—HOISTS THE AMERICAN FLAG IN CALIFORNIA—COL. BENTON'S ACCOUNT OF THE CONQUEST OF CALIFORNIA—KIT CARSON'S ACCOUNT OF A NIGHT ATTACK BY A PARTY OF TLAMATH INDIANS—PARDON OF PICO—SECRETARY MARCY'S ACCOUNT OF THE CONQUEST OF CALIFORNIA—ESTABLISHES THE INDEPENDENCE OF CALIFORNIA.

In preparing his reports for the press the remainder of 1844 was occupied. In the spring of the following year, Fremont set out on a third expedition, which comprehended in its design an exploration of the interior region known as the Great Basin, and the maritime country of Oregon and California. But the leading idea of the journey was an examination of the overland communication with the ocean, and to this the others, though of great and special interest, were incidental and subordinate.

To this special object his general plan of surveys had been gradually directed, and his visit to California in the preceding winter had given to it point and increased attraction. The beauty of the country, and its grand commercial advantages, had indelibly impressed themselves on his mind, and he had, in consequence, decided to make it a future home for himself and his family.

After some months spent in examining the head-waters of the great rivers which flow to either ocean, the party descended at the beginning of winter to the Great Salt Lake, and in October encamped on its south-western shore, in view of that undescribed country which at that time had not been penetrated, and which vague and contradictory reports of Indians, represented as a desert without grass or water.

Their previous visit to the lake had given it a somewhat familiar aspect, and on leaving it they felt as if about to commence their journey anew. Its eastern shore was frequented by large bands of Indians, but here they had dwindled down to a single family, which was gleaning from some hidden source enough to support life, and drinking the salt water of a little stream near by, no fresh water being at hand. This offered scanty encouragement as to what they might expect on the desert beyond.

At its threshold and immediately before them was a naked plain of smooth clay surface, mostly devoid of vegetation—the hazy weather of the summer hung over it, and in the distance rose scattered, low, black and dry-looking mountains. At what appeared to be fifty miles or more, a higher peak held out some promise of wood and water, and towards this it was resolved to direct their course.

Four men, with a pack animal loaded with water for two days, and accompanied by a naked Indian—who volunteered for a reward to be their guide to a spot where he said there was grass and fine springs—were sent forward to explore in advance for a foothold, and verify the existence of water before the whole party should be launched into the desert. Their way led toward the high peak of the mountain, on which they were to make a smoke signal in the event of finding water. About sunset of the second day, no signal having been seen, Fremont became uneasy at the absence of his men, and set out with the whole party upon their trail, travelling rapidly all the night. Towards morning one of the scouts, Archambault, was met returning.

The Indian had been found to know less than themselves, and had been sent back, but the men had pushed on to the mountains, where they found a running stream, with wood and sufficient grass. The whole party now lay down to rest, and the next day, after a hard march, reached the stream. The distance across the plain was nearly seventy miles, and they called the mountain which had guided them Pilot Peak. This was their first day's march and their first camp in the desert.

A few days afterwards the expedition was divided into two parties—the larger one under the guidance of Walker, a well-known mountaineer and experienced traveller, going around to the foot of the Sierra Nevada by a circuitous route which he had previously travelled, and Fremont, with ten men, Delawares and whites, penetrating directly through the heart of the desert.

They had been travelling a week, during which they had seen human beings only on one occasion, and at the close af a hard day's journey, in which they had failed to find water, had turned into a mountain where some appearances of timber and grass gave promising indications of a good camp.

They followed up a dry stream bed, until they were nearly two thousand feet above the plain and towards the summit of the mountain, where they found a spring sufficiently large for the camp wants, with grass abundant, and pine wood and cedar to keep up the night fires; for it was November, and the newly-fallen snow already marked out the higher ridges of the mountains.

They were surprised to see tracks of a naked foot near the spring, which had been recently cleaned out, but there were no other indications of human life. Supper was over, and they were about the fire, when Carson who was lying on his back with his pipe n his mouth, his hands under his head and his feet to the fire, suddenly exclaimed, half rising and pointing to the other side of the fire—"Good God! look there!" In the blaze of the fire, peering over her skinny, crooked hands, which shaded her eyes from the glare, so as to enable her to see the men, was standing an old woman, apparently eighty years of age, nearly naked, her grizzly hair hanging down over her face and shoulders. She had evidently thought it a camp of her people, and in the grateful warmth of the fire had already begun to talk and gesticulate, when her open mouth was suddenly paralysed and her face blanched with fright, as she saw the faces of the whites.

With a natural instinct she turned to escape, but the men had gathered round her, and she made them comprehend that she had been brought there and left by her people—that she was very old and could gather no more seeds, and was no longer good for anything, and that she was going to die when the snows got deep.

She was greatly alarmed and eager to get away, and as the hunters had been successful that day, she was plentifully supplied with the meat of mountain sheep, which she ran off with as soon as it was given to her. She had not gone twenty steps before it was remembered that she had no fire and probably no means of making one; and one of the men, seizing a brand, ran after her, but to no purpose—she had dodged down into the brush and in the darkness could not be found.

Some days afterwards, travelling along the foot of a mountain, the arid country covered with dwarf shrubs, a light volume of smoke was seen rising from a ravine. Riding cautiously up, they discovered a single Indian on the border of a small creek. He was standing before a little fire, naked as he was born, apparently thinking, and looking at a small earthen pot which was simmering over the fire, filled with the common ground-squirrel of the country. Another bunch of squirrels lay near it, and close by were his bow and arrows. He was a well-made, good-looking young man, about twenty-five years of age. Although so taken by surprise that he made no attempt to escape, and evidently greatly alarmed, he received his visitors with forced gaiety and offered them part of his *pot au feu* and his bunch of squirrels. He was kindly treated and some little presents made him, and the party continued their way.

His bow was handsomely made, and the arrows, of which there were about forty in his quiver, were neatly feathered, and headed with obsidian, worked into spear-shape by patient labor.

After they had separated, Fremont found that his Delawares had taken a fancy to the Indian's bow and arrows, and carried them off. They carried them willingly back, when they were reminded that they had exposed the poor fellow to almost certain starvation by depriving him, in the beginning of winter, of his only means of subsistence, which it would require months to replace.

There were no tracks around, to indicate the presence of other Indians in the neighborhood, nor was it probable there were any within twenty or thirty miles. The difficulty of subsistence reduces this people nearly to the condition of animals, and scatters them, during the greater part of the year, sometimes singly, sometimes in families, until the spring or (in certain places) the fishing season brings them together again.

One day the party had reached one of the lakes lying along the foot of the Sierra Nevada, which was their appointed rendezvous with their friends, and where, at this season, the scattered Indians of the neighborhood were gathering, to fish. Turning a point on the lake shore, a party of Indians, some twelve or fourteen in number, came abruptly in view. They were advancing along in Indian file, one following the other, their heads bent forward, and eyes fixed on the ground. As the two parties met, the Indians did not turn their heads or raise their eyes from the ground, but passed silently along. The whites, habituated to the chances of savage life, and always uncertain whether they should find friends or foes in those they met, fell readily into their humor, and they too passed on their way without word or halt.

It was a strange meeting: two parties of such different races and different countries, coming abruptly upon each other, with every occasion to excite curiosity and provoke question, pass in a desert without a word of inquiry or greeting—without any show of friendship or attempt at hostility.

Shortly after this rencontre, the divided parties met at their appointed place, where a river, to which they gave Walker's name, discharges into the lake.

There was a place on the lake where beds of rushes made good pasturage for their half-starved animals, and here the two parties remained some days together.

It was now mid-winter, they were out of provisions—and there was no game. The heavy snows might be daily expected to block up the passes in the great Sierra, if they had not already fallen, and with all their experience it was considered too hazardous to attempt the passage with the *materiel* of a whole party; it was arranged therefore that Walker should continue with the main party southward along the Sierra, and enter the valley of the San Joaquin by some one of the low passes at its head, where there is rarely or never snow. Fremont undertook, with a few men, to cross directly westward over the Sierra Nevada to Sutter's Fort, with the view of obtaining there the necessary supplies of horses and beef cattle with which to rejoin his party.

He encountered the obstacles which these formidable mountains always present in winter, but had the good fortune to get through the passes before they were choked by the snows, and reached Sutter's Fort in safety.

The necessary supplies were obtained without difficulty, and in the middle of December he proceeded with his party—now numbering in all about sixteen—to meet his main camp at the appointed place of rendezvous, travelling in a southeasterly direction up the valley of the San Joaquin.

After some days' travel, leaving the Mercedes river, they had entered among the foot hills of the mountains, and were journeying through a beautiful country of undulating upland, openly timbered with oaks, principally evergreen, and watered with small streams. In the beauty and varied character of its scenery, this tract is one of the most remarkable in Southern California.

Travelling along, they came suddenly upon broad and deeply-worn trails, which had been freshly travelled by large bands of horses, apparently coming from the settlements on the coast. These and other indications warned them that they were approaching villages of the Horse-Thief Indians, who appeared to have just returned from a successful foray. With the breaking up of the missions many of the Indians had returned to their tribes in the mountains. Their knowledge of the Spanish language, and familiarity with the ranches and towns, enabled them to pass and repass, at pleasure, between their villages in the Sierra and the ranchos on the coast. They very soon availed themselves of these facilities to steal and run off into the mountains bands of horses, and in a short time it became the occupation of all the Indians inhabiting the southern Sierra Nevada, as well as the plains beyond.

Three or four parties would be sent at a time from different villages, and every week was signalized by the carrying-off of hundreds of horses to be killed and eaten in the interior. Repeated expeditions had been made against them by the Californians, who rarely succeeded in reaching the foot of the mountains, and were invariably defeated when they did.

As soon as the fresh trail had been discovered, four men, two Delawares with Maxwell and Dick Owens, two of Fremont's favourite men, were sent forward upon the trail. The rest of the party had followed along at their usual gait, but Indian signs became so thick, trail after trail joining on, that they started rapidly after the men, fearing for their safety. After a few miles ride, they reached a spot which had been the recent camping ground of a village, and where abundant grass and good water suggested a halting place for the night. It was, evidently, a favorite encampment of the Horse Thieves, as horse-bones whitened the ground in every direction. They immediately set about unpacking their animals and preparing to encamp.

While thus engaged, they heard what seemed to be the barking of many dogs, coming apparently from a village, not far distant; but they had hardly thrown off their saddles when they suddenly became aware that it was the noise of women and children shouting and crying; and this was sufficient notice that the men who had been sent ahead had fallen among unfriendly Indians, so that a fight had already commenced.

It did not need an instant to throw the saddles on again, and leaving four men to guard the camp, Fremont, with the rest, rode off in the direction of the sounds.

They had galloped but half a mile, when crossing a little ridge, they came abruptly in view of several hundred Indians advancing on each side of a knoll, on the top of which were the men, where a cluster of trees and rocks made a good defence. It was evident that they had come suddenly into the midst of the Indian village, and jumping from their horses, with the instinctive skill of old hunters and mountaineers as they were, had got into an admirable place to fight from.

The Indians had nearly surrounded the knoll, and were about getting possession of the horses as Fremont's party came in view. Their welcome shout as they charged up the hill was answered by the yell of the Delawares as they dashed down to recover their animals, and the crack of Owen's and Maxwell's rifles. Owens had singled out the foremost Indian, who went headlong down the hill, to steal horses no more.

Profiting by the first surprise of the Indians, and anxious for the safety of the men who had been left in camp, the whites immediately retreated towards it, checking the Indians with occasional rifle shots, with the range of which it seemed remarkable that they were acquainted.

Night was drawing on as they reached their camp, the Indians scattered through the woods and rocks about, whence they kept up animated harangues to the whites.

Many of them had been mission Indians, and spoke Spanish well. "Wait," they said, "*Esperate Carrajos* —wait until morning. There are two big villages close by; we have sent for the chief: he'll be down before morning with all the people, and you will all die. None of you shall go back; we will have all your horses."

The whole camp were on guard until daylight. As soon as it was dark, each man crept to his post. They heard the women and children retreating towards the mountains, but nothing disturbed the quiet of the camp, except when one of the Delawares shot at a wolf as it jumped over a log, and which he mistook for an Indian. As soon as it grew light they took to the most open ground, and retreated into the plain. This was a village of Chauchiles Indians, and the locality has since become well known under the name of Mariposas.

The party again, by a more circuitous route, pushed on to their rendezvous with the main camp.

In his search after his companions, Fremont entered into high and rugged mountains, where he was shut in by the winter's snows, from which he extricated himself with great difficulty, and with the loss of all his cattle.

After a delay of some weeks both parties descended into the "Great California Valley," glad of their escape from suffering, and confident of again enjoying the hospitable welcome they had received the year before. Leaving them in the valley of the San Joaquin, Fremont proceeded alone to Monterey, to make known to the authorities the condition of his party, and obtained permission to recruit and procure the supplies necessary to proceed on his exploration.

Journeying in the security of this permission, he was suddenly arrested in his march, near Monterey, by an officer at the head of a body of cavalry, who bore him a violent message from the commanding officer in California—Gen. Castro—commanding him to retire instantly from the country.

This message—peremptory and rude, denouncing the party as highwaymen and robbers, and inexplicable to Fremont—was the result of orders from the city of Mexico, directing that, in the event Fremont repeated his visit to California, he and his party should be seized and sent prisoners to Mexico, as had happened to Pike in his expedition to New Mexico.

The General's rude message met with a suitable response. Fremont refused to follow a course for which he was totally unprepared. He was in no condition to throw his party into the desert from which they had just issued, but retired into the "Pico del Gabellan," (Hawk's Peak), a rough mountain overlooking the plains of San Juan and Monterey. He chose, near the summit, a strong position, which he strengthened by a rude fort of felled oak trees, over which he hoisted the American flag. The position was strong, powder and ball plenty, and the men were the flower of our western frontier. For three days they remained encamped, during which they saw Castro, at the mission of San Juan, in the plain immediately below them, preparing his forces, scaling his cannon, and gathering in the force of the country, which he strengthened by Indians.

The country was thrown into great excitement, and the serious condition of affairs is very clearly shown by the following letter from the United States Consul at Monterey to the Consul at Mazatlan:

"CONSULATE OF THE UNITED STATES,
MONTEREY, CALIFORNIA, *March* 9, 1846.

"Sir: Enclosed with this you will receive several copies of correspondence in this town for the present week; also an official letter for the captain of any of our ships-of-war you may have in your port on your receiving this letter. It is impossible to say whether Señor Castro, the Prefects and the General will attack Captain Fremont; we expect such will be the case.

"I am just informed by Señor Arce, the general's secretary, who has just come in from the general's camp, (San Juan), that the whole country will be raised to force Capt. Fremont, if they required so many. Señor Arce further says, that the camp of the Americans is near Mr. Hartwell's rancho on a high hill, with his flag flying; of the latter I am not certain. As you are acquainted with this country and its people, you will advise with our naval captains on the subject of sailing immediately for this port.

"If the vessel is not actually obliged to go elsewhere, it is my earnest desire she sails for Monterey on the receipt of this, although everything may end pleasantly amongst us.

"Believe me to be, yours sincerely,

"THOMAS O. LARKIN.

"To John Parrot, Esq., United States Consul, Mazatlan."

Two couriers were sent to Fremont's camp by Mr. Larkin. One, an American, failed to get through; the other, a native Californian, succeeded in reaching his camp, after a narrow escape from being shot by Fremont's men.

He brought back a note in pencil, from Captain Fremont,* and reported that two thousand of his countrymen could not compel him to leave the country, although his party was so small.

The following is Fremont's note to the consul, dated:

"MARCH 10, 1846.

"MY DEAR SIR: I this moment received your letters, and without waiting to read them, acknowledge the receipt, which the courier requires, immediately.

"I am making myself as strong as possible, in the intention that if we are unjustly attacked, we will fight to extremity, and refuse quarter, trusting to our country to avenge our death. No one has reached our camp, and from the heights we are able to see the troops (with the glass) mustering at St. John's and preparing cannon. I thank you for your kindness and good wishes, and would write more at length as to my intentions, did I not fear that my letter would be intercepted. We have in no wise done wrong to the people or the authorities of the country,

* These papers are on file in the State Department.

and if we are hemmed in and assaulted here, we will die, every man of us, under the flag of our country.

"Very truly yours,

"J. C. Fremont.

"Thomas O. Larkin, Esq., *Consul for the United States, Monterey.*"

They remained in their encampment several days, in hourly expectation of an attack. The men were strongly disposed to surprise Castro's camp in the night, but Fremont was unwilling to compromise his government and the safety of the settlers in the country, by any violent act on his part. Towards the close of the fourth day, while they sat in council on the difficulties of their position, the flag which had been hoisted on a tall sapling which had been trimmed into a flag-staff, suddenly fell, staff and all, to the ground. It was ominous. The men looked at each other doubtingly, and Fremont with great presence of mind availed himself of the incident to decide their course. "Men," said he, that means saddle up,"—and before morning they were many miles distant on the flank of the San Joaquin valley.

During the night a messenger from Castro, (Gilroy, of the valley of San Juan), reached the deserted camp, where he found the fires still burning. He brought with him a letter from Castro, offering to Fremont a cessation of hostilities, and proposing they should join their forces and declare the country independent of Mexico, and march against Governor Pico, who was in the southern part of the territory.

Fremont now quietly and without molestation continued his journey northward, up the valley of the

Sacramento, into Oregon. For what followed, we avail ourselves of the succinct, but thrilling account given by Col. Benton, in the second volume of his "Thirty Years' View."

"Turning his back on the Mexican possessions, and looking to Oregon as the field of his future labors, Mr. Fremont determined to explore a new route to the Wah-lah-math settlements and the tide-water region of the Columbia, through the wild and elevated region of the Tlamath lakes. A romantic interest attached to this region from the grandeur of its features, its lofty mountains and snow-clad peaks, and from the formidable character of its warlike inhabitants. In the first week of May he was at the north end of the great Tlamath lake, and in Oregon—the lake being cut near its south end by the parallel of 42° north latitude. On the eighth day of that month a strange sight presented itself—almost a startling apparition—two men riding up and penetrating a region which few ever approached without paying toll of life or blood. They proved to be two of Mr. Fremont's old *voyageurs*, and quickly told their story. They were part of a guard of six men conducting a United States officer, who was on his trail with despatches from Washington, and whom they had left two days back, while they came on to give notice of his approach, and to ask that assistance might be sent him. They themselves had only escaped the Indians by the swiftness of their horses. It was a case in which no time was to be lost, nor a mistake made. Mr. Fremont determined to go himself; and taking ten picked men, four of them Delaware Indians, he took down the western shore of the lake on the morning of the 9th, (the direction the officer was to come), and made a ride of sixty miles without a halt. But to meet men, and not to miss them, was the difficult point in this trackless region. It was not the case of a high road, where all travellers must meet in passing each other: at intervals there were places—defiles, or camping grounds—where both parties must pass; and watching for these, he came to one in the afternoon, and decided that, if the party was not killed, it must be there that night. He halted and encamped; and, as the sun was going down, had the inexpressible satisfaction to see the four men approaching. The officer proved to be a lieutenant of the United States marines, who had been dispatched from Washington the November previous, to make his way by Vera Cruz, the City of Mexico and Mazatlan, to Monterey, in Upper California, deliver despatches to the United States consul there; and then find Mr. Fremont, wherever he should be. His despatches for Mr. Fremont were only a letter of introduction from the Secretary of State, (Mr. Buchanan), and some letters and slips of newspapers from Senator Benton and his family, and some verbal communications from the Secretary of State. The verbal communications were that Mr. Freemont should watch and counteract any foreign scheme on California, and conciliate the good will of the inhabitants towards the United States. Upon this intimation of the government's wishes, Mr. Fremont turned back from Oregon, in the edge of which he then was, and returned to California. The letter of introduction was in the common form, that it might tell nothing if it fell into the hands of foes, and signified nothing of itself; but it accredited the bearer, and gave the stamp of authority to what he communicated; and upon this Mr. Fremont acted; for it was not to be supposed that Lieut. Gillespie had been sent so far, and through so many dangers, merely to deliver a common letter of introduction on the shores of the Tlamath lake."

The events of the night referred to by Mr. Benton, and of a few succeeding days, are graphically told by Carson himself, in an article furnished to the Washington *Union* of June 16th, 1847, from which we make the following extract:

"'Mr. Gillespie had brought the Colonel letters from home—the first he had had since leaving the States the year before—and he was up, and kept a large fire burning until after midnight; the rest of us were tired out, and all went to sleep. This was the only night in all our travels, except the one night on the island in the Salt Lake, that we failed to keep guard; and as the men were so tired, and we expected no attack now that we had sixteen in the party, the Colonel didn't like to ask it of them, but sat up late himself. Owens and I were sleeping together, and we were waked at the same time by the licks of the axe that killed our men. At first, I didn't know it was that; but I called to Basil, who was that side—'What's the matter there?—What's that fuss about?'—he never answered, for he was dead then, poor fellow, and he never knew what killed him—his head had been cut in, in his sleep; the other groaned a little as he died. The Delawares (we had four with us) were sleeping at that fire, and they sprang up as the Tlamaths charged them. One of them caught up a gun, which was unloaded; but, although he could do no execution, he kept them at bay, fighting like a soldier, and didn't give up until he was shot full of arrows—three entering his heart; he died bravely. As soon as I had called out, I saw it was Indians in the camp, and I and Owens together cried out 'Indians.' There were no orders given; things went on too fast, and the Colonel had men with him that didn't need to be told their duty. The Colonel and I, Maxwell, Owens, Godey, and Stepp, jumped together, we six, and ran to the assistance of our Delawares. I don't know who fired and who didn't; but I think it was Stepp's shot that killed the Tlamath chief; for it was at the crack of Stepp's gun that he fell. He had an English half-axe slung to his wrist by a cord, and there were forty arrows left in his quiver—the most beautiful and warlike arrows I ever saw. He must have been the bravest man among them, from the way he was armed, and judging by his cap. When the Tlamaths saw him fall, they ran; but we lay, every man with his rifle cocked, until daylight, expecting another attack.

"'In the morning we found by the tracks that from fifteen to twenty of the Tlamaths had attacked us. They had killed three of our men, and wounded one of the Delawares, who scalped the chief, whom we left where he fell. Our dead men we carried on mules; but, after going about ten miles, we found it impossible to get them any farther through the thick timber, and finding a secret place, we buried them under logs and chunks, having no way to dig a grave. It was only a few days before this fight that some of these same Indians had come into our camp; and, although we had only meat for two days, and felt sure that we should have to eat mules for ten or fifteen days to come, the Colonel divided with them, and even had a mule unpacked to give them some tobacco and knives.'

"The party then retraced its way into California, and two days after this rencontre they met a large village of Tlamaths—more than a hundred warriors. Carson was ahead with ten men, but one of them having been discovered, he could not follow his orders, which were to send back word and let Fremont come up with the rest in case they found Indians. But as they had been seen, it only remained to charge the village, which they did, killing many, and putting the rest to flight. The women and children, Carson says, we didn't interfere with; but they burnt the village, together with their canoes and fishing nets. In a subsequent encounter, the same day, Carson's life was imminently exposed. As they galloped up he was rather in advance, when he observed an Indian fixing his arrow to let fly at him. Carson levelled his rifle, but it snapped, and in an instant the arrow would have pierced him, had not Fremont, seeing the danger, dashed his horse on the Indian and knocked him down. 'I owe my life to them two,' says Carson—'the Colonel and Sacramento saved me.' Sacramento is a noble Californian horse which Captain Sutter gave to Colonel Fremont in 1844, and which has twice made the distance between Ken tucky and his native valley, where he earned his name by swimming the river after which he is called, at the close of a long day's journey. Notwithstanding all his hardships—for he has travelled everywhere with his master—he is still the favorite horse of Colonel Fremont."

We resume the extract from Benton's "Thirty Years' View:"

"It was in the midst of such dangers as these, that science was pursued by Mr. Fremont; that the telescope was carried to read the heavens; the barometer to measure the elevations of the earth; the thermometer to gauge the temperature of the air; the pencil to sketch the grandeur of mountains, and to paint the beauty of flowers; the pen to write down whatever was new, or strange, or useful in the works of nature. It was in the midst of such dangers, and such occupations as these, and in the wildest regions of the Farthest West, that Mr. Fremont was pursuing science and shunning war, when the arrival of Lieutenant Gillespie, and his communications from Washington, suddenly changed all his plans, turned him back from Oregon, and opened a new and splendid field of operations in California itself. He arrived in the valley of the Sacramento in the month of May, 1846, and found the country alarmingly and critically situated. Three great operations, fatal to American interests, were then going on, and without remedy, if not arrested at once. These were—1. The massacre of the Americans, and the destruction of their settlements, in the valley of the Sacramento. 2. The subjection of California to British protection. 3. The transfer of the public domain to British subjects. And all this with a view to anticipate the events of a Mexican war, and to shelter California from the arms of the United States.

"The American settlers sent a deputation to the camp of Mr. Fremont, in the valley of the Sacramento, laid all these dangers before him, and implored him to place himself at their head and save them from destruction. General Castro was then in march upon them: the Indians were incited to attack their families, and burn their wheat-fields, and were only waiting for the dry season to apply the torch. Juntas were in session to transfer the country to Great Britain: the public domain was passing away in large grants to British subjects: a British fleet was expected on the coast; the British vice-consul, Forbes and the emissary priest, Macnamara, ruling and conducting everything, and all their plans so far advanced as to render the least delay fatal. It was then the beginning of June. War had broke out between the United States and Mexico, but that was unknown in California. Mr. Fremont had left the two countries at peace when he set out upon his expedition, and was determined to do nothing to disturb their relations: he had even left California to avoid giving offence; and to return and take up arms in so short a time was apparently to discredit his own previous conduct, as well as to implicate his government. He felt all the responsibilities of his position; but the actual approach of Castro, and the immediate danger of the settlers, left him no alternative. He determined to put himself at the head of the people, and to save the country. To repulse Castro was not sufficient: to overturn the Mexican government in California, and to establish Californian Independence, was the bold resolve, and the only measure adequate to the emergency. That resolve was taken, and executed with a celerity that gave it a romantic success. The American settlers rushed to his camp—brought their arms, horses and ammunition—were formed into a battalion; and obeyed with zeal and alacrity the orders they received. In thirty days all the northern part of California was freed from Mexican authority—Independence proclaimed—the flag of Independence raised—Castro flying to the south—the American settlers saved from destruction; and the British party in California counteracted and broken up in all their schemes.

"This movement for independence was the salvation of

California, and snatched it out of the hands of the British at the moment they were ready to clutch it. For two hundred years—from the time of the navigator Drake, who almost claimed it as a discovery and placed the English name of New Albion upon it—the eye of England has been upon California; and the magnificent bay of San Francisco, the great seaport of the North Pacific Ocean, has been surveyed as her own. The approaching war between Mexico and the United States was the crisis in which she expected to realize the long-deferred wish for its acquisition; and carefully she took her measures accordingly. She sent two squadrons to the Pacific as soon as Texas was incorporated—well seeing the actual war which was to grow out of that event—a small one into the mouth of the Columbia, an imposing one to Mazatlan, on the Mexican coast, to watch the United States squadron there, and to anticipate its movements upon California. Commodore Sloat, commanding the squadron at Mazatlan, saw that he was watched, and pursued by Admiral Seymour, who lay along side of him, and he determined to deceive him. He stood out to sea, and was followed by the British Admiral.

"During the day he bore west, across the ocean, as if going to the Sandwich Islands: Admiral Seymour followed. In the night the American commodore tacked, and ran up the coast towards California: the British Admiral, not seeing the tack, continued on his course, and went entirely to the Sandwich Islands before he was undeceived. Commodore Sloat arrived before Monterey on the second of July, entering that port amicably, and offering to salute the town, which the authorities declined on the pretext that they had no powder to return it—in reality because they momentarily expected the British fleet. Commodore Sloat remained five days before the town, and until he heard of Fremont's operations; then believing that Fremont had orders from his government to take California, he having none himself, he determined to act himself. He received the news of Fremont's successes on the 6th day of July: on the 7th he took the town of Monterey, and sent a dispatch to Fremont. The latter came to him in all speed, at the head of his mounted force. Going immediately on board the commodore's vessel, an explanation took place. The commodore learnt with astonishment that Fremont had no orders from his government to commence hostilities—that he acted entirely on his own responsibility. This left the commodore without authority for having taken Monterey; for still at this time, the commencement of the war with Mexico was unknown. Uneasiness came upon the commodore. He remembered the fate of Captain Jones in making the mistake of seizing the town once before in time of peace. He resolved to return to the United States, which he did—turning over the command of the squadron to Commodore Stockton, who had arrived on the 15th. The next day (16th) Admiral Seymour arrived; his flagship, the Collingwood, of 80 guns, and his squadron the largest British fleet ever seen in the Pacific. To his astonishment he beheld the American flag flying over Monterey, the American squadron in its harbor, and Fremont's mounted riflemen encamped over the town. His mission was at an end. The prize had escaped him. He attempted nothing further, and Fremont and Stockton rapidly pressed the conquest of California to its conclusion. The subsequent military events can be traced by any history; they were the natural sequence of the great measure conceived and executed by Fremont before any squadron had arrived upon the coast, before he knew of any war with Mexico, and without any authority from his government, except the equivocal and enigmatical visit of Mr. Gillespie. Before the junction of Mr. Fremont with Commodores Sloat and Stockton, his operations had been carried on under the flag of Independence—the Bear Flag, as it was called—the device of the bear being adopted on account of the courageous qualities of that animal (the white bear), which never gives the road to men—which attacks any number—and fights to the last with increasing ferocity, with amazing strength of muscle, and with an incredible tenacity of the vital principle—never more

FREMONT'S PARDON OF DON PICO—"OVERCOME WITH EMOTION, HE FLUNG HIMSELF UPON THE FLOOR BEFORE COL. FREMONT, CLASPED HIS KNEES CONVULSIVELY, SWORE ETERNAL FIDELITY TO HIM AND HIS, AND BEGGED THE PRIVILEGE OF FIGHTING AND DYING FOR HIM"—PAGE 145

formidable and dangerous than when mortally wounded. The Independents took the device of this bear for their flag, and established the independence of California under it: and in joining the United States forces, hauled down this flag and hoisted the flag of the United States. And the fate of California would have been the same whether the United States squadrons had arrived or not, and whethe. the Mexican war had happened or not. California was in a revolutionary state, already divided from Mexico politically, as it had always been geographically. The last governor-general from Mexico, Don Michel Toreno, had been resisted, fought, captured and shipped back to Mexico, with his 300 cut-throat soldiers. An insurgent government was in operation, determined to be free of Mexico, sensible of inability to stand alone, and looking, part to the United States, part to Great Britain for the support which they needed. All the American settlers were for the United States protection and joined Fremont. The leading Californians were also joining him. His conciliatory course drew them rapidly to him. The Picos who were the leading men of the revolt (Don Pio, Don Andres, and Don Jesus,) became his friends. California, became independent of Mexico by the revolt of the Picos, and independent of them by the revolt of the American settlers, had its destiny to fulfill—which was, to be handed over to the United States. So that its incorporation with the American Republic was equally sure in any and every event."

The following incident illustrates the conciliatory policy of Col. Fremont, towards the Picos, which Col. Benton refers to in the last preceding paragraph, as well as the sagacity and judgment—to say nothing of the generosity with which he discharged his duties as an officer during this critical period.

One of the Picos, the brother of the governor of California, had been dismissed by Fremont on parole, and was recaptured in the act of breaking it. He was heading an insurrection which might have proved fatal to the American army; and the American soldiers clamored for his head. Pico was brought before Fremont, identified, tried by a court martial, and condemned to death. Through the whole examination and the delivery of the sentence, he remained cool and composed, and received his last sentence with true Castilian dignity. The hour of twelve was fixed for the execution. About an hour before, an unusual noise was heard without, and before one had time to ascertain its cause, a company of ladies and children rushed into the room to which the colonel had retired, threw themselves on their knees, and with the eloquence which only such an emergency could inspire, begged that the husband and father might be spared. The stern officer who was himself both a husband and a father, and whose thoughts were suddenly hurried back over the wilderness, and the mountain, to their distant homes in the East, was unprepared for this appeal, and surrendered to the impulses of humanity without resistance. Raising the broken hearted mother, he exclaimed, but with choaking utterance, "he is pardoned." He would have turned to escape the grateful blessings which were invoked upon his head, and from witnessing the tears of joy which followed the tears of despair, from their now delighted eyes, but they would not permit it. As the shortest and fittest way of closing the trying scene, Col. Fremont sent for the prisoner to receive his pardon, in the presence of his family. When Pico entered the room, the countenances of all present told him of his good fortune, and when it was confirmed by the word of the Colonel, he was for a moment speechless. He had borne misfortune and disgrace with firmness, but the news of his pardon was too much for him. Overcome with emotion, he flung himself upon the floor before Colonel Fremont, clasped his knees convulsively, swore eternal fidelity to him and his, and begged the privilege of fighting and dying for him. From that day forth, Col. Fremont had no firmer friend than his former inveterate antagonist, Pico.

The prudence, heroism, skill, and endurance displayed by Col. Fremont, in the conquest of California, furnished the administration at Washington, with one of its most grateful and decisive triumphs. The following passages from the annual report of Mr. Marcy, then Secretary of War, bearing date December 6th, 1846, will show the importance which President Polk and his cabinet, attached to the services of the young hero, in securing that triumph.

MR. MARCY'S REPORT ON FREMONT'S EXPLORATIONS.

WAR DEPARTMENT, *Dec.* 5, 1846

* * * * * *

"In May, 1845, John C. Fremont, then a brevet captain in the corps of Topographical Engineers, and since appointed a lieutenant colonel, left here under orders from this department to pursue his explorations in the regions beyond the Rocky Mountains. The objects of this service were, as those of his previous exploratious had been, of a scientific character, without any view whatever to military operations. Not an officer nor soldier of the United States army accompanied him; and his whole force consisted of sixty-two men, employed by himself for security against Indians, and for procuring subsistence in the wilderness and desert country through which he was to pass.

"One of the objects he had in view was to discover a new and shorter route from the western base of the Rocky Mountains to the mouth of the Columbia river. This search, for a part of the distance, would carry him through the unsettled, and afterward through a corner of the settled parts of California. He approached these settlements in the winter of 1845–'6. Aware of the critical state of affairs between the United States and Mexico, and determined to give no cause of offence to the authorities of the province, with commendable prudence he halted his command on the frontier, one hundred miles from Monterey, and proceeded alone to that city to explain the object of his coming to the commandant general, Castro, and to obtain permission to go to the valley of the San Joaquim, where there was game for his men and grass for his horses, and no inhabitants to be molested by his presence. The leave was granted; but scarcely had he reached the desired spot for refreshment and repose, before he received information from the American settlements, and by expresses from our Consul at Monterey, that General Castro was preparing to attack him with a comparatively large force of artillery, cavalry and infantry, upon the pretext that, under the cover of a scientific mission, he was exciting the American settlers to revolt. In view of this danger and to be in a condition to repel an attack, he then took a position on a mountain overlooking Monterey, at a distance of about thirty miles, entrenched it, raised the flag of the United States, and with his own men, sixty-two in number, awaited the approach of the commandant general.

From the 7th to the 10th of March, Colonel Fremont and his little band maintained this position. General Castro did not approach within attacking distance, and Colonel Fremont, adhering to his plan of avoiding all collisions, and determined neither to compromit his government nor the American settlers, ready to join him at all hazards, if he had been attacked, abandoned his position, and commenced his march for Oregon, intending by that route to return to the United States. Deeming all danger from the Mexicans to be passed, he yielded to the wishes of some of his men who desired to remain in the country, discharged them from his service, and refused to receive others in their stead, so cautious was he to avoid doing anything which would compromit the American settlers or give even a color of offence to the Mexican authorities. He pursued his march slowly and leisurely, as the state of his men and horses required, until the middle of May, and had reached the northern shore of the greater Tlamath Lake, within the limits of the Oregon Territory, when he found his further progress in that direction obstructed by impassable snowy mountains and hostile Indians, who, having been excited against him by General Castro, had killed and wounded four of his men, and left him no repose either in camp or on his march. At the same time information reached him that General Castro, in addition to his Indian allies, was advancing in person against him with artillery and cavalry, at the head of four or five hundred men; that they were passing around the head of the Bay of San Francisco to a rendezvous on the north side of it, and that the American settlers in the valley of the Sacramento were comprehended in the scheme of destruction meditated against his own party.

Under these circumstances, he determined to turn upon his Mexican pursuers, and seek safety both for his own party and the American settlers, not merely in the defeat of Castro, but in the total overthrow of the Mexican authority in California, and the establishment of an independent government in that extensive department. It was on the 6th of June, and before the commencement of the war between the United States and Mexico could have there be known, that this resolution was taken; and, by the 5th of July, it was carried into effect by a series of rapid attacks, by a small body of adventurous men, under the conduct of an intrepid leader, quick to perceive and able to direct the proper measures for accomplishing such a daring enterprise.

On the 11th of June a convoy of 200 horses for Castro's camp, with an officer and 14 men, were surprised and captured by 12 of Fremont's party. On the 15th, at daybreak, the military post of Sanoma was also surprised and taken, with nine brass cannon, 250 stand of muskets, and several officers and some men and munitions of war.

"Leaving a small garrison at Sanoma, Colonel Fremont went to the Sacramento to rouse the American settlers; but scarcely had he arrived there, when an express reached him from the garrison at Sanoma, with information that Castro's whole force was crossing the bay to attack that place. This intelligence was received in the afternoon of the 23d of June, while he was on the American fork of the Sacramento, 80 miles from the little garrison at Sanoma; and, at 2 o'clock on the morning of the 25th, he arrived at that place with 90 riflemen from the American settlers in that valley. The enemy had not yet appeared. Scouts were sent out to reconnoitre, and a party of 20 fell in with a squadron of 70 dragoons (all of Castro's force which had crossed the bay), attacked and defeated it, killing and wounding five, without harm to themselves; the Mexican commander, De la Torre, barely escaping with the loss of his transport boats and nine pieces of brass artillery, spiked.

"The country north of the bay of San Francisco being cleared of the enemy, Colonel Fremont returned to Sanoma on the evening of the 4th of July, and on the morning of the 5th, called the people together, explained to them the condition of things in the province, and recommended an immediate declaration of independence. The declaration was made, and he was selected to take the chief direction of affairs.

"The attack on Castro was the next object. He was at Santa Clara, an entrenched post on the upper or south side of the Bay of San Francisco, with 400 men and two pieces of field artillery. A circuit of more than a hundred miles must be traversed to reach him. On the 6th of July the pursuit was commenced, by a body of 160 mounted riflemen, commanded by Colonel Fremont in person, who, in three days, arrived at the American settlements on the Rio de los Americanos. Here he learnt that Castro had abandoned Santa Clara, and was retreating south towards Ciudad de los Angeles (the city of the Angels), the seat of the Governor General of the Californias, and distant 400 miles. It was instantly resolved on to pursue him to that place. At the moment of departure the gratifying intelligence was received that war with Mexico had commenced; that Monterey had been taken by our naval force, and the flag of the United States there raised on the 7th of July; and that the fleet would co-operate in the pursuit of Castro and his forces. The flag of independence was hauled down, and that of the United States hoisted, amidst the hearty greetings and to the great joy of the American settlers and the forces under the command of Colonel Fremont.

"The combined pursuit was rapidly continued; and on the 12th of August, Commodore Stockton and Colonel Fremont, with a detachment of marines from the squadron and some riflemen, entered the City of the Angels, without resistance or objection; the Governor General, Pico, the Commandant General Castro and all the Mexican authorities, having fled and dispersed. Commodore Stockton took possession of the whole country as a conquest of the United States, and appointed Colonel Fremont Governor, under the law of nations; to assume the functions of that office when he should return to the squadron.

"Thus, in the short space of sixty days from the first decisive movement, this conquest was achieved by a small body of men, to an extent beyond their own expectation; for the Mexican authorities proclaimed it a conquest, not merely of the northern part, but of the whole province of the Californias.

"The Commandant General, Castro, on the 9th of August, from his camp at the Mesa, and next day 'on the road to Sonora,' announced this result to the people, together with the actual flight and dispersion of the former authorities; and at the same time, he officially communicated the fact of the conquest to the French, English, and Spanish Consuls in California; and to crown the whole, the official paper of the Mexican government, on the 16th of October, in laying these official communications before the public, introduced them with the emphatic declaration, 'The loss of the Californias is consummated.'

"The whole province was yielded up to the United States, and is now in our military occupancy. A small part of the troops sent out to subject this province will constitute, it is presumed, a sufficient force to retain our possession, and the remainder will be disposable for other objects of the war.

* * * * * * * * *

"W. L. MARCY.

"TO THE PRESIDENT OF THE UNITED STATES."

The extraordinary journey of Fremont, with ninety riflemen, to succor the American garrison at Sanoma, which the Secretary of War deems worthy of such specific commendation, was altogether surpassed, a few months later, when impelled by motives equally humane and patriotic, he rode nine hundred and sixty miles in seven days, through a rough and dangerous country, to inform General Kearney of an impending insurrection in Lower California. An account of this extraordinary feat, in which, however, the distance is under-stated, was prepared for the Washington Intelligencer in 1848, by one who became acquainted with the incidents from the lips of one of the party, and is every way worthy of being preserved among the choicest memorials of the young conqueror and explorer of California. We quote it as published in the National Intelligencer of Nov. 22, 1847.

THE EXTRAORDINARY RIDE OF LIEUT. COL. FREMONT, HIS FRIEND DON JESUS PICO, AND HIS SERVANT, JACOB DODSON, FROM LOS ANGELES TO MONTEREY AND BACK IN MARCH, 1847.

"This extraordinary ride of 800 miles in eight days, including all stoppages and near two days' detention—a whole day and a night at Monterey, and nearly two half days at San Luis Obispo—having been brought into evidence before the Army Court Martial now in session in this city, and great desire being expressed by some friends to know how the ride was made, I herewith send you the particulars, that you may publish them if you please, in the *National Intelligencer* as an incident connected with the times and affairs under review in the trial, of which you give so full a report. The circumstances were first got from Jacob, afterwards revised by Col. Fremont, and I drew them up from his statement.

" The publication will show, besides the horsemanship of the riders, the power of the California horse, especially as one of the horses was subjected, in the course of the ride, to an extraordinary trial in order exhibit the capacity of his race. Of course this statement will make no allusion to the objects of the journey, but be confined strictly to its performance.

" It was at daybreak on the morning of the 22d of March, that the party set out from La Cuidad de los Angeles (the city of the Angels) in the southern part of Upper California, to proceed, in the shortest time, to Monterey on the Pacific coast, distant full four hundred miles. The way is over a mountainous country, much of it uninhabited, with no other road than a trace, and many defiles to pass, particularly the maritime defile of *el Rincon* or Punto Gordo, fifteen miles in extent, made by the jutting of a precipitous mountain into the sea, and which can only be passed when the tide is out and the sea calm, and then in many places through the waves. The towns of Santa Barbara and San Luis Obispo, and occasional ranches, are the principal inhabited places on the route. Each of the party had three horses, nine in all, to take their turns under the saddle. The six loose horses ran ahead, without bridle or halter, and required some attention to keep to the track. When wanted for a change, say at the distance of twenty miles, they were caught by the *lasso*, thrown either by Don Jesus or the servant Jacob, who, though born in Washington, in his long expeditions with Col. Fremont, had become as expert as a Mexican with the lasso, as sure as the mountaineer with the rifle, equal to either on horse or foot, and always a lad of courage and fidelity.

"None of the horses were shod, that being a practice unknown to the Californians. The most usual gait was a sweeping gallop. The first day they ran one hundred and twenty-five miles, passing the San Fernando mountain, the defile of the Rincon, several other mountains, and slept at the hospitable ranche of Don Thomas Robberis, beyond the town of Santa Barbara. The only fatigue complained of in this day's ride was in Jacob's right arm, made tired by throwing the lasso, and using it as a whip to keep the loose horses to the track.

"The next day they made another one hundred and twenty-five miles, passing the formidable mountain of Santa Barbara, and counting upon it the skeletons of some fifty horses, part of near double that number which perished in the crossing of that terrible mountain by the California battalion, on Christmas day, 1846, amidst a raging tempest, and a deluge of rain and cold more killing than that of the Sierra Nevada—the day of severest suffering, say Fremont and his men, that they have ever passed. At sunset, the party stopped to sup with the friendly Captain Dana, and at nine at night San Luis Obispo was reached, the home of Don Jesus, and where an affecting reception awaited Lieutenant-Colonel Fremont, in consequence of an incident which occurred there that history will one day record; and he was detained till 10 o'clock in the morning receiving the visits of the inhabitants (mothers and children included), taking a breakfast of honor, and waiting for a relief of fresh horses to be brought in from the surrounding country. Here the nine horses from los Angeles were left, and eight others taken in their place, and a Spanish boy added to the party to assist in managing the loose horses.

"Proceeding at the usual gait till eight at night, and having made some seventy miles, Don Jesus, who had spent the night before with his family and friends, and probably with but little sleep, became fatigued, and proposed a halt for a few hours. It was in the valley of the Salinas (salt river called *Buena Ventura* in the old maps), and the haunt of marauding Indians. For safety during their repose, the party turned off the trace, issued through a *cañon* into a thick wood, and laid down, the horses being put to grass at a short distance, with the Spanish boy in the saddle to watch. Sleep, when commenced, was too sweet to be easily given up, and it was half way between midnight and day, when the sleepers were aroused by an *estampedo* among the horses, and the calls of the boy. The cause of the alarm was soon found, not Indians, but white bears—this valley being their great resort, and the place where Colonel Fremont and thirty-five of his men encountered some hundred of them the summer before, killing thirty upon the ground.

"The character of these bears is well known, and the bravest hunters do not like to meet them without the advantage of numbers. On discovering the enemy, Colonel Fremont felt for his pistols, but Don Jesus desired him to lie still, saying that 'people could scare bears;' and immediately hallooed at them in Spanish, and they went off. Sleep went off also; and the recovery of the horses frightened by the bears, building a rousing fire, making a breakfast from the hospitable supplies of San Luis Obispo, occupied the party till day-break, when the journey was resumed Eighty miles, and the afternoon brought the party to Monterey.

"The next day, in the afternoon, the party set out on their return, and the two horses rode by Col. Fremont from San Luis Obispo, being a present to him from Don Jesus, he (Don Jesus) desired to make an experiment of what one of them could do. They were brothers, one a grass younger than the other, both of the same color (cinnamon), and hence called *el cañalo*, or *los cañalos*, (the cinnamon or the cinnamons.) The elder was to be taken for the trial; and the journey commenced upon him at leaving Monterey, the afternoon well advanced. Thirty miles under the saddle done that evening, and the party stopped for the night. In the morning the elder cañalo was again under the saddle for Col. Fremont, and for ninety miles he carried him without a change, and without apparent fatigue. It was still thirty miles to San Luis Obispo, where the night was to be passed, and Don Jesus insisted that cañalo could do it, and so said the horse by his looks and action. But Col. Fremont would not put him to the trial, and, shifting the saddle to the younger brother, the elder was turned loose to run the remaining thirty miles without a rider. He did so, immediately taking the lead and keeping it all the way, and entering San Luis in a sweeping gallop, nostrils distended, snuffing the air, and neighing with exultation at his return to his native pastures; his younger brother all the time at the head of the horses under the saddle, bearing on his bit, and held in by his rider. The whole eight horses made their one hundred and twenty miles each that day (after thirty the evening before), the elder cinnamon making ninety of his under the saddle that day, besides thirty under the saddle the evening before; nor was there the least doubt that he would have done the whole distance in the same time if he had continued under the saddle.

"After a hospitable detention of another half a day at San Luis, Obispo, the party set out for Los Angeles on the same nine horses which they had rode from that place, and made the ride back in about the same time they had made it up, namely, at the rate of 125 miles a day.

"On this ride, the grass on the road was the food for the horses. At Monterey they had barley; but these horses, meaning those *trained and domesticated*, as the cañalos were, eat almost anything of vegetable food, or even drink, that their master uses, by whom they are petted and caressed, and rarely sold. Bread, fruit, sugar, coffee, and even wine (like the Persian horses), they take from the hand of their master, and obey with like docility his slightest intimation. A tap of the whip on the saddle, springs them into action; the check of a thread rein (on the Spanish bit) would stop them: and stopping short at speed they do not jostle the rider or throw him forward. They leap on anything —man, beast, or weapon, on which their master directs them. But this description, so far as conduct and behavior are concerned, of course only applies to the trained and domesticated horse.

CHAPTER VIII.

CONQUEST OF CALIFORNIA COMPLETED—JOINS COMMODORE STOCKTON—DESCRIPTION OF HIS PARTY ON ITS ARRIVAL AT MONTEREY—ORGANIZES THE CALIFORNIA BATTALION—IS APPOINTED MAJOR—ORIGIN OF THE CONTROVERSY BETWEEN COMMODORE STOCKTON AND BRIGADIER GENERAL KEARNEY—COMMODORE STOCKTON'S REPORT OF THE CONQUEST OF SOUTH CALIFORNIA—INSURRECTION OF THE WAH-LAH-WAH-LAH INDIANS QUELLED—CAPITULATION OF COUENGA—FREMONT GOVERNOR OF CALIFORNIA.

AMPLER details of some of the events which preceded the capitulation of Couenga so eloquently grouped by Col. Benton, are necessary to a perfect appreciation of the military and administrative ability displayed by Col. Fremont in the emancipation of California.

Castro's first hostile message reached him in the midst of his scientific employments about eight leagues from Monterey on the 3d of March, 1846. By the 1st of July he had scattered the combinations of Mexicans and Indians that had been formed against him. On the 4th of July he was elected governor of California by the revolutionists, and on the 10th about sunset, he received the gratifying intelligence, that encouraged by his success in the interior, Commodore Sloat had taken Monterey, and that the American flag had been flying from the fort since the 7th. He immediately set out for the commodore's quarters, with his troops of 160 mounted riflemen, in order to secure the co-operation of the only branch of the American military service in force in that quarter of the globe. He reached Monterey on the 19th of July. It so happened that the British ship of war Collingwood, of 80 guns, had arrived about a week after the capture. Had she arrived a week sooner it is generally conceded that the place could not have been taken without a contest with her commander Sir George Seymour, the people of the place having entered into arrangements with a view of transferring their allegiance to Great Britain. Among the officers of the Collingwood who happened to be at Monterey and saw Fremont enter the place with his company, was Lieutenant Frederick Walpole, of the Collingwood, who has given his impressions of the spectacle in a very readable book which he published on his return to England, entitled "Four years in the Pacific, in her Majesty's Ship 'Collingwood,' from 1844 to 1848."

"During our stay in Monterey," says Mr. Walpole, "Captain Fremont and his party arrived. They naturally excited curiosity. Here were true trappers, the class that produced the heroes of Fennimore Cooper's best works. These men had passed years in the wilds, living upon their own resources; they were a curious set. A vast cloud of dust appeared first, and thence in long file emerged this wildest wild party. Fremont rode ahead, a spare, active-looking man, with such an eye! He was dressed in a blouse and leggings, and wore a felt hat. After him came five Delaware Indians, who were his body-guard, and have been with him through all his wanderings; they had charge of two baggage horses. The rest, many of them blacker than the Indians, rode two and two, the rifle held by one hand across the pommel of the saddle. Thirty-nine of them are his regular men, the rest are loafers picked up lately; his original men are principally backwoodsmen, from the State of Tennessee and the banks of the upper waters of the Missouri. He has one or two with him who enjoy a high reputation in the prairies. Kit Carson is as well known there as 'the Duke' is in Europe. The dress of these men was principally a long loose coat of deer skin, tied with thongs in front; trowsers of the same, of their own manufacture, which, when wet through, they take off, scrape well inside with a knife, and put on as soon as dry; the saddles were of various fashions, though these and a large drove of horses, and a brass field-gun, were things they had picked up about California. They are allowed no liquor, tea and sugar only; this, no doubt, has much to do with their good conduct; and the discipline, too, is very strict. They were marched up to an open space on the hills near the town, under some large fires, and there took up their quarters, in messes of six or seven, in the open air. The Indians lay beside their leader. One man, a doctor, six feet six high, was an odd-looking fellow. May I never come under his hands!"

Contemporaneously with the arrival of Fremont's party at Monterey, Commodore Stockton entered the harbor in command of the Frigate Congress. Commodore Sloat, then in command of the Pacific squadron, who had been greatly embarrassed by the position he found himself placed in by the capture of Monterey, which he had made under the impression that

Fremont's movements in the north had been conducted under orders from Washington, determined, after some hesitation, to transfer the command of the fleet to Commodore Stockton, and return to the United States.

The same day that Commodore Stockton took command of the squadron, he requested Col. Fremont to organize, and take the command, with the rank of major, of what soon became famous as the "California battalion." The colonel complied with the commodore's request, waiving the rights which he might have asserted as the conqueror and liberator of the country, and at once entered cordially into the plans of the commodore for the subjugation of South California, which was in a state of insurrection. As the most unpleasant and momentous personal controversy that Col. Fremont has ever been engaged in, originated in his acceptance of this command from Commodore Stockton—and as the events have been the subject of a protracted judicial scrutiny, we shall probably discharge our duties most acceptably as his biographer, by relying for our record of the events out of which the controversy originated, and which are spread over the remainder of his sojourn in California as an American officer, upon official documents and such public records as give events in the most compact and accessible form. With this view, we submit the following dispatch from Commodore Stockton, which was written in 1848, and gives a very detailed account of his movements after taking command of the Pacific fleet in July, 1846.

In perusing this dispatch, the reader is requested to note those passages in which the commodore discusses certain differences between himself and General Kearney, in regard to their respective powers—differences which resulted in Mr. Fremont's abandoning the army as a profession, the following year. It should also be borne in mind, that this dispatch is in some sort the commodore's defence of himself, inasmuch as he was necessarily implicated in the guilt of issuing any orders which it was unlawful for another party to obey.*

REPORT OF COMMODORE STOCKTON OF HIS OPERATIONS ON THE COAST OF THE PACIFIC.†

"WASHINGTON, D. C., February 18, 1848.

"SIR: On my return from California in November last, the circumstances of the times seemed to present reasons for delaying a full report of my transactions and operations on the coast of the Pacific.

"The authority under which I had acted was questioned or denied; the validity of much that had been done was doubted, and investigations were on foot in which the propriety of my proceedings might be brought to the especial notice of the Executive.

"After a full consideration of the circumstances, to which it is unnecessary here further to allude, it appeared to me decorous and respectful, to withhold, for a brief period, my own views of the questions in which I was to some extent implicated, and to leave the Executive to learn the details of those transactions

*In a communication addresssed to the court-martial by which Col. Fremont was subsequently tried for disobeying orders of Gen. Kearney in conflict with orders he had previously received with a commission, from Commodore Stockton, the commodore, in explaining the testimony which he had given before the court, remarks: "For each and every of the acts of Lieut. Col. Fremont, performed under my authority and in obedience to my orders, I cannot but feel that in some form or other I am responsible, if the acts were in themselves illegal or in the execution of them, criminal."

† From Executive Document No. 1, accompanying the President's message at the 2nd Session of the Thirtieth Congress, December, 1848.

from other quarters. The period, however, has now arrived in which I feel that I can, without the imputation of improper feelings or motives, lay before the Executive, in a tangible and official form, a narrative of the occurrences which I directed in California; explain the circumstances wihch induced the course which I pursued, the motives by which I was guided, the objects which I designed to accomplish, and thus to put the President in possession of ample means to form a judgment upon my conduct. It appears now to be no longer questioned that I actually possessed and exercised the power of governor of California and commander-in-chief of the forces of the United States in that quarter, and that, whether rightfully or wrongfully, I executed the duties and administered the functions appertaining to these high offices, for the administration of which I am alone responsible. The dispatches which were from time to time addressed to the Department were designed to furnish the government with accurate information of what transpired; but, under the circumstances in which they were prepared, it did not enter into my purpose to give a general narrative of the entire operations. Opening a full view of the circumstances which influenced my judgment in selecting the course which was adopted, and the policy by which that course was determined, with your permission I beg leave, at this time, to perform this duty; the obligations to do which, at this juncture, seem to me more imperative, since it appears that in an official communication addressed to the Department by my successor in command, I am in the most explicit terms censured for premature as well as injudicious action. With what of propriety or of professional courtesy this condemnation has been passed by an officer of equal rank with myself, without any report or communication to him of what had occurred, or the reasons by which I was governed, is not so apparent. Under the instructions from the Department, I arrived, in command of the United States Frigate Congress, at the harbor of Monterey, about the middle of July, 1846. The American flag was there flying. I immediately went on board the United States frigate Savannah, then lying off that town and, in conformity with my orders, I reported myself to Com modore Sloat as forming part of the Squadron then under his command. From him I learned that in the preceding month of June, while lying off Mazatlan, he had received intelligence that war had commenced between the United States and Mexico; that he had forthwith proceeded to Monterey, landed a force, and hoisted the flag of the United States without resistance. In the course of our interview, Commodore Sloat apprised me of his intention to return in a short time to the United States, whereby the command of the squadron would devolve upon me In this position it became my duty to examine into the state of affairs, and, in view of the responsibility which was about to rest upon me, to obtain all the information which would enable me to exercise a proper judgment as to the ulterior measures to be pursued. The result of my inquiries and investigations showed me that the position I was about to occupy was an important and critical one. The intelligence of the commencement of hostilities between the two nations, although it had passed through Mexico, had reached Commodore Sloat in advance of the Mexican authorities. When he made his first hostile demonstrations, therefore, the enemy, ignorant of the existence of the war, had regarded his acts as an unwarrantable exercise of power by the United States, and the most lively indignation and bitter resentment pervaded the country.

"The public functionaries of the territory were not slow in availing themselves of this feeling, and endeavored to stimulate it to the highest possible degree. A proclamation was put forth, denouncing in the most unmeasured terms all foreigners; but it was unquestionably aimed principally at the citizens of the United States, and such others as sympathized with them. Two or three were, in fact, murdered, and all were led to apprehend extermination from the sanguinary feeling of resentment which was everywhere breathed.

"The local legislature was in session. Governor Pio Pico had assembled a force of about seven hundred or one thousand men, supplied with seven pieces of artillery, breathing vengeance against the perpetrators of the insult and injury which they supposed to have been inflicted. These hostile demonstrations were daily increasing, and by the time that the command devolved on me by the departure of Commodore Sloat, the situation of things had assumed a critical and alarming appearance. Every citizen and friend of the United States throughout the territory was in imminent jeopardy; he could count upon no security for either property or life. It was well known that numerous emigrants from the United States were on their way to Upper California. These, marching in small and detached parties, encumbered with their wives and children and baggage, uninformed of the war and consequently unprepared for attack, would have been exposed to certain destruction.

"It was also ascertained that, in the anticipation of the eventful conquest of the country by the United States, many of those in the actual possession of authority were preparing for this change by disposing of the public property, so that it might be found in private hands when the Americans should acquire possession, believing that private rights would be protected and individual property secure. Negotiations were in actual progress thus to acquire three thousand leagues of land, and to dispose of all the most valuable portions of the territory appertaining to the missions at nominal prices, so that the conquerors should find the entire country appropriated to individuals, and in hands which could effectually prevent sales to American citizens, and thus check the tide of emigration, while little or no benefit would result to the nation from the acquisition of this valuable territory.

"All these considerations, together with others of inferior moment, seemed to make prompt and decisive action an imperative duty. To retain possession merely of a few seaports, while cut off from all intercourse with the interior, exposed to constant attack by the concentrated forces of an exasperated enemy, appeared wholly useless. Yet to abandon ground which we had occupied, to withdraw our forces from these points, to yield places where our flag had been floating in triumph, was an alternative not to be thought of, except as a last resource. Not only would all the advantages which had been obtained be thus abandoned, and perhaps never be regained without great expenditure of blood and treasure, but the pride and confidence of the enemy would be increased to a dangerous extent by such indications of our weakness and inability to maintain what we had won.

"Previous to the departure of Commodore Sloat, he had, at my instance, and upon my representations, placed at my disposal the United States sloop-of-war Cyane, as well as the forces on shore. I immediately apprised Captain Fremont, then of the topographical corps, with whom I had previous communications, of the position in which I was placed, and that I had determined upon my plan of operations.

"Captain Fremont and Lieutenant Gillespie, of the marine corps, had already raised a body of 160 volunteers, prepared to act according to circumstances. I informed those gentlemen that if they, together with the men whom they had raised, would volunteer to serve under my command so long as I should remain in California and require their services, that I would form them into a battalion, appointing the former major and the latter captain. These arrangements were all completed in the course of the 23d of July, and my letters of that date to Commodore Sloat, to Commander Du Pont, and Captain Fremont, on the file in the Department, will have apprised you of my movements.

"It was thus that the battalion of California volunteers was organized, which subsequently, under its gallant officers, took so patriotic and efficient a part in the military operations in that territory. It was received into the service of the United States to aid the navy, as essential as well to the maintenance of the position we then occupied as to execute the plans which I had contemplated in the interior.

"A few days subsequently, Commodore Sloat sailed in the Levant, thus devolving upon me the command of the entire force, both afloat and on shore. That force then consisted of the frigates Congress and Savannah, sloops-of-war Portsmouth, Cyane, and Warren, and the store-ship Erie. The Portsmouth was at San Francisco, the Congress and Savannah at Monterey, the Cyane had been sent with the California battalion to San Diego, the Warren was at Mazatlan, and the Erie at the Sandwich Islands. The force to be employed on land consisted of 360 men, furnished from the Congress, provided with about 90 muskets and bayonets, some small cannon procured from the merchant-vessels, and the battalion of volunteers, all indifferently provided with the appendages of an army.

"Leaving the Savannah at Monterey, for its protection, I sailed about the first of August, in the Congress, for San Pedro. This town is situated about 28 miles from Ciudad de los Angeles, in the vicinity of which the enemy was stated to be. On the way to San Pedro, we landed at Santa Barbara, of which we took possession, and, leaving a small force for its defence, proceeded to San Pedro, where we arrived on the 6th of August. Here information was received of the arrival of the Cyane at San Diego, of the landing of the battalion, and supply of horses. We immediately commenced the landing of our forces from the frigate. On the following day two persons arrived representing themselves to be commissioners sent from General Castro, authorized to enter into negotiations with me, and bearing a letter from the general, which is already in possession of the Department. Before, however, they would communicate the extent of their power or the nature of their instructions, they made a preliminary demand that the further march of the troops must be arrested, and that I must not advance beyond the position which I then occupied. This proposition was peremptorily declined. I announced my determination to advance; and the commissioners returned to their camp without imparting further the objects of the proposed negotiations.

* * * * * * *

Having completed all the arrangements which time and circumstances permitted, and dispatched a courier to Major Fremont, apprising him of my movements, we commenced our march towards the camp of the enemy on the 11th of August. In the course of the afternoon of that day information reached us that the enemy's force, instead of awaiting our approach, had dispersed; that they had buried their guns, and that the governor and general had retreated, as was supposed, towards Sonora. We continued our march towards Ciudad de los Angeles, and on the 13th, having been joined by Major Fremont with about 120 volunteers under his command, we marched into the city, which we quietly occupied.

"After the dispersement of the army of the enemy, the flight of the general and governor-in-chief out of the territory, a number of the officers of the Mexican army were captured and made prisoners of war. Among these were Jose Maria Flores, whose name hereafter will appear prominently, and Don Andres Pico, brother of Governor Pio Pico. These officers were released upon their parole of honor not to bear arms against the United States pending the war, unless exchanged; with what of fidelity they performed this obligation will appear in the sequel. The people in general came in, tendered their submission to our authority, and promised allegiance to our government. Every indication of a hostile force had now disappeared from the country, tranquillity was restored, and I forthwith determined to organize a temporary civil government to conduct public affairs and to administer justice as in time of peace. Various considerations prompted to this course. It appeared to me that the existence of such a government, under the authority of the United States, would leave no pretence upon which it might be urged that the conquest of the country had not been accomplished. While merely the military power exercised power, enforcing its authority by martial law, and executing its functions through the instrumentality of a regular military force, nothing could be regarded as settled, and opposition to its

THE EXTRAORDINARY RIDE OF COL. FREMONT AND PARTY, 800 MILES IN EIGHT DAYS—PAGE 152.

power would be considered as a lawful opposition to a foreign enemy. When, however, the whole frame of civil administration should be organized—courts and judges performing their accustomed functions—public taxes and imposts regularly collected and appropriated to the ordinary objects and purposes of government—any opposition might be justly deemed a civil offence, and the appropriate punishment inflicted in the ordinary course of administering justice.

"Indeed, the law military appeared to me wholly inadequate to the emergency. It could not reach many of the objects over which a salutary control ought to be exercised. It could not effectively administer the property or sufficiently guard private rights. A civil government which should, through its various functionaries, pervade the entire country, exercise a superintendence over all the inhabitants, discover, restrain, and punish, all acts of insubordination, detect and check all attempts at a hostile organization, recognize and sanction the possession, use, and transfer of property, inflict upon criminals the appropriate punishment, and remedy injuries inflicted upon individuals, seemed not only an important instrument in the accomplishment of the objects which I had in view, but essential to the attainment of the ends of the government. It appeared to me desirable that the actual possession and exercise of power should be transferred, with the least possible delay, from the military to civil functionaries.

"Under our institutions the military is regarded as inferior to the civil authority, and the appropriate duty of the former is to act as auxiliary to the latter. Such being the general character of our institutions, it seemed in the first degree desirable that the inhabitants of the country should, as soon as practicable become familiar with them, that they might perceive and appreciate their importance and their value, their capacity to maintain right and redress wrong, and, in the protection afforded to persons and property, to recognize a guarantee of all their individual rights. The marked contrast which would thus be afforded to their former institutions and rulers would reconcile the Mexican portion of the population to the change; while the American inhabitants would gratefully witness an administration of law and justice analogous to that to which they had been accustomed at home. Actuated by such considerations, I gave my immediate attention to the establishment, upon a permanent basis, of a civil government throughout the country, as much in conformity with the former usages of the country as could be done in the absence of any written code. A tariff of duties was fixed, and collectors appointed. Elections were directed to be held for the various civil magistrates; Major Fremont was appointed military commandant of the territory, and Captain Gillespie military commandant of the southern department. The battalion of volunteers was ordered to be augmented to three hundred; and, contemplating soon to leave the territory, I determined on my departure to appoint Major Fremont Governor of California. He was apprised of these intended arrangements, and instructed to meet me at San Francisco on the 25th of October, for the purpose of consummating them. These acts and intentions were officially communicated to the Department in my several dispatches.

"This exposition of my operations and acts will, I trust, prove satisfactory to the Executive, and be a sufficient reply to Commodore Shubrick's charge of premature action. In a state of actual war against a foreign enemy, I found myself at the head of a force and in command of means competent to take and hold possession of an important part of the hostile territory. I found that before the command had devolved upon me the flag of my country had been raised in some parts of California. Important interests were involved; to stop short would have led to their absolute sacrifice, accompanied by great individual loss and suffering. No middle course was open to my choice. The alternative was the subjection of the entire province to our authority, or its total abandonment. In such a position I could not hesitate as to the line of duty. Empowered to conduct the war against Mexico according to the exigency of circumstances and my own judgment, I determined to support the honor of my flag and to promote what I regarded as the best interest of the nation. Having achieved the conquest of the country, and finding my military strength ample to retain it, the establishment of a civil government naturally and necessarily resulted. The omission to do this would have marred the entire plan and stamped a character of imbecility and instability upon the whole operation. My views of the interests of my country were decisive; as to the expediency of my measures, the estimate I entertained of my authority impressed upon them the sanction of duty. The arrangements having been thus completed, I determined to leave California under the administration of the civil authority, and with the squadron under my command, aided by a volunteer corps raised for the purpose, to sail for the southern part of Mexico, capture Acapulco, and, having secured proper positions on the coast, to march into the interior, advance towards the city of Mexico, and thus to co-operate with the anticipated movements of General Taylor, or produce a powerful diversion which would materially aid him in his operations. My dispatches have already put the Department in possession of these plans.

"About the 2d of September I left Ciudad de los Angeles, embarked on board the Congress on the 3d, and on the 5th sailed for Santa Barbara. Having taken on board the small detachment which had been landed at this place, we proceeded to Monterey, where everything was found tranquil. The people appeared to be quite satisfied with the state of affairs. Information was here received leading to the apprehension that Sutter's settlement on the Sacramento was threatened with an attack by a body of one thousand Wah-lah-wah-lah Indians. The Savannah was immediately ordered to San Francisco; Lieutenant Maddox, of the marine corpse, appointed military commandant of the middle department, and, other necessary arrangements having been made, I proceeded in the Congress to San Francisco, which place I reached in a few days. It soon appeared that the reports in regard to the Wah-lah-wah-lah Indians had been greatly exaggerated. They were not so numerous as had been represented, had they any hostile intentions.

We deem it proper to interrupt the commodore's narrative at this point, for the purpose of giving Upham's fuller and more authentic account of this Wah-lah-wah-lah insurrection, in the quieting of which Col. Fremont displayed a degree of judgment and discretion which Commodore Stockton does not seem to have had the means of appreciating. Mr. Upham says: *

"At this time an additional panic arose from the report of an Indian invasion from the north. It was said that one thousand Wah-lah-wah-lahs were advancing to attack Sutter's Fort. The whole country was aroused, and every element of disposable force was drawn out to meet the threatened danger. Fremont had already assembled a body of several hundred western riflemen towards the completion of his California battalion, when the news reached him. He was quite confident that the story was exaggerated; but it was necessary to restore security in the northern frontier. He took three tried men with him, and went directly to meet the Wah-lah-wah-lahs. He found them much less numerous than had been represented, but assembled in considerable force, and in a state of the greatest exasperation. He went, with his three men, directly into their midst. One of them knew him, and all gathered round him to tell their wrongs. They had been robbed, and one of their best young men killed by the whites. He promised them redress if they would follow his advice. He told them that he was going to the south,

* Upham's Life of Fremont, p. 242.

and could not attend to them until the spring, but that he would then meet them, at a place agreed upon, and have justice done them. He advised them, in the mean time, to go off on a winter hunt—said that he would let one of his own men go with them, to hold over them the United States flag, and that whoever struck that flag struck him. They were perfectly subdued by his talk, and manner of treating them: at once gave up their plan of attacking the whites; and agreed to go off on a winter hunt. They gave him ten of their young braves to go with him, who proved themselves among the best in his battalion. In the spring of the year, he met them, although at a great inconvenience, and gave them of his own horses until they were satisfied. In this way he not only stopped an Indian war, and recruited his own ranks, but he taught a lesson which it would be well to have inculcated upon those who undertake to grapple with our Indian difficulties, and enforced upon the administration of that department of our government."

The commodore continues:

About the 30th of September, a courier arrived from Captain Gillespie, despatched by that officer to convey to me the information that an insurrection had broken out at Ciudad de los Angeles, and that he was besieged in the government-house at that place by a large force. I immediately ordered Capt. Mervine to proceed in the Savannah to San Pedro, for the purpose of affording aid to Captain Gillespie. Major Fremont was at Sacramento when the news of the insurrection reached him, and, having formed the determination to march against the insurgents with the force he could muster, amounting to about one hundred and twenty men, was preparing to move. I sent a request to him forthwith to join me at San Francisco with his command, and to bring with him as many saddles as he could procure. While awaiting the arrival of Major Fremont I detached officers in various directions for the purpose of procuring volunteers to join the battalion, and engaged the merchant-ship Sterling to take them down to Santa Barbara.

"About the 12th of October, Major Fremont arrived at San Francisco, and immediately embarked on board the Sterling, with about one hundred and sixty volunteers. He was directed to proceed to Santa Barbara, there to procure horses to march to Ciudad de los Angeles, while I, with the Congress, was to sail to San Pedro, and by that route advance towards the same point. The insurgents were represented to be encamped in the neighborhood of that city. The Congress and Sterling sailed in company from San Francisco, but separated the same evening in a fog. Between San Francisco and Monterey we spoke a merchant-vessel from the latter port, with dispatches from Lieutenant Maddox, apprising me that Monterey was threatened with an attack, and that he was in want of immediate assistance. We ran into the Bay of Monterey, landed two officers with fifty men and some ordnance. Having thus strengthened that post, I proceeded to San Pedro. On my arrival on that place, about the 23d of October, I found the Savannah frigate. Captain Mervine informed me that Captain Gillespie, with the volunteers under his command, was on board his vessel, having left Ciudad de los Angeles, under a capitulation entered into with General Flores, the leader of the insurrection—one of the Mexican officers who, having been made prisoner of war, had been released on his parole.

"Captain Mervine further informed me that, about two weeks before, he had landed with his sailors and marines for the purpose of marching in conjuntion with Captain Gillespie and his detachment of volunteers to Ciudad de los Angeles. He had not carried any artillery with him; that about twelve miles from San Pedro he encountered a party of the insurgents with one piece of artillery; a battle ensued; that several charges had been Made upon the insurgents' gun, but it was impossible to capture it, as, whenever he approached, they hitched their horses to it and retreated. Having sustained a loss of several men killed and wounded, he retired with his force and re-embarked.

"Proper arrangements having been made during the night, in the morning we landed a strong force with several pieces of artillery, once more hoisted the flag of the United States at San Pedro, and formed our camp there. The insurgent force in the vicinity was supposed to number about eight hundred men. Our authority was necessarily limited to the portion of territory in our actual possession or within the range of our guns. The in surgents, in the undisturbed occupancy of the interior, and watchful of our every movement, could, at their pleasure, threaten us with an attack by night or day, and had the precaution to remove beyond our reach every horse and all the cattle which might have been available either for food or transportation.

"The roadstead at San Pedro was also a dangerous position for men-of-war, being exposed to the storms which at that season of the year rage with great violence upon the coast.

"This consideration decided me to proceed to San Diego, which, although the entrance was obstructed by a bar which had never been passed by a vessel of equal draught of water with the Congress, might, I hoped, be crossed; and, if the passage should prove practicable, would be found a convenient and safe harbor. We did not, however, leave San Pedro until I had been compelled to relinquish all expectation of the co-operation of Major Fremont from whom I had not heard a word since we parted off San Francisco, nor until the officers and men had become completely exhausted by their incessant duties on shore, in guarding the camp from attack and pursuing small parties of the insurgents who approached us. Having embarked the men belonging to the squadron, and volunteers under Captain Gilles pie, I sailed for San Diego in the Congress.

"On my arrival off the harbor of San Diego, I received information from Lieutenant Minor that the town was besieged by the insurgents, that his stock of provisions was small, and that he was in the want of an additional force. He gave it as his opinion that the Congress might be got over the bar. In attempting this, however, the ship struck, and her position was so dangerous that we were compelled to return to the anchorage out side.

"On the following day the Malek Adhel, a prize to the United States ship Warren, arrived from Monterey with dispatches from Lieutenant-Colonel Fremont. I thus received information from that officer that on his way to Santa Barbara he met the merchant-ship Vandalia, from San Pedro, by whom he was informed of the state of affairs at the South; that it would be impossible for him to procure horses at Santa Barbara, in consequence of which he had proceeded to Monterey, and would employ all diligence in preparing his force to march for Ciudad de los Angeles.

"Lieutenant Minor was directed to send the ship Stonington, then lying in the harbor of San Diego, with as many volunteers as could be spared, to Ensanado, about ninety miles below San Diego, for the purpose of procuring animals, which he was instructed to have driven into San Diego. Without a supply of horses and beeves, it was not prudent to commence our march. Captain Mervine was dispatched in the Savannah to Monterey, to aid Lieutenant-Colonel Fremont in his preparations to march, and, having myself gone to San Pedro, returned with all convenient speed to San Diego.

"About thirty or forty miles from that place, our progress was arrested by a calm. My anxiety on account of Lieutenant-Colonel Fremont, and my desire to go to his assistance was so great, that a boat was immediately dispatched with Lieutenant Tilghman, the bearer of a communication addressed to Lieutenant George Minor, in command at San Diego, apprising that officer that on my arrival I would be ready to take the field in person, and with an additional force of two hundred and fifty men from the ship, to take up the line of march for Ciudad de los Angeles.

Lieutenant Minor was directed to arrange with Lieutenant Tilghman, the commanding officer of the artillery, and Mr. Southwick, commanding officer of the engineers, to have the horses necessary for the transportation of the guns and ammunition.

"Notwithstanding my first unsuccessful attempt to get into the harbor of San Diego, it was an object of too great importance to be abandoned, unless from the absolute impossibility of effecting it. The bar and channel were again, on my return, examined and buoyed, and a second attempt made. After crossing the bar, the ship grounded, and in such a situation that it became expedient to prepare her spars to shore her up, to prevent her from tumbling over. While thus occupied, the insurgents commenced an attack upon the town, and, notwithstanding the perilous condition of the frigate, and the necessity of employing the crew in extricating her from her position, a portion of them was simultaneously engaged in landing from the ship, in boats, to take part in the fight. In executing my orders in reference to those two distinct objects at the same time, the conduct of the officers and men under my command was such as to command my warmest commendation. Everything was performed with the regularity and order of the ordinary duties of the vessel. Having accomplished a landing of the men from the ship, the attack of the insurgents was successfully repelled by the combined force under the command of Lieutenant Minor and Captain Gillespie.

"The situation of the place was found to be most miserable and deplorable. The male inhabitants had abandoned the town, leaving their women and children dependent upon us for protection and food. No horses could be obtained to assist in the transportation of the guns and ammunition, and not a beef could be had to supply the necessary food; some supplies of provisions were furnished from the ship. The expedition to the southward for animals, under the command of Captain Gibson, of the battalion, had succeeded in driving about ninety horses, and two hundred head of beef-cattle into the garrison.

"The horses were, however, much worn down, and it was supposed a fortnight's rest would be required before they would be fit for service. During the time required for resting the horses, we were actively employed in the construction of a fort, for the more complete protection of the town, mounting guns, and in making the necessary harness, saddles, and bridles. While the work of preparation necessary for our march to meet Lieutenant-Colonel Fremont at Ciudad de los Angeles was thus going on, we sent an Indian to ascertain where the principal force of the insurgents was encamped. He returned with information that a body of them, about fifty strong, was encamped at San Bernardo, about thirty miles from San Diego. Captain Gillespie was immediately ordered to have as many men as he could mount, with a piece of artillery, ready to march, for the purpose of surprising the insurgents in their camp. Another expedition, under the command of Captain Hensley, of the battalion, was sent to the southward for animals, who, after performing the most arduous service, returned with five hundred head of cattle, and one hundred and forty horses and mules. About the 3d of December, two deserters from the insurgents, whose families lived in San Diego, came into the place, and reported themselves to Lieutenant Minor, the commander of the troops. On receiving information of the fact, I repaired to Lieutenant Minor's quarters, with my aid-de-camp, Lieutenant Gray, for the purpose of examining one of these men. While engaged in this examination, a messenger arrived with a letter from General Kearney, of the United States army, apprising me of his approach, and expressing a wish that I would open a communication with him, and inform him of the state of affairs in California.

"Captain Gillespie was immediately ordered to proceed to General Kearney's camp, with the force which he had been directed to have in readiness, carrying a letter which I wrote to

General Kearney. Captain Gillespie left San Diego at about half-past seven o'clock the same evening, taking with him one of the deserters to act as a guide in conducting General Kearney to the camp of the insurgents. The force which accompanied Captain Gillespie consisted of a company of volunteers, composed of Acting Lieutenant Beale, Passed Midshipman Duncan, ten carbineers from the Congress, Captain Gibson, and twenty-five of the California battalion. Mr. Stokes, who was the bearer of the letter from General Kearney, was also of the company. In the evening of December 6th, Mr. Stokes returned to San Diego, to inform me that General Kearney, on the morning of that day, had attempted to surprise the insurgents, under the command of Captain Andres Pico, in their camp at San Pasqual; that he had been worsted in the action which ensued, but to what extent he was unable to say, as he had left the field before the battle was concluded. He, however, was under the impression that General Kearney had lost a number of men, killed and wounded.

"The following morning, Lieutenant Godey, of the California battalion, with two men, came into San Diego with a letter from Captain Turner, of the dragoons, informing me that General Kearney had had a fight with a considerable body of the Mexicans; that he had about eighteen killed, and fourteen or fifteen wounded; and suggesting the propriety of dispatching, without delay, a considerable force to his assistance. Preparations were immediately made to dispatch a detachment for this purpose. Captain Turner had not mentioned the strength on either side, and Lieutenant Godey was not able to inform me. From the information, however, I deemed it advisable to proceed in person, with all the force that could be spared from the garrison, to form a junction with him. Two days' provisions were ordered to be prepared, and the advance, with two field-pieces, under Acting Lieutenant Guest, was directed to march forthwith to the mission of San Diego, where it was my intention to join it with the rest of the force the next morning. Before, however, the advance had moved, an Indian came in from General Kearney. From the information he gave, I judged that the necessity for immediate assistance was much more urgent than had been previously supposed. Anticipating great difficulty and delay from the want of animals to drag the artillery, should I march with my entire force, and believing, from the representations now made, that the force of the Californians was less than had been supposed, and consequently, that a portion of my command would be sufficient for the purpose, I determined not to move in person, but to send on, as rapidly as possible, an effective body of men. About ten o'clock at night, Acting Lieutenant Beale, of the Congress, arrived from General Kearney's camp, and confirmed the worst accounts we had received, and the importance of prompt assistance. The advanced body, increased to the number of 215 men, was placed under the command of Lieutenant Gray, my aid-de-camp, with orders to proceed directly to the camp of General Kearney. The order was successfully performed, and Lieutenant Gray having accomplished it, returned to San Diego, accompanied by the general. On their arrival, General Kearney, his officers and men, were received by all the garrison in the kindest and most respectful manner. So far as my observation extended, no civility or attention was omitted. Having sent with Captain Gillespie every horse that was fit for use to General Kearney, I was without one for my own accommodation. I was therefore compelled, on foot, to advance and receive the general, whom I conducted to my own quarters, until others more agreeable to him could be prepared. The arrival of General Kearney was to me a source of gratification, although it was my decided opinion—which as yet I have seen no reason to change—that, under the circumstances that existed, I was entitled to retain the position in which I was placed of commander-in-chief; yet, in consideration of his high standing in the army, his long experience as a soldier, the importance of military science and skill in the movements that were to be made in the interior of the country, I immediately determined to yield all personal feelings of ambition, and to place in his hands the supreme authority. In accordance with this determination, I tendered to General Kearney the position of commander-in-chief, and offered to accompany him as his aid.

"This proposition was on more than one occasion renewed, and with all sincerity and singleness of purpose. The responsibility of moving from San Diego, and leaving the safety of the ships, deprived of so large and efficient a portion of their crews, was of itself a momentous one. This, however, in the discharge of duty, I felt no inclination to shrink from. But the fate of the territory itself might depend upon the issue of a battle to be fought on shore against an army organized to encounter us. The nature of the service and the importance of the stake, it seemed to me, appertained rather to a general in the army than a captain in the navy. Whatever ambition I might feel for distinction, either on my account or on that of the gallant officers and men under my command, was voluntarily and deliberately offered as a sacrifice to a paramount sense of duty. The offers thus made were, however, on every occasion distinctly and positively declined by General Kearney, who, on his side, offered to accompany me in the capacity of my aid, and tendered to afford me the aid of his head and hand.

"A day or two after his arrival at San Diego, General Kearney removed from my quarters to others which at his instance had been provided for his accommodation. Before leaving, however, he handed me his instructions from the War Department. On reading them, I came to the conclusion that he had submitted them to my perusal to afford me the gratification of perceiving how entirely I had anticipated the views of the government in the measures which I had adopted. In return, I exhibited some of my own dispatches to the Department. Subsequently, and before leaving San Diego, General Kearney mentioned the subject of his instructions from the War Department, and seemed to intimate that he ought of right to be the governor of the territorv. His language, however, though perhaps sufficiently explicit, was not very intelligible to me, as I was at a loss to reconcile the assertion of such a claim of right with his repeated refusal to accept the offer, which I had more than once made to him, to devolve upon him the supreme command in the territory. The subject, however, was discussed between us without any interruption of that harmony which had commenced on our first interview.

"A few days before I expected to take up the line of march, I addressed a note to the general, expressing a wish that he would accompany me. In his reply he repeated the language which he had before employed—that he would so accompany me, and afford me the aid of his head and hand. Accordingly, on the morning of our departure he appeared upon the ground. After the troops had been paraded, and were nearly ready to commence the march, as I was about to mount my horse, General Kearney approached me and inquired who was to command the troops, I replied, Lieutenant Rowan was to have the command. On his expressing a wish that he should himself command them, I replied, that he should have the command. The different officers were at once convened, and informed that General Kearney had volunteered to command the troops, and that I had given him the appointment, reserving my own position as commander-in-chief. This arrangement having been made, we proceeded on the march.

* * * * * * * * * *

"On the morning of the day we marched into Ciudad de los Angeles, General Kearney came to me with Mr. Southwick, who was acting as engineer, to ascertain from me by what road I intended to enter the city. He requested Mr. Southwick to mark on the sand the position of the city, and the different roads leading into it. I selected the plainest and broadest road, leading into the main street of the city; and when we marched into the city, I led the way with the advance-guard. My position as commander-in-chief was again distinctly recognized in a letter of January 13, addressed to me by General Kearney, as *Governor of California, commanding United States forces.*

A few days after we had taken Ciudad de los Angeles, Lieut. Colonel Fremont arrived with his part of the battalion.

"With the firm convictions which existed upon my mind as to my rights and authority as commander-in-chief, and the obligations which all officers and men under my command were under to obey implicitly all my orders, I should not only have felt it to be my right, but a matter of imperative duty, to assert and maintain my authority, if necessary, by a resort to force. I continued this exercise of the power of commander-in-chief without its having been denied or questioned by any person, as far as I was informed, up to the 16th of January, when I received a letter of that date from General Kearney, which is now on file in the Department, in which he demands that I will cease all further proceedings relating to the formation of a civil government for the territory. In my reply of the same date to that letter (which, I think, is also on file in the Department), I suspended General Kearney from his volunteer command under me, when he again became Brigadier-General Kearney, over whom I never attempted or desired to have any command or control.

"I exercised no authority in the territory after I left San Diego, except that which was induced by the receipt of a letter from Lieutenant-Colonel Cook, informing me that he had received information that a French schooner had been landing some guns on the Southern coast, and that General Bustamente, with 1,500 Mexicans, was approaching the territory. I wrote to Lieutenant-Colonel Cook that I would go in search of them as soon as possible. I went down the coast 120 miles, landed and mounted some of my men, and went in pursuit. It turned out to be a false alarm. After performing this last service in California, I returned, *via* San Diego and Monterey, to San Francisco, where I gave up the command of the frigate Congress, and returned to the United States by way of the Rocky Mountains.

"The California battalion (Fremont's) was organized under my own personal direction and authority, under a special condition that it should act under my orders as long as I might remain in California and require its services. It was paid by my orders, as long as I had anything to pay with. The officers derived their appointments exclusively from me. It was never, in any form or manner, mustered into the service of the United States as a part of the army or connected with it. It was exclusively and essentially a navy organization. The battalion was entirely composed of volunteers, organized under my authority, but with their own free consent, according to the terms of a distinct and specific agreement to obey my orders and to serve while I should require their services. These men were not of that kind of *personnel* which sometimes composes regular armies: they were principally free American citizens who had settled in California; they were men of respectability, of influence, and of property; they were no ordinary men, because, when told that I had offered them as pay ten dollars a month, they said that they would not accept that pay—that it would not pay their expenses—but that they would volunteer to serve under my command without compensation.

"This was the origin, character, and position of the battalion when engaged, in co-operation with the squadron under my command, in accomplishing the objects which I had in view.

"Such was the posture of things when General Kearney arrived in California, and when he joined me in San Diego. He brought with him a very inconsiderable force, wholly insufficient of itself to accomplish the important objects of tranquilizing the province and subjecting it to the authority of the Union, by the suppression of the insurrection which had been organized for the purpose of recovering the positions we occupied, overthrowing the government we had organized, and expelling us from the country, if, indeed, it had proved itself able to defend itself without our aid. * * * * *

"The battalion was never placed under the command of General Kearney by me, and was not subjected to his orders. It still remained in immediate subordination to me and to my authority. Up to the period last mentioned,—viz.: the date of our occupation of Ciudad de los Angeles, the only authority which General Kearney had exercised, while he accompanied me, was simply that authority which he had asked me to give him, and which he had voluntarily accepted at my hands.

"No one has ever pretended—I certainly never claimed—that I possessed any right or authority to command General Kearney as such. All the power which I ever claimed or exercised over him was derived from his volunteering to aid me and to act under my orders. This connection, being purely one created by mutual consent, was, at any time, dissoluble at the will of either of the parties. As I could not originally have compelled General Kearney to assume the position he held, neither had I any authority to detain him in it one moment against his inclination. He might, at any time, have laid down his character as a volunteer under me, and resumed his official rank and rights as brigadier-general in the army of the United States.

"In his capacity of brigadier-general, however, he had no authority to command me or any portion of my force. I was as independent of him as he confessedly was of me. If the force which I had brought ashore from the squadron constituted a portion of the navy—if the California battalion, which I had raised and organized, was ever rightfully subject to my orders—both were as independent of General Kearney, or any other officer of the army, as I myself was.

"Nor have I ever questioned, much less denied, the authority of General Kearney to assume command over and give his orders to Lieutenant-Colonel Fremont. He might, at any time, without my controverting his power, have directed Lieutenant-Colonel

Fremont to leave my command, to terminate his connection with me as a volunteer under my command, and to report to him for orders. With any such exercise of authority I should never have interfered; whether rightfully or wrongfully exercised was not for me to judge. That was a matter dependent upon the relative rights and duties of the parties themselves, as fixed by the military law, and to be decided by military authority.

I did, however, and do still, deny that General Kearney, while occupying the position of volunteer under my command, had any authority whatever, as brigadier-general, over any portion of the forces serving under me. I deny that after the character of volunteer was laid down, and that of brigadier-general resumed, he had, as such, any authority, nor could the Secretary of War give him any such authority over any portion of the force which I had organized. Whatever authority he might lawfully exercise over Lieutenant-Colonel Fremont personally, I deny that it reached to the battalion organized under me and by me placed under the command of that officer. And, finally, I deny that General Kearney could rightfully control me in my conduct as governor of California, more especially after having explicitly refused to accept the supreme authority when voluntarily tendered to him.

"I have the honor to be, faithfully,

"Your obedient servant,

"R. F. STOCKTON.

"To the HON. JOHN Y. MASON,

"*Secretary of the Navy, Washington, D. C.*"

All that remains to be told of the conquest of California by Col. Fremont, is given with sufficient minuteness in the following extract from Mr. Upham's memoir:

"On the 27th of December, the battalion entered without resistance the town of Santa Barbara, where it remained recruiting until the 3d of January, 1847. On the 11th of January, while pursuing their march, they were met by two Californians, riding in great haste, bareheaded, who informed them that the American forces, under Commodore Stockton, had retaken Los Angeles, after a victorious engagement with the insurgent forces. The enemy's force was understood to be in the vicinity, and the next day two California officers came into camp to treat for peace. After full consultation, articles were agreed upon on the 13th of January, 1847. They stipulated that all California should deliver up their arms, return peaceably to their homes, not take up arms again during the war between the United States and Mexico, and assist and aid in keeping the country in a state of peace and tranquillity. Any Californian or citizen of Mexico, who might desire to do so, was permitted to leave the country, and none be required to take the oath of allegiance to the United States, until a treaty of peace should be signed and made between the United States and Mexico. The articles of capitulation were signed by officers duly commissioned for the purpose, and approved by 'J. C. Fremont, Lieutenant-Colonel U. S. Army, and Military Commandant of California, and Andres Pico, Commandant of Squadron and Chief of the National forces of California.'

"This was the 'Capitulation of Couenga.' It terminated the war so far as California was concerned. No hostile arm was ever again lifted, except in the ordinary form of local Indian outbreaks, within the limits of that State, against the authority of the United States. It secured reconciliation as well as peace. It is in evidence, on the records of the government, that the final conquest of California could not have been accomplished by any force then on the Pacific coast, without the aid of the California battalion; and that, had it not been consummated by the Treaty of Couenga, a 'bloody, vexatious, and predatory warfare,' would surely have been protracted for an indefinite length of time. The whole western slope of the Sierra Nevada would have afforded safe retreats, inaccessible to naval and even regular military forces, from which ravaging parties would have rushed down upon the plains, and where insurrectionary movements would have been fomented perpetually. Fremont terrified the Californians and the Indians by the celerity and boldness of his movements, and he conquered their hearts by the good conduct of his men, and the moderation and clemency of his policy."

In a dispatch from General Kearney, to the War Department at Washington, dated Ciudad de los Angeles, January, 14th, 1847, he says:

"This morning, Lieutenant-Colonel Fremont, of the regiment of mounted riflemen, reached here with four hundred volunteers from the Sacramento; the enemy capitulated with him yesterday, near San Fernando, agreeing to lay down their arms, and we have now the prospect of having peace and quietness in this country, which I hope may not be interrupted again."

CHAPTER IX.

ORIGIN OF THE CONTROVERSY BETWEEN COLONEL FREMONT AND GENERAL KEARNEY—IS ORDERED BY GENERAL KEARNEY NOT TO RE-ORGANIZE THE CALIFORNIA BATTALION—HIS REPLY—GENERAL KEARNEY CLAIMS THE COMMAND OF THE CALIFORNIAN ARMY—COMMODORE STOCKTON REFUSES TO YIELD IT—THEIR CORRESPONDENCE—NEW INSTRUCTIONS FROM WASHINGTON—KEARNEY TAKES THE COMMAND—FREMONT IS ORDERED HOME—HOSTILE CORRESPONDENCE WITH COL. MASON—ARRESTED AT FORT LEAVENWORTH—INVITED TO A PUBLIC DINNER AT ST. LOUIS—LETTER DECLINING THE INVITATION—ARRIVES AT WASHINGTON.

THE differences between General Kearney and Commodore Stockton, alluded to in the foregoing dispatch, originated primarily in the indefiniteness of the instructions which were issued from the seat of government. Those addressed to the naval commanders on the Pacific, in their judgment justified the organization of a military force and a civil government in California, and under those instructions Commodore Stockton authorized Fremont to organize the California battalion and take its command with the title of Major. By virtue of those, he likewise took the necessary steps for the organization of a civil government for California and invested Fremont with the title and responsibilities of Governor.

As soon as these results were consummated, Kit Carson was sent with an escort of fifteen men to bear the intelligence overland to Washington, as soon as possible. Just as he had crossed the desert and was approaching the American frontier, he was met by General Kearney with a small force of dragoons marching westward, under instructions from his government to conquer California and organize a civil government in the territory, a work which had already been successfully accomplished.

Upon learning what had occurred, Kearney insisted upon Carson's returning with him as his guide to California, having forwarded the dispatches to Washington by another messenger of his own selection. Upon the general's arrival at Los Angeles, the capital of California, and the seat of the new government, the contest soon rose between himself and Commodore Stockton, which is referred to in the commodore's dispatch. The process by which Colonel Fremont became involved in this controversy is obvious. He held a commission in the army as lieutenant of topographical engineers, and as such was primarily subject to the orders of his superior general officer of the army. He had since yielded to the exigencies of the occasion, and from motives and for reasons which cannot be impeached, waived any privileges he might have claimed, as the real conqueror of North California, and in point of rank, the superior representative of the army on the Pacific coast, and with his men, volunteered to serve under Commodore Stockton in the farther prosecution of the war in South California, the subjugation of which could not be so successfully effected without the aid of a fleet. By accepting the governorship of California, a vacancy had been created in the command of the California battalion and other changes had become necessary. The first intimation which Colonel Fremont received of General Kearney's intention to test the validity of Commodore Stockton's acts through him, was conveyed in the following note.

"HEADQUARTERS, ARMY OF THE WEST,
"CIUDAD DE LOS ANGELES, *January* 16, 1847.

"By direction of Brigadier General Kearney, I send you a copy of a communication to him from the Secretary of War, dated June 18, 1846, in which is the following, 'These troops and such as may be organized in California will be under your command.' The general directs that no change will be made in the organization of your battalion of volunteers or officers appointed in it, without his sanction or approval being first obtained.

"WM. F. EMORY.
"*Lieutenant and Acting Assistant Adjutant General.*"

This note at once raised the question whether he was to obey General Kearney, and thereby, so far as his example could go, invalidate the acts of Commodore Stockton, in which he had co-operated, or obey Commodore Stockton, and so far as his decision would go, sustain the validity of those proceedings which he believed to be both legal and patriotic. If he took the former course he incurred the liability to be arraigned and, in his judgment, justly disgraced for disobeying an officer whose rank and authority he had deliberately recognized; and he further incurred the charge of base ingratitude towards an officer whose courtesy and confidence he had shared, whose conduct he had approved, and who unexpectedly found himself in a situation to need the support of his friends. Fremont was incapable of deserting either a friend or what he deemed his post of duty; he accordingly addressed to General Kearney the following reply on the following day:

COL. FREMONT TO GENERAL KEARNEY.

"CIUDAD DE LOS ANGELES, *Jan.* 17, 1847.

"SIR: I have the honor to be in receipt of your favor of last night, in which I am directed to suspend the execution of orders which, in my capacity of military commandant of this territory, I had received from Commodore Stockton, governor and commander-in-chief, in California. I avail myself of an early hour this morning to make such a reply as the brief time allowed for reflection, will enable me.

"I found Commodore Stockton in possession of the country, exercising the functions of military commandant and civil governor, as early as July of last year; and shortly thereafter I received from him the commission of military commandant, the duties of which I immediately entered upon, and have continued to exercise to the present moment.

"I found also, on my arrival at this place, some three or four days ince, Commodore Stockton still exercising the functions of civil and military governor, with the same appparent deference to his rank on the part of all officers (including yourself), as he maintained and required when he assumed them in July last.

"I learned, also, in conversation with you, that on the march from San Diego, recently, to this place, you entered upon, and discharged duties implying an acknowledgment on your part, of supremacy to Commodore Stockton.

"I eel, therefore, with great deference to your professional and personal character, constrained to say that, until you and Commodore Stockton adjust between yourselves, the question of rank, where I respectfully think the difficulty belongs, I shall have to report and receive orders, as heretofore, from the commodore.

"With considerations of high regard, I am, sir, your obedient servant,

"J. C. FREMONT,
"*Lieutenant-Colonel, U. S. Army, and Military*
"*Commandant of the Territory of California.*"

"Brigadier-General S. W. KEARNEY,
"U. S. Army."

The same day that General Kearney addressed the note above quoted, to Mr. Fremont, a yet more serious correspondence commenced between him and Commodore Stockton. We give it at length with the introductory remarks of Commodore Stockton's biographer, who evidently wrote under the eye and approval of the commodore:

"Fremont throughout the California war, was strictly and technically in the naval service, under Commodore Stockton. He had taken service under him with an express agreement that he would continue subject to his orders as long as he continued in command in Callifornia. This engagement both he and Captain Gillespie had entered into from patriotic motives, and to render the most efficient service to the country. He visited California originally upon topographical, and not on military duty. His volunteering under Stockton on special service, was a patriotic impulse, in complying with which the government were in honor bound to sustain him. He therefore, very properly refused to violate his agreement with Stockton, and unite with Kearney against him.

"Having failed to compel Fremont to acknowledge his authority, the general addressed himself to the commodore and demanded that he should abdicate the command-in-chief.

"The commodore considering the subjugation of California complete, and that no further hostilities were likely to take place, was of opinion that he might now relinquish his governorship, and command-in-chief, and return to his ships. But, having informed the government that upon that event he intended to appoint Colonel Fremont governor, he now proceeded to carry that design into execution.

"General Kearney, learning this to be the purpose of the commodore, and desirous of exercising the functions of governor himself, addressed to him the following letter, which, with the ensuing correspondence, will apprise the reader of the true relations of the parties better than we could state them.

GENERAL KEARNEY TO COMMODORE STOCKTON.

"HEADQUARTERS, ARMY OF THE WEST,
"CIUDAD DE LOS ANGELES, *January* 16, 1847.

"SIR: I am informed that you are now engaged in organizing a civil government, and appointing officers for it in this territory. As this duty has been specially assigned to myself, by orders of the President of the United States, conveyed in letters to me from the Secretary of War, of June 3, 8, and 18, 1846; the original of which I gave to you on the 12th, and which you returned to me on the 13th, and copies of which I furnished you with on the 26th December, I have to ask if you have any authority from the President, from the Secretary of the Navy, or from any other channel of the President, to form such government and make such appointments.

"If you have such authority, and will show it to me or furnish me with a certified copy of it, I will cheerfully acquiesce in what you are doing. If you have not such authority, I then demand that you cease all further proceedings relating to the formation of a civil government for this territory, as I cannot recognize in you any right in assuming to perform duties confided to me by the President.

"Very respectfully your obedient servant,

"S. W. KEARNEY,

"*Brigadier-General, United States Army*

"Commodore R. F. STOCKTON, Acting Governor of California."

COMMODORE STOCKTON TO GENERAL KEARNEY.

"HEADQUARTERS, CIUDAD DE LOS ANGELES, *Jan.* 16, 1847.

"SIR: In answer to your note received this afternoon, I need say but little more than that which I communicated to you in a conversation at San Diego—that California was conquered, and a civil government put into successful operation, that a copy of the laws made by me for the government of the territory, and the names of the officers selected to see them faithfully executed, were transmitted to the President of the United States before you arrived in the territory.

"I will only add, that I cannot do anything nor desist from doing anything on your demand, which I will submit to the President and ask for your recall. In the meantime you will consider yourself suspended from the command of the United States forces in this place.

"Faithfully, your obedient servant,

"R. F. STOCKTON,

"*Commander-in-chief.*

"To Brevet Brigadier-General S. W. KEARNEY."

GENERAL KEARNEY TO COMMODORE STOCKTON.

"HEADQUARTERS, ARMY OF THE WEST,
CIUDAD DE LOS ANGELES, *Jan.* 17, 1847.

"SIR: In my communication to you of yesterday's date I stated that I had learned that you were engaged in organizing a civil government for California. I referred you to the President's instructions to me (the original of which you have seen) and copies of which I furnished you, to perform that duty, and I added that if you had any authority from the President, or any of his organs, for what you were doing, I would cheerfully acquiesce, and if you had not such authority I demanded that you would cease further proceedings in the matter.

"Your reply of the same date refers me to a conversation held at San Diego, and adds that you cannot do anything or desist from doing anything or alter anything on your (my) demand. As, in consequence of the defeat of the enemy on the 8th and 9th inst., by the the troops under *my command*, and the capitulation entered into on the 13th inst. by Lieutenant-Colonel Fremont with the leaders of the Californians, in which the people under arms and in the field agree to disperse and remain quiet and peaceable, the country may now, for the first time, be considered as conquered, and taken possession of by us; and as I am prepared to carry out the President's instructions to me, which you oppose, I must, for the purpose of preventing a collision between us and possibly a civil war in consequence of it, remain silent for the present, leaving with you the great responsibility of doing that for which you have no authority, and preventing me from complying with the President's orders.

"Very respectfully, your obedient servant,

"S. W. KEARNEY,

"*Brigadier-General, United States Army.*

"Commodore R. F. STOCKTON, Acting Governor of California."

The motives which actuated Col. Fremont in electing to pursue the course which he did upon the arrival of Gen. Kearney, are scarcely open to misconstruction. There happens, however, to be the best of evidence in regard to them in a letter addressed to Col. Benton at the time of the collision which reveals in all the confidence of personal friendship, the innermost secrets of his heart. In that letter, he says:

* * * "When I entered Los Angeles I was ignorant of the relations subsisting between these gentlemen, having received from neither any order or information which might serve as a guide in the circumstances. I therefore, immediately on my arrival, waited upon the governor and commander-in-chief, Commodore Stockton; and, a few minutes afterwards, called upon General Kearney. I soon found them occupying a hostile attitude, and each denying the right of the other to assume the direction of affairs in this country.

"The ground assumed by General Kearney was, that he held in his hand plenary instructions from the President directing him to conquer California, and organize a civil government, and that consequently he would not recognize the acts of Commodore Stockton.

"The latter maintained that his own instructions were to the same effect as Kearney's; that this officer's commission was obsolete, and never would have been given could the government have anticipated that the entire country, seaboard and interior, would have been conquered and held by himself. The country had been conquered and a civil government instituted since September last, the constitution of the territory, and appointments under the constitution, had been sent to the govvernment for its approval, and decisive action undoubtedly long since had upon them. General Kearney was instructed to conquer the country, and upon its threshold his command had been nearly cut to pieces, and, but for relief from him (Commodore Stockton) would have been destroyed. More men were lost than in General Taylor's battle of the 8th. In regard to the remaining part of his instructions, how could he organize a government without first proceeding to disorganize the present one?

His work had been anticipated; his commission was absolutely void, null, and of no effect.

"But if General Kearney believed that his instructions gave him paramount authority in the country, he made a fatal error on his arrival. He was received with kindness and distinction by the commodore, and offered by him the command of his land forces. General Kearney rejected the offer and declined interfering with Commodore Stockton. This officer was then preparing for a march to Ciudad de los Angeles, his force being principally sailors and marines, who were all on foot (fortunately for them), and who were to be provided with supplies on their march through an enemy's country where all the people are cavalry. His force was paraded, and ready to start, 700 in number, supported by six pieces of artillery. The command, under General Stockton, had been conferred upon his first lieutenant, Mr. Rowan. At this juncture General Kearney expressed to Commodore Stockton his expectation that the command would have been given to him. The commodore informed the general that Lieutenant Rowan was in his usual line of duty, as on board ship, relieving him of the detail and drudgery of the camp, while he himself remained the commander-in-chief; that if General Kearney was willing to accept Mr. Rowan's place, under these circumstances, he could have it. The general assented. Commodore Stockton called up his officers and explained the case. Mr. Rowan gave up his post generously and without hesitation; and Commodore Stockton desired them clearly to understand that he remained the commander-in-chief; under this arrangement the whole force entered Angeles; and on the day of my arrival at that place General Kearney told me that he did then, at that moment, recognize Commodore Stockton as governor of the territory.

"You are aware that I had contracted relations with Commodore Stockton, and I thought it neither right nor politically honorable to withdraw my support. No reason of interest shall ever compel me to act towards any man in such a way that I should afterwards be ashamed to meet him."

Early in the spring, new instructions, bearing date Nov. 5th, reached Commodore Stockton, which put an end to the latter's supremacy in that quarter. In his dispatch, the Secretary of the Navy says:

"The President has deemed it best for the public interests, to invest the military officer commanding, with the direction of the operations on land, and with the administrative functions of the government over the people and territory occupied by us. You will relinquish to Col. Mason, or to General Kearney, if the latter shall arrive before you have done so, the entire control over these matters, and turn over to him all papers necessary to the performance of his duties."

Instructions of a corresponding import were of course received from the War Department, by General Kearney, and with them, or not long afterwards, a dispatch from Mr. Marcy, of which the following is an extract:

EXTRACT FROM INSTRUCTIONS TO BRIGADIER-GENERAL KEARNEY.

"WAR DEPARTMENT, *June*, 11, 1847.

* * * * * * * * *

"When the dispatch from this Department was sent out in November last, there was reason to believe that Lieutenant-Colonel Fremont would desire to return to the United States, and you were then directed to conform to his wishes in that respect. It is not now proposed to change that direction. But since that time it has become known here that he bore a conspicuous part in the conquest of California, that his services have been *very valuable* in that country, and doubtless will continue to be so should he remain there.

"Impressed, as all engaged in the public service must be, with the great importance of harmony and cordial co-operation in carrying on military operations in a country so distant from the seat of authority, *the President is persuaded that when his defi-*

nite instructions were received, all questions of difficulty were settled, and all feelings which had been elicited by the agitation of them had subsided.

"Should Lieut. Col. Fremont, *who has the option to return or remain*, adopt the latter alternative, the President does not doubt you will employ him in such a manner as will render his services most available to the public interest, having reference to his extensive acquaintance with the inhabitants of California, and his knowledge of their language, qualifications independent of others, which it is supposed may be very useful in the present and prospective state of our affairs in that country. * * *

"Very respectfully your ob't servant,

"W. L. MARCY, *Secretary of War*."

The "definite instructions" to which reference is here made were never communicated to Colonel Fremont, and their suppression was very justly esteemed by him a grievance for several reasons, and among others, because they show that by the President's directions it was at Col. Fremont's option whether he would remain in California or not, an option, however, which was denied him by General Kearney.

Early in March, and after taking the supreme command in California, Gen. Kearney addressed Col. Fremont the following letter:

GEN. KEARNEY TO COL. FREMONT.

"HEADQUARTERS, 10TH MILITARY DEPARTMENT,
MONTEREY, U. C., *March* 1, 1847.

"SIR: By Department orders, No. 2, of this date (which will be handed to you by Captain Turner, 1st Dragoons, A.A.A.G., for my command) you will see that certain duties are there required of you as commander of the battalion of California volunteers.

"In addition to the duties above referred to, I have now to direct that you will bring with you, and with as little delay as possible, all the archives and public documents and papers which may be subject to your control, and which appertain to the government of California, that I may receive them from your hands at this place, the capital of the Territory.

"I have directions from the general-in-chief not to detain you in this country against your wishes, a moment longer than the necessities of the service may require; and you will be at liberty to leave here after you have complied with these instructions, and those in the order referred to.

"Very respectfully your obedient servant,

"S. W. KEARNEY,

"*Brig. Gen., and Governor of California.*

"Lt. Col. J. C. FREMONT, Regt. of Mtd. Riflemen,
Com'g. Bat. of California Vols.,
Ciudad de los Angeles."

About a month later, he received the following order from Gen. Kearney:

"HEADQUARTERS, 10TH MILITARY DEPARTMENT,
MONTEREY, CALIFORNIA, *March* 28.

"SIR: This will be handed to you by Col. Mason, 1st Dragoons, who goes to the southern district, clothed by me with full authority to give such orders and instructions upon all matters, both civil and military, in that section of the country, as he may deem proper and necessary. Any instructions he may give you, will be considered as coming from myself."

A few weeks later Col. Fremont received orders from General Kearney to report himself at Monterey with such of the members of his topographical corps as were still under pay, prepared to set out at once for Washington. Col. Fremont then applied for permission to join his regiment under General Taylor's command, supposed to be on its way to Vera Cruz. This request was refused without explanation or apology, and on the 14th of June Col. Fremont addressed General Kearney as follows:

FROM COL. FREMONT TO GENERAL KEARNEY.

"NEW HELVETIA, UPPER CALIFORNIA, *June* 14, 1847.

"SIR: In a communication which I received from yourself in March of the present year I am informed that you had been directed by the commander-in-chief not to detain me in this country against my wishes longer than the absolute necessities of the service might require.

"Private letters in which I have entire confidence further inform me that the President has been pleased to direct that I should be permitted the choice of joining my regiment in Mexico, or returning directly to the United States. An application which I had the honor to make to you at the Ciudad de los Angeles for permission to proceed immediately to Mexico, having been rejected, and the duties of the exploring expedition which had been confided to my direction, having been terminated by yourself, I respectfully request that I may now be relieved of all connection with the topographical party which you have taken under your charge, and be permitted to return to the United States. Travelling with a small party by a direct route, my knowledge of the country and freedom from professional business, will enable me to reach the States some forty or fifty days earlier than yourself, which the present condition of affairs and a long absence from my family make an object of great importance to me.

"It may not be improper to say to you that my journey will be made with private means, and will not therefore, occasion any expenditure to the government. I have the honor to be, with much respect, your obedient servant,

"J. C. FREMONT,
'*Lieut. Colonel, Mounted Riflemen.*

"Brigadier-General S. W. KEARNEY, Commanding, &c."

To this request Col. Fremont received the following reply:

GENERAL KEARNEY TO COL. FREMONT.

"CAMP NEAR NEW HELVETIA, CALIFORNIA, *June* 14, 1847.

"SIR: The request contained in your communication to me of this date, to be relieved from all connection with the topographical party (nineteen men) and be permitted to return to the United States with a small party made up by your private means, cannot be granted.

"I shall leave here on Wednesday, the 16th instant, and I require of you to be with your topographical party in my camp (which will probably be fifteen miles from here) on the evening of that day, and to continue with me to Missouri.

"Very respectfully, your obedient servant,

"S. W. KEARNEY.

"*Brigadier-General.*

"Lieut. Col. FREMONT, Regiment Mounted Riflemen,
"New Helvetia."

The appointment of Mason to the command of the Southern District with the authority over Fremont, conferred by the order of the 28th of March proved to the latter a source of extreme irritation and annoyance, and was near producing much more serious results. Mason seemed to share the grudge which General Kearney bore to Fremont, and to take pleasure in doing whatever seemed calculated to mortify and humiliate him, for which, if he chose to avail himself of them, of course he had abundant opportunities in his new position. Fremont subsequently came to the conclusion that Mason wished to provoke a challenge, and then by selecting a weapon with which he was very expert—a double-barrelled shot-gun, which Fremont knew nothing about—to shoot him. If such was his purpose, he accomplished it, so far as provoking the challenge, and having the choice of his favorite weapon.* He was in the habit of sending for Fremont several times a day, to come to his quarters, which were at the house of an unfriendly resident at los Angeles, to be questioned in the presence of other officers with whom he had no social relations, and who, it is alleged, were in attendance for the purpose of being used as witnesses. One day he directed Fremont to bring to him the one hundred and twenty horses which he had sent to grass in the country, to recruit for a march into Mexico, which he at that time contemplated, to join General Taylor, little dreaming, that even then, his enemies were collecting their evidence, and perfecting their arrangements to have

* The following paragraph from the Sporting Magazine, vol. 4, p. 533, will explain Colonel Mason's preference for so unusual and unofficer-like a weapon for the settlement of an affair of honor.

"The drawing herewith sent is a sketch of a scene, in which Captain R. B. Mason, as frequently happens, acted a conspicuous part.

"A party of six gentlemen left St Louis about 10 o'clock A. M., with the intention of hunting a few acres of high grass on the American bottom, and, if possible, killing a deer or two. We no sooner arrived at the high grass than old Rock broke forth in full cry. His deep-mouthed tones were barely heard before two fine does bounced in front of Mr. Henderson, but two far off for a successful shot, making directly for Captain Mason, who wheeled his horse directly around; and, as rapidly as the occasion required, raised his gun with his right hand, holding the bridle reins with the left, as represented in the drawing—fired both barrels in quick succession, bringing down dead in their tracks, one with each barrel. It was the work of an instant, and the effect was like magic. It may not be amiss to state that Captain Mason always shoots, when mounted, as represented in the plate; and I have seen him kill grouse on the wing and knock down deer on the jump, in that manner, and sometimes when his horse was nearly at his speed."

him sent home in disgrace. The order to produce the horses was esteemed an insulting one, under the circumstances, and the time within which it was to be executed too limited. Mason sent for Fremont twice in the course of the same afternoon, to come to his quarters to answer about the horses. Fremont resented what he esteemed the brutality of Mason's course and manner, to which Mason replied, "None of your insolence, or I will put you in irons." The sequel justified Fremont's suspicions that the order to bring up the horses was a mere pretext for insulting him; for when brought, they were turned over to Mason's friendly witness, who sold them for one, two, and three dollars apiece. Fremont's friends saw that Mason's designs were mischievous, and they urged the colonel to restrain his feelings to the utmost. He did so until the remark above quoted was uttered, when his indignation knew no bounds. But even here his coolness, which had so often served him in more trying situations, did not forsake him. He at once asked Mason if he held himself personally accountable for what he said. Mason replied that he did, whereat Fremont leaped upon his horse, dashed back to his quarters, and wrote two notes, the first asking a retraction of the offensive words, and another based upon his probable refusal to make a retraction, conveying a challenge, and dispatched both by his friend Major P. B. Reading. These notes and Colonel Mason's reply to the first, ran as follows:

FREMONT TO MASON.

"Ciudad de los Angeles, *April* 14, 1847.

"Sir: I have the honor to request through my friend, Major P. B. Reading, who will hand you this note, that you apologize for the injurious language applied to me this day.

"Very respectfully, your obedient servant,
"J. C. FREMONT,
"*Lieut. Col. Mounted Riflemen.*

"Col. R. R. MASON,
"Col. Dragoons, Ciudad de los Angeles."

MASON TO FREMONT.

"ANGELES, *April* 14, 1847.

"SIR: I have just received your note of this evening, and can only repeat in writing, what I stated to you verbally, when we parted, viz.: 'I thought you intended to be so. You best knew whether you did or did not.' Your not disavowing it, left me to infer that I was not mistaken; with that impression upon my mind, I can say nothing more until it be removed.

"I am, respectfully, your obedient servant,
"R. B. MASON.

"Lieut. Col. J. C. FREMONT,
"Mounted Riflemen."

FREMONT TO MASON.

"CIUDAD DE LOS ANGELES, *April* 14, 1847.

"SIR: An apology having been declined, Major Reading will arrange the preliminaries for a meeting, requiring personal satisfaction.

"Very respectfully, your obedient servant,
"J. C. FREMONT.
"*Lieut. Col. Mounted Riflemen.*

"COL. R. B. MASON,
"First Dragoons, Ciudad de los Angeles."

No further answer was received from Mason that

evening; but relying on the verbal acceptance and designation of weapons, loading and time, Col. Fremont's friends proceeded to hunt up a double barrelled gun. Col. Fremont had no such weapon, and had never used such a one. But he was ready by daybreak, with the requisite gun and shot, but nothing was heard farther of Mason until towards noon, when Capt. Smith of the dragoons, arrived with the following note:

MASON TO FREMONT.

"ANGELES, *April* 15, 1847.

"SIR: With a view to the adjustment of my *private affairs*, it is necessary that I return to Monterey, before I afford you the meeting you desire. We shall probably reach there within a a few days of each other, I will then, as soon as circumstances permit, arrange the necessary preliminaries for the meeting.

"I am respectfully, your obedient servant,

"R. B. MASON.

"Lieut. Col. FREMONT,
"Mounted Riflemen."

To which Fremont replied:

"CIUDAD DE LOS ANGELES, *April* 15, 1847.

"SIR: I am in receipt of your letter of this date, and in reply have the honor to state that I will hold myself in readiness for a meeting at Monterey, at such time as you may designate.

"I am, very respectfully, your obedient servant,

"J. C. FREMONT,
"*Lieut. Col. Mounted Riflemen.*

"Col. R. B. MASON,
"First Dragoons, Ciudad de los Angeles."

The duel was thereby adjourned to Monterey; but no note was received from Mason fixing a time.

A day or two after these notes passed, Col. Mason went to Monterey. After his arrival there, Gen. Kearney came down to Los Angeles, and had a conversation with Col. Fremont on the subject of the duel, saying he forbade it, and had left an order at Monterey to that effect. Fremont soon followed to Monterey. On arriving there, Capt. Tyler, an intimate of Mason's, called on Col. Fremont, said that he did not come by direction of Mason, that he had talked with him about it, that Mason did not intend to insult him, &c. Col. Fremont paid no attention to this, went to Col. Mason's quarters, was invited to sit down but did not, saying that he came to let Col. Mason see that he was in Monterey, and then walked away.

Soon after quitting Col. Mason's quarters an order from Gen. Kearney was delivered to Col. Fremont by the adjutant general in these words:

"HEADQUARTERS, TEN MILE DEPOT,
"MONTEREY, CAL., *May* 4, 1847.

"SIR: It has been reported here, by some of the discharged men of the battalion of California volunteers, just arrived from Pueblo de los Angeles, that a challenge has passed between Col. Mason, of the 1st dragoons, and yourself, the meeting to take place at or near Monterey.

"As I am about leaving here for the South, in consequence of rumors of an excitement among the people in that district of country, it becomes my duty to inform you that the good of the public service, the necessity of preserving tranquillity in California, imperiously require that the meeting above referred to should not take place at this time, and in this country, and you are hereby officially directed by me to proceed no further in this matter

"A similar communication has been addressed to Colonel Mason.

"Very respectfully,

"Your obedient servant,

"S. W. KEARNEY, *Brigadier General.*

"Lieutenant-Colonel FREMONT,

"Regiment Mounted Rifles, Monterey."

"N.B.—A letter to same purport, and of same date, addressed to Col. Mason."

Soon after the receipt of the foregoing, came the following letter from Mason himself to Fremont.

MONTEREY, *May* 19, 1847.

"SIR: The affair between us has been made public here by the arrival, about the 4th instant, of some of the discharged men of the late battalion of California volunteers from Los Angeles.

"I did not expect that this affair would have gained publicity until it had finally been terminated, but it has turned out otherwise. The result is, it has come to the knowledge of the general, and you doubtless have received, as well as myself, a communication from him upon the subject. This unforeseen and unexpected circumstance, together with reasons which you will find in the copy of a letter on the next page, dated on the 4th of the present month, renders it proper that the meeting should be postponed to some future time and place.

"I am inclined to believe that, under the existing state of things, you will at once see the propriety of this course.

"I am, respectfully,

"Your obedient servant,

"R. B. MASON.

"Lieut. Col. FREMONT."

The letter referred to by Mason, and a copy of which was sent with his own, in his own handwriting, said as follows:

U. S. SHIP COLUMBUS.
MONTEREY, *May 4th*, 1847.

"MY DEAR COLONEL: A party of Californian volunteers, recently under Lieut. Col. Fremont, have just arrived on their way to the north. They state publicly that at Puebla a challenge had passed between yourself and Lieut. Col. Fremont, and that on the arrival of the latter here, a hostile meeting would take place. I learn that this statement is generally credited on shore. As your personal friend, and the friend of your public character, this statement has given me great pain. You cannot but be sensible that, in the present condition of things in California, personal collisions between the officers must be highly injurious to the public interest. You cannot but know that it is the duty of all of us to suppress for the moment every angry feeling of a personal nature, and to give ourselves zealously, cordially, and exclusively to the public service. Permit me to appeal to your patriotism, and to your sense of public duty, and upon these grounds to entreat that any contemplated hostile meeting may be postponed. Elsewhere, and at another time, it may not be improper, but there, in the present distracted state of affairs, it could have no other result than to injure the public, and to injure your military reputation.

"I remain, very truly,
"Your friend, &c.,
"JAMES BIDDLE.

"Col. MASON, U. S. Army, Monterey."

To these two letters Col. Fremont returned this answer:

"MONTEREY, *May 22d*, 1847.

"SIR: I have the honor to acknowledge the receipt, on yesterday, of your note of the 19th instant, accompanied by a copy of a letter from Commodore Biddle to yourself.

"The object of your note appears to be to induce me to consent to a further, and indefinite postponement of a meeting. If such be your desire I am willing to comply with it, trusting that you will apprise me of the earliest moment at which the meeting can take place consistently with your convenience and sense of propriety.

"I am most respectfully,

"Your obedient servant,

"JOHN C. FREMONT.

"Col. R. B. MASON, Monterey."

MASON TO FREMONT.

MONTEREY, CAL., *May* 24, 1847.

"SIR: I have the honor to acknowledge the receipt of your letter of the 22d instant. I shall certainly promptly inform you when the peculiar official obligations, under which I find myself placed in this country, are so far removed as to enable me to meet you.

"I am, respectfully,

Your obedient servant,

"R. B. MASON.

"Lieutenant-Colonel J. C. FREMONT, U. S. A."

The following letter from Major Reading to Colonel Fremont at Monterey, immediately after this second adjournment took place, supplies some additional details. It ran as follows:

MAJOR READING TO COLONEL FREMONT.

"MONTEREY, CAL., *May* 27, 1847.

"DEAR SIR: In reply to your favor of yesterday, I will state that immediately after having delivered your challenge to Colonel Mason, he informed me that he would give you the desired meeting, *and said to me*, in order that there might be as little delay as possible, he would inform me (though informally) that he would select double-barrelled shot-guns as the weapons to be used on the occasion. I replied to him at once that I should lose no time in obtaining such a weapon for Colonel Fremont—that in the morning I should have him provided with a good gun. When I delivered the challenge to Colonel Mason, it was about eight o'clock in the evening, though you received this written acceptance, through his friend Captain Smith, near noon the following day, in which he proposed that the meeting should take place at Monterey, distant from the Puebla de los Angeles about four miles. This gave us considerable surprise, as we expected and were fully prepared to have taken the field that day—forming our opinions from the character of his conversation to me the preceding evening.

"Since that period, your correspondence with Colonel Mason contains the history of this affair.

"I am, most respectfully, your very obedient servant,

"R. B. READING.

"Lieutenant-Colonel J. C. FREMONT, U. S. A."

It was the opinion of Col. Benton, and he so publicly expressed himself in the Senate, that the three letters of Biddle, Kearney, and Mason, were collusive, got up in concert among them, and all looking to the extrication of Mason, and not to the laws of honor, or of martial or municipal law, or common humanity; all of which would have required two of the concern (Biddle and Kearney) to have used their official authority and their personal influence to have put an end to so savage a duel. Kearney's conduct in adjourning and licensing the duel—for in his order he did both—was particularly exceptionable, for by the 26th of the rules and articles of war, it is made "the duty of every officer commanding an army, regiment, post, or detachment, who is knowing to a challenge being given or accepted by any officer, non-commissioned officer, or soldier, under his command, or has reason to believe the same to be the case, *immediately to arrest and bring to trial such offenders.*"

Nothing further was heard from Mr. Mason for over three years. Soon after the events just recited, Col. Fremont was sent home by Gen. Kearney under arrest. In the fall of the following year he returned overland to California, and as he entered the territory from the east, Col. Mason left by a steamer from the west, for the United States. In 1850 Fremont went to Washington as United States senator. Just at the close of the session, and when he was about starting again with his family for California, he received a note from Col. Mason—the first since that of May, 1847—informing him that if he would come out to St. Louis (where Mason was then residing) he should have the satisfaction which he (Mason) had promised him just three years and a-half before. Of course Col. Fremont paid no attention to the letter. He sailed in a few days for California, whither the intelligence not long after followed, of Col. Mason's death.

We will now resume the thread of our narrative.

General Kearney broke up his camp near Sutter's fort on the day after issuing the order of the 14th of June, and set out for the United States, attended by Col. Fremont, who was treated, however, with deliberate disrespect throughout the journey. The party reached Fort Leavenworth about the 22d of August. On that day General Kearney sent for him, and directed Lieut. Wharton to read to him a copy of the first paragraph of an order he had just issued of that date, as follows:

"FORT LEAVENWORTH, *August* 22*d*, 1847.

"Lieutenant Col. Fremont, of the regiment of mounted riflemen, will turn over to the officers of the different departments at this post, the horses, mules, and other public property in the use of the topographical party now under his charge, for which receipts will be given. He will arrange the accounts of these men (nineteen in number) so that they can be paid at the earliest possible date. Lieutenant Colonel Fremont having performed the above duty will consider himself under arrest and will then repair to Washington City and report himself to the Adjutant General of the Army." * * *

Thus, like Columbus, Col. Fremont returned from the discovery and conquest of a New World beyond the Rocky Mountains, a prisoner and in disgrace. Like Columbus his achievements and rapid promotion, had awakened the jealousy of certain sordid hearts and narrow minds, and like Columbus, instead of being permitted to continue his researches in the vast region which he had first brought within the reach of science, he was required to come home and defend himself from the attacks of men who had just sense enough to envy his successes without the ability to achieve them.

Col. Fremont repaired at once to Washington, where he arrived on or about the 16th of September. His journey led him through St. Louis, the first city that he entered upon his return to his native country after a most eventful absence of nearly two years. The history of his brilliant achievements had preceded him, and the reception which he met with, compensated him to some extent for the indignities to which he had been subjected in his tedious journey over the plains from California. He was immediately addressed by a large number of the most respectable citizens of St. Louis, who, after congratulating him upon his safe arrival and recapitulating his claims to public admiration, tendered him an invitation to a public dinner, as a token of their esteem and regard. He was touched by this most seasonable evidence of undiminished confidence, and immediately addressed them the following reply:

LETTER FROM COL. FREMONT TO THE CITIZENS OF ST. LOUIS.

"ST. LOUIS, *August 30th*, 1847.

"GENTLEMEN: I had the pleasure this morning to receive your letter of this date, in which, with many kind assurances of welcome and congratulations on my return, you honor with the strong expression of your approbation, my geographical labors during the recent explorations in Oregon and North California, and the military operations in which sudden emergencies involved me in California.

"I beg you to receive my earnest acknowledgments for the very favorable notice you have bestowed upon the published results of those expeditions, and I regret that events which interrupted, and more recent circumstances which abruptly terminated the last exploration, will permit me to give only a brief and imperfect account of California, and of the intervening basin, which it had been the great object of the expedition to explore and determine.

"The labor of many years in the interest of science, undertaken and sustained with only a distant hope of gaining your good opinion, has received, in the rapid progress of events, an earlier reward than I could possibly have hoped for or anticipated; but I am free to say that the highest pleasure I received from the perusal of your letter, was derived from your decided approval of my political course in North California. Circumstances there made us, in connection with the emigrants to that country, involuntary witnesses, and unwilling actors at the birth of a great nation, but to which we now consider it our great good fortune to have aided in securing the blessings of peace with civil and religious liberty.

"Placed in a critical and delicate position, where imminent danger urged immediate action, and where the principal difficulty lay in knowing full well what must be done; where in a struggle barely for the right to live, every effort to secure our safety involved unusual and grave responsibilities, I could only hope from your forbearance a suspension of judgment until, with full possession of facts, you would be able to determine understandingly.

"I had the gratification, on my arrival, to find that neither remoteness of situation, nor the more immediately important and interesting events at home, had diverted your attention from our conduct, but from a knowledge only of the leading occurrences in California, it had been fully justified and sustained.

"I regret that, under present circumstances, I cannot have the pleasure of meeting you at the dinner you have done me the honor to offer me, but I beg you to accept the assurances of the high and grateful sense which I entertain of your kindness and regard, and the very flattering manner in which you have expressed it.

"With sentiments of respect and consideration, I am, gentlemen, your very obedient servant,

"J. C. FREMONT."

CHAPTER X.

FREMONT ARRIVES AT WASHINGTON—DEMANDS A COURT MARTIAL—ILLNESS AND DEATH OF HIS MOTHER—COURT MARTIAL ORDERED—ITS ORGANIZATION AND PROGRESS—FREMONT'S DEFENCE—VERDICT OF THE COURT—SENTENCE REMITTED BY THE PRESIDENT—RESIGNS HIS COMMISSION AND RETIRES FROM THE ARMY.

THE fame of Col. Fremont's arrest preceded him across the Alleghanies, and some days before his arrival at Washington, had penetrated the seclusion of his widowed mother's home at Aiken, in South Carolina. Her heart had not been properly prepared for such tidings, and the pleasure which he naturally expected from rejoining his family was destined to be qualified by one of the severest trials he had yet known. He found letters at Washington informing him that his mother was dangerously ill. Without delay, he asked for leave of absence to join her, and it was granted on the following day; but before availing himself of it, he addressed the following manly letter to the adjutant general, in relation to his position in the service:

LETTER FROM COL. FREMONT TO THE ADJUTANT GENERAL.

C STREET, WASHINGTON, *Sept. 17th*, 1847.

TO THE ADJUTANT GENERAL:

"SIR: According to the orders of Brigadier General Kearney,

I have the honor to report myself to you in person, in a state of arrest, and to make the following requests:

"1. A copy of the charges filed against me by the said general.

"2. A copy of the orders under which the said general brought back from California to the United States myself and the topographical party of which I had the command.

"3. A copy of the communications from Senator Benton, asking for my arrest and trial on the charges made in the newspapers against me, and which application from him I adopt and make my own.

"4. That charges and specifications, in addition to those filed by General Kearney, be made out in form against me, on all the newspaper publications which have come or shall come to the office, oral or written.

"5. That I may have a trial as soon as the witnesses now in the United States can be got to Washington; for, although the testimony of the voice of California, through some of its most respectable inhabitants, is essential to me, and also that of Commodore Stockton, who has not yet arrived from that province, yet I will not wish the delay of waiting for these far distant witnesses, and will go into trial on the testimony now in the United States, part of which is in the State of Missouri, and may require thirty days to get into Washington. I therefore ask for a trial at the end of that time.

"These requests I have the honor to make, and hope they will be found to be just, and will be granted. I wish a full trial, and a speedy one. The charges against me by Brigadier General Kearney, and the subsidiary accusations made against me in newspapers, when I was not in this country, impeach me in all the departments of my conduct (military, civil, political, and moral), while in California, and, if true, would subject me to be cashiered and shot, under the rules and articles of war, and to infamy in the public opinion.

"It is my intention to meet these charges in all their extent and for that purpose to ask a trial upon every point of allegation or insinuation against me, waiving all objections to forms and technicalities, and allowing the widest range to all possible testimony.

"These charges and accusations are so general and extensive as to cover the whole field of my operations in California, both civil and military, from the beginning to the end of hostilities; and as my operations, and those of which I was the subject or object, extend to almost every act and event which occurred in the country during the eventful period of those hostilities, the testimony on my trial will be the history of the conquest of California, and the exposition of the policy which has been heretofore pursued there, and the elucidation of that which should be followed hereafter. It will be the means of giving valuable information to the government, which it might not otherwise be able to obtain, and thus enlighten it, both with respect to the past and the future. Being a military subordinate, I can make no report, not even of my own operations; but my trial may become a report, and bring to the knowledge of the government what it ought to know, not only with respect to the conduct of its officers, but also in regard to the policy observed, or necessary to be observed, with regard to the three-fold population (Spanish, Americans, Anglo-Americans, and Aboriginal-Americans), which that remote province contains. Viewed under these aspects of public interests, my own personal concern in the trial—already sufficiently grave—acquires an additional and public importance; and for these high objects, as well as to vindicate my own character from accusations both capital and infamous, it is my intention to require and to promote the most searching examination into everything that has been done in that quarter.

"The public mind has become impressed with the belief that great misconduct has prevailed in California; and, in fact, it would be something rare in the history of remote conquests and governments, where every petty commander might feel himself invested with proconsulate authority, and protected by distance from the supervision of his government, if nothing wrong or culpable has been done by the public agents of the United States in that remote province. The public believes it, and the charges filed against me by Brigadier General Kearney—the subsidiary publications made against me whilst I was not in the country—my arrest on the frontier, and the premonitory rumor of that event—the manner of my being brought home for trial, not in irons, as some newspapers suppose, but in chains stronger than iron, and with circumstances of ostentation and galling degradation—have all combined to present me as the great malefactor, and the sole one. Heretofore I have said nothing, and could have said nothing in my own defence. I was ignorant of all that was going on against me; ignorant of the charges sent from California; ignorant of the intended arrest, and of the subsidary publications to prejudice the public mind. What was published in the United States in my favor, by my friends, was done upon their own views of things here, and of which I knew nothing. It was only on my arrival at the frontiers of the United States, that I became acquainted with these things, which concerned me so nearly. Brought home by General Kearney, and marched in his rear, I did not know of his design to arrest me until the moment of its execution at Fort Leavenworth. He then informed me that, among the charges he had preferred, were mutiny, disobedience of orders, assumption of powers, &c., and referred me to your office for particulars. Accordingly I now apply for them, and ask for a full and speedy trial, not only on the charges filed by the said general, but on all accusations contained in the publications against me.

"The private calamity which has this evening obtained for me permission from the Department to visit South Carolina, does not create any reason for postponement or delay of the trial, or in any way interfere with the necessary preliminaries. Hoping, then, sir, that you will obtain and communicate to me an early decision of the proper authorities on these requests.

"I remain your obedient servant, JOHN C. FREMONT.

"*Lieut. Col., Mounted Rifles.*"

Having dispatched this letter, Col. Fremont set out

at once for the bedside of his mother. He did not arrive at Washington until Thursday, the 16th of September. On the following Monday he was in Charleston. The melancholy issue of his visit was briefly told in the following paragraph which appeared in the *Charleston Mercury* of Sept. 21:

"We regret to learn that Col. Fremont did not reach Aiken to see his mother alive. She died but a few hours before his arrival. He accompanied her remains the next day to Charleston, and, after witnessing the last sad rites, left the evening following on his return to Washington. In his affliction, rendered doubly poignant by his deep disappointment in not receiving her parting look of recognition after his long and eventful absence, he has the sympathy of our entire community.

"The marked and brilliant career of Col. Fremont, has arrested general attention and admiration, and has been watched with lively interest by his fellow citizens of South Carolina. Charleston particularly is proud of him and the reputation which he has at so early an age achieved for himself. She claims as something in which she too has a share. But for the melancholy circumstance attending his visit, our city would have manifested by suitable demonstration their respect for him, and their continued confidence in his honor and integrity. It will require something more than mere accusation to sully them in the minds of the people of Charleston. Some months since a sword was voted to him by our citizens, the individual subscriptions to which were limited to $1 ; it now awaits his acceptance at a suitable opportunity. We are happy to learn that the ladies of Charleston propose, by a similar subscription, to furnish an appropriate belt to accompany the sword, an evidence that they too can appreciate the gallantry and heroism which have so signally marked his career, and have thrown an air of romance over the usually dry detail of scientific pursuits."*

* The sword and belt referred to in the foregoing paragraph were presented to Col Fremont soon after the opening of Congress by one of the

In compliance with Col. Fremont's request for a speedy trial, a General Court Martial, to consist of thirteen members, was ordered to assemble on the 2d of November, at Fort Monroe, in Virginia, which place afterwards, upon application of the accused, was changed to the arsenal at Washington City, and the following officers were detailed to hold the court:

Brevet Brigadier-General G. M. BROOKE, *Colonel 5th Infantry*,
Colonel S. CHURCHILL, *Inspector General*,
Colonel J. B. CRANE, *1st Artillery*,
Brevet Colonel M. M. PAYNE, *4th Artillery*,
Brevet Colonel S. H. LONG, *Corps of Topographical Engineers*,
Lieutenant-Colonel R. E. D. RUSSEY, *Corps of Engineers*,
Lieutenant-Colonel J. P. TAYLOR, *Subsistence Department*,
Brevet Lieutenant-Colonel H. K. CRAIG, *Ordnance Department*,
Major R. S. BAKER, *Ordnance Department*,
Major J. D. GRAHAM, *Corps of Topographical Engineers*,

representatives from South Carolina. The sword was a splendid piece of workmanship, silver and gold mounted. The head of the hilt, around which is coiled a rattlesnake belonging to the old arms of the State, is formed to represent the summit of the Palmetto tree. On the guard is a map, with the word "Oregon," partly unrolled, to display the coast of the Pacific Ocean. On the scabbard, which is gold, are two silver shields hung together, with the words "California" and "1846," respectively. Below them is the following inscription:

Presented,
BY THE CITIZENS OF CHARLESTON,
TO LIEUTENANT-COLONEL
JOHN CHARLES FREMONT.
A MEMORIAL OF THEIR HIGH APPRECIATION
OF THE GALLANTRY AND SCIENCE
HE HAS DISPLAYED IN HIS
SERVICES IN OREGON AND CALIFORNIA.

Still lower down on the scabbard is a representation of a buffalo hunt.

And elegant and costly gold-mounted belt, having the present arms of the State on its clasp, presented by the LADIES OF CHARLESTON, accompanied the sword.

Major R. Delafield, *Corps of Engineers*,

Brevet Major G. A. McCall, *Assistant Adjutant-General*, afterwards excused on account of ill health, and Colonel T. F. Hunt, *Deputy Quarter Master General*, appointed in his place,

Major E. W. Morgan, *11th Infantry*.

Capt. John F. Lee, of the Ordnance Department, was appointed judge advocate of the court, and Col. Thos. H. Benton, father-in-law, and Wm. Carey Jones, brother-in-law of the accused, were selected to conduct the defence.

The charges against him were three in number. 1. Mutiny. 2. Disobedience of the Lawful Command of a Superior Officer, and 3. Conduct to the Prejudice of Good Order and Military Discipline.

The trial commenced on the 2d day of November, 1847, and concluded on the 31st of January, 1848, when a verdict of guilty was brought in on each of the charges, and Col. Fremont was sentenced to be dismissed from the service.

The interest of this, probably the most memorable military trial ever held in the United States, has long since passed away. The principal prosecutor was called to his last account a few weeks after the trial closed, and there are few, if any, left who care now to inquire into the motives which actuated him in the course he chose to pursue towards his gallant subordinate. The general tenor of the controversy has been disclosed in the preceding pages. Such additional information as may be requisite to an appreciation of Col. Fremont's motives in the delicate situation in which he was placed between the rival commanders, may be found in the masterly defence which he read to the court, and which we now submit to the reader with entire confidence, that whatever may be his judgment as to the technical propriety of the verdict, he will be constrained to admit, that had Fremont omitted to coöperate with Stockton when and as he did, or had he abandoned him afterwards, as General Kearney directed him to do, and when his abandonment might have been construed into a condemnation of a course of action which he not only approved but advised, he would have justly forfeited, not only his own self-respect, but that generous public sympathy which actually stripped the verdict of all its terrors, even before it reached him.

DEFENCE OF LIEUT. COL. FREMONT.

"MR. PRESIDENT: The crimes with which I stand charged are, 1. MUTINY. 2. DISOBEDIENCE OF ORDERS. 3. CONDUCT PREJUDICIAL TO GOOD ORDER AND DISCIPLINE. Either of these would be sufficiently grave in itself; united, they become an assemblage of crimes probably never before presented against an American officer. They descend from the top to the bottom of the military gradation of crime; from that which is capital and infamous, to what involves but little of disgrace or punishment; but from the whole of which it becomes me to defend myself, and from each, in its order, according to the degree of its enormity.

"The crime of mutiny stands at the head of military offences, and, in this case, is presented with all the aggravations of which it is susceptible; rank in the offender—time of war—in a foreign country—base and sordid motive—willful persistence.

"It is the most dangerous of military crimes, and, therefore, the most summarily and severely punished. Any officer present at a mutiny becomes the judge and punisher of the offence upon the instant, and may kill the mutineer upon the spot, without trial or warning. More than that, he becomes a great offender himself if he does not do his utmost to suppress the mutiny which he witnesses, and may be punished with death, or such other punishment as a court-martial may award. It is the only case in which death may be inflicted without trial ; in all other cases, the supposed offender is presumed to be innocent until he is convicted, and cannot be punished until he has been tried.

"Of this great crime, with all the aggravations of which it is susceptible, I am charged to have been guilty, and continuously so, from the 17th day of January, 1847, to the 9th day of May following, both days inclusive ; during all which time I was liable to have been killed by any officer present who believed me guilty. I was not killed ; but am now here to be tried, and with the presumption of guilt against me from the fact of being ordered to be tried.

"The order to put an officer upon trial is a declaration, virtually so, on the part of the high authority giving the order, of probable guilt. It is equivalent to the '*true bill*' endorsed by the grand jury on the bill of indictment ; and, in this case, is equivalent to three such endorsements on three separate bills, for three several crimes ; for the order for my trial extends to the three different charges upon which I am arraigned, and with the trial of the whole of which this court is charged.

" utiny is not defined in the United States rules and articles of war, or in the British mutiny act from which they are copied, and the decisions, as to what will constitute the crime, are very various in both countries. I only refer to this want of definition of the offence, and to these various decisions, to say that I have no objection, in my own case, to have my conduct judged by any case that was ever decided to be mutiny, either in this country or in Great Britain, strange and extraordinary as some of these cases may appear.

"The first act of this crime, alleged against me, is found in this letter, set cut as the basis of specification first in charge first.—(*See letter of January* 17, 1847, *page* 192.)

"If this letter is mutiny, Mr. President, I shall now add another aggravation to the five aggravations already attending it ; I shall justify it before this court ! and now most respectfully declare that I would write the same letter over again under the same circumstances. But being prosecuted for it, I am bound to defend myself, and proceed to do it.

"I am happy to find that my rights, in one respect, are at least equal to theirs—that of stating my own case as fully as they stated theirs, and showing how I became principal in a contest which was theirs before I heard of it, or came near them; and which, as suggested heretofore, ought to have been settled between themselves, or by the government, whose authority they both bore. A subordinate in rank, as in the contest, long and secretly marked out for prosecution by the commanding general, assailed in newspaper publications when three thousand miles distant, and standing for more than two months before this court to hear all that could be sworn against my private honor as well as against my official conduct, I come at last to the right to speak for myself.

"In using this privilege, I have to ask of this court to believe that the preservation of a commission is no object of my defence. It came to me, as did those which preceded it, without asking, either by myself, or by any friend in my behalf. I endeavored to resign it in California, through General Kearney, in March last (not knowing of his design to arrest me), when it was less injurious to me than it is at present. Such as it now is, it would not be worth one moment's defence before this court. But I have a name which was without a blemish before I received that commission; and that name it is my intention to defend.

In the winter of 1845–6, I approached the settled parts of Upper California with a party of sixty-two men and about two hundred horses, in my third expedition of discovery and topographical survey in the remote regions of the great West.

"I was then brevet captain in the corps of topographical engineers, and had no rank in the army, nor did an officer or soldier of the United States army accompany me.

"The object of the expedition, like that of the two previous ones, was wholly of a scientific character, without the least view to military operations, and with the determination to avoid them, as being not only unauthorized by the government, but detrimental or fatal to the pursuit in which I was engaged. The men with me were citizens, and some Delaware Indians, all employed by myself on wages, and solely intended for protection against savages, and to procure subsistence in the wilderness, and often desert country, through which I had to pass.

"I had left the United States in May, 1845—a year before the war with Mexico broke out; but I was aware of the actual state of affairs between the two countries, and being determined to give no cause of offence to the Mexican authorities in California, I left my command at the distance of about two hundred miles from Monterey, and proceeded, almost alone, to the nearest military station, that of New Helvetia (or Sutter's fort), and obtained a passport (which I now have) for myself and attendants to proceed to Monterey, the residence of the commandant general or deputy governor, General Castro.

"Arrived at Monterey, I called upon the commandant and other authorities, in company with the United States consul, and with all the formalities usual on such occasions, and was civilly received. I explained to General Castro the object of my coming into California, and my desire to obtain permission to winter in the valley of the San Joaquin, for refreshment or repose, where there was plenty of game for the men and grass for the horses, and no inhabitants to be molested by our presence. Leave was granted, and also leave to continue my explorations south to the region of the Rio Colorado and of the Rio Gila.

"In the last days of February, I commenced the march south, crossing into the valley of the Salinas, or Buenaventura, and soon received a notification to depart, with information that Gen. Castro was assembling troops with a view to attack us, under the pretext that I had come to California to excite the American settlers to revolt. The information of this design was authentic, and with a view to be in a condition to repel a superior force, provided with cannon, I took a position on the Sierra, called the Hawk's Peak, entrenched it, raised the flag of the United States, and awaited the approach of the assailants.

"At the distance of four miles we could see them, from the Sierra, assembling men and hauling out cannon; but they did not approach nearer; and after remaining in the position from the 7th to the 10th of March, and seeing that we were not to be attacked in it, and determined not to compromise the government of the United States, or the American settlers, who were ready to join me at all hazards, I quit the position, gave up all thoughts of prosecuting my researches in that direction, and turned north towards Oregon.

"Disappointed in the favorite design, of examining the southern parts of the Alta California, and the valley of Rio Colorado and Gila, I formed another design which I hoped would be of some service to my country, that of exploring a route to the Wah-lah-math settlements in Oregon, by the Tlamath lakes; and thence to return to the United States by a high northern route, exploring the country in that direction. In pursuance of this plan, and before the middle of May, we had reached the northern shore of the Great Tlamath lake, within the limits of Oregon, when we found our further progress in that direction obstructed by impassable mountains, and hostile Indians, of the formidable Tlamath tribes, who had killed or wounded four of our men, and left us no repose either upon the march or in the camp.

"We were now at the north end of the Greater Tlamath lake, in the territory of Oregon, when on the morning of the 9th I was surprised to find ride up to our camp two men—one turned out to be Samuel Neal, formerly of my topographical party, and his companion, who quickly informed me that a United States officer was on my trail, with dispatches for me, but he doubted whether he would ever reach me; that he and his companions had only escaped the Indians by the goodness of their horses; and that he had left the officer, with three men, two days behind.

"Upon the spot I took nine men, four of them Delaware Indians, coasted the western shore of the lake for sixty miles, and met the party.

"The officer was Lieutenant Gillespie. He brought me a letter of introduction from the Secretary of State (Mr. Buchanan), and letters and papers from Senator Benton and his family. The letter from the secretary imported nothing beyond the introduction, and was directed to me in my private or citizen capacity. The outside envelope of a packet from Senator Benton was directed in the same way, and one of the letters from him, while apparently of mere friendship and family details, contained passages enigmatical and obscure, but which I studied out, and made the meaning to be that I was required by the government to find out any foreign schemes in relation to the Californias, and to counteract them. Lieutenant Gillespie was bearer of dispatches to the United States consul at Monterey, and was directed to find me wherever I might be; and he had, in fact, travelled above six hundred miles from Monterey, and through great dangers, to reach me.

"He had crossed the continent through the heart of Mexico, from Vera Cruz to Mazatlan, and the danger of his letter falling into the hands of the Mexican government had induced the precautions to conceal their meaning. The arrival of this officer, his letter of introduction, some things which he told me, and the letter from Senator Benton, had a decided influence on my next movement.

"Three men were killed in our camp by the Indians, the night Lieutenant Gillespie delivered his letters. We returned to the camp at the north end of the lake, pursued and waylaid, but killing two of the assailants without loss.

"I determined to return to the unsettled parts of the Sacramento, and did so. Soon the state of things in California was made known to me; Gen. Castro approaching with troops; the Indians of California excited against us; the settlers in danger as well as ourselves, and all looking to me for help.

"We made common cause, and I determined to seek safety, both for them and ourselves, not merely in the defeat of Castro, but in the total overthrow of Mexican authority in California, and the establishment of an independent government in that extensive province. In concert, and in co-operation with the American settlers, and in the brief space of about thirty days, all was accomplished north of the Bay of San Francisco, and independence declared on the 5th day of July. This was done at Sonoma, where the American settlers had assembled. I was called, by my position, and by the general voice, to the chief direction of affairs, and on the next day, at the head of 160 mounted riflemen, set out to find Gen. Castro. He was then at Santa Clara, on the south side of the bay, in an entrenched camp, with 400 men and some pieces of artillery. We had to make a circuit round the head of the bay, and on the 10th day of July, when near Sutter's fort, we received the joyful intelligence that Commodore Sloat was at Monterey; had taken it on the 7th, and that war existed between the United States and Mexico. Instantly we pulled down the flag of independence, and ran up that of the United States.

"A dispatch from Commodore Sloat requested my co-operation, and I repaired with my command (160 mounted rifles) to Monterey. I was ready to co-operate with him, but his health requiring him to return to the United States, he relinquished the command to Commodore Stockton. He (Commodore Stockton) determined to prosecute hostilities to the full conquest of the country, and asked not co-operation, but service under him. He made this proposal in writing to Lieutenant Gillespie and myself. We agreed to it, and so did our men, the latter, as Commodore Stockton so emphatically testified before this court, refusing to stickle about terms and pay, giving their services first, and trusting their government, far distant as it was, to do them justice.

"Commodore Stockton has proved the terms of our engagement with him, and that we became a part of the naval forces under his command. I went under him with pleasure. I was glad to be relieved from the responsibilities of my position. At the same time I had no doubt but that the riflemen with me would have chased Castro, with his troops, out of the country, and that the Californian population might be conciliated. If Commodore Stockton had not taken the command and lead in the war, I should have continued the work as I had begun it, with the men of my topographical party, and the American settlers, and had not, and have not, a doubt of our success.

"We (Lieutenant Gillespie and myself) joined Commodore Stockton and myself for the public good, and with some sacrifice of our independent positions. Neither of us could have been commanded by him except upon our own agreement. I belonged to the army, and was at the head of the popular movement in California. The common voice of the people called me to the head of affairs, and I was obeyed with zeal and alacrity. Lieutenant Gillespie was of the marines, and was, besides, on special duty, by orders of the President, and no officer of any rank could interfere with him. We might have continued our independent position, and carried on the war by land. We judged it best for the United States to relinquish that independence, take service under Commodore Stockton, obey him; and we did so. His testimony is complete on this point. We became part of the naval forces. We went under the command of the naval commander on that station; and it was to the naval commanders there that the President had specially assigned the conquest of California. The California battalion of mounted riflemen was then organized, Commodore Stockton appointing all the officers, myself being appointed major, and Lieutenant Gillespie captain. From that time we were part of the naval forces for the conquest of the country.

"I omit details of naval or military events, in order to come to the point which concerns me.

"On the 13th of August, 1846, Commodore Stockton, as conqueror, took possession of the City of the Angels, the seat of the governors general of California. On the 17th he issued a proclamation, or decree, as such, for the notification and government of the inhabitants, followed by many others in the same character, and for the better government of the conquered country.

"On the 28th of August, he communicated all these acts to the government at home, stating in the communication that, when he should leave California, he should appoint Major Fremont governor, and Captain Gillespie secretary. Four days before that time, namely, on the 24th of August, and in anticipation of his own speedy return to the sea, for the protection of American commerce and other objects, he appointed me military commandant of the territory, and charged me with enlisting a sufficient force to garrison the country, and to watch the Indians and other enemies. In that letter is this paragraph: '*I propose, before I leave the territory, to appoint you to be governor, and Captain Gillespie to be secretary; and to appoint also the council of state, and all the necessary officers. You will, therefore proceed to do all you can to further my views and intentions thus frankly manifested. Supposing that by the 25th of October you will have accomplished your part of these preparations, I will meet you at San Francisco on that day, and place you as governor of California.*'

"A copy of this letter, with a copy of all the rest of the acts of Commodore Stockton, as governor and commander-in-chief in California, was sent to the Navy Department at the time (August, 1846), by Mr. Christopher Carson, who was met by General Kearney, below Santa Fe, on the Rio Grande, and turned back, the dispatches being sent on by Mr. Fitzpatrick, and were communicated to Congress with the annual message of the President of December, 1846, and are printed in the documents attached to the message, from page 668 to 675, inclusively." * * * * * * *

"It is then certain that, in November, 1846, the President had full knowledge of Commodore Stockton's intention to appoint me governor, when he should return to his ship, to wit, by the 25th of October; and in his message spoke of all his acts in organizing a civil government in a way to imply entire approbation. At the same time that Commodore Stockton sent his dispatches, I also wrote to Senator Benton, giving a brief account, for his own information, of what had taken place in California, and especially on the great point of having joined the American settlers in raising the flag of Independence, and overturning the Mexican government in California. It was done before we had knowledge of the war. I felt all its responsibilities, moral and political, personal and official. It was a resolve made by me, not merely upon serious but upon long and painful reflection. I wrote to Senator Benton, if my conduct was not approved, to give in my resignation, and sent a blank for him to fill up to that effect. Happy had it been for me had the government *then* disapproved my conduct!

"And here it becomes me to state something, which justice to myself and others, and regard for history, requires to be known. A few facts and dates will establish a great point.

"Commodore Sloat arrived at Monterey on the 2d day of July; he did not take it; he hesitated. On the 7th, he did. He had by that time heard of my operations, and supposed I had positive instructions. On the 15th of July, Commodore Stockton arrived; on the 16th, Admiral Seymour, in the Collingwood, of 80 guns; on the 19th, the mounted force, under Lieutenant Gillespie and myself. Upon priority of time in some of these events probably depended the fate of California. Commodore Sloat's action was determined by mine. His action, on the 7th, anticipated the arrival of Admiral Seymour, who found the American flag flying where it is probable he came prepared to be invited to raise the British.

"California was saved, and also the grant of the three thousand square leagues of land to the Irish priest, Macnamara (all the original papers of which I have, to deliver up to the government), was left incomplete, and the land saved, as well as the scheme of colonization defeated. History may some day verify these events,* and show that the preservation of California, and the defeat of the three thousand square leagues grant, covering the valley of the San Joaquin, was owing to the action which determined the action of Commodore Sloat.

"I left Los Angeles early in September. The insurrection broke out there in the same month, and soon spread over all the southern half of California. It extended to near Monterey. It delayed Commodore Stockton's return to the sea, and deferred my own appointment as governor. Instead of being occupied in arrangements to be at San Francisco, on the 25th of October, to be placed '*as governor over California*,' I was engaged, with

* A Catholic priest, named Eugenio Macnamara, in the year 1845 and the early part of 1846, was domesticated with the British legation at the city of Mexico. During that time he made application for a grant of land for the purpose of establishing a colony in California. He asked for a square league, containing, 4,428 acres, to be given to each family, and that each child of a colonist should have half a square league. The territory to be conveyed to him should be around San Francisco Bay, embrace three thousand square leagues, and include the entire valley of the San Joaquin. He agreed to bring a thousand families at the beginning. His object is stated in his memorial to the Mexican President, in these words:

"I propose, with the aid and approbation of your excellency, to place in Upper California, a colony of Irish Catholics. I have a triple object in making this proposition. I wish, in the first place, to advance the cause of Catholicism. In the second, to contribute to the happiness of my countrymen. Thirdly, I desire to *put an obstacle in the way of further usurpations on the part of an irreligious and anti-Catholic nation.*"

His proposal was favorably entertained by the central government. It was referred, for a final decision, to the landholders and local authorities of California. Conventions were about being held to perfect the arrangement. Macnamara was landed, from the British frigate Juno, one of Sir George Seymour's fleet, at Santa Barbara, just at this time. Every thing was ripe for a final settlement of the whole matter; and by virtue of this grant of land to Macnamara, the whole country would have passed under British protection.—*Upham's Life of Fremont*, p. 229.

h e other means than personal influence, in raising men from the American settlements, on the Sacramento, to go south to suppress the insurrection.

"With a small body of men, hastily raised for the emergency, I embarked, according to Commodore Stockton's orders, first, in boats to descend the bay of San Francisco, and then, in the ship Sterling, to go down the coast to Santa Barbara. We had left our horses, and expected to obtain remounts when we landed. Two days after our departure from San Francisco, we fell in with the merchant ship Vandalia, from which I learned, and truly, that no horses could be had below; that, to keep it out of our hands, the Californians had driven all their stock into the interior, and that San Diego was the only point left in possession of the Americans. I therefore determined to return to Monterey, and make the march overland. I did so, and there I learned, or the 27th of October, that I had been appointed lieutenant-colone in the army of the United States. It was now the month of December, the beginning of winter, and the cold distressing rains had commenced. Everything had to be done and done quickly, and with inadequate means. In a few weeks all was ready; 400 men mounted; three pieces of artillery on carriages: beef cattle procured; the march commenced, I omit its details to men tion the leading events, a knowledge of which is essential to my defence. We made a secret march of 150 miles to San Louis Obispo, the seat of a district commandant; took it by surprise, without firing a gun; captured the commandant, Don Jesus Pico, the head of the insurrection in that quarter, with thirty-five others, among them the wounded captain who had commanded at La Natividad. Don Jesus was put before a court martial for breaking his parole, sentenced to be shot, but pardoned. That pardon had its influence on all the subsequent events; Don Jesus was the cousin of Don Andreas Pico, against whom I was going, and was married to a lady of the Cavillo family; many hearts were conquered the day he was pardoned, and his own above all. Among the papers seized, was the original dispatch of General Flores, which informed us of the action of San Pasqual, but without knowing who commanded on the American side. Don Jesus Pico attached himself to my person, and remained devoted and faithful under trying circumstances. We pursued our march, passing all the towns on the way without collision with the people, but with great labor from the state of the roads and rains. On Christmas day, 1846, we struggled on the Santa Barbara mountains in a tempest of chilling rains and winds, in which a hundred horses perished, but the men stood to it to their honor. They deserve mention, for they are not paid yet.

"We passed the maritime defile of the Rincon, or Punta Gorda, without resistance, flanked by a small vessel which Commodore Stockton had sent to us, under Lieutenant Selden of the navy. A corps of observation, of some 50 or 100 horsemen, galloped about us, without doing or receiving harm: for it did not come within my policy to have any of them killed. It was the camp of this corps which Captain Hamlyn passed, to give me Commodore Stockton's orders, which he found in the "camp of the willows," as said in his testimony. The defile of San Fernando was also passed, a corps which occupied it falling back as the rifles advanced. We entered the plain of Couenga, occupied by the enemy in considerable force, and I sent a summons to them to lay down their arms, or fight at once. The chiefs desired a parley with me in person. I went alone to see them (Don Jesus Pico only being with me). They were willing to capitulate to me; the terms were agreed upon. Commissioners were sent out on both sides to put it into form. It received the sanction of the governor and commander-in-chief, Commodore Stockton, and was reported to the government of the United States. It was the capitulation of *Couenga*. It put an end to the war and to the feelings of war. It tranquilized the country, and gave safety to every American from the day of its conclusion.

"My march from Monterey to Los Angeles, which we entered on the 14th of January, was a subject for gratulation. A march of

400 miles through an insurgent country, without spilling a drop of blood—conquering by clemency and justice—and so gaining the hearts of all, that, until troubles came on from a new source, I could have gone back, alone and unarmed, upon the trail of my march, trusting for life and bread to those alone among whom I had marched as conquerer, and whom I have been represented as plundering and oppressing? I anticipate the order of time, but preserve the connection of events by copying here from an original private letter to Senator Benton, written at Los Angeles, the 3d of February, 1847, received by him in May at St. Louis, and sen t to the President for his reading, whose endorsement is on the back, in his own handwriting, stating it to have been received from Mr. Christopher Carson on the 8th of June.

"Had it not been for the treatment I have received, the secret purpose to arrest, the accumulated charges, the publications against me, and other circumstances of the prosecution, I should have been willing to have read that paper to the court as my sole defence against this charge of mutiny; as things are, I copy from it merely some passages, which illustrate what I have said of the effects of that march from Monterey, and the capitulation of Couenga.

"'Knowing well the views of the cabinet, and satisfied that it was a great national measure to unite California to us as a sister State, by a voluntary expression of the popular will, I had in al my marches through the country, and in all my intercourse with the people, acted invariably in strict accordance with this impression, to which I was naturally further led by my own feelings. I had kept my troops under steady restraint and discipline, and never permitted to them a wanton outrage, or any avoidable destruction of property or life. The result has clearly shown the wisdom of the course I have pursued. * * * *

"'Throughout the California population, there is only one feeling of satisfaction and gratitude to myself. The men of the country, most forward and able in the revolution against us, now put themselves at my disposition, and say to me, "*Viva usted seguro, duerme usted seguro*" (live safe, sleep safe), "we ourselves will watch over the tranquillity of the country, and nothing can happen which shall not be known to you." The unavailing dissatisfaction on the part of (our)own people, was easily repressed; the treaty was ratified.'

"'I terminate my narrative at the capitulation of Couenga because at that point I got into communication with my two superiors, became involved in their difficulties, and the events began for which I am prosecuted.

"From this point the evidence begins. My narrative, intended to be brief and rapid, was necessary to the understanding of my position in California, and brings me to the point of the particular offences charged against me.

"Mutiny is first in the order of the charges, and the first specification under it is, for disobeying the negative order of General Kearney, in relation to the re-organization of the California battalion.

"Governor Stockton gave me an order to re-organize it, General Kearney sent me an order not to re-organize it; this on the 16th of January, in the night. The next morning I informed General Kearney, by letter, that I though the and Governor Stockton ought to adjust the question of rank between themselves; and, until that was done, I should have to obey Commodore Stockton, as theretofore; and gave some statement of facts and reasons for my justification.

"This letter constitutes the alleged act of mutiny; the ingredient of a corrupt motive, in trying to trade for a governorship, has been since added; and now, let the accuser and prosecuting witness speak for himself.

"On the first day of his examination, General Kearney testifies thus:

"'On the day subsequent, viz., on 17th of January, Lieutenant Colonel Fremont *came* to my quarters, and in conversation, I asked him whether he had received my communication of the day previous; he acknowledged the receipt of it, and stated that he had written a reply and left it with his *clerk* to be copied.

"'About this time, a *person* entered the room with a paper in his hand, which Lieutenant Colonel Fremont took, overlooked, and then used the pen upon my table to sign it; his *clerk* having told him that the signature was wanting to it. *He* then handed it to me. At my request, Lieutenant Colonel Fremont took a chair by my table while I read the letter.

"'Having finished the reading of it, I told him I was an older man than himself; that I was a much older soldier than himself; that I had a great respect and regard for his wife, and great friendship for his father-in-law, Colonel Benton, from whom I had received many acts of kindness; that these considerations induced me to volunteer advice to him; and the advice was, that he should take the letter *back* and *destroy it; that I was willing to forget it.* Lieutenant Colonel Fremont *declined* taking it back, and told me that Commodore Stockton would support him in the position taken in that letter. I told him that Commodore Stockton *could not* support him in disobeying the orders of his *senior officer*, and that if he *persisted* in it he would *unquestionably ruin himself.* He told me that Commodore Stockton was *about to organize* a civil government, and *intended* to appoint him *governor* of the territory. I told him Commodore Stockton had no such authority, that authority having been conferred on me by the President of the United States. *He asked me whether I would appoint him governor?* I told him that I expected shortly to leave California for Missouri; that I had, previously to leaving Santa Fe, asked permission to do so, and was in hopes of receiving it; that, as soon as the country should be quieted, I should, most probably, organize a civil government, and *that I at that time knew of no objection to appointing him as the governor.* He then stated to me that he would *see* Commodore Stockton, and that unless he appointed him governor *at once*, he would *not obey his orders;* and he left me.'

"This is the evidence on which the prosecution rests the conviction, both for the fact, and its imputed base motive; and at this point the defence begins, and will be directed at once to both motive and fact, with the belief of showing each to be untrue

"*First*, as to the probability of this testimony in all that imputes the dishonorable conduct to me, which is presented as the motive of the meeting.

"I hold it to be improbable on its face, and self-evidently unworthy of credit. It represents me as coming to General Kearney's quarters without invitation, signing a letter in his presence which I had directed to be brought after me, giving it to him to read, and refusing to take it back and accept his pardon and oblivion for having written it. The writing of the letter was avowed at the outset of the trial; the question now is upon what passed at the time of its delivery. The letter contained reasons which placed my refusal to obey his order on high grounds of fact and law; the testimony presents me as descending at once from all those high reasons to the low and base proposal of virtually selling myself to the best bidder himself or Commodore Stockton, for a governorship. According to the testimony, the proposal was abrupt.

"'He asked me whether I would appoint him governor?' and this sudden offer to sell myself, in a case in which the purchaser would be about as censurable as the seller, far from exciting indignation, seems to have been courteously entertained; and far from being instantly rejected, seemed to be accepted, provided a little time was given for payment. 'I (General K.) then told him that I expected shortly to leave California for Missouri, &c., &c., and that I, at that time, knew of no objections to appointing him as governor.' Thus, he had no objections to the transaction—only wanted a little time for performance. I, on the contrary, was for prompt work; for the testimony immediately says: 'He then stated to me that he would see Commodore Stockton, and unless he appointed him governor at once, he would not obey his orders; and he left me.'

"This is the spirit of trade, with its very language and action, with the clear implication that I immediately went to Commodore Stockton, and not coming back, had received the appointment at once. Now, all this is too cool and quick.

"It is improbable on its face, especially coupled with the

fact that I left the letter in his hands, after his warning of unquestionable ruin, which now constitutes the alleged act of mutiny, and so put myself completely in his power, both for the fact and the alleged motive. The testimony is improbable.

"*Secondly*, I hold it to be invalidated on the cross-examination.

"This is the next point of view in which I propose to examine this part of the testimony. After his examination came his cross-examination; and by means of that probe and sharp searcher after truth, came out many circumstances to invalidate the first swearing. Thus, the testimony opens with saying 'Lieutenant Colonel Fremont came to my quarters,' &c., the inference being, that I came of my own head; and, from the sudden manner in which I opened the subject, the further inference being, that I came for the governorship; and third inference being, from my sudden exit and eagerness to see Commodore Stockton, that my whole business was to see from which I could get the governorship the soonest. Now, if I did not come of my own head—if General K. himself actually sent for me, and desired to see me on business—then all these inferences, so injurious to me, fall to the ground; and the very first words spoken by the witness, though literally true, become untrue testimony, and impart a character to the interview which the truth requires to be reversed. Now let us see how the fact is.

"On the eighth day of the trial, this question was put to General Kearney: 'Did he (Lieutenant Colonel Fremont) come of his own head (as your statement implies), or did you invite him?'

"The answer to that question was this: 'I have no recollection of having invited him to come.' On hearing this answer a small slip of paper with a few words written upon it was exhibited to the witness, and this question addressed to him: 'Is this paper an original?' The word original was used on purpose to remind the witness of what had occurred on the first day of the trial, and to show the court that the implication then gratuitously raised against me as a person who would destroy originals, was about to receive a retributive rebuke. To this question and slip of paper, the witness answered: 'That is my writing, and that is my note.'

"The note was then read and was in these words:

"'JANUARY 17.

"'DEAR COLONEL: I wish to see you on business.

"'S. W. KEARNEY,
"'*Brigadier General.*'"

"This settled the question of the coming, and not only showed that it was upon General Kearney's invitation that I came his quarters on that day, but that it was an invitation in writing, and to a business interview that I was invited, and consequently that it was his seeking and not mine that brought us together, and his business, not mine, that was the object of the interview. The production of this little original worked this great change in the character and effect of the evidence; it reversed the character of the coming, and destroyed all the implications arising from a voluntary coming of my own head, and for a purpose of my own.

"But suppose this little original had been actually lost or destroyed, then the first answer of General Kearney, that he had no recollection of having invited me to come, would have stood with the effect of an affirmation that he had not invited me, and would have left in full force all the injurious implications resulting from a gratuitous visit on such an occasion, and with such a conversation sworn against me.

"As I would have suffered from implications in the first state of his evidence, I claim the benefit of them in its corrected form; and, further, I present it as an instance of the infirmity of his memory.

"The want of recollection in the witness in this important particular, I am instructed by counsel to say, goes to the invalidation of his testimony with respect to the whole interview. The circum stance was an important one. It was a key to the character of the interview: it decided the character of the interview as being at his instance or mine. It decided it to be a business interview, and that business his, and not mine. It precludes the idea of my coming to him for any purpose whatever; it fixes the fact that he sent to me for a purpose, and that not a common one, as he invited me to an interview, which was a private one, at his own quarters. General Kearney was then in the crisis of his difficulties with Governor Stockton; he was making a last effort to get me to join him.

"The next circumstance of invalidation which I mention, arising from his own testimony, is in this statement: 'He told me that Commodore Stockton was *about* to organize a civil government, and *intended* to appoint him governor of that territory.' Now, it appears by his own letter to Commodore Stockton of the 16th of January, that he knew that Governor Stockton was then engaged in appointing civil officers for the territory; that, as to *intending* to appoint me, I could not have said so, because I had been virtually appointed since September of 1846, and actually commissioned the day before; and finally, that Governor Stockton had made known to General Kearney at St. Diego, in December, that he intended to appoint me, and had so informed the government at Washington. (Ninth day's testimony.)

"The next circumstance, to invalidate the witness upon his own swearing, is, what he says he stated in reply to the request to be appointed governor, namely, 'that he (General Kearney) at that time knew of no objection to appointing him governor, when he left the country,' &c., &c. Time is the material point in this statement, and this point the witness has fortunately made clear both by collocation and cross examination. It is placed near the end of the interview, and after the act of meeting, with all its aggravations. had been consummated in his presence; and the cross-examination took place on the ninth day of the trial, and shows that it was after the supposed crime, for which I am now prosecuted, was consummated in his presence, that he was able to see no objection to appointing me governor of California.

"From this it results that my conduct that day did not appear to be mutiny, or, that mutiny was no objection to his appointing me governor of California. In either event, I present the circumstance as invalidating his testimony, as it is impossible to reconcile the opposite opinions of my conduct which the declaration of that day, and the prosecution of this day present.

"The next invalidating circumstance which I draw from the cross-examination, is, in the difference which it exhibits to the first day's testimony in relation to this alleged application for the governorship, and the answer to it. The first day's testimony professes to give the interview full and complete, and in the exact words of each speaker; the cross-examination on the 10th day makes material variations. The first day's testimony says: "He asked me whether I would appoint him governor?' That is a single question as to the fact. The cross-examination adds another, as to time, by adding, 'and when?'—and that led to a corresponding difference in the answer, by substituting 'a month or six weeks,' for 'shortly.' The cross-examination of the same day, and of the 9th also, brought the fact of two material omissions in that report of the conversation of the 17th. One related to the fact of Lieutenant Colonel Fremont's urging him (General Kearney) to have a personal intervies with Governor Stockton, and expressing the belief that all difficulties between them could be settled in such an interview; the other, in bringing out the fact that I appeared to be greatly distressed at the differences between the two superior officers. Neither of these important facts are mentioned in the direct testimony, purporting to be verbally exact, and precisely full, neither more nor less; but, not only are these points omitted, but, as told, there is no part of the conversation to which they could be applicable—no place where they would fit in; from which the conclusion is inevitable, that some whole topics, and of a very different kind from these related, were forgotten in that report of a conversation.

"To be distressed at the state of things, between the two superiors, was a different thing from making dissensions between them; to endeavor to get them together for the purpose of reconciliation, was very different from committing mutiny against one of them. Yet these circumstances, so important to the fair and just understanding of my conduct and feelings, are wholly omitted in the direct testimony, and only imperfectly got out in the cross-examination, without the topics to which they belong, and without showing a place in the reported conversation to which they could be applicable, or made to fit; thereby implying greater omissions than have been discovered. As if to deprive me of the merit which these disclosures implied, the witness added, 'Lieutenant Colonel Fremont might have effected an interview between Commodore Stockton and myself; perhaps there were but few others at Los Angeles who could have done it.'

"I certainly believe I could have effected the interview. Governor

Stockton had no objection to it, but General Kearney's sudden departure the next morning, without notice to me, frustrated any such attempt at reconciliation.—(Tenth day's testimony, near the close.)

"The next invalidating circumstance, drawn from the cross-examination in relation to the same point, is, in not suppressing or endeavoring to suppress, the alleged mutiny at the time it is charged to have been committed.

"The eighth article of war, copied from the British mutiny act, is imperative that, 'any officer, non-commissioned officer, or soldier, who, being present at any mutiny or sedition, does not use his utmost endeavor to suppress the same, or coming to the knowledge of any intended mutiny, does not, without delay, give information thereof to his commanding officer, shall be punished, by the sentence of a general court martial, with *death*, or otherwise, according to the nature of his offence.' As a further test to ascertain General Kearney's opinion of my conduct on that day, the following question was put to him: 'Did you do your utmost to suppress the mutiny of which Lieutenant Colonel Fremont is charged with being guilty in your quarters, and in your presence?' The judge advocate reminded the witness of his privilege to refuse to answer where he might subject himself to a penalty, but the witness did not claim his privilege, and answered: 'Nothing further passed between Lieutenant Colonel Fremont and myself in the interview, than what I have stated;' (adding, the next day, 'to the best of my recollection.')

"This is clear, that General Kearney did nothing to suppress the supposed mutiny, and equally clear that he gives no reason for not doing so. He was in his own quarters—in the house where his troops were quartered—and he testified that he does not think Commodore Stockton would have used force. The inference is, that either he did not consider it mutiny then, or that he had some reason, not yet told, for not doing his duty. The former is the probable one, because it corresponds with the contemporary declaration of knowing no objection to appointing me governor, and for the further reason that it appears, from his own evidence, that he gave me, in the month of March, several orders to execute, implying trust and confidence, and wholly inconsistent with his duty, under the eighth article of war, and wholly inconsistent with military usage, if he then believed me to be guilty of mutiny.

"For these reasons, I consider his testimony further invalidated upon his own evidence, drawn out upon his own examination.

The next circumstance to invalidate the testimony of this witness, arising out of his own cross-examination, is what relates to the bearer of my letter of the 17th of January.

"In his direct testimony, General Kearney spoke of him as being my clerk. As I kept no clerk, and knowing that Lieutenant Talbott had copied the letter, and that Mr. Christopher Carson had brought it to me (for in my anxiety at the state of things, and hope for some better understanding, I went in such haste to General Kearney's quarters, on receiving his invitation, as to leave my letter in the hands of a copyist, to be sent after me), I undertook to turn his mind toward the right person, by asking who the person was who brought that letter. To that question he answered: 'I do not know. I had never seen him before; nor do I know that I have ever seen him since.' I then put the question direct: 'Was not that person Mr. Christopher Carson? To which the answer was: 'I think not.' This answer terminated the interrogatories upon that point; and, according to the evidence, the fact was established that not only it was not Mr. Carson who brought the letter, but that it was some strange person whom General Kearney had never seen before or since. The defect of memory became so glaring in this instance that it was deemed essential by my counsel to expose it; and something, like a Providence, enabled me to do so.

"Mr. Carson, the best witness, had returned to California; Lieutenant Talbott, who copied the letter, and sent him with it, was the next best witness; and he had been ordered to Mexico by sea. In passing some of the Florida reefs, the vessel he was in was wrecked, but the lives of the passengers were saved, and Lieutenant Talbott, with his command, had returned to Charleston. Hearing all this, an order and summons were dispatched for him; he came; and, being examined before this court, he testified to the facts that he had copied the letter at my request, and sent it after me by Mr. Carson to General Kearney's quarters. Captain Hensley gave corroborating testimony; and thus the fact established by General Kearney's testimony, that it was not Mr. Carson who brought the letter, nor any person that General Kearney had ever seen before or since, was entirely disproved. Certainly the fact in itself, as to who brought the letter, was not very material; but it became eminently so from the answers of the witness. For General Kearney not to know Kit

Carson; not to remember him when he brought the letter on which this prosecution is based; to swear that he had never seen the man before or since, who brought that letter, when that man was the same express from Commodore Stockton and myself from whom he got the dispatches; whom he turned back from the confines of New Mexico, and made his guide to California; the man who showed him the way, step by step, in that long and dreary march; who was with him in the fight of San Pasqual: with him on the besieged and desolate hill of San Bernardo; who volunteered, with Lieutenant Beale and the Indians, to go to San Diego for relief, and whose application to go was at first refused, 'because he could not spare him;' who was afterwards the commander of the scouts on the march from San Diego to Los Angeles; not to know this man who had been his guide for so many months, and whom but few see once without remembering; and not only not to know him, but to swear that he had never seen him before or since. This, indeed, was exhibiting an infirmity of memory almost amounting to no memory at all.

"In that point of view I present it to the Court, and to invalidate all the testimony of General Kearney, with respect to my words, or his words in that alleged conversation of the 17th of January. Acts and facts are more easily remembered than words; persons and things seen are more easily remembered than expressions heard; and after forgetting his own act, in writing to me to come to see him on business; after forgetting the fact of seeing the famous Kit Carson bring the letter which he has so long saved for this prosecution, I am instructed, by counsel, to say that the law discredits him as a witness.

"*Thirdly*. Discredited by his own conduct.

"I hold that the charge is discredited by General Kearney's own conduct at the time, in not reporting it to Governor Stockton or to the government of the United States. In neither of the two letters written by him to Governor Stockton, on the same day when my alleged offer to sell the California battalion to him for a governorship, accompanied by a menace of revolt against Governor Stockton, is testified to have taken place, is the remotest hint or allusion to any such transaction. Now, whatever may have been General Kearney's opinion of his own rights, and of the refusal of Governor Stockton to recognize his claims, considerations of public duty ought to have prompted him, before going away and leaving the interests of the country entirely in the hands of Governor Stockton, with a known intention of presently committing them to me, ought to have induced him to warn that officer of my conduct, and threat of sedition, if any such had taken place.

"On the other hand, if considerations of public duty are not the motive that had influence with him, but, instead, his private resentments, these also, whether against Commodore Stockton, myself, or both, would equally have prompted him to the disclosure, had there been any to make; for, if after being informed of such insubordination, Governor Stockton had still persisted in his intentions towards me (continuing my command, and leaving me in the governorship), the witness would have fastened upon both a corrupt intrigue and collusion; or, if Governor Stockton had acted upon the information, as would have been proper to act, and as he probably would have acted, namely taken away my command, and possibly seized my person, then that 'UNQUESTIONABLE RUIN,' intimated as in reserve for me, would have been soon accomplished.

"Had that which is now charged upon me actually taken place, the suppression of the fact, at that time, when fresh and working in the mind of the witness, as it must have done, cannot, with the reasons and inducements which existed for its disclosure, be accounted for on any known principle of human conduct.

"Besides these two letters to Governor Stockton of that day, both silent on this charge, the witness also wrote to the War Department on the same day, and reporting both Governor Stockton and myself, as refusing to obey him, or the instructions of the President; and neither in that letter is there the slightest hint or allusion to any such transaction as General Kearney has now testified to.

"There is a case at the Old Bailey where a person was convicted and executed, mainly on the presumption which a very similar omission to this raised. It was the case of Governor Wall, tried at the Old Bailey, 1802, on a charge of murder, committed, under color of official duty, in the punishment of a soldier at Goree, off the coast of Africa, twenty years before.

"The soldier was punished with eight hundred lashes, in consequence of which he died two days after. The defence set up, was, that a part of the troops of the garrison were in a state of MUTINY, of which the soldier punished was the ringleader; and that the punishment was inflicted under the article of war which requires an officer present at a mutiny to do his utmost to suppress it.

"The prosecution proved *that Governor Wall went away from the place on the day following the alleged acts of mutiny, and with him two officers; and that, arriving in England, he reported, in writing, to the government concerning the affairs of the garrison* BUT MADE NO MENTION OF THE ALLEGED MUTINY.

"The lord chief baron, Mac Donald, dwelt upon that omission, and pointed it out to the jury. There was other evidence on the point of MUTINY or no mutiny; but it was nearly balanced, and this omis sion became the great point in the case. The governor was convicted; and notwithstanding the most powerful efforts to obtain his pardon, the king (George III.) refused to grant it; and he was hung at Tyburn, according to his sentence, and his body given up to the surgeons to be dissected and anatomized.

"The presumption raised in the present instance is stronger than in the one I have quoted. There the report referred only to the affairs of the garrison generally; here it relates exclusively to the subject now in issue. There, if there had been a *mutiny*, there was no occasion for the action of the government; for the mutiny, such as it was, had been suppressed and the mutineers punished; here the report was specially for the action of the government on the case stated. There, the omission was merely a matter left out, not affecting, in any way, what was put in; here the omission is of the material part, and without which not only an imperfect but a false view is given to the whole. There, the letter was written six weeks after the occurrence, and at a great distance from the scene of it; here it was written on the spot—the same day. All the reasons for General Kearney to have *reported* my alleged mutiny, and the base motive for it in the imputed attempted bargaining about the governorship, are infinitely stronger than in the case of Governor Wall. The omission was a heavy circumstance against him in this case; it must be more so in the present one; and authorizes me to say that the testimony of the witness here is discredited by his own conduct, at the time of these imputed offences.

"*Fourthly.* I now take a more decided view of this testimony in relation to governorship, and say that besides being improbable on its face, invalidated on the cross-examination, and discredited by his own conduct, it is disproved by facts and witnesses. The imputed bargaining for the governorship is the point of the mutiny and the base and sordid cause of it. Now, if there was no bargaining, or attempt at it, for the governorship, then there was no mutiny; and the whole charge, with its imputed motive and inferences, falls to the ground. And, now, how was the fact? That as early as August, 1846, Governor Stockton, of his own head, selected me for his successor as governor and commander-in-chief in California. That he informed me of it at the time by letter, and also informed the government of the United States of it, and had actually fixed the 25th day of October, 1846, for his own return to his squadron, and for my installation as governor, and was only delayed in that intention by the breaking out of the insurrection. That he informed General Kearney of all this at San Diego, by giving him a copy of his official dispatch to the government to read; that, arriving at Los Angeles in January, he immediately proceeded to consummate his delayed intention, making all preparations for his own departure and for my installation, appointing me governor in form, appointing a secretary of my choice, appointing the council, immediately filling up my place in the California battalion by promoting Captain Gillespie to be major; and all these things done and completed by the 16th, and so known generally at the time, and actually known to General Kearney himself, as appears by his own letter, of that date, to 'acting Governor Stockton,' forbidding the appointments; and also by his cross-examination before this court.

"The following are passages from the letter:

"'I am informed that you are now engaged in organizing a civil government, and appointing officers for it in this territory.' 'If you have not such authority (from the President), I then demand that you cease all further proceedings relating to the formation of a civil government for this territory, as I cannot recognize in you any right in assuming to perform duties confided to me by the President.'—(Tenth day.)

"The cross-examination of the same day fully sustains the assertion that, on the 16th, General Kearney knew that Governor Stockton was appointing the governor and secretary for California, and his letter to the department, of the same date (16th), shows that he not only knew it, but reported it. These facts disprove the assertion that, on the 17th, I asked General Kearney for the governorship of California; disprove the assertion that I would see

Commodore Stockton, and, unless he gave it at once, I would not obey his orders. The facts disprove it, for all the forms of bestowing the appointment had been completed the day before, while the appointment itself had been virtually and actually made for near six months before.

"I will now proceed to the positive testimony of an unimpeached and unimpeachable witness, to disprove the testimony of General Kearney in relation to this governorship.

"Colonel Wm. H. Russell, a witness introduced on the thirty-sixth day of the trial, testified that he was sent by Lieutenant Colonel Fremont from the plains of Couenga, about the 13th of January, to Los Angeles, to ascertain who was in chief command, and to make report of the capitulation of Couenga. I leave out, at this time, all notice of his testimony, except what relates to the governorship. He says he went first to General Kearney's quarters; afterwards to Commodore Stockton's; returned, by invitation of General Kearney, and supped and slept at his quarters. On his return the chief conversation took place, and now the very words of the witness shall be given. Colonel Russell says: 'In that conversation he (General Kearney) expressed great pleasure at Colonel Fremont's being in the country; spoke of his eminent qualifications for the office of governor, from his knowledge of the Spanish language, of the manners of the people, &c.; and of his (General Kearney's) intention to have appointed him governor, if the instructions he brought from the Secretary of War had been recognized in California.' 'It (the conversation about the governorship), was a subject of very much conversation, protracted to a late hour in the night. He told me of his civil appointments in New Mexico, and of his determination to have appointed Colonel Fremont governor.' 'He said that so soon as he could organize a civil government, it was his intention to return to the United States, and finding so suitable a person as Colonel Fremont in the country to take the place of governor, his design need not be long postponed. I do not pretend to quote his exact words.'

"On the the thirty-eighth day of the trial, and after objections to certain questions to Colonel Russell had been sustained by the court, his direct examination was resumed, and he testified (after stating that he rode out the next morning and met Lieut. Colonel Fremont, then entering Los Angeles, at the head of his battalion),

I informed him (Lieutenant Colonel Fremont) that both General Kearney and Commodore Stockton were anxious to confer upon him the office of Governor, and his only difficulty would be in the choice between them.' 'Commodore Stockton informed me, on the evening of the 13th, on my second interview with him, that he intended to confer the office of governor on Lieutenant Colonel Fremont, as I understood, immediately on his arrival at Los Angeles. I think it was a matter of ordinary publicity throughout the city.' 'On the morning, as I suppose, of the 16th, I was at Commodore Stockton's quarters, and he informed me that the commission for Lieutenant Colonel Fremont as governor, and my own as secretary of state, were then in the act of being made out by his clerk, and desired me to ask Lieutenant Colonel Fremont to be at his quarters by a given hour, when the commissions would be ready for delivery. I made this communication to Lieutenant Colonel Fremont, and at the appointed time returned with him to Commodore Stockton's quarters, when he (the commodore) accordingly handed the commissions to each of us.

" 'I want to qualify here, as I am told there is some discrepancy about dates. I presume it was the 16th, because the commissions bear that date, and for the further reason that it was within two or three days of the arrival of Lieutenant Colonel Fremont at Los Angeles.' This was on the direct examination.

" On the cross-examination, on the fortieth day of the trial, the witness (Colonel Russell) in reply to questions, confirmed all that he had said, and added: 'That in all the conversations I had with General Kearney on that evening 13th January), I understood it to be his wish to appoint Lieutenant Colonel Fremont as governor, if he could rightfully do so.'

" And thus, I say that the testimony of General Kearney is disproved by the positive testimony of an unimpeached, an unimpeachable witness, as well as by established facts.

"*Fifthly.* I say that this statement, that I asked General Kearney for the governorship, is disavowed by the entire tenor of my life. I have neither begged nor bargained for offices. My first appointment, as second lieutenant of topographical engineers, was given me by President Jackson, Mr. Poinsett being Secretary at War, when I was far distant on the Upper Mississippi, assisting M. Nicollet in his great survey of that region. My brevet of captain was given me by President Tyler, Mr. Wilkins being Secretary at War, without solicitation from myself or friends. The appointment of lieutenant colonel came to me in California, when I was not even thinking of it; and I am assured by Senator Benton, that it was President Polk's own act, not only unasked by him, but that he refused to consent that any friend should name such a thing to the President.

"The three appointments given to me by Commodore Stockton (those of major of the California battalion, military commandant of California, and governor and commander-in-chief, in California), were all given of his own head, without solicitation or hint from me. Such has been the uniform tenor of my life in respect to office, and General Kearney is no exception to it.

"The uniform conduct of my life disavows the application which he says I made to him; and I claim the benefit of that disavowal in a case where a request would be infamous, which I never made, when it might have been done with honor.

"*Sixthly.* Having shown that this testimony of General Kearney is improbable on its face, invalidated on his own cross-examination, discredited by his own conduct, disaproved by positive testimony, and disavowed by the tenor of my life, I now come to the last, and only remaining species of testimony—that of my own declaration. Happily I have no new declaration to make; I have only to show the statement which I made for the eye of private friendship, in the mere course of narrative, and as a circumstance in the history of the transaction, near twelve months ago, when the event was fresh, no question about it, and none of any kind ever expected. In that private letter to Senator Benton, already referred to, written at Los Angeles, and dated the 3d day of February, 1847, are these words:

"'*Both offered me the commission and post of governor; Commodore Stockton, to redeem his pledge to that effect, immediately, and General Kearney offering to give the commission in four or six weeks.*'

This is what I then wrote for the eye of private friendship, and what I now produce to this court as my own testimony in this case. IT IS TRUE. And I now owe it to myself, to my friends, and to good men, whose esteem I desire to possess, to declare, and to make the declaration upon responsibilities infinitely Higher than those of military honor or commission, that Brigadier General Kearney, in all that he has testified in relation to this governorship, has borne false witness against me.

"I dismiss this topic, the only one in the multiplied charges against me which concerns my honor, with the reflection which springs of itself from the case and finds a response in every generous mind, that General Kearney himself undertook to seduce me with this governorship, and failing to do so, has raised against me the false accusation of applying to him for it, and has sworn to it.

"And I here close my defence, both as to the fact and the motive, of specification first, in charge first, for the crime of mutiny.

"I proceed now to defend the same act under a different charge; for it so happens in this trial that the same set of acts are placed under different charges, some under two charges, namely, mutiny and disobedience of orders; and some under three, the same act, in some instances, being carried out under the charge of conduct prejudicial to good order and discipline, as well as under the heads of mutiny and disobedience of orders.

"I refer to a paper, heretofore filed, for the opinion which my counsel entertain of these multiplied charges upon the same set of acts. They consider them as so many different trials for the same thing, and wholly unjustified by the practice which admits less degrees of the same offence to be found, according to the proof produced on the trial. Here the charges are on the same acts for different kinds of offences, and the same evidence adduced under each, and the same that was adduced before the trial, when the charges were framed, as before this court, when they are tried. My counsel instruct me to say it is a clear case of two trials and three trials for the same matter; but I take no legal objection to it.

"To save the labor of re-stating questions, and of re-producing proofs as many times as the same specifications are repeated under different charges, I prefer to pursue each one, when I begin it, through all the charges; and thus finish with it complete, and have all my trials over upon it, before I begin with another. This method will be convenient to me, and probably no disadvantage to the prosecution, as it will get all the chances of conviction, which the multiplied charges require, though, perhaps, not in the order they would regularly imply.

"I begin with my letter to General Kearney, of the 17th of January, which he produces under the charge of disobedience of orders, as well as under that of mutiny, and as evidence to prove both, and which I produce as containing the facts and the law which disprove each. That letter is in these words. (See letter of Jan. 17, 1847, p. 192.)

"This letter was signed in the quarters of General Kearney, and in his presence, and delivered to him by myself. He read it in my presence, and has produced it here as evidence against me, and, in so doing, has made it evidence against himself. What he did not then deny, he admitted; and I will show, from his own testimony, that that is the case with the whole letter. He contradicted no part of it, therefore he admitted every part of it; and this results from his own swearing, in which he professes to give an exact verbal account, no more, no less, of all that passed at that interview, of the letter, from my *entrance*, at the beginning, to my *exit* at the end; and not one word of my letter contradicted in the whole account. I will now analyze its statements of law and fact, so far as they apply to this charge of disobedience of orders, and show it to be a complete refutation of the charge founded upon it. The letter is the text of my defence, and the development of its positions will make its leading argument. I am advised by counsel that it is complete in itself, and such as it was written that morning, needs no aid from subsequent reflection or legal advice; and on that letter, as it is, both for the law and the fact, I stand all the multiplied trials which are founded upon it.

"*First.* It fixes the *time* of sending the countermanding order to me—a most material point which could not be fixed by any examination, or cross-examination of General Kearney. All the multiplied questions put to him, and by all parties, the judge advocate, myself, and the court, left the *time* of the day uncertain, and led to a wrong time, as being at some period of the day, and even the fore part of the day, of the 16th of January. (See 8th and 9th days of the testimony.) My letter fixes the time; it opens with fixing it. It fixes it to the *night.* The first line acknowledges the receipt of your favor (*i. e.* the countermanding order) *of last night.* No denial was made of having sent this order at night; and thus that period was confessed.

"*Second.* It fixes the character in which I myself was then acting, and a knowledge of which was so material to the case, and so difficult to be obtained from the prosecuting witness. It shows that

I was military commandant of the territory; and that the order I was required to cease from executing was an order in relation to the battalion under my command as military commandant. It fixes the fact that the order came to me in that capacity; for so my letter asserts, and it was not contradicted by General Kearney when read by him.

"*Third.* It fixes the character of Commodore Stockton in giving me the order to reorganize the battalion; for it names him as giving the order, and describes him as governor and commander-in-chief in California.

"*Fourth.* It fixes the fact that on my arrival at Los Angeles (14th January), Commodore Stockton was exercising the functions of civil and military governor with apparent deference to take his rank by General Kearney, for that is asserted in the letter, and was not contradicted by him.

"*Fifth.* It also fixes the fact that, on the march from San Diego to Los Angeles, General Kearney discharged duties implying the supremacy of Commodore Stockton; for that is asserted to have been learnt by me, from conversations with General Kearney himself, and was not denied by him.

"These important facts, five in number, are fixed and established by the letter; for they were not denied when the letter was read. I am advised by council that the law takes for confessed whatever is said to a man in his presence, and not contradicted, at the time, by him. General Kearney's testimony, professing to give a full account of all that was said, on both sides, during the whole interview at the reception of the letter, is silent upon all these points; and it is too late now to think of contradicting what was then, by all the rules of evidence, irrevocably admitted. That letter and its delivery in his presence, and being read in my presence, besides containing the facts of the case, and the law of the case, becomes also the evidence of the case. If that order had not been written or sent in the *night*, that was the time for General Kearney to have said so. If the order had not been intended for me, in my capacity of *military commandant of the territory*, that was the time for him to have corrected my error. If Commodore Stockton was not then *governor and commander-in-chief in California*, then was the time for him to have told me so. If Commodore Stockton had not been exercising the functions of *military commander and civil governor*, from the month of July preceding, then was the time for him to have contradicted the assertion of it in my letter. If I had not found the commodore exercising the *same functions* on my arrival at Los Angeles, three days before, with apparent deference on the part of all officers, General Kearney inclusive, that was the time for him to have denied the assertion, or, at all events, to have protested against the inclusion of himself in that obedient and deferential class of officers. If I had not learnt in conversation with himself that, in the march from San Diego, and also there, at Los Angeles, he had not entered upon and discharged duties implying, *on his part*, an acknowledgment of Commodore Stockton's *supremacy* then was the time for him to have told me that I labored under a total mistake in my misunderstanding of his conversations.

"If there was no question of *rank* then (on the 17th) depending between himself and Governor Stockton, he ought to have said so. If it had not been right for me to remain as I was *until they adjusted that question*, then was the time for him to say so to me. If the *difficulty* was not between the two superiors alone, then was the time for him to have cast it upon me. If I had ever *reported* to him, or *received orders* from him, surely it was the time to tell me so when he was reading that last paragraph of my letter, in which the contrary is asserted in the declaration, that I should have to *report* and to *receive orders* '*as heretofore*,' from Commodore Stockton. If all, or any of these points were not true, *then* was the *time*, and *there* was the *place*, and *that* was *the occasion*, to have denied them. Denial, omitted then, cannot be supplied now. And both law, reason, and justice, require my uncontradicted letter of that day to remain as established truth in the question between General Kearney and myself.

"Clear and strong in its facts, the letter is equally just and legal in its conclusions. It does not refuse obedience to General Kearney, but defers it until he and Commodore Stockton adjust the question of rank between themselves; it respectfully suggests to him that the settlement of the difficulty belongs to himself and Commodore Stockton; and concludes with stating that until this rank is so adjusted, I would have to report and receive orders, as heretofore, from Commodore Stockton. Now all this, I am advised by counsel, is both law and reason; and to prove this law, and this reason, is now my duty before this court.

"I proceed to do it:

"*First.* It shows that there was a question of rank admitted by General Kearney to be depending between himself and Commodore Stockton. He wished to settle it by giving me a contradictory order. I declined the responsibility, and I think rightfully. For, in the first place, it is not for the subordinate to decide between his superiors. He has no legal power to do so; no legal power to require submission from the one decided against; and if he used physical force, it might indeed be a case of mutiny, and that in its proper sense of a military rebellion. Besides, decide which way he might, his danger would be the same. Having no right or power to decide between them—my duty being passive and not active—the only safe or legal course open to me was to remain as I was, reporting to, and receiving orders from Commodore Stockton. I considered the question to lie between the two superiors, and that seems to be their own opinion of it, from their correspondence at the time (16th and 17th of January). The concluding words of General Kearney's letter to Commodore Stockton, of the 17th of January (eighth day of the trial) are express to that point. Those words are too material to paraphrase or put off with a reference; they are these:

"'*And as I am prepared to carry out the President's instructions to me, which you oppose, I must, for the purpose of preventing a collision between* US, *and possibly to prevent a civil war* IN CONSEQUENCE *of it, remain* SILENT *for the* PRESENT, *leaving with* YOU *the great* RESPONSIBILITY *of doing* THAT *for which you have no authority, and* PREVENTING ME *from complying with the President's* ORDERS.'

"This extract and the whole contemporaneous correspondence between the two superior officers, beginning at San Diego when I was on the march from Monterey, shows that the contest was between them; and it shows also the serious point at which it had arrived. The time of writing the letter, from which this extract is taken, is now the material point, and that was sufficiently ascertained on the cross-examination of General Kearney on the eighth day. It was ascertained to have been written after my refusal to obey him against Commodore Stockton. The conclusion is inevitable. That refusal prevented the *collision* and *the civil war* which the letter mentioned, as being for the present prevented. I prevented it. My reward has been to have the war directed against myself, and to be tried for capital and infamous crimes, with base and sordid motives attributed to me.

"The question now is disobedience of orders—the order not to re-organize the California battalion being the specification.

"In the British service, from whose rules and articles of war our own are copied, and where there is a judge advocate general to direct court martial proceedings with uniformity, the character or qualities of the order, disobedience to which is criminal, are already defined. At page 89 of Hough, edition of 1825, is found this definition of such an order:

"In the absolute resistance of, or refusal of obedience to, a present and *urgent* command, conveyed either orally or in *writing*, and directed to be obeyed with promptitude, by the non-compliance with which some immediate act necessary to be done might be impeded or defeated, as high an offence is discoverable as can well be contemplated by the military mind; inasmuch as the principle which it holds out, would, if encouraged or not suppressed by some heavy penalty, forbid or preclude a reliance on the execution of any military measure. It is this positive disobedience, therefore, evincing a *refractory* spirit in the INFERIOR, an active opposition to the commands of a SUPERIOR, against which it must be supposed the severe penalty of the article is principally directed.'

"From this definition of the kind of order which the rules and articles of war contemplate, it is clear that it is not *every* order, and merely because it is an order, given by a superior to an inferior, that entitles itself to implicit obedience. On the contrary it must have certain indispensable requisites to entitle itself to that obedience; and among these are: 1st, legality; 2d, necessary for the public service; 3d, urgent; by the non-compliance with which some immediate act necessary to be done is defeated or impeded; and that the disobedience must be of a kind to evince a refractory spirit.

"I have to answer that the order given by General K. possessed none of these requisites, and that disobedience drew after it no injury to the public service, and that my refusal to obey it was not in a refractory spirit.

"1. It was not a legal order, and this for reasons which I shall fully show in the proper place.

"2. It was a mere experimental order of contradiction, to try a question of rank, and against the public service, as the state of the battalion required it to be re-organized, the time for which many of the men and officers were engaged having expired, and to give it a major in the place of myself, made governor.

"3. So far from being for the public service, it would seem from the sentence in General Kearney's letter to Commodore Stockton of the 17th of January (already quoted), in relation to a collision between them, and possibly a civil war, that the battalion was wanted for forcibly asserting his right to the governorship against Commodore Stockton. The letter can have no other meaning; and this interpretation of it is, moreover, borne out by his letter of the same date to the department, by his testimony before the court, and by the testimony of Lieutenant Emory.

"4. The battalion was not, and never had been, under the orders of General Kearney; was not such troops as his instructions contemplated, and several of its officers were from the navy, over whom he could have no control.

"5. General Kearney was, at the time of giving the order, suspended from the command of the forces at that place by order of Governor Stockton.

"6. If not suspended at the time he wrote and sent the order, then he was himself in mutiny against his own commander, and endeavoring to induce me 'to join' in it, and thus was in the commission of the double offence of mutiny himself, and endeavoring to make another join him in it.

"7. General Kearney has not shown for what purpose he gave the order against re-organization, but it appears evident it was for an unlawful purpose, *to wit*, for the purpose of keeping the battalion together in his own hands to be used against Gov. Stockton. On his cross-examination (eighth day) he *seems* to have known nothing about what he was doing in giving this order, on which I am now doubly prosecuted. To the question: 'Did you know what was the nature of the re-organization commanded by Governor Stockton, of the battalion under Lieutenant Colonel Fremont, and forbid by you?' he answered, 'I do not. I learned that Commodore Stockton was about to re-organize that battalion, and I forbid it.' Thus, a battalion raised, officered, commanded, and organized by Governor Stockton, and being a part of his forces for the conquest, preservation, and government of California, was forbid to be *re*-organized by General Kearney, without knowing what the actual organization was, or what the re-organization would be. He heard something was to be done—he knew not what—and he forbid it. Surely he should tell what purpose he had in view.

"8. It was an order that I could not obey without rebelling against the authority by which the battalion was raised and from which I held my commission as its commander.

"From all this it appears that the order not to re-organize the battalion has none of the requisites of an order entitled to obedience; that it was not a lawful order; that it was not intended for the public service; that there was no necessity for it; that no injury to the public service accrued from non-obedience to it; that the refusal to obey it, so far from being in a refractory spirit, was a mere determination to remain as I was, and as I had been, under Commodore Stockton's command until my superiors settled their own dispute. And I am now advised by counsel to say that that decision was legally right.

"In opposition to all this, General Kearney urges, in support of his right to command me, *first*, his rank as brigadier general; *secondly*, his instructions to take command of the troops organized in California; *thirdly*, that I had put myself under his command by reporting to him on the 13th of January. I deny all three of his positions:

"1. As brigadier general he had no right to give me any order in relation to Commodore Stockton's forces. He admits this with respect to the sailors and marines; also, with respect to that part of the battalion which was detached, and under the command of Captain Gillespie; it was equally illegal to interfere with that part of the commodore's forces which was under my command.

"2. His instructions to take command of the troops organized in California did not apply to those raised by the navy; they did not apply to such forces as I commanded, and of which nothing was known at Washington when the instructions were given.

"3. His pretension that I put myself under his command by reporting to him, and on which he mainly relies, is as unfounded as all the rest, but requires a more detailed and precise examination. He lays great stress upon this alleged reporting, and shall have the full benefit of his own testimony in support of his pretension. In his direct examination, he said: 'About the 14th of January, 1847, I received from Lieutenant Colonel Fremont a communication dated the day previous, upon the march, and dated January 13, 1846 (presumed to be written by mistake for 1847), and which I furnished together with the charges, to the adjutant general.'

"The paper was read, as follows:

'ON THE MARCH, *January*, 13, 1846.

'"DEAR SIR: I have the honor to report to you my arrival at this place with 400 mounted riflemen and six pieces of artillery, in cluding among the latter two pieces lately in the possession of the Californians. Their entire force, under the command of Don Andres Pico, have this day laid down their arms and surrendered to my command.

"'Very respectfully, your obedient servant,

"'J. C. FREMONT,

"'*Lieutenant Colonel U. S. army, and Military*

"'*Commandant of the Territory of California.*

"'Brigadier General S. W. KEARNEY.'

"'On the day of the receipt of that report (viz.: of the 13th January), Lieutenant Colonel Fremont, at the head of a battalion of volunteers, entered the city of Los Angeles. On the 16th January an order was sent to him, relating to this battalion, by my direction, and signed by Lieutenant Emory, a copy of which I have furnished, and which I can identify if shown to me.

"'This is a copy of the order furnished to him by Lieutenant Emory.

"The paper was read, as follows:

"'HEAD QUARTERS, UNITED STATES ARMY,
CIUDAD DE LOS ANGELES, *Jan.* 16, 1847.

"'By direction of Brigadier-General Kearney, I send you a copy of a communication to him from the Secretary of War, dated June 18th, 1846, in which is the following: "These troops, and such as may be organized in California, will be under your command." The General directs that no change will be made in the organization of your battalion of volunteers, or officers appointed in it, without his sanction or approval being first obtained.

"'Very respectfully,

"'WM. H. EMORY,

"'*Lieutenant and Acting Assistant Adjutant General.*

"'Lieut. Col. J. C. FREMONT,

"'*Mounted Riflemen, Commanding*

"'*Battalion California Volunteers.*'

"On his cross-examination, General Kearney thus testifies in relation to that battalion, and the brief note which he treated as a military report for duty: '*The California battalion was under my command from the time of Lieutenant-Colonel Fremont's reporting to me on the 13th of January.*' He, therefore, swears to the fact of my *reporting* to him, and also being *under* his command; and this double swearing becomes the corner-stone of his accusation. Twice afterwards he swears to the same effect, thus: '*I was a brigadier-general in the army, and the accused was a lieutenant-colonel in it. I was in command of the battalion of the time*' (to wit: 16th and 17th). And again: '*I made no attempt to get the command; the battalion was already under me.*'

"In this way, and by dint of his own swearing, he gets me, as he swears, under his command, and thereby acquires the right to give me orders, with the resulting consequences of mutiny and disobedience if I did not obey them; and all these rights and consequences flowing from the word *report*, as found in my note of the 13th January to him.

"Now let us see with how much truth and justice this is done. From the testimony in chief, at the opening of the trial, quoted above, it would seem that, of my own head, on the 13th day of January, I reported myself and battalion, in the military sense of the word, to General Kearney for duty; that after thus reporting, and without anything else passing upon the subject, and after I had voluntarily put myself and my battalion under the command of General Kearney, I did, on the 17th, refuse to obey the order of General Kearney, in relation to said battalion, and thus became guilty of two crimes—mutiny, for which I might have been lawfully killed on the spot; and disobedience of orders, for which I may be sentenced to be shot or cashiered, or otherwise punished by this court.

"The first words of the testimony imply voluntary communication. The words are: 'about the 14th of January, 1847, I received from Lieutenant-Colonel Fremont a communication, dated the day previous, upon the march, &c., which I furnished, together with the charges to the adjutant general.' This testimony presents a voluntary act on my part, a movement of my own head, uninfluenced by any previous act of General Kearney; and so stood the case on the direct examination, on the first day of the trial.

"On the seventh day the cross-examination reached this point, and the recorded testimony shows as follows:

"Question. Did you, at Los Angeles, from the 10th to the 13th of January inclusive, address notes to Lieutenant-Colonel Fremont, and if so, how many, and for what object?

"Answer. Between those dates I addressed, I think, three communications to Lieutenant-Colonel Fremont. * * * The object of my communication was to inform Lieutenant-Colonel Fremont of our being in possession of Los Angeles, and having a strong force, &c.

"Question. Were they official orders, or familiar notes of information in regard to impending military events, and desiring information of Lieutenant-Colonel Fremont's movements in return?

"Answer. They were what are termed semi-official, written in a familiar manner, and of which I have no copies. I keep a copy of all my official communications.

"Question. Did either of those notes give the information that Governor Stockton was at Angeles?

"Answer. I have no recollection of it.

"Question. Did either of those notes, dated at 6 o'clock in the evening of the 6th of January, contain these words; 'Dear Fremont: I am here in possession of this place, with sailors and marines. We met and defeated the whole force of the Californians the 8th and 9th. They have not now to exceed 300 men concentrated. Avoid charging them, and come to me at this place. Acknowledge the hour of receipt of this, and when I may expect you Regards to Russell?'

"Answer. I cannot answer, but I think it highly probable it did. As I stated before, I kept no copies of those semi-official papers.

"Question. Did you address the accompanying letter to Lieutenant-Colonel Fremont, and at the time of its date?

"Answer. That is my writing and that is my note.

"The letter was read, as follows:

"'PUEBLA DE LOS ANGELES,
Sunday, Jan. 10, 1847—4 P. M.

"'DEAR FREMONT: We are in possession of this place, with a force of marines and sailors, having marched into it this morning. Join us as soon as you can, or let me know if you want us to march to your assistance. Avoid charging the enemy; their force does not exceed four hundred, perhaps not more than three hundred. Please acknowledge the receipt of this, and dispatch the bearer at once.

"'Yours,

"'S. W. KEARNEY,

"'*Brigadier-General, U. S. Army.*

"'Lieut. Colonel J. C. FREMONT,

"'*Mounted Rifles, Com., &c.*'

"Question. Did you also address this one to him, and at the time of its date?

"The witness, having examined the paper, said: That is my writing, and that is my note.

"It was read, as follows:

"'CIUDAD DE LOS ANGELES,
Jan. 13, 1847—12 *o'clock, noon.*

"'DEAR FREMONT: We are in force in this place—sailors and marines. Join us *as soon as possible.*

"'We are ignorant of your movements, and know nothing of you further than your armistice of yesterday.

"'Yours,

"'S. W. KEARNEY,

"'*Brigadier-General.*

"'Lieut. Colonel J. C. FREMONT.'

"Question. Did you also address this to him, and at the time it bears date?

"Answer. That is my writing and that is my note.

"It was read, as follows:

"'PUEBLA DE LOS ANGELES,
Jan. 12, 1847—*Tuesday*, 6 P. M.

"'DEAR FREMONT: I am here in possession of this place, with sailors and marines. We met and defeated the whole force of the Californians, the 8th and 9th. They have not now to exceed 300 men concentrated. Avoid charging them, and come to me at this place.

12

"'Acknowledge the hour of receipt of this, and when I may expect you. Regards to Russell.

"'Yours,

"'S. W. Kearney,

"'*Brigadier-General.*

"'Lieut. Colonel J. C. Fremont.'

"Question. Did you also write this one to him, and were the first two of the five words (*do not* charge the enemy) underscored by you, as they now appear?

"Answer. That is my writing, and that is my note, and though I have no recollection of underscoring these words, I have no doubt but I did so.

"The note was read, as follows:

"'Ciudad de los Angeles,
January 13, 1847—2 p. m.

"'Dear Fremont: We have been here since the 10th. I have plenty of marines and sailors. We know nothing of you, except your armistice of yesterday, signed by yourself. I have sent several letters to you, and fear they have been intercepted, as I have received no answer. Come here *at once*, with your whole force, and join us; or if you cannot, let me know it, and I will go to you. The enemy cannot *possibly* have near you more than 300, most probably not more than 150 men. Acknowledge the *hour* of receiving this, and send back the bearer *at once*, and write but little, as it may get into the hands of the enemy, instead of mine.

"'We defeated the enemy on the 8th and on the 9th, during our march. Since then they have been much scattered, and several, no doubt, gone home.

"'I repeat, we are ignorant of everything relating to your command, except what we conjecture from your armistice, signed by yourself. Success to you!

"'Yours,

"'S. W. Kearney,

"'*Brigadier General.*

"'*Do not* charge the enemy.

"'Lieutenant Colonel J. C. Fremont,
"'*Mounted Rifles, &c.*'

"This is what is shown by the cross-examination! The note of the 13th, so far from being voluntary, that it was actually pulled and dragged out of me by General Kearney, by dint of repeated, urgent solicitations, and affectionate notes, all requiring information of my position and movements, and all concealing the fact that Commodore Stockton was with him at Los Angeles, and his commander-in-chief. "Dear Fremont," four times repeated, and four applications for informations of him, show the character of the notes sent and the object of sending them; that they were familiar notes of information, such as are written in all services and between officers of all ranks, and which are used for no purpose in the world except for the sake of the information they contain. But, while the notes show this, the cross-examination was impotent to gain the same knowledge, either of their number, object, or contents. To the question, How many of these notes? he answers three, he 'thinks.' Not being in the habit of destroying originals, I produce him four. To the question, With what object? he replies that it was to give him (myself) information of his (General Kearney's) being in possession of Los Angeles, &c., &c. The notes being read show that, in addition to that information to me, they desired information from me also. To the inquiry whether either of these notes gave information that Governor Stockton was at Los Angeles? the answer is, 'I have no recollection of it.'

"The notes themselves being read, each one shows that the presence of Governor Stockton was not even hinted. The same four notes tell something else very incompatible with the testimony of a previous day; they tell Lieutenant-Colonel Fremont the force gone against him may be 300 or 400 men. In the previous swearing are these words: "And a small party under Don Andreas Pico—*which party I have never understood to have exceeded fifty or sixty men*—went to Couenga, and entered into capitulation with Lieutenant-Colonel Fremont.

"From these notes, then, the great fact was brought out that the communication, presented as a voluntary act, was extracted from Lieutenant-Colonel Fremont by General Kearney himself; that instead of being a military reporting for duty, it was a reporting for information only; that, instead of being an official communication, it was a familiar private note, in answer to familiar, private, and apparently most affectionate notes.

"Upon their face they contradicted the swearing of General Kearney; and it is further contradicted by facts and circumstances drawn from himself or from authentic sources. The direct testimony at the opening of the trial, says: 'On the day of the *receipt* of that letter, &c., &c., Lieutenant-Colonel Fremont, at the head of a battalion of volunteers, entered the city of Los Angeles." Now, all the testimony agrees (and such is the fact) that on my entrance into Los Angeles with my battalion, I went direct to the quarters assigned it by Governor Stockton through Colonel Russell;

then reported in person to Governor Stockton, and afterwards called on General Kearney.

"That note so extracted from me, and so perverted, did not fetch itself to Los Angeles. Some person must have brought it, and did; and that person was Col. W. H. Russell; and he has given an account of his mission, and of his conversation with General Kearney, wholly incompatible with the present imputed intention of that note. On the 37th day of that trial, that witness (Colonel Russell) was introduced, and the second question put to him (the first being only to show his rank in the Californian battalion) was this: 'Were you sent to Los Angeles, from the plains of Couenga, by Lieutenant-Colonel Fremont? If so, at what time, and for what purpose?' and the answer was: 'I was sent by Lieutenant-Colonel Fremont from the plains of Couenga, about the 13th of January, 1847, for the purpose of ascertaining who was in chief command, and to make report of the capitulation made on that day to whomsoever I should find in the chief command at Los Angeles.' The next question: 'Will you state how you executed that mission?' Answer. 'I went to the quarters of General Kearney first, and inquired of him whether his arrival in the country had superseded Commodore Stockton, who, before, had been recognized as chief commander. From General Kearney I learned that Commodore Stockton was still in chief command, and by him I was directed to make my report to the commodore.' This was the testimony of Colonel R. on that point on his examination in chief. On my cross-examination (39th) day the following questions were put by the judge advocate:

"'Do you recollect General Kearney told you expressly that he was serving under Commodore Stockton, or did he say anything more explicit than, as was said by you, that Commodore Stockton was in chief command, and you would carry your report of the capitulation to him?

"Answer. 'He told me distinctly that he was serving under Commodore Stockton, and had been doing so from San Diego.'

"Question by judge advocate. 'Was Captain Turner present at that interview?'

"Answer. 'I am not positive, but believe he was.'

"On the fortieth day of the trial, the court took up the cross-examination; and, on this point, with the following results:

"Question. 'When you were sent to Los Angeles, to ascertain who was in command, had you any orders what to do if you found the chief command claimed by both Commodore Stockton and General Kearney.'

"Answer. 'My instructions from Lieutenant-Colonel Fremont were to proceed to Los Angeles, and carefully to inquire as to who was in chief command, and to make my report accordingly. No such contingency was contemplated, I think, by Lieutenant-Colonel Fremont, when he dispatched me on that mission, as the command being claimed by them both.'

"Question by a member. 'Why did you first report to General Kearney rather than to Commodore Stockton?'

"Answer. '*I bore a letter* to General Kearney from Lieutenant-Colonel Fremont, *in acknowledgment* of one received by Lieutenant-Colonel Fremont *from* General Kearney, and for the further reason that we were totally ignorant of the object of General Kearney's being in the country, and my orders from Lieutenant-Colonel Fremont were that I should ascertain all about it.'

"Question by the court. 'State all the conversation which passed between you and Lieutenant-Colonel Fremont on the subject of choice of commanders, after you returned and reported to him the result of your visit to Los Angeles?'

"Answer. 'I met Lieutenant-Colonel Fremont at the head of his battalion, on the morning of the 14th of January (as I stated in my chief examination), about five or six miles from Los Angeles, and told him I had had much conversation with both General Kearney and Commodore Stockton, touching their respective positions in the country. That I was satisfied, from what had occurred, that General Kearney was a better friend of his than Commodore Stockton; but from General Kearney's own admission, I regretted to have to give it as my opinion that we should have to look to Commodore Stockton still as commander-in-chief. That I found Commodore Stockton exercising the functions of commander-in-chief, and submitted to implicitly, as I thought, by General Kearney. This was the substance of my communication to Lieutenant-Colonel Fremont; and he, I think, with equal reluctance, at the time, came to the same conclusion.'

"This is the testimony of the witness who bore the note which is represented here (and made the foundation of the prosecution against me), as a military report, to put myself and my battalion under orders of General Kearney, and actually so placing myself and battalion under his orders.

"From all the testimony of Colonel Russell, it seems clear that General Kearney undertook to gain me over to his side by flatteries, by offering the governorship of California, and by exciting resentment against Commodore Stockton; and failing by all of these means to accomplish that purpose, he tried the experiment of an order upon me, with the menace of 'unquestionable ruin,' which ruin, it would seem, he has been laboring ever since to effect.

"That this construction was not put upon my note at the time it was received, seems clear from official cotemporaneous acts of General Kearney himself. Thus, on the 14th day of January, he writes to the War Department, from Los Angeles, that 'this morning Lieutenant-Colonel Fremont, of the regiment of mounted riflemen, *reached here* with 400 volunteers,' &c., &c. No word of reporting to him, or placing myself and battalion under his command. Surely that was the time to have communicated to the War Department such an essential piece of intelligence. In the concluding part of the same letter he says: 'On their their arrival (troops from New York and New Mexico) I shall, agreeably to the instructions of the President of the United States, have the management of affairs in this country, and will endeavor to carry out his views in relation to it,' words which necessarily mean that he did not consider himself entitled to command until the arrival of those troops, or else that he intended to avail himself of those troops to obtain command.

"The letters of the 16th and 17th of January, from General Kearney to Commodore Stockton, are significant at this point. 1. They are totally silent on the subject of my having placed myself and the battalion under his command. 2. They show the whole contest, up to the 17th, to be between the two superiors. 3. The letter of the 17th shows a shifting of the grounds of his claim to command in California, basing it on *his* victories of the 8th and 9th, and the capitulation of the enemy to me on the 13th. The words of the letter, significant of this change, are: 'As in consequence of the defeat of the enemy on the 8th and 9th instant by the troops under my command, and the capitulation entered into on the 13th instant, by Lieutenant-Colonel Fremont with the leaders of the Californians, in which the people under arms and in the field agree to disperse and to remain quiet and peaceable, the country may now, for the first time, be considered as conquered and taken possession of by us, and as I am prepared to carry out the President's instructions to me, which you oppose, I must, for the purpose of preventing a collision between us, and possibly a civil war in consequence of it, remain silent for the present, leaving with you the great responsibility of doing that for which you have no authority, and preventing me from complying with the President's orders.'

"The value of this testimony, which would make me to have reported to General Kearney, and placed myself and battalion under his command, must now be understood. I undertake to say there is no authentic modern instance of a note, as innocent in itself, and extracted from the writer under such circumstances, so totally perverted from its meaning, and made the foundation of such a prosecution as I have endured.

"If men are to be capitally and infamously tried for such a note, no one is safe in writing.

"I am charged here with a great military crime. I should have been guilty, not only of it, but of an inexcusable breach of faith, if I *had* made a report of myself and battalion to General Kearney, and so placed under the command of that officer the troops raised by the means and authority of Commodore Stockton, and by him intrusted to me.

"I now close this defence to specification first, of charge two, for disobedience of lawful orders.

"The second specification, under the head of mutiny, is for raising and attempting to raise troops, on the 25th of January, 1847; and is in these words.

"'*Specification* 2. In this, that he, Lieutenant-Colonel John C. Fremont of the regiment of mounted riflemen, United States army, being in command of a battalion of volunteers organized in California, which were placed by the aforesaid orders of the Secretary of War, of June 18, 1846, under the command of Brigadier-General Kearney, did issue an order to Captain J. K. Wilson, at Angeles, January 25, 1847, in the following words, to wit:

"'ANGELES, *January* 25, 1847.

"'SIR: You are hereby authorized and directed to raise a company of men to constitute the second company of artillery in the California service, and for that purpose are detached from your present command.

"'You will please report the number you will be able to enlist with as little delay as possible. You are authorized to enlist the men for three months, and to promise them as compensation $25 per month

"'Respectfully,

"'J. C. FREMONT,

"'*Lieut. Col. commanding California force in U. S. service.*

"'To Captain S. K. WILSON,

"'*Light Artillery.*'

"'Thereby raising and attempting to raise troops, in violation and contempt of the lawful command aforesaid of his superior officer, Brigadier-General Kearney, of date January 16, 1847, and thereby acting openly in defiance of, and in mutiny against, the authority of his superior officer aforesaid, by raising and attempting to raise troops, and by proclaiming himself to be, and assuming to act as commander of the United States forces in California.'"

The same act is specification No. 2, in charge, for disobedience of orders—the orders charged to have been disobeyed being the order of January 16, 1847, against the organization of the California battalion.

"I will consider both of these specifications together, and arrange the matter of defence under these general heads: 1. That I was, at that time, governor and commander-in-chief in California. 2. That General Kearney had no right to command the battalion at that time. 3. That the order of the 16th of January, 1847, besides being illegal in itself, had no relation to any other change in the battalion than the one intended at the time it was given.

"1. That I was then governor and commander-in-chief in California is proved by the testimony of Commodore Stockton, and the production of the original commission; and his right to bestow that commission upon me resulted from his own right to constitute himself governor. Both acts were done under the law of nations; and by virtue of the right of conquest; by virtue of the orders and instructions of the President of the United States, charging the naval commanders in the Pacific ocean, exclusively, with the conquest and civil government of California, until relieved under the instructions of the 5th of November, 1846. These instructions did not arrive until after the alleged commission of the act of mutiny and disobedience now under examination; and, when they did arrive, were never communicated to me at all.

"I am advised by counsel, that the appointment of himself as governor, by Commodore Stockton, was a valid appointment under the law of nations; and that upon the same principle, his appointment of myself as his successor was equally valid; and that in neither case was the approval of the President of the United States necessary to the validity of the appointment, though each revocable by him at his pleasure; and therefore proper to be made known to him. This I am advised is the law; but being now prosecuted for mutiny and for disobedience of orders, in assuming and usurping the governorship of California, and it being the President alone who could order my trial in this case (accused as I am by my commanding general), it becomes material to show that this appointment, and the intention to make it long before it was made, was duly communicated to him, and, while not disapproved, was impliedly sanctioned, and never revoked. For the fact of the communication of the intention to appoint me his successor, I refer to Governor Stockton's official dispatch of August 28, 1846, from Los Angeles, sent in by Mr. Carson; and for the fact of his communicating the fact of his having appointed me, I refer to his official dispatch of January 22, 1847, from San Diego. The first of these dispatches arrived by the hands of Mr. Fitzpatrick early in November, 1846, and their general contents were noticed by the President in his annual message of December following, and in the reports of the Secretaries of War and Navy, and all in terms of general approval. Passages from this message and these reports have been already quoted, and require no repetition; and from them and from the communication of Governor Stockton's acts as governor, to Congress, at the time by the administration, I assume it to be proved that the intent to appoint me governor was known to the government in November, 1846, and not disapproved by it. The dispatch of the 22d January, 1847, was received from Lieutenant Gray of the navy, in the month of April following; and, so far as I can learn, his act was not disavowed in appointing me governor. Even if it was, the disavowal could only operate from the time it would be known to me, which it never was.

"The commission from Governor Stockton was in these words:

"'To all whom it may concern, greeting: Having, by authority of the President and Congress of the United States of North America, and by right of conquest, taken possession of that portion of territory heretofore known as Upper and Lower California, and having declared the same to be a territory of the United States, under the name of the territory of California, and having established laws for the government of the same territory, I, Robert F. Stockton, governor and commander-in-chief of the same, do in virtue of the authority in me vested, and in obedience to the aforementioned laws, appoint J. C. Fremont, Esq., governor and commander-in-chief of the territory of California, until the President of the United States shall otherwise direct.

"'Given under my hand and seal on this sixteenth day of January, [SEAL.] Anno Domini one thousand eight hundred and forty-seven, at the Ciudad de los Angeles.

"'R. F. STOCKTON, *Governor, &c.*'

"On this state of facts, I maintain that I was duly and legally governor and commander-in-chief in California at the time of the act done, which is charged as mutiny and as disobedience of orders, in the two specifications, under the two charges referred to.

"2. That General Kearney had no right to command the battalion at that time.

"The facts and the arguments in support of this proposition are the same which have been already used in answer to specifications first in both the first charges, with the addition of arguments to show that Gen. Kearney had no more right, at that time, to command me, in my governorship of California, than he had to command Governor Stockton while in the same office; and that, in fact, this prosecution, in the specifications under consideration, is nothing but a continuation of the contest which began at San Diego with Governor Stockton, and which ought to have been finished with him.

"General Kearney claimed authority to command the battalion, first, by virtue of his instructions, and next, by the assumption that I had put myself under his command. I presume this latter ground has been effectually disposed of heretofore. The first one has received some answers, and has others to receive. It has been argued from the beginning—from San Diego to this place, and from December, 1846, to this time—that the instructions to General Kearney were conditional: '*Should you conquer and take possession of New Mexico and California or considerable places in either, you will establish temporary civil governments therein.*' These instructions are evidently conditional, and only applicable to a country unconquered, and without a civil government. On the contrary, before General Kearney left New Mexico he had '*positive*' (using the word of his order) information that all this was already done, and immediately acted upon that '*positive*' intelligence, by diminishing the force with which he had set out. He met Mr. Christopher Carson, bearer of official dispatches from Governor Stockton, and of private letters from myself, learned the true state of things from him, turned him back as his guide, reduced '*the army of the West*,' with which he was to conquer California, to an escort for his personal safety in travelling through the country, and went on, as the sequel showed, not to execute government orders, already executed by others, but (what is rarely seen in any military service) to take from others the fruits of their toils, hardships, dangers, and victories. He took the bearer of dispatches, sent by the real conquerors, to guide him—show him the way—to the conquered country; before he arrived there, sent for aid from the conqueror, and received it in a handsome detachment, nearly equal to half his force, and after fighting an action with that aid, was four days upon a hill in a state of siege, from which he was relieved by two hundred and fifteen men sent out by Commodore Stockton to conduct him into San Diego, where he was safe. This was not the conquest of California, nor was the plain of San Pasqual, or the hill of San Bernardo, the conquest of '*considerable places*' in that province, so as to give a right to govern it. The subsequent operations were under the command of Commodore

Stockton; and it is because he should appear as conqueror, in order to get a right under his instructions to the governorship, that the claim has been set up by General Kearney to have commanded the troops to Los Angeles, and gained the victories of the 8th and 9th of January, and, thereupon, in conjunction with the capitulation of Couenga, started a new claim to the governorship, on the assumption that he had just conquered the country. This new claim is started in the letter of 17th January, 1847, from General Kearney to Commodore Stockton, and clearly shows his own views, at that time, of the conditional nature of his instructions. The letter has been quoted. Its effective and applicable words at this point are, 'As, in consequence of the defeat of the enemy on the 8th and 9th instant, by the troops under *my* command, and the capitulation entered into on the 13th instant by Lieutenant-Colonel Fremont with the leaders of the Californias, &c., the country may *now*, for the *first* time, be considered as *conquered*, and taken *possession* of by us; and as I am prepared to carry out the President's instructions to *me*, which *you* oppose,' &c., &c.

"This extract shows General Kearney's own opinions of his instructions at the time he wrote that letter, and that they were conditional upon the fact of conquering and taking possession of the country. It shows his opinion; but, if the facts were not as he supposed, to wit, that *he* was commander-in-chief in the actions of the 8th and 9th, and that the country was then, for the *first* time, conquered and taken possession of; if these facts fail him as they do, then his new claim to command in California fails also; and Commodore Stockton, as commander-in-chief on the 8th and 9th, becomes the second time the conqueror. That the rest may be well conceived, from the circumstances under which they were issued, as well as from their terms.

"The navy had been charged, from the beginning of the war (and before it in anticipation), with the exclusive conquest, preservation and government, in California. In giving a military officer orders to go into California to conquer, &c., &c., the contingency that everything required to be done might have been already done, was too obvious to be overlooked, and would naturally be provided for in making the military instructions conditional.

"The naval instructions say: 'Previous instructions have informed you of the intentions of this government, pending the war with Mexico, to take and hold possession of California. * * * * The object of the United States is, under its right as a belligerent nation, to possess itself entirely of Upper California. * * * The object of the United States has reference to ultimate peace with Mexico; and if, at that peace, the basis of the *uti possidetis* shall be established, the government expects, *through your forces*, to be in actual possession of Upper California. * * * This will bring with it the necessity of a civil administration. Such a government should be established under your protection. * * * For your further instruction, I inclose to you a copy of confidential instructions from the War Department to Brigadier General Kearney, who is ordered overland to California. You will also communicate your instructions to him, and inform him that they have the sanction of the President.'

"These instructions were not received by Commodore Stockton, but were anticipated by him, and this anticipation obtained for him the express approbation of the President. The dispatch of the 5th of November, from the Secretary of the Navy to the commodore, contained this clause in reference to his operations in California: 'And it is highly gratifying that so much has been done in anticipation of the orders which have been transmitted.'

"This was written near four months after the transmission of the orders of July 12, and is a full ratification of all that had been done in anticipation of them.

But a higher view remains to be taken of the conditional character of the instructions to General Kearney, a view which involves their absolute repeal and nullity, unless understood conditionally; and I am advised by counsel that even that understanding of them cannot save them from the fate of total abrogation until subsequently revived by the instructions of the 5th of November, 1846. A few dates and facts establish this view. The instructions to General Kearney, on which he relies for his authority, are dated the 3rd and 18th of June, 1846. Now, it so happens that, on the 12th day of July, in the month following, instructions of the most peremptory character were dispatched to Commodore Sloat to conquer, hold, and govern California, and to let General Kearney know of these instructions, and that they had the sanction of the President. Here are extracts from the orders to Commodore Sloat; and, although they did not reach his hands, nor those of his successor, Commodore Stockton, until after the country was conquered, yet, I am advised to say, their effect is the same upon this prosecution. This is not case of an officer prosecuted for not obeying instructions, in which case it must be shown they came to his hands; but it is a prosecution against me, as successor to Governor Stockton, for doing what the instructions commanded. In this case, the anticipation of the orders is an additional merit in complying with them; and such is the case with the orders in question.

"These instructions are near a month later than those to General

Kearney, and not only especially confide the conquest, preservation, and civil government of California to the naval commanders, but require the naval forces to hold the country till the peace, and direct General Kearney to be informed accordingly; and further informed that all this instruction to the naval commanders had the sanction of the President.

"I, with the battalion I commanded, was part of the naval force to which this duty was confided. (Commodore Stockton's testimony, 37th day.) This order remained in force until the instructions of the 5th of November arrived in California, which was not until the 13th day of February, 1847, AND WHICH WERE NEVER COMMUNICATED TO ME, AND OF WHICH I REMAINED TOTALLY IGNORANT TILL SINCE THE COMMENCEMENT OF THIS TRIAL. Neither General Kearney, Commodore Shubrick, or Commodore Biddle, communicated them to me, although I was then governor and commander-in-chief in California, under the commission of Commodore Stockton, to whom the instructions of the 5th of November were addressed; nor were they communicated to Commodore Stockton himself, until more than a month after they had been received. They were evidently concealed from me, for a purpose not yet explained. By these instructions the military and civil duties, confided to the navy, were transferred to the commanding officer on land; another proof that the land-officer did not then possess them, and that officer was specially named as General Kearney or Colonel Mason.

"The instruction says: 'The President has deemed it best, for the public interests, to invest the *military* officer commanding with the direction of the operations on *land*, and with the *administrative* functions of government over the people and territory occupied by us. You will *relinquish* to Colonel Mason, or to General Kearney, if the latter shall arrive before you have done so, the entire control over these matters, and 'turn over' to him all papers necessary to the performance of his duties. If officers of the navy are employed in the performance of civil or military duties, you will withdraw or continue them, at your discretion, taking care to put them to their appropriate duty in the squadron, if the army officer commanding does not wish their services on land.'

"Until this dispatch was received by the naval commanders, those of July the 12th abrogating those to General Kearney, remained in full force; and it was only by virtue of these orders, of the 5th of November, that he acquired the command, militarily or civilly, in California. And it is in evidence that Commodore Shubrick had received these instructions, of the 12th of July, at the time that General Kearney visited him at Monterey, and had consultations with him, and was sent by him in a ship to Yerva Buena, and that he made known to General Kearney, at that time, that the naval commanders were charged with the whole conquest, defence and government of California; and that they (General Kearney and Commodore Shubrick) mutually agreed not to disturb the existing state of affairs until the government had further been heard from.

"It is clear that the instructions to the different branches of the service were not properly consistent, and that concurrences might have arisen under them that would have necessarily produced a conflict of authority; but it is also clear that it was the intent of the government that the right and duty of the navy to conquer, preserve and govern California should remain complete and entire until the arrival of the instructions of November 5th, and that no concurrence did arise that, under the plain interpretation of the army instructions, could justify a collision. All this is fairly stated by the Secretary of the Navy, Mr. Mason, under the express orders of the President, in a dispatch of the 14th of June, 1847, directed to the naval commanding officer on the California station.

"That dispatch contains these passages:

"'The *misapprehension* between the commanding officers of the army and navy in California, which is mentioned in the letter of Commodore Shubrick, above referred to, must long since have been removed by *the very explicit instructions which have since been received in that country.* * * * * At the commencement of the war with Mexico the United States had no military force in California of any description whatever, *and the conquest of that country was from necessity, therefore, devolved exclusively upon the navy.* * * The conquest brought with it the necessity of a temporary civil government, and, on the 12th of July, 1846, Commodore Sloat was informed that *such a government should be established under his protection.* Contrary to all expectation this dispatch did not reach California *until the arrival there of General Kearney*

"'On the 5th of November, 1846, Commodore Stockton was informed that the President has deemed it best for the public interests to invest the military officer commanding *with the direction of the operations on land, and with the administrative functions over the people and territory occupied by us.* He was also directed to relinquish to Colonel Mason, or to General Kearney, if the latter should arrive before he had done so, the entire control over these matters, and to turn over to him all papers necessary to the performance of his duties. *It was believed that even this dispatch might anticipate the arrival in California of General Kearney.*

"'SIMILAR instructions were communicated to Commodore Stock

ton under date of *January* 14, 1847, and were renewed to Commodore Shubrick under date of *May* 10, 1847. A copy of these last instructions, which on this subject are very full and distinct, are herewith enclosed.'

"All these dispatches were too late. The mischief was all done before they arrived, and they leave the naval officers completely justified, and General Kearney wholly without excuse for attempting to make himself governor of California in a case not contemplated by his instructions, and in which he would have to commence with disorganizing an established civil government before he could begin to organize one. His whole conduct, from the day he met Mr. Carson, was contrary to the intent and meaning of his instructions. He was to conquer California; it was already conquered. He was to establish a civil government; it was already done. He was to lead an army to California; he took only a personal escort. He turned back two-thirds of his dragoons; he should have turned back the whole, and himself with them. He should not have applied to Governor Stockton to send him aid to San Pasqual, and to the hill of San Bernardo, if he intended to contend with him for supremacy after he got there. He should not have attempted to found a claim to the governorship on the victories of the 8th and 9th of January, after the refutation of his claim by Commodore Stockton at San Diego. He should not have pretended to have been commander-in-chief on the march to Los Angeles, in order to found upon it a claim to the governorship in right of conquest. He should not, even if the letter of his instructions had borne him out (which they did not), have attempted to take the fruits of conquest from those who had conquered the country before he came to it, and without whose helping hand he could not have got to it.

"I have now made clear the right of Governor Stockton, under whom I held the governorship of California at the time of the act done, which is charged in the specifications under examination to be governor himself, upon his own assumption of the office, and afterwards to appoint me his successor; and that these governorships were valid under the law of nations, until disapproved by the President, or the incumbents in some way lawfully relieved or discharged. Having done this, I am instructed by counsel to resume my original position, as in the letter of the 17th January, in declaring that all this difficulty in California was a question between my two superiors, which should have been settled by the government between them, and not settled in my person by trying me for mutiny and disobedience against one of them—charges to which I might have been well exposed in disobeying the other. And I am further instructed by counsel to renew, and to repeat, in the most solemn manner, the PROTEST heretofore filed in the War Office by them, in my name, against the ILLEGALITY and INJUSTICE of thus trying me for the acts of Commodore Stockton and General Kearney, or for declining the responsibility of settling their disputes of authority.

"2. The second head of my defence, in answer to these two specifications is, that General Kearney at that time had no right to command the battalion to which the order of the 16th of January was applicable. The argument heretofore made on this point, is referred to without repeating it, to show that this battalion was part of the naval forces under Commodore Stockton, and that it was my duty, as stated in my letter of the 17th of January, to continue to receive orders from him in relation to it.

"3. The third head of my defence to these two specifications is, that the order of the 16th of January, 1847, besides being illegal in itself, had no relation to any other change in the battalion than the changes intended at the time it was given. This illegality has been heretofore shown, both as being issued without authority by General Kearney, but also because it was in positive violation of the rights of the men, most of whom had engaged for the expedition alone, and that being over, were entitled, by their contract and by law, to their discharge. Many were accordingly discharged, and others engaged, and all for the necessary service of the country, and under my authority as governor and commander-in-chief. The nullity of the order, as being founded on the familiar note of information *extracted from me* by General Kearney, and perverted into a military official report, placing myself and the battalion under his command, has heretofore been shown; and the facts and arguments adduced on that point are now referred to, without being repeated, as applicable to this order of the 16th of January, at its present reproduction, and as often as it shall be produced hereafter. Illegal and null as it was for the purpose of its issue, it is clear this order had no relation, at the time it issued, to anything but the re-organization then intended, and which resulted from discharges proper to be made, and promoting Captain Gillespie into my place, I being that day commissioned as governor and commander-in-chief, to take effect on Commodore Stockton's departure. The circumstances of the order, delivered in the night, limited it to that immediate impending operation. The charges, as preferred by General Kearney, so limited it, he having testified before this court that he preferred but a single charge (understood to be mutiny); that these were not his charges; that they had been changed. This can only mean that *he* has not extended the order of the 16th of

January to subsequent acts—to changes subsequently made in the battalion. With this corresponds his testimony before this court (9th day, near the close), that he left no orders for me when he left Los Angeles. The question then put to General Kearney on this point was, '*Did you leave any orders for Lieutenant-Colonel Fremont, or take leave of him, or give notice to him of your going away, or let him know where you were going?*' The answer is, 'I did not;' this answer applying categorically and negatively to all four points of the interrogatory, and establishing the fact that General Kearney left Los Angeles without leaving any orders for me, without taking leave of me, without giving me notice that he was going away, and without letting me know where he was going; and I am instructed by counsel to say, that it is carrying the doctrine of constructive criminality rather too far (even if General Kearney had been my lawful and acknowledged commander), to construe into the crimes of mutiny and disobedience of orders, and of conduct prejudicial to good order and discipline, any act done after he was gone, when I had no possible guide but my own discretion.

"*Specification* 3, under the charge of mutiny, and also for disobedience of orders, is, for the order of Louis McLane, Esq., of the United States navy, in his character of major of artillery in the California service, to make further enlistments, and to examine into the defences of the country. The answer to this specification is the same as heretofore, both with respect to General Kearney's authority, and my own rights and duties as governor and commander-in-chief in California, and the nullity and inapplicability of the order of January 16th, 1847.

"*Specification* 4, under the charge of mutiny, is based on the letter of February 7th, 1847, to Commodore Shubrick—a letter which is set out in full in the specification.

"The offence imputed is twofold; first, mutiny, in assuming to be governor; and second, mutiny, in endeavoring to entice Commodore Shubrick to countenance and abet me.

"The letter was written in answer to one from Commodore Shubrick to me, and I received another in reply; that in reply I will now introduce, to show that at least Commodore Shubrick himself did not look upon what I had written in the light in which the ingenuity of this prosecution has contrived to represent it.

"'U. S. SHIP INDEPENDENCE,
HARBOR OF MONTEREY, *February* 13, 1847.

"'SIR: I have the honor to acknowledge the receipt of your letter of the 7th instant, and shall detain your courier as short a time as possible for my answer, and will also avail myself of your kind offer, to forward dispatches to the United States.

"'When I wrote to you on the 25th ultimo, I was not informed of the arrival of Brigadier General Kearney in California, and addressed you as the senior officer of the army in the territory; on the 28th, however, having understood that the general was at Los Angeles, I addressed a similar letter to him.

"'On the 8th instant, General Kearney arrived in this harbor, in the sloop-of-war, Cyane, and left by the same conveyance on the 11th, for San Francisco. While the general was here, we consulted fully, as enjoined on me by my instructions, and on him by his, on the measures necessary to be taken by us for the security of the territory of California.

"'I am looking daily for the arrival of Commodore Stockton in this harbor, when I shall, of course, receive from him a full account of the measures taken by him while in command of the squadron.

"'It is to be hoped that the pleasure of the President of the United States on the subject of the organization of a civil government, and of the measures taken by Commodore Stockton and yourself, may be soon known, and it will give me pleasure at all times to co-operate with the civil government, as well as with the military commander-in-chief, for the peace and security of the territory.

"'I regret to say that, not anticipating any unusual draft on them, the funds brought by me are barely sufficient, with the most economical expenditure, to meet the wants of the squadron.

"'I am, very respectfully, sir, your most obedient servant,

"'W. BRANFORD SHUBRICK,

"'*Commander-in-chief, U. S. naval forces.*

"'Lieutenant Colonel FREMONT, &c., &c., &c.'

"The plain deductions of this letter are, that Commodore Shubrick and General Kearney, having met at Monterey, had consulted together, compared their several instructions, agreed upon their respective powers, and arranged the course of action they judged proper. All this appears in the third paragraph. What the course of action agreed upon was, is to be drawn from the fifth paragraph; and the necessary inference is, that it had been found either not competent, or not proper, to disturb the existing state of affairs, before 'the pleasure of the President' should be further ascertained. The letter does not bear any other interpretation; so that, whatever the tenure of my office as governor may have been previously, this amounts in the legal phrase, to *quieting me in possession*, by common consent, till such time as the government at home should direct differently or definitively. This is the plain import of the letter, and if anything contrary to it was intended, I never heard of it, nor was anything contrary done, till more than two weeks after the contingency reserved (farther instructions from the government) had happened. That I did not misconstrue this letter, as I received it then, and as circumstances justified my construction of it, is rendered certain by the additional light which I have upon it now. This additional light is found in the dispatch of Commodore Shubrick to the government, of even date with the above letter to me. In this dispatch is the following:

"'SIR: Since my letters of the 26th, 27th, and 28th ultimo, no important change, so far as I can learn, has taken place in the territory. The people seem to be settling down into quiet acquiescence *in the change of government.* Those best acquainted with their temper and disposition, do not apprehend further disturbance of the peace of the country.

"'General Kearney arrived here on the 8th, in the sloop-of-war Cyane; and, after the adoption of such measures as we thought necessary here, *I sent him to San Francisco*, in the Cyane, to which place I should have accompanied him, but that I am looking daily for the arrival of Commodore Stockton from San Diego, and it is important that I should receive his reports before I go further.

"'You will have learned ere this that an unfortunate difference has taken place between Commodore Stockton and General Kearney, and between the general and Colonel Fremont, growing out of the *appointment of Colonel Fremont as civil governor of California by the commodore*, and the refusal of the colonel to recognize the authority of the general.

"'I have, as enjoined on me by my instructions, exchanged opinions with General Kearney, and shall *continue to concert* with him *such measures as may seem best* for keeping quiet possession of California.

"'With regard to the civil government of territory, *authority* for the establishment of which is contained in your instructions to Commodore Sloat, of 12th July last, which I received by the Lexington, measures have been, in my opinion, *prematurely taken* by Commodore Stockton, and *an appointment of governor made*, of a gentleman who, I am led to believe, is not acceptable to the people of California; *but* as the intention to make the appointment was, I understand, communicated to the President as early as August last, and information as to his wishes may be soon expected, *I have determined to await such information*, and confine myself for the present, to arrangements for the *quiet possession of the territory*, and for the blockade of the coast of Mexico.'

"Now, this is conclusive of Commodore Shubrick's intentions and opinions, his views of his authority, and of the manner he determined to exercise it. It is conclusive that though he was pleased to impute *precipitancy* to the action of Commodore Stockton, and had been 'led to believe' that the appointment made by him was not of the right sort of a person, yet that he did not question its legality, nor the authority for making it. It is also conclusive that whatever doubts he had as to the *propriety* of the appointment made by Commodore Stockton, he did not feel authorized, even under the powers which he held, to disturb it; or at least that he declined to do so. Not to disturb, was to continue; '*to await*' the information from the government, concerning the appointment, was to recognize the appointment in the meantime, and, in effect (if that had been necessary), to confirm it.

"Such was the action of Commodore Shubrick after a comparison of his instructions with those of General Kearney, after consultation with that officer; and such was the effect of that action upon my appointment.

"I now proceed to show that, in determining on this course of action, Commodore Shubrick had the agreement and acquiescence of General Kearney. This appears in the official dispatch of the letter of 15th March, which, after relating his meeting with Commodore Shubrick at Monterey, on the 8th of February, proceeds as follows:

"'On my showing to Commodore Shubrick my instructions from the War Department, of June 3d and 18th, 1846, he was at once prepared to pay *all proper respect* to them; and being at that time the commander-in-chief of the naval forces on this station, he acknowledged me as *the head and commander of the troops* in California, which Commodore Stockton and Lieutenant-Colonel Fremont had hitherto refused. He then showed me the instructions to Commodore Sloat of July 12th, from the Navy Department, received by the Lexington, at Valparaiso, on the 2d December, and which he had brought with him from there; and, as they contained *directions for Commodore Sloat to take charge of the civil affairs in California*, I immediately told Commodore Shubrick that *I cheerfully acquiesced*, and was ready to afford him any assistance in my power. We *agreed* upon our separate *duties;* and *I* then went to the bay of San Francisco, taking with me Lieutenant Halleck, of the engineers, besides Captain Turner and Lieutenant Warner, when was made a reconnoissance of the bay, with a view to the selection of sites for fortifications, for the protection of shipping in the harbor and the security of the land forces.'

"This establishes that General Kearney acknowledged the *authority* of Commodore Shubrick over the civil affairs of the territory, and *acquiesced* in the determination of that officer not to disturb Commodore Stockton's appointment until further information from the government; and that the two *agreed* upon their separate duties in the premises. This letter also establishes another important circumstance, viz.: the true weight and value attached by General Kearney himself to his instructions. '*On showing to Commodore Shubrick my instructions, he was at once prepared to pay all proper respect to them, and being at that time commander-in-chief of the naval forces, he acknowledged me* AS THE HEAD AND COMMANDER OF THE TROOPS," &c. The latter part of the sentence rests entirely upon General Kearney; the letter of Commodore Shubrick, containing nothing of the sort, and the phrase used in it towards General Kearney, viz.: '*I sent him* in the Cyane,' &c., would seem to imply the contrary. But grant General Kearney's position, and it results that in his own estimation a '*proper respect*' to his instructions only required him to be acknowledged as 'the head and commander *of the troops*,' and that he did not consider himself entitled under them to interfere with the civil affairs. General Kearney adds, after stating that 'he acknowledged me as the head and commander of the troops,' the words, '*which Commodore Stockton and Lieutenant-Colonel Fremont had hitherto refused.*' Now, what is the testimony to this point? Commodere Stockton testifies: 'After General Kearney arrived, and in my quarters and in presence of two of my military family, *I offered* to make him *commander-in-chief over all of us.* He said *no;* that the *force was mine.*'

"The agreement as to their respective powers, between Commodore Shubrick and General Kearney, and the determination of the former, with the acquiescence of the latter, that the state of affairs then existing should await further information from home, was, no doubt, the legal and proper course, and had it been continued in, every thing would have proceeded harmoniously. It was continued in, so far as appears, until after the receipt of the instructions, which they had determined to await. The wrong consisted in not obeying those instructions. I put out of view entirely, in this connection, my right to be lawfully and regularly *relieved*, and plant myself on the express letter of the instructions of the 5th November. These are mandatory to the naval commanders to *relinquish* the control of the civil administration, and to '*turn over*' the papers connected with it. The only way in which they could be *obeyed* was for that commander to inform me of the order he had received, and take from my hands the office, and the archives connected with it, that he might, as directed, 'relinquish' and 'turn them over' to General Kearney. For some purpose yet unexplained—unless its object is seen in this prosecution—they were not obeyed. I was kept in ignorance of the wishes of the government, and General Kearney undertook by wrongful orders to get possession from me of what he could only lawfully receive from Commodore Shubrick.

"And on this I leave the defence of this act, both where it is charged as mutiny, and where as an offence against discipline.

"*Specification* 5, under the charge of mutiny, is based on the letter to Mr. Willard Hall and charged as a design to persuade him (Mr. Hall) to aid me in my mutiny against General Kearney. The first answer of Mr. Hall to the first question put to him (31st day) entirely negatived that charge. On the day after Mr. Hall came into court, and desired to explain his testimony. The explanation went to show that by the expression in the letter, 'cannot suffer myself to be interfered with by another,' that General Kearney was meant. The answer to the next question however, was, that General Kearney was not there at the time, and that Mr. Hall did not know where he was, and so negatived the 'explanation.' Moreover, as I was not in mutiny myself, I could not have been inciting others to mutiny. The letter itself is all the defence which I make to this specification.

"*Specification* 6, under the charge of mutiny, is based on the purchase of an island near the mouth of the San Francisco Bay, for the United States, taking the title to the United States, and promising the payment of $5,000.

"My answer appears upon the face of the papers, that it was done as governor, and for the benefit of the United States; a fact which, if I understand the prosecution, and the decision of this court, refusing to receive any evidence to the point, is admitted.

"*Specification* 7, under the charge of mutiny, and specification 4, under the charge of disobedience of orders, are for the same act or acts, and will be considered together. Not mustering the men of the California battalion for payment is one of the points of the charge: the evidence shows that the men, without exception, refused to be mustered. The officers, whose pay would not be materiallly affected, were willing to be mustered. Not marching the battalion to Yerba Buena, and ordering it to remain at San Gabriel, and ordering Captain Owens not to deliver up the cannon of the battalion, are the essential points of the rest of the specification, with the aggravation of not obeying the orders brought by Captain Turner, after promising to do so, and disregarding the proclamation of General Kearney and Commodore Shubrick.

"The order by Captain Turner was delivered on the 11th of March on the 16th I gave my orders to Captain Owens, based upon my intended visit to Monterey, and on their face intended to keep the troops in a condition to sustain themselves, or to repel actual invasion.

"No notice of the President's instructions of the 5th of November was sent to me, nor did the joint proclamation, or any other paper that I ever saw, refer to them. I was then governor and commander-in-chief in California, and had a right to be regularly relieved, if any instructions had terminated my power, and no one had a right to depose me by force and violence.

"The statement which I shall now make, is based upon the evidence given by different witnesses, who testified to the points I shall mention, of whom Major Gillespie, Colonel Russell, Lieutenant Minor, of the navy, Captain Cooke, Lieutenant Loker, were the principal.

"After the capitulation of Couenga, the country immediately subsided into profound tranquillity, and security of life, person, and property, became as complete as in any part of the United States. Travelling or at home, single or in company, armed or defenceless, all were safe. Harmony and good will prevailed, and no trace of the suppressed insurrection, or of resentment for what was passed, was anywhere seen. I lived alone, after a short time, in the ancient capital of the governors general of Los Angeles, without guards or military protection; the battalion having been sent off nine miles to the mission of San Gabriel. I lived in the midst of the people in their ancient capital, administering the government, as a governor lives in the capital, of any of our States.

"Suddenly, and in the beginning of the month of March, all this was changed. 'Men, armed to the teeth, were galloping about the country.' Groups of armed men were constantly seen. the whole population was in commotion, and everything verged towards violence and bloodshed. For what cause? The approach of the Mormons, the proclamations incompatible with the capitulation of Couenga, the prospect that I was to be deposed by violence, the anticipated non-payment of government liabilities, and the general insecurity which such events inspired. Such was the cause. I determined to go to Monterey to lay the state of things before General Kearney, and gave all the orders necessary to preserve tranquillity while I was gone. I then made that extraordinary ride of which testimony has been given. General Kearney is the only witness before the court of what took place at Monterey. He seems to know but of two events in my interview with him: that I insulted him, and offered to resign my commission. It can hardly be supposed that I rode 400 miles to Monterey, in less than four days, and back in the same time for such purposes; yet these are the only things done in that visit, as established by the testimony before the court. To the question, whether I did not mention the government liabilities, the answer was that he did not recollect it, but would have refused if the application had been made.

That I was interrogated in presence of a witness, and admonished of the importance of any answers, is proved by himself. It was at that time already resolved, as has since appeared, to arrest and try me for mutiny, so that something of more importance to me still seemed to be impending. A little time was allowed for me to consider. No communication was made to me of the instructions of November 5th. Supposing that I was to be deposed by force and violence, I submitted, in order to prevent that consequence, and the injurious results to the public service that would follow such a contest, and returned to Los Angeles.

"These are the meagre facts which the evidence discloses, and on which I rely for my defence to all the allegations of this specification.

"But I think proper to add, that the orders embraced in the specification, though they were all complied with, as far as the state of the country would allow, were, with a single exception—that of re-mustering the battalion—illegal. The instructions of the 5th of November direct that the *naval commander* shall 'relinquish' to General Kearney, or Colonel Mason, the control of the civil administration, and 'turn over' all papers connected with it. Simple obedience to the instructions themselves, therefore, made their communication to me, and my consequent regular and lawful relief from the governorship, necessary, and all orders of General Kearney, or any other person, inconsistent with that, were unlawful, while the one concerning the archives were contrary to the express letter of the instructions.

"*Specification* 8, under the charge of mutiny, and 5, under that of disobedience of orders, are based on the same act, and receive the same answer with the last mentioned specification.

"*Specification* 9, of mutiny, is based upon the act of ordering the collector at San Pedro, on the 21st of March, to receive government paper in discharge of public dues, &c.; and the answer to it is, that the order, in writing, of that day was to cover a verbal order previously given, the officer wishing the written order for his justification; that neither Commodore Shubrick nor any other person gave me any notice of the President's instructions of November 5, 1846, and that I had not then, nor until a week afterwards at Monterey, yielded to what I believed to be a design to depose me, by force and violence, from the governorship of California.

"*Specification* 10, of the charge of mutiny, and 6, of disobedience of orders, all refer to acts done when I was governor and commander-in-chief in California, and are in alleged violation of the order of January 16, 1847. I refer to my previous answers to show that I was governor at that time, and to show the nullity and inapplicability of the orders of January 16, 1847.

"*Specification* 11, of mutiny, and 7, of disobedience of orders, are based on the same act: that of not obeying the order to repair to Monterey, given to me on the 26th and 28th days of March. This failure to obey that order is sufficiently accounted for in the testimony, which shows the danger of travelling at that time; and there was nothing on its face, or in the testimony in relation to it, which showed it to be urgent, or that the public service required risks of person or life in attempting to comply with it. The words, 'I desire to see you in this place,' &c., &c., as used in the order, seems not to come within the meaning of an order to be obeyed at all hazards; and the first clause of the order, written on the 28th day of March, directing me to consider all instructions coming from him (Colonel Mason) as if they had come from General Kearney himself, seemed to encourage the same idea of the want of urgency in the desire to see me at Monterey.

"The following is the clause of that order:

"'HEAD-QUARTERS, 10TH MILITARY DEPARTMENT,
"'MONTEREY, CALIFORNIA, *March* 28, 1847.

"'SIR: This will be handed to you by Colonel Mason, 1st dragoons, who goes to the southern district, clothed by me with full authority to give such orders and instructions upon all matters, both civil and military, in that section of country, as he may deem proper and necessary. Any instructions he may give to you will be considered as coming from myself.'

"The execution of his own order, and of consequent additional orders given to me by Colonel Mason, occupied so much time that it became impossible to reach Monterey within the period fixed by him, and delayed my departure until it was further interfered with by the condition of the country.

"As a further answer to all the orders given to me on and after the 1st of March, 1847, I am advised by counsel to say that they are in violation of the orders of General Scott, of November 3d, 1846, to Gen. Kearney, viz.:

"'It is known that Lieutenant-Colonel Fremont, of the United States rifle regiment, was, in July last, with a party of men, in the service of the United States topographical engineers, in the neighborhood of San Francisco, or Monterey bay, engaged in joint operations against Mexico with the United States squadron on that coast. Should you find him there, it is desired that you do not detain him against his wishes a moment longer than the necessities of the service may require.'

"This order was carried out by Colonel Mason, and came to the hands of General Kearney before any orders issued by him with respect to me on the 1st March, on which day he addressed an official letter to me, reciting that he had the directions of the general-in-chief not to detain me against my wishes a moment longer than the necessities of the service required, and leaving me at '*liberty*' to leave the country, after I had complied with the instructions in the letter and with the orders referred to. I rely upon the concluding paragraph of this official letter to prove that General Kearney, *at that time*, could not have considered criminal, and worthy of the prosecution now carried on, any act of mine previous to the writing of that letter.

"The following is the letter:

"'HEAD-QUARTERS, 10TH MILITARY DEPARTMENT,
"'MONTEREY, U. C. *March* 1, 1847.

"'SIR: By department orders, No. 2, of this date, which will be handed to you by Captain Turner, 1st dragoons, A. A. A. G., for my command, you will see that certain duties are there required of you as commander of the battalion of California volunteers.

"'In addition to the duties above referred to, I have now to direct that you will bring with you, and with as little delay as possible, all the archives and public documents, and papers, which may be subject to your control, and which appertain to the government of California, that I may receive them from your hands at this place, the capital of the territory. I have directions from the general-in-chief not to detain you in this country against your wishes a moment longer than the necessities of the service may require, and you will be at liberty to leave here after you have complied with these instructions, and those in the "orders" referred to.

"'Very respectfully, your obedient servant,

"'S. W. KEARNEY

"'*Brigadier General and Governor of California.*

"'To Lieut. Col. J. C. FREMONT,

"'*Regiment of Mounted Riflemen, commanding Battalion of California Vols., Ciudad de los Angeles.*'

"Having now answered all the specifications under the charges of mutiny and disobedience of orders, I have to say that five of the same acts on which these specifications are founded, are also laid under the charge of conduct prejudicial to good order and discipline. I am advised by counsel that offences enumerated in the rules and articles of war cannot be prosecuted among the non-enumerated offences of the 99th article of war (Hough, page 630), but I take no exception to any illegality or any irregularity, if such there be in the charges, and make the same answers to these five specifications, under the charge under which they are last found, as was made under the two preceding charges.

"I have deemed it my duty to reply to each specification, because it is the duty of the court to find upon each, and because it is right to show my conduct consistent and proper with all points. I obeyed orders, after the 1st of March, to avoid bloodshed and violence. Not relieved, as governor, and deeming them illegal, I obeyed. Now, being put upon my trial, according to law, I claim the benefit of law, and to be considered governor until I was relieved. In themselves, most of the specifications, after the first leading ones, are either cumulative or insignificant in the presence of the grave ones which precede them, and which would hardly, of themselves, have been considered worthy of such a prosecution, and while replying separately to each of these minor and cumulative accusations, I refer to the main leading argument at the opening of the charges of mutiny, in usurping the office of governor, and disobedience to the order of January 16, 1847, as presenting the general and sustained defence which the gravity of the charges required.

"I now come to a different part of my defence—but of which I fairly gave notice to the court, and through it to the prosecution, at an early stage of this trial—that of impeaching the *motives* and *the credit* of the prosecuting witness. To do this is both legal and fair, where there is just ground for it; and that is abundantly the case in this instance. A prosecutor should have none but public motives; his testimony should be scrupulously fair towards the accused. If he contradicts other witnesses, which General Kearney has so much done, it becomes necessary to weigh their respective credit; and in doing this I have a right, and moreover, it is my duty to myself and to others, to produce instances of erroneous testimony he may have exhibited, either from defect of memory, or from evil intent; and for that purpose to contrast his own testimony with itself where it varies, or with that of other witnesses where they contradict him. To this part of my defence I now proceed, and speak first of the acts which go to the motives of the prosecutor:

"1. Giving me no notice of his intended arrest. He admits that this arrest was resolved upon in January, 1847, and that I had no notice of it until I was actually arrested on the frontiers in the latter part of August following. Others were informed of it, but not myself, the one above all others the most interested to know. I was brought across the continent in a state of virtual imprisonment, to be tried for a multitude of offences, charged to have been committed on the shores of the Pacific, without the warning which would enable me to bring evidence to meet a single charge; while my accuser and general, brought with him all that he deemed necessary either of written evidence, or of witnesses to insure my conviction. It is impossible, in my opinion, to reconcile this conduct with any fair and honorable motive. It laid me under the necessity of choosing between a trial, brought on by surprise, and almost without the means of defence, or of suffering ruinous charges, enforced by newspaper publications, to hang over my head. The latter, according to Major Cooke's testimony, seems to have been General Kearney's calculation; and as I deemed the effect of such impending charges and publications would be worse than any conviction, I was forced into a trial, unprepared for it, to take the chance of any testimony that might be found.

"2. Denying me the privilege of going to Mexico to join my regiment when I had made preparation of sixty men and a hundred and twenty horses to do so, and had not the least doubt of reaching General Taylor's camp, and thence going to the regiment, expected (according to information received from Washington), to be on the road from Vera Cruz to Mexico. I expected to reach it in July, which would have been in time for the great operations impending, and since so gradually executed. The refusal to let me go did me many injuries which a soldier can feel; and, besides, left me involved in debts for my preparations, and was further, in violation of General Scott's directions, not to detain me in the country, against my wishes, a moment longer than the necessities of the service required; and, also, in violation of his own official letter to me of March 1, 1847, leaving me at liberty to quit the country when I pleased, after complying with a few small orders, not amounting to "*necessities*" of the service, but which were complied with.

"3. Taking away from me the command of my topographical party, taking away the scientific instruments which I had so long used; leaving behind my geological and botanical specimens of near two years' collection; leaving behind the artist of the expedition (Mr. Kern), with his sketches and drawings; leaving behind my assistant (Mr. King), he and Mr. Kern both standing in a relation to be material witnesses to me in any inquiry into my conduct; denying me the privilege of returning to the United States by any new route, which would enable me to correct previous explorations, or add to geographical and scientific knowledge;

making me follow on his trail in the rear of his Mormon escort. All this after he had, in conformity to General Scott's instructions, previously left me at '*liberty*' to quit California when I pleased, after executing the few small orders above referred to.

"4. Interfering with Commodore Biddle to detain Major Gillespie in California, an officer known to have been intimately associated with me in California, and who, arriving a fortnight after this trial had commenced, has shown himself to be a material witness for me. The fact of interference is admitted; the circumstances attending it are most suspicious; the reasons given for it most inadequate, and, besides, contradicted by the fact that Major Gillespie was soon after allowed "*to go about the country*,' and did not do the mischief which had been apprehended from his being at large. The detention of Major Gillespie was the detention of Commodore Stockton and his party; so that this interference delayed the arrival not only of Major Gillespie, but of Commodore Stockton, Captain Hensley, and other material witnesses who came with him.

"5. Not communicating to me his knowledge of the instructions of the 5th of November and 12th of July, 1846, when a knowledge of those instructions was so necessary for the safe guidance of my conduct. The excuse, in relation to that of the 5th of November, that he was not in the habit of communicating instructions to juniors, is invalidated by the fact of the previous communication of those of June, 1846, when I was equally junior militarily, and before I had become governor and commander-in-chief.

"6. Making injurious representations to the War Department against me and against the battalion under my command, without giving me any knowledge of such representations, and which I have only found out in the progress of this trial, in searching for testimony in the department.

"7. My reception at Monterey on March 26th, for the nature of which I *now* refer entirely to General Kearney's testimony. I made a most extraordinary ride to give information to prevent an insurrection. I asked an interview on business, and had it granted, and found Colonel Mason with him. The only thing, it would seem, that I came for in that interview, was to insult General Kearney and to offer my resignation; and he does not even know what I went for. Certainly the public service, to say nothing of myself as an officer, required a different kind of reception from the one I received.

"8. The order given to Colonel Mason on the 28th of March (after what had happened in his presence on the 26th), to proceed to Los

Angeles, where I was, with the power and authority over me, of which I was officially advised by letter of that date. I now only mention the order, in connection with my reception at Monterey, as represented by General Kearney, and add nothing to it. I do not go beyond the evidence.

"9. The fact of not *relieving* me in some legal form from the duties of governor of California, after the President's instructions of the 5th of November arrived, and concealing from me all knowledge of those instructions, while putting the interrogatories, the answers to which he has sworn he warned me might be of so much importance.

"10. The march of the Mormons upon Los Angeles, when I was expected to be there, and would have been, except for the urgent business which carried me to Monterey—the '*crushing*' that might have taken place, if a '*revolt*' of the people had not been apprehended—and all the circumstances of that movement I leave where the evidence placed it.

"11. The conduct of Colonel Mason to me at Los Angeles (so far as the evidence discloses it), is by me referred to the full authority over me with which he was clothed by General Kearney, and of which I was notified in this clause of General Kearney's official letter to me:

"'SIR: This will be handed to you by Colonel Mason, 1st dragoons, who goes to the southern district, clothed by me with full authority to give such orders and instructions in that section of the country as he may deem proper and necessary. Any instructions he may give to you will be considered as coming from myself.'

"12. The exhibition of myself and the citizens of my topographical party at Monterey, on the 30th May—the circumstances of the march from that place to Fort Leavenworth, and the manner of the arrest there—I leave in like manner where the evidence placed it; giving it as my opinion, in the twelve instances enumerated, besides in many others to be seen in the testimony, that no presumption of acting from a sense of public duty can outweigh the facts and appearances to the contrary, and that all these twelve instances, and others to be seen in the testimony, go to impeach his motives in this prosecution.

"I now proceed to the last point of my defence—the impeachment of the credit of General Kearney as a witness before this court. The law gives me the right to do so. Morality condemns the exercise of that right, unless sternly justified by credible evidence. I feel so justified.

I also feel that this case, above all others, admits of the exercise of all the rights against this witness which the law and the evidence allow to the accused.

"It is a case in which the witness comprises, in his own person, the character of accuser, prosecutor, leading witness, commanding general, arresting officer—and bringing me, by virtue of his superior rank, three thousand miles across the continent, to be tried, without warning, upon unknown charges, or to be ruined by infamous accusations hanging over me and urged in the newspapers. This is the case, and I claim in it the right of impeaching the credit of the witness, both upon his own swearing and that of others.

"Referring then to the points on which the credit of the witness is already impeached in other parts of the defence, I will first call attention, under this head, to what relates to the expedition of December and January, 1846 and 1847, from San Diego to Los Angeles, and especially with reference to the testimony concerning *the command of the troops* in that expedition. This is a matter on which General Kearney lays great stress throughout, bottoming, at one time, his claim to chief authority in the province, mainly on the results of that expedition, and his alleged command of it. I shall, consequently, examine and test what he says in relation to it, with some minuteness.

"And first as to the point, *at whose instance was the expedition raised and marched?* There is a great discrepancy here. In General Kearney's letter of 17th January, to the department he says:

"'I have to state that *the march of the troops from San Diego to this place was reluctantly consented to by Commodore Stockton, on my urgent advice* that he should not leave Lieutenant-Colonel Fremont unsupported to fight a battle on which the fate of California might, for a long time, depend; *the correspondence to prove which is now with my papers at San Diego*,' &c., &c.

"In his cross-examination, on the fourth day of the trial, he says:

"'In the latter end of December, an expedition was organized at San Diego to march to Los Angeles to assist Lieutenant-Colonel Fremont; *and it was organized in consequence, as I believe, of this paper, which is a copy of a letter from me to Commodore Stockton*,' (referring to his letter of December 22, hereafter quoted.)

"Let us contrast this first positive assertion, and second more reserved declaration of belief, with facts, with other testimony, and finally with the 'proof' which General Kearney tenders.

"Commodore Stockton testifies:

"'After General Kearney arrived (on the 12th December), and in my quarters, and in presence of two of my military family, I offered to make him commander-in-chief over all of us, and I offered *to go* as his aid-de-camp. He said no; that the force was mine; and he *would go* as my aid-de-camp, or accompany me.'

"Now, '*to go*' where? to '*accompany* where?

"This, if not sufficiently explicit, is made entirely so by the certificate of Messrs. Spieden and Moseley, of the navy, offered by Commodore Stockton, in corroboration, under the sanction of his oath, and, of course, forming a proper interpretation of his words. This certificate is as follows:

"'We, the undersigned, were present at a conversation held between Commodore Stockton and General Kearney, at San Diego, shortly after the arrival of the general, in which conversation the commodore offered to give to General Kearney the 'command-in-chief' *of the forces he was preparing to march with to the Ciudad de los Angeles, and to act as his aid-de-camp. This offer the general declined,* but *said he would be most happy to go with the commodore as his aid-de-camp,* and assist him with his head and hand.

"'WILLIAM SPIEDEN, *U. S. N.*
"'SAMUEL MOSELEY, *U. S. N.*

"'SAN DIEGO, *February* 5, 1847.'

"Again Commodore Stockton testifies that, at a subsequent interview, a few days afterwards he made to General Kearney 'the same offer, in pretty much the same language, and received pretty much the same answer.'

"It is certain, then, that General Kearney's letter of the 22d December was *not* the inducing cause of the expedition, as '*believed*,' in General Kearney's testimony, and that 'the march of the troops' was *not* a matter that Commodore Stockton 'reluctantly assented to,' as *asserted* in General Kearney's official letter; and it is also certain that General Kearney could not have supposed either to be the case, for he had been informed ten days before of the design to send the expedition; that it was 'preparing to march;' and he had been twice offered, and had twice declined the command of it.

"Commodore Stockton further testifies:

"I now set to work to make the best preparations I could to commence our march for the Ciudad de los Angeles. During this time an expedition that had been sent to the south for horses returned, and brought with it a number of horses and cattle. Captain Turner was allowed to take his pick of the horses for the dragoons. After he had done so he wrote to me this note:

" 'SAN DIEGO, *December* 23, 1846.

" 'COMMODORE: In compliance with your verbal instruction to examine and report upon the condition of the public horses turned over to me for the use of C Company, 1st dragoons, I have the honor to state that, in my opinion, not one of the horses referred to is fit for dragoon service, being too poor and weak for any such purpose; also, that the company of dragoons, under my command, can do much better service on foot than if mounted on those horses.

" 'I am, sir, with high respect, your obedient servant,

" 'H. S. TURNER,

" '*Captain 1st Dragoons commanding company C.*

" 'Commodore R. F. STOCKTON,

" '*United States Navy, Commanding, &c. &c.*'

"The exact day of the return of this expedition for horses and cattle does not appear. But, as there had been time for Captain Turner to be allowed to 'take his pick' from the horses, examine them, and make a report upon them by the 23d of December, it is nearly certain that it must have returned by the 22d; and hence it would seem that General Kearney's letter, sent to Commodore Stockton in the night of the last mentioned day, in which he 'recommends' the expedition, and in which he claims the whole merit of the march, and to have induced Commodore Stockton reluctantly to consent to it, was not written till he had not only been repeatedly informed that the expedition was in preparation, and he had been twice offered the command of it, but not till the horses and cattle for its use had actually arrived, and probably a part of them turned over to his own company of dragoons. This, indeed, is rendered nearly certain by the fact that the preparations for the expedition were so far advanced that Commodore Stockton's general orders for the march were issued on the day next following General Kearney's letter, which he pretends, under oath to have been the inducing cause of the expedition.

"But General Kearney is entitled to the benefit of the '*proof*' which he vouches to the department in this passage of his letter:

" 'I have to state that the march of the troops from San Diego to this place was reluctantly consented to by Commodore Stockton, on my urgent advice that he should not leave Colonel Fremont unsupported to fight a battle on which the fate of California might for a long time depend; *the correspondence to prove which is now with my papers at San Diego*, and a copy of which will be furnished to you on my return to that place.'

"This 'correspondence,' as he certifies it on the 12th day of the trial, consists of three letters and Commodore Stockton's general orders for the march. I will set out all of them:

"'SAN DIEGO, *December* 22, 1846.

"'DEAR COMMODORE: If you can take from here a sufficient force to oppose the Californians, now supposed to be near Pueblo, and waiting for the approach of Lieutenant-Colonel Fremont, I advise that you do so, and that you march with that force as early as possible in the direction of the Pueblo, by which you will either be able to form a junction with Lieutenant-Colonel Fremont, or make a diversion very much in his favor.

"'I do not think that Lieutenant-Colonel Fremont should be left unsupported to fight a battle upon which the fate of California may, for a long time, depend, if there are troops here to act in concert with him. Your force, as it advances, might surprise the enemy at the St. Louis Mission, and make prisoners of them.

"'I shall be happy, in such an expedition, to accompany you, and to give you any aid, either of head or hand, of which I may be capable.

"'Yours truly,
"'S. W. KEARNEY,
"'*Brigadier General.*

"'To Commodore STOCKTON,
"'*Commanding United States Forces, San Diego.*'

"'HEADQUARTERS, SAN DIEGO, *December* 23, 1846.

"'DEAR GENERAL: Your note of yesterday was handed to me *last night* by Captain Turner, of the dragoons.

"'In reply to that note, *permit me to refer you to the conversation held with you yesterday morning at your quarters.* I stated to you *distinctly* that I *intended* to march upon St. Louis Rey *as soon as possible*, with a part of the force under my command, and that I was *very desirous* to march on to the Pueblo *to co-operate with Lieutenant-Colonel Fremont;* but my movements after, to St. Louis Rey, would depend entirely upon the information that I might receive as to the movements of Colonel

Fremont and the enemy. It might be necessary for me to stop the pass of San Felipe, or march back to San Diego.

"'Now, my dear general, if the object of your note is to advise me to do anything which would enable a large force of the enemy to get into my rear and cut off my communication with San Diego, and hazard the safety of the garrison and the ships in the harbor, you will excuse me for saying I cannot follow any such advice.

"'My PURPOSE *still is* to march for St. Louis Rey *as soon as I can get the* DRAGOONS *and riflemen mounted*, which I hope to do in two days.

"'Faithfully, your obedient servant,

"'R. F. STOCKTON,

"'*Commander-in-chief and governor of the territory of California.*

"'To Brigadier General S. W. KEARNEY,

"'*United States Army.*'

"'SAN DIEGO, *December* 23, 1846.

"DEAR COMMODORE: I have received yours of this date, repeating, as you say, what you stated to me yesterday; and in reply I have only to remark that, *if I had so understood you*, I certainly *would not have written* my letter to you of last evening.

"'You certainly could not for a moment suppose that I would advise or suggest to you any movement which might endanger the safety of the garrison and the ships in the harbor.

"'My letter of yesterday's date stated that 'if you can take from here,' &c., of which you were the judge, and of which I knew nothing.

"'Truly yours,

"'S. W. KEARNEY,

"'*Brigadier General.*

"'Commodore R. F. STOCKTON,

"'*Commanding U. S. Navy, &c., San Diego.*'

"'GENERAL ORDERS:

"'The forces composed of Captain Tilghman's company of artillery, a detachment of the 1st regiment of dragoons, companies A and B of the California battalion of mounted riflemen, and a detachment of sailors and marines, from the frigates Congress and Savannah and the ship Portsmouth, will take up the line of march *for the Ciudad de los Angeles* on Monday morning, the 28th instant, at 10 o'clock, A. M.

"'By order of the commander-in-chief.

'"J. ZIELAN,

"'*Brevet Captain and Adjutant.*

"'SAN DIEGO, *December* 23, 1846.'

"The character of this correspondence entirely destroys General Kearney's asseverations; both the one in his report that Commodore Stockton 'reluctantly consented' to the march of the troops, and the one before the court that he 'believed' that the expedition was organized in consequence of his letter of advice.

"Commodore Stockton's letter is explicit both of his present and previous '*intention*,' '*desire*,' and '*purpose*,' to march '*as soon as possible*;' while the reference to the dragoons, which were General Kearney's especial corps, shows that the subject of the expedition must have been previously entertained between the two correspondents. Allow General Kearney, however, the benefit of any misunderstanding, touching Commodore Stockton's disposition and intentions, that he may have been under when he wrote his letter, the commodore's reply corrects all such mistakes, and leaves General Kearney's subsequent assertions on this head direct contradictions of the declarations of Commodore Stockton.

"The next question in connection with this expedition is *who was its commander?* General Kearney says *he* was; Commodore Stockton, sustained by the testimony of many others says *he* was. As it could not have had *two commanders*, at the same time, I will compare the testimony. General Kearney's claim first comes to attention in a letter to the department of which the following is the first paragraph:

"'HEADQUARTERS, ARMY OF THE WEST,
"'CIUDAD DE LOS ANGELES, *Jan.* 12, 1847.

"'SIR: I have the honor to report that, at the request of Commodore R. F. Stockton, United States navy (who in September last assumed the title of governor of California), I consented to TAKE COMMAND of an expedition to this place (the capital of the country), and that on the 29th December, *I left San Diego* with about 500 men, consisting of 60 dismounted dragoons, under Captain Turner, 50 California volunteers, and the remainder of marines and sailors, with a battery of artillery; Lieutenant Emory (topographical engineer) acting as assistant adjutant general. *Commodore Stockton accompanied us.*'

"Here the claim to have been the commander is plain, unequivocal, and unconditional. In his letter to me, however, of same date (January 12th), he expresses it perhaps even more strongly; since Commodore Stockton is not mentioned at all, and the pronoun 'I' and 'me' exclude the idea of any participant in the 'possession' or command:

"'Puebla de los Angeles,
"'January 12, 1847—Tuesday, 6 p. m.

"'Dear Fremont: *I am here in possession of this place, with sailors and marines.* We met and defeated the whole force of the Californians the 8th and 9th. They have not now to exceed 300 men concentrated. Avoid charging them, and come to *me* at this place.

"'Acknowledge the hour of receipt of this, and when I may expect you. Regards to Russell.

"'Yours,
"'S. W. Kearney
"'*Brigadier General.*

"'Lieutenant-Colonel Fremont.'

"At the next step, General Kearney slightly varies his claim, and admits some qualification to the completeness of his command. This is on his cross-examination. (Fourth day of the trial.)

"'In the latter end of December, an expedition was organized at San Diego to march to Los Angeles, to assist Lieutenant-Colonel Fremont, and it was organized in consequence, as I believe, of this paper, which is a copy of a letter from me to Commodore Stockton of (December 22). Commodore Stockton, at that time, was acting as governor of California, so styling himself. * * * * He determined on the expedition, and on the morning of the 29th December the troops were paraded at San Diego for the march. The troops consisted of about five hundred sailors and marines, about sixty dragoons, and about forty or fifty volunteers. While they were on parade, Commodore Stockton called several officers together; Captain Turner, of the dragoons, and Lieutenant Minor, of the navy, I know were there, and several others. He then remarked to them to the following purport; 'Gentlemen, General Kearney has kindly consented to take the command of the troops on the expedition; you will, therefore, look upon him as your commander. *I shall go along as* GOVERNOR *and commander-in-chief in* CALIFORNIA.' 'We marched toward Los Angeles,' &c. * * * * 'The troops, *under my command,* marched into Los Angeles on the 10th of January,' &c.

"At the next stage, in reply to a question of the judge advocate, he returns to the positive and unconditional assertion of command:

"By the act of Commodore Stockton, who styled himself governor of California, the sailors and marines were placed UNDER MY COMMAND, on the 29th December, 1846, for the march to Los Angeles. I COMMANDED

THEM ON THE EXPEDITION; Commodore Stockton accompanied us. I exercised no command whatever over Commodore Stockton, *nor did he exert any whatever over me.*'

"Afterward (fourteenth day) under examination by the court, and when information had been received here of the arrival of Commodore Stockton in the country, the witness greatly modified his position on this point, and admits several acts of authority done on the march by Commodore Stockton, and that he 'felt it his duty' to 'consult the wishes of the commodore.'

"'I found Commodore Stockton, on my arrival at San Diego, on the 12th December, 1846, in command of the Pacific squadron, having several ships, either two or three, in the harbor at that place. Most of his sailors were on shore. He had assumed the title of Governor of California in the month of August previous. *All at San Diego addressed him as 'governor.'* I DID THE SAME.

"'After he had determined on the march from San Diego to Los Angeles, the troops being paraded for it on the 29th December, he, in the presence of several officers, among whom was myself, Captain Turner, of the dragoons, and Lieutenant Minor, of the navy, and others, whose names I do not recollect, remarked to them: 'Gentlemen, General Kearney has kindly consented to take command of the troops in this expedition; you will therefore consider him as your commander. *I will go along as* GOVERNOR *and commander-in-chief* IN CALIFORNIA.' *Under Commodore Stockton's directions every arrangement for the expedition was made. I had nothing whatever to do with it.* We marched from San Diego to Los Angeles. Whilst on the march, a few days before reaching Los Angeles, a commission of two citizens, as I believe, on behalf of Governor Flores, came to Commodore Stockton with a communication to him as governor, or commander-in-chief in California. *Commodore Stockton replied to that communication without consulting me.* On the march I at no time considered Commodore Stockton under my direction; nor did I at any time consider myself under his. His assimilated rank to officers of the army at that time was, and now is, and will for upwards of a year remain, that of a colonel.

"'Although I did not consider myself *at any time or under any circumstances, as under the orders of Commodore Stockton*, yet, as so large a portion of my command was of sailors and marines, I felt it my duty on all important subjects *to consult his wishes, and, as far as I consistently could do so, to comply with them.*'

"But it was not till the fifty-first day of this trial, when he had had the benefit of several weeks' reflection, added to information of the character of the testimony delivered by Commodore Stockton and others, and when he came into court fortified with his own questions, drawn up by himself to square with pre-arranged answers, that he could be brought to the point of admitting that, during the march, the commodore exercised the prerogative of sending him what he calls 'messages,' but the commodore calls 'orders' and had directed many movements of the expedition. But even this day's admissions are so reluctant, and with so many reservations, that for the plain facts other testimony must necessarily be brought in.

"General Kearney recites twice, and with much particularity, in his testimony to this point, *his* version of what Commodore Stockton said to the troops before marching from San Diego on the subject of command; laboring by an ingenious turn of the last clause, to draw a distinction between the commander-in-chief *in the territory*, and the commander-in-chief *of the troops*. This is his precise version of Governor Stockton's remarks: 'Gentlemen, General Kearney has kindly consented to take command of the troops in this expedition; you will therefore look upon him as your commander. *I shall go along as* GOVERNOR *and commander-in-chief* IN CALIFORNIA.

"This fine-spun distinction seems, in fact, the corner stone of General Kearney's claim to have been the commander of the expedition, for while he constantly persists in that pretension, he as constantly admits that Commodore Stockton was the Governor and commander in the territory.

"I do not refer to this because I attach any value to the point in itself. For any argument that I desire, the version given by General Kearney would answer as well as any other; for if Commodore Stockton was governor and commander-in-chief *of California*, his authority was sufficient for my case, since Los Angeles, where I believe the charges are all laid, is certainly within that province. But the distinction drawn in the version given by the witness was considered important by him, and that version is contradicted; and this is the point of view in which I present it. It is contradicted by Commodore Stockton, Lieutenant Gray, Lieutenant Minor, and the certificate of Lieutenant Rowan, all whose concurrent testimony affirms that Commodore Stockton's reservation of authority related to the commander-in-chief of the *expedition*, without the words of qualification to which General Kearney testifies; and it is worthy of note that, though a witness of the prosecution, Captain Turner was present at the address, the prosecution have not thought proper to bring him to sustain General Kearney thus contradicted.

"A few detached passages from the testimony will show how materially General Kearney is contradicted, in other respects, upon this point of the command:

"*General Kearney:* 'By the act of Commodore Stockton, the sailors and marines were placed under *my command. I commanded them* on the expedition.'

"*Commodore Stockton:* 'During which march I performed *all the duties* which I supposed devolved on the *commander-in-chief.*'

"*General Kearney:* 'I exercised no command whatever over Commodore Stockton, *nor did he exert any whatever over me.*'

"*Commodore Stockton:* 'I was *in the habit* of sending my aid-de-camp *to General Kearney* to inform *him* what time *I wished* to move in the morning; and I *always* decided on the *route* we should take, and *when* and *where* we should *encamp.*'

"*General Kearney:* 'The troops *under my command* marched into Los Angeles, on the 10th of January.'

"*Commodore Stockton:* 'And when we marched into the city, *I led the way, at the head of the advanced guard.*'

"*General Kearney:* 'On the march, I at no time considered Commodore Stockton under my direction, *nor did I, at any time, consider myself under his.*'

"*Commodore Stockton:* 'I observed the guns being unlimbered; I was told it was done *by order of General Kearney* to return the fire of the enemy; *I ordered the guns limbered up*, and the forces to cross the river before a shot was fired.' 'I observed that the men of the right flank had been formed into a square, *and General Kearney at their head.* I sent my aid-de-camp, Mr. Gray, *to General Kearney with* INSTRUCTIONS *to move that square*, and two pieces of artillery, immediately up the hill.'

"*General Kearney:* 'During our march, many messages were brought to me from Commodore Stockton; those messages I looked upon as *suggestions* and *expressions of his wishes.* I have, *since then*, learned that he considered them in the light of orders.'

"*Commodore Stockton:* 'I sent for Captain Emory; I asked him by whose order the camp was making below the hill. He said, *by General Kearney's order.* I told him to go to General Kearney, and tell him that it was *my order* that the camp should be immediately moved to the top of the hill.' 'I sent my aid-de-camp, Mr. Gray, to General Kearney, *with instructions* to move,' &c. 'The witness (Commodore Stockton), in enumerating *some* of the *orders given* and *some* of the details, executed by himself, meant merely to cite instances in which *General Kearney re-*

cognized and acknowledged his (the witness's) *command-in-chief on the field of battle*, as well as *in the march*.'

"*General Kearney:* 'During our march, his (Commodore Stockton's) authority and command, *though it did not extend over me, or over the troops which he had himself given me*, extended far beyond,' &c.

"*Commodore Stockton:* 'Commodore R. F. Stockton begs leave to add, &c., that he wishes to be understood as meaning distinctly to convey the idea that General Kearney was fully invested with the command of the troops in the battles of the 8th and 9th of January, SUBJECT *to the orders of him, the witness, as* COMMANDER-IN-CHIEF. Most and nearly all the execution of details was confided to General Kearney as SECOND in command.' 'He could not attempt to enumerate and specify the many and important acts of General Kearney *as* SECOND *in command*.' 'When the troops arrived at San Bernardo, I made my head-quarters a mile, or two miles, in advance of the camp; and *I* SENT *to General Kearney to send me the marines and a piece of artillery, which was immediately done*.' '*I* ORDERED *the troops all to lie down*,' &c. '*After having* DIRECTED *the troops* to be formed, &c., *I took the marine guard* and two pieces of *artillery*,' &c. 'On my return, I gave ORDERS where the different *officers* and *troops* were to be quartered, and ORDERED the same *flag*,' &c.

"*General Kearney:* 'I exercised no command whatever over Commodore Stockton, *nor did he exert any whatever over me*.'

"*Lieutenant Gray:* 'Question. Did you bear an *order* from Commodore Stockton on the 8th of January, in the field, to General Kearney?—if so, state the order and all the circumstances.

"'Answer. I did bear *an order* from Commodore Stockton to General Kearney on the 8th of January, on the field of battle. The enemy had been observed to withdraw his guns from the height. The Commodore directed me to go to General Kearney, and say to him, to send a square and a field-piece immediately up on the height, to prevent the enemy's returning with their guns. I went and gave him *the order*, and on my return to Commodore Stockton, observed the division, or square, of General Kearney moving toward the hill.

"'Question. Did you bear that order to General Kearney in your character of aid-de-camp to Commodore Stockton, the commander-in-chief?

"'Answer. Yes.

"'Question by the judge advocate. Do you recollect the words and manner in which you delivered that order; did you deliver it, so that General Kearney must have received it as an order, or merely as a suggestion?

"'Answer. I carried it *as an order*, in the usual, respectful way. How General Kearney received it, I, of course, cannot say. He did not show by his manner, that it was disagreeable to him, according to the best of my recollection.'

"Finally, I shall conclude this point, by showing that General Kearney did not, and could not, at any time, have considered himself the commander of the expedition, or of the troops composing it, and was not so considered by the army officers who had accompanied him into California, and were there. Because,

"1. The place which General Kearney held in the expedition was that which had been before assigned to a lieutenant of the navy, serving under Commodore Stockton, and this General Kearney knew. This is the testimony of Commodore Stockton:

"'After the forces had been paraded preparatory to the march, and I was about mounting my horse, General Kearney came to me and inquired, "who was to command the troops?" I said to him, *Lieutenant Rowan, first lieutenant of the Cyane, would command them.* He gave me to understand that *he* would like to command the troops, and after some further conversation on the subject, *I agreed to appoint him to the command*, and immediately sent for Lieutenant Rowan,' &c.

"2. Because, at the moment of receiving the appointment, he was informed that the command-in-chief was reserved by Commodore Stockton. This is Commodore Stockton's testimony to this point:

"'I immediately sent for Lieutenant Rowan, and, assembling the officers that were near at hand, stated to them that General Kearney had *volunteered* to take command of the troops, but that I *retained my own position as commander-in-chief*. I directed my aid-de-camp, and the commissary who was with me, to *take a note* of what I said on the occasion.'

"And to the same effect is the testimony of Lieutenant Gray and Lieutenant Minor, and the certificate of Lieutenant Rowan.

"3. Because both General Kearney and the officers under him, received and obeyed the orders of Commodore Stockton, in some instances in opposition to those first given by General Kearney, both on the march and in the battles. The evidence on this point need not be recapitulated. Commodore Stockton testifies to it, Lieutenant Gray testifies to it, Lieutenant Minor testifies to it, and Lieutenant Emory testifies to have received and obeyed orders from Commodore Stockton.

"4. Because Lieutenant Emory, attached to General Kearney's dragoon escort, and acting as assistant adjutant general, did not make his official report of losses in action in the expedition to General Kearney, but to

Commodore Stockton. True, General Kearney says this was done 'witnout his knowledge or consent;' but that is only the stronger proof that he was not regarded or respected as the commander-in-chief, even by his confidential supporters and military family.

"5. Because he admitted to Colonel Russell, as appears repeatedly in Colonel Russell's testimony, that he was serving *under* Commodore Stockton, and had been serving under him from San Diego.

"6. Because when I delivered to him, and he read in my presence, my letter to him of 17th January, in which is this passage:

"'*I learned also in conversation with you, that on the march from San Diego, recently, to this place, you entered upon, and discharged duties implying an acknowledgment on your part* OF SUPREMACY *to Commodore Stockton*,' he made no denial of it, or objection to it.

"7. Because on the 16th of January he applied, in writing, to Commodore Stockton, 'advising' and 'offering' 'to take one-half' of the command, and march to form a junction,' &c., addressing Commodore Stockton in that letter as 'governor of California, *commanding United States forces*.'

"On the eighth day of the trial General Kearney testified as follows:

"Question.—Do you know whether the officers of the battalion raised it and marched it under commission from Commodore Stockton?

"Answer.—I have always understood that Lieutenant-Colonel Fremont had raised that battalion under the direction of Commodore Stockton.

"Question.—With what commission?

"Answer.—*I never heard of Commodore Stockton conferring a commission on Lieutenant-Colonel Fremont, further than having appointed him military commandant of California.*

"The object of this inquiry was not, by any means, to get an opportunity to discredit the witness. The object was to ascertain before the court that the battalion was enlisted, organized, and officered exclusively under naval authority, and so, of course, subject to the orders of the naval commander; and also to ascertain if these facts were not within the knowledge of the witness when he attempted to get command of the battalion in opposition to Commodore Stockton; both being inquiries pertinent to the issues of the trial, and the facts being what was desired. But the nature of the last answer was such as to leave the original inquiries unsettled, and to open a *new one*.

"The answer was this: '*I never heard* of Commodore Stockton's conferring a commission on Lieutenant-Colonel Fremont, further than having ppointed him *military commandant* of California.'

"And the new question raised was whether, in fact, the witness had '*never heard*' of a matter so notorious in that country. Accordingly, on the next day General Kearney having mentioned the receipt on the 16th of December, 1846, of a certain communication from Commodore Stockton, this question was put.

"Question.—Did not Commodore Stockton, in that communication, *inform you* that Captain Fremont had been appointed by him MAJOR, and Lieutenant Gillespie, of the marines, captain in the California battalion?

"And a copy of the paper having been shown to the witness, he answered:

"Answer.—Among the papers sent to me by Commodore Stockton on the 16th of December, *was* a copy of his letter to the Navy Department, dated August 28, 1846, the second paragraph of which states that he had organized a Californian battalion of mounted riflemen, by the appointment of all the necessary officers, and received them as volunteers in the service of the United States; *that Captain Fremont was appointed major, and Lieutenant Gillespie, captain of the battalion.*

"Again, on the 13th day of the trial, two other papers were shown to the witness, with this question:

"Were not copies of these two papers, describing him (Fremont) as *Major* Fremont, among those furnished to you by Commodore Stockton at San Diego. And were not copies of them filed in the War Department by you since your return from California, and after your arrival in this city in September last?

"Answer.—(After reading over the papers,) I think that copies of these papers *were furnished to me by Commodore Stockton.* To the latter part of the question, 'were they not filed by you in the War Department since your return from California, and after your arrival in this city in September last?' I see on the papers the certificate of Captain Townsend that I did so; *I think Captain Townsend is mistaken.*

"But on the following day he admitted that Captain Townsend was *not* mistaken; that the papers had been put into his hands by Commodore Stockton in December, 1846, and had been filed by him in the war office as late as the 21st of September last. From all this, however, it only resulted that he had *seen* of the appointment of Fremont as major: that he had '*never heard*' of it, was not yet disproved.

"This was accomplished in his testimony on the ninth day, when he admitted as follows:

"'Commodore Stockton *did* inform me, in the conversation alluded to between us, that California had been conquered in July and August of the same year (this conversation was held in December), and that *Major Fremont* had gone to the north to raise men,' &c.

"In the same connection, and for the same purpose, the question arose, whether Lieutenant Gillespie, of the marine corps, was not also an officer of the battalion; and the answer of the witness was again such as not only to leave the original question open, but to raise the new one, which brings the subject within this branch of my defence. The witnesses' answer was as follows:

"'Captain Gillespie had marched with me from San Diego to Los Angeles, and was serving under me. *If his company was with the California battalion* I DID NOT KNOW IT.'

"It appeared, however, on examination, that the same communication (of 28th August, 1846), that informed the witness that Fremont had been appointed major of the battalion, also informed him that Gillespie had been appointed captain in it. It further appeared, that in the surgeon's list of killed and wounded in the actions of the 8th and 9th of January, furnished by Lieutenant Emory to General Kearney, and by him sent to the department, Captain Gillespie is reported as an officer of the California battalion; and Captain Gillespie himself gave the following emphatic testimony:

"'Question. Did you at any time communicate to General Kearney your rank and position in the California battalion? If so, when and where was that communication made?

"Answer. *I did communicate to General Kearney my position in the battalion*, on the 5th of December, 1846, about one o'clock in the day, in the mountains about half way between Santa Maria and Santa Isabel. When I met him I was at the head of a detachment of volunteers and sailors, I having been ordered by Commodore Stockton to proceed to Warner's Pass to communicate with General Kearney.'

"These inquiries concerning the raising and officering of the battalion were matters connected intimately with the issues of the trial, and the answers of the witness seem to indicate a consciousness of it. But I do not desire to present them in any other light than as instances of defective and equivocating memory, and in that view, affecting the general credit of his testimony.

"Under the same infirmity of memory I am willing to class the extraordinary facility of *omission* betrayed by the witness, in his manner, which seems to be habitual, of *half-telling*, where *whole-telling* is essential. Thus: On the third day of the trial he commences an answer in these words: 'About the 14th of January, 1847, *I received* from Lieutenant Colonel Fremont a communication, dated,' &c.,—the inference being, of course, that my communication was voluntary; the fact (and most important one, too,) being, that it was drawn out by no less than *four* importunate letters that I had before received. Again, in continuation of the same narration: 'On the day subsequent, viz., on the 17th of January, Lieutenant-Colonel Fremont *came to my quarters*, and in conversation,' &c.,—the inference being, of course, that I went at my own instance, whereas the fact (most material and relevant, and deciding the character of the interview) turned out, that I went in compliance with the written request of the witness to see me 'on business.' Again, same day: 'I was first *met* by a detachment from Commodore Stockton,' &c. . . . 'It *came* from Commodore Stockton, *to give* me information,' &c.; the inference being, that it went voluntarily, or was sent by Commodore Stockton of his own motion; the important fact appearing, however, when Commodore Stockton came on the stand, three weeks after, that it was sent out at the written request of General Kearney, for a party 'to open communication with him,' &c. So, in the same letter, making this application, he writes to Commodore Stockton as follows: '*Your express, by Mr. Carson, was met on the Del Norte, and your mail must have reached Washington at least ten days since,*'—omitting the material fact, that Mr. Carson, in addition to being *met*, was likewise *turned back;* and leaving the inference, that he had gone on. Again, in his testimony on the sixth day of the trial, speaking of his position on the hill of San Bernardo, the witness says: 'I stated to the doctor and others, that we would leave next morning, which we accordingly did; *Lieutenant Gray, of the navy, with a gallant command of sailors and marines, having come into our camp the night previous,*'—the inference being, that Lieutenant Gray and his command came voluntarily, or by chance, into the camp; the fact being, that it was a detachment of two hundred and fifteen men, sent from San Diego expressly for the relief of General Kearney's camp, and in pursuance of his repeated urgent calls for succor—one of them (that by Lieutenant Beale, Mr. Carson, and the Indian) conveyed through the enemy's lines and an insurgent population, under circumstances of devotion and courage unsurpassed, but no mention of which is found in the official report, or any part of the testimony of General Kearney.

"I give these as examples, taken only from two days' proceedings, of a vast deal of the same sort of testimony, running through General Kearney's examination.

"The testimony of General Kearney, *in relation to the charges*, is the next point to which I advert, under this head of my defence. On the sixth day of the trial, General Kearney testifies as follows:

"'The charges on which Lieutenant-Colonel Fremont is now arraigned are not my charges. I preferred a single charge against Lieut. Colonel Fremont. The charges on which he is now arraigned have been changed from mine.' * * * * * * * * * *

"Question (by Lieutenant-Colonel Fremont). Did you give any information to the person who drew up the seventh specification under the first charge, in relation to the cannon?

"Answer. I DID NOT.

"This testimony was promptly communicated to the War Office, by my counsel, for the purpose of ascertaining upon *whose* (if not General Kearney's), information the charge had been drawn up, as matter necessary to be known, unless I would proceed in my defence against unknown and secret prosecutors; the adjutant general, by direction of the Secretary of War, returned for answer the emphatic assurance, that the charges and specifications produced to the court, '*were based upon facts alleged and officially reported to the department by General Kearney; and it is not known or understood that any charge or specification has been introduced, based on facts derived from any other source whatever.*'

"In addition to this positive contradiction by the department, the charges came to the court certified upon their face as being preferred '*upon information of Brigadier General S. W. Kearney;*' and myself and counsel are further informed, by the judge advocate, that the seventh specification of the first charge *is copied literally from the charge furnished by General Kearney in his own hand-writing.*

"This inquiry into the charges, leads naturally to the subject upon which that inquiry arose, viz.: a certain *mountain howitzer*, lost by General Kearney at the battle of San Pasqual, and recovered by me at the capitulation of Couenga. The inquiry was not originally made, with any view or expectation that an untrue answer would be given to it, and hence an opportunity arise for contradicting the testimony of the witness. On the contrary, the object of the inquiry was truth. It was to ascertain whether the recovery by me, of a cannon so lost by General Kearney, had been reported by him to the department; and, if not, the argument would be to the impeachment of the temper and motive towards me; for the loss of cannon is always a source of mortification, and its recovery a subject of gratulation and honorable report. It turned out that the recovery had *not* been reported, but to escape the inference thus raised the witness pleaded want of sufficient knowledge of the fact. This, then, became the point at issue; and to say that this is an incidental question, upon which the answer of the witness must suffice, whether true or false, is to say that he may escape from the consequences of one wrong, by committing a greater; that a fact cannot be proved going to impeach his motives if he chooses to deny it with a falsehood. But it is the rule of law and justice that 'a man shall not profit by his own wrong;' and, therefore, I did not consider myself concluded by the answer of the witness; but, finding by inspection of the charges, that the witness (who I had understood was the sole accuser against me) had sufficient knowledge concerning the cannon, to impute the *having* of it to me *as a crime*, I inferred that he ought to have had sufficient knowledge of it, to report the *gaining* of it *to my credit*. Hence, I continued the inquiry with the following question:

"'In the seventh specification, under the first charge, you charge Lieutenant-Colonel Fremont with refusing to give up two cannon which had been brought from Fort Leavenworth, and which were then at San Gabriel. Will you state what cannon they were, how they were brought from Fort Leavenworth, and how they got to San Gabriel?'

"And hence arose the sweeping declarations already examined, that these charges 'were not his;' that they 'had been changed from his;' and that he 'did not' furnish the information concerning the cannon on which the seventh specification of charge first was drawn up. After which he continued his answer in these words:

"'The two howitzers, however, referred to, *are* the two howitzers brought by the first dragoons from Fort Leavenworth to California; one of them, as was previously stated, was lost at San Pasqual; the other we took with us.'

"'Question. Do you know that one of those cannon was the one lost by you at San Pasqual?

"'Answer. I DO NOT.'

"Two days after, he comes into court with this 'explanation:' 'In reading over in the papers this morning the proceedings of Monday, I find the following question put to me by the accused, and my answer thereto, as follows:

"'Question. Do you know that one of those cannon was the one lost by you at San Pasqual?

"'Answer. I do not.'

"'I have now to explain that *I had no personal knowledge of it; I had a knowledge of it* FROM AN OFFICIAL REPORT made to my staff officer BY LIEUTENANT COLONEL COOKE.'

"Now, on this point, General Kearney is contradicted by his own witness; for Lieutenant Colonel Cooke testifies to having received *from* General Kearney orders in relation to the cannon *before* he ever made any report on the subject.

"This is from Major Cooke's testimony in chief, delivered on the fourteenth day of the trial:

"'On *the 24th of March*, I rode out from Los Angeles to the mission of San Gabriel, accompanied, &c. I called on Captain Owens at his quarters, and shortly after asked to look at the artillery. He showed them to me in the court of the mission, and I observed two *mountain howitzers*, which I believed had been brought to that country by the dragoons. *I had received verbal instructions from General Kearney*, by Captain Turner, *to have them turned over to company C, under my command;* and had, *before I left town*, ordered mules and drivers to be sent after THEM.'

"This relates to occurrences of *the 24th of March*, whilst the verbal instructions' referred to, afterward ascertained to be written memoranda, were issued from Monterey about the *1st of March*, and the only report made upon the subject by Major Cooke was of *March 25th.*

"This is Major Cooke's testimony to these points (eighteenth day of the trial):

"'Question. Is your letter or report of the 25th March, which was read in your cross-examination of Thursday, your official report to your superior officer? and does it refer to the same events as those narrated in your testimony? and did you ever make any other official report of those occurrences to General Kearney, or to any other officer for him?

"'Answer. *It was my official report. It refers to the same subject as my evidence in chief.* I do not remember having made *any* OTHER *report to him or to any one else.*

"'Question. Did you have any verbal or special order in relation to ordnance, arms, &c.?

"'Answer. I had some verbal orders in relation to arms, communicated, however, in the form of *written memoranda.* * * * I have them not here. I lost all my papers by an accident, &c.

"'Question. Will you state the tenor of those orders and instructions, giving the words as far as possible, and whom they came from?

"'Answer. THEY CAME FROM GENERAL KEARNEY. I was directed, I believe, *to put the* HOWITZERS in charge of the dragoons. * * * * I received, *at the same time* an *official letter* from General Kearney.'

"A copy of this official letter was produced the next day, and found to be dated at Monterey, March 1, which fixes the time of those 'verbal orders' or 'written memoranda.' Finally, on the nineteenth and twentieth days of the trial, Major Cooke again testifies, concerning the same verbal instructions as follows:

"'Under ordinary circumstances, I should have deemed it my duty to have enforced my orders in relation to the artillery, founded on the verbal orders *of the general.* The verbal orders alluded to might be considered as giving higher importance, in my view, to the *object to be attained,* which was to turn over to company C, 1st dragoons, *the two mountain howitzers.*'

"From all which, it results that General Kearney's first information concerning the cannon was *not* received through Major Cooke's report, but that the report resulted, in fact, from orders about the cannon, given by General Kearney several weeks before the report was made.

"The first great allegations, then, made by General Kearney to escape from the original simple and comparatively innocent fact supposed by the inquiry concerning the cannon, are contradicted, in their whole essence, by the official assurance of the Secretary of War, by the charges as they are certified by the judge advocate to the court, and by the original draft of accusations against me in General Kearney's own hand; while his subsequent 'explanation' to escape from *this* labyrinth, by attempting to draw a distinction between *personal knowledge* and *official knowledge* involves him in the repudiation of his own orders, and in a double contradiction with himself and with Major Cooke, his own witness.

"I think it proper, I think it my duty, to introduce here some maxims of the law, which, I am advised, are recognized in all courts.

"Where it turns out that a witness's testimony is corruptly false in any particular, it should be entirely disregarded by the jury.

"A witness's credibility being seriously impeached by written, or other plain, deliberate contradictory statement by him, and not supported, ought, it would seem, to be entirely rejected.

"But where a party speaks to a fact, in reference to which he cannot be presumed liable to mistake, if the fact turn out otherwise, it is extremely difficult to exempt him from the charge of deliberate falsehood; and courts of justice, under such circumstances, are bound upon principles of law, morality, and justice, to apply the maxim, '*falsus in uno, falsus in omnibus.*'—FALSE IN ONE, FALSE IN ALL. (See Phillips on Evidence, vol. iii. pp. 397 and 772.)

"MR. PRESIDENT: The length of this defence precludes the necessity of recapitulation. I omit it, and go to the conclusion with a few brief reflections, as pertinent, I trust, as they are true.

"I consider these difficulties in California to be a comedy—(very near being a tragedy)—of three errors: *first*, in the faulty orders sent out from this place; *next*, in the unjustifiable pretensions of General Kearney; *thirdly*, in the conduct of the government in sustaining these pretensions. And the last of these errors I consider the greatest of the three.

"Certainly the difficulties in California ought to be inquired into; but how? Not by prosecuting the subordinate, but the principals; not by prosecuting him who prevented, but him who would have made civil war If it was a crime in me to accept the governorship from Commodore Stockton, it was a crime in him to have bestowed it; and in either event, crime or not, the government which knew of his intention to appoint me, and did not forbid it, has lost the right of prosecuting either of us.

"My acts in California have all been with high motives, and a desire for the public service. My scientific labors did something to open California to the knowledge of my countrymen; its geography had been a sealed book. My military operations were conquests without bloodshed; my civil administration was for the public good. I offer California, during my administration, for comparison with the most tranquil portion of the United States: I offer it in contrast to the condition of New Mexico during the same time. I prevented civil war against Governor Stockton, by refusing to join General Kearney against him: I arrested civil war against myself, by consenting to be deposed—offering at the same time to resign my post as lieutenant colonel in the army.

"I have been brought as a prisoner and a criminal from that country. I could return to it, after this trial is over, without rank or guards, and without molestation from the people, except to be importuned for the money which the government owes them.

"I am now ready to receive the sentence of the court."

The reading of this defence, which occupied three sessions of the court, was concluded on the 26th of January, 1848. The three succeeding days were spent in deliberating upon the case, and on the day following, January 31, the court rendered its verdict of "guilty" on all the charges, and sentenced the accused to be dismissed from the service.

Accompanying the verdict, were the following papers, which were directed to be made parts of the record. The first, signed by the President of the Court, Bt. Brig. General Brooke, Lieut. Col. Taylor, and Major Baker, was as follows:

"Under the circumstances in which Lieutenant-Col. Fremont was placed between two officers of superior rank, each claiming to command-in-chief in California—circumstances in their nature calculated to embarrass the mind, and excite the doubts of officers of greater experience than the accused: and, in consideration of the important professional services rendered by him, previous to the occurrence of the acts for which he has been tried, the undersigned, members of the court, respectfully commend Lieutenant-Colonel Fremont to the lenient consideration of the President of the United States."

The other, signed by Lieutenant Colonel Long, Lieutenants-Colonel Morgan, and Major Delafield, was a follows:

"Under all the circumstances of this case, and in consideration of the distinguished professional services of the accused, previous to the transactions for which he has now been tried, the undersigned beg leave to recommend him to the clemency of the President of the United States."

President Polk refused to confirm the verdict of the court, as to the first charge, but "approved" of the sentence, which, however, he immediately remitted. The following was his order in the case:

"Upon an inspection of the record, I am not satisfied that the facts proved in this case constitute the military crime of 'mutiny.' I am of opinion that the second and third charges are sustained by the proof, and that the conviction upon these charges warrants the sentence of the court. The sentence of the court is therefore approved; but, in consideration of the peculiar circumstances of the case, of the previous meritorious and valuable services of Lieutenant-Colonel Fremont, and of the foregoing recommendations of a majority of the members of the court, the penalty of dismissal from the service is remitted.

"Lieutenant-Colonel Fremont will accordingly be released from arrest, will resume his sword, and report for duty.

"JAMES K. POLK."

Upon receiving notice of the result of the trial, Colonel Fremont addressed the following letter to the Adjutant-General:

"WASHINGTON CITY, C Street, *Feb.* 19, 1848.

"SIR: I have this moment received the general order, No. 7 (dated the 17th instant), making known to me the final decision in the proceedings of the general court-martial, before which I have been tried; and hereby send in my resignation of lieutenant-colonel in the army of the United States.

"In doing this, I take the occasion to say that my reason for resigning is that I do not feel conscious of having done anything to merit the finding of the court; and, this being the case, I cannot, by accepting the clemency of the President, admit the justice of the decision against me.

"Very respectfully your obedient servant.

"J. C. FREMONT."

The President did not act upon this resignation for some time, and as the President's acceptance was necessary to give it legal effect, Col. Fremont addressed the adjutant-general a note to that effect on the 14th of March, and received a reply on the following day announcing the acceptance of his resignation from that date. Thus, on the 15th day of May, 1848, and in the 34th year of his age, Col. Fremont's connection with the military profession terminated, and his manhood once more resumed its natural proportions.*

* "In pursuance of his original intentions as communicated to the government in August, 1846, Commodore Stockton appointed Colonel Fremont civil governor of California, and Colonel William H. Russell, secretary. Governor Fremont immediately entered on the duties of his office, and the people acquiesced in his exercise of authority.

"The commodore and his maritime army returned to the squadron.

"The performance of his duties as governor of California by Col. Fremont were incompatible with the authority which General Kearney attempted to exercise over him by virtue of seniority of rank, notwithstanding the President and Secretary of War both justified the appointment of Colonel Fremont by Commodore Stockton, as civil governor of California, yet nevertheless he was permitted to be brought to trial on charges of disobedience preferred by General Kearney. He was found guilty on several charges and specifications, by a court evidently disposed to favor General Kearney. The finding of the court was approved in part by the President, but the sentence remitted.

"Indignant with the injustice and inconsistency manifested by the government, Colonel Fremont promptly resigned his commission in the army.

"Towards the close of the Mexican war, the army was powerful and popular at Washington. The *esprit de corps* of military gentlemen was piqued and offended with Fremont's deference to a naval commander, and his sacrifice was demanded. The President and Secretary of War had not the moral courage and firmness which the occasion required, and Colonel Fremont was driven from the army."—*Life of Commodore Stockton*, p. 154.

CHAPTER XI.

COLONEL FREMONT PROJECTS A FOURTH EXPLORING EXPEDITION—CALIFORNIA CLAIMS BILL—SPEECHES OF SENATORS BENTON, CLARKE AND DIX—MAP AND GEOGRAPHICAL MEMOIR—REPORT OF SENATOR BREESE—PROFESSOR TORREY'S PLANTÆ FREMONTIANÆ—GOLDEN MEDAL FROM THE KING OF PRUSSIA—LETTER FROM HUMBOLDT—FOUNDER'S MEDAL FROM THE ROYAL GEOGRAPHICAL SOCIETY OF LONDON—LETTERS FROM JOHN M. CLAYTON AND ABBOTT LAWRENCE—REPLY OF COLONEL FREMONT.

When Mr. Fremont abandoned the profession for which he had accomplished himself, and sat himself down the morning after his resignation was accepted, to determine what useful end the remainder of his life should be devoted to, he was but thirty-four years of age. Within that period he had attached his name imperishably to the historical, geographical, scientific and political history of his country. The highest peak of the longest chain of mountains on this continent had accepted his name in token of his being its first explorer; the plants which bloomed on its sides and in its valleys, had received from him their nomenclature; as the deliverer of California from Mexican misrule, he had identified himself for ever with the most durable traditions of that wonderful State; as a geographer he had won the homage of the whole scientific world; and finally he had achieved among his own countrymen a popularity more unanimous and more universal than had ever before been enjoyed by any one of his years. These reflections were well calculated to sooth any mortification, if he had felt any, at the result of the court martial. Starting life without means and aided only by the friends he had made himself, and his own energies, he had reached distinction before he had reached the maturity of his faculties; and, before most men have begun their career he was covered with honors enough for the close of his.

None of these considerations, however, disposed him to idleness. On the contrary his plans for a laborious and useful future were soon formed. While in California he had made arrangements for the purchase of the tract of land known as the Maraposas, of the value of which he had informed himself during his third expedition. Upon this he determined to settle as soon as he had demonstrated the practicability of uniting the Atlantic and Pacific States by a public highway. This he resolved to do before allowing himself any but necessary repose, and soon made his arrangements for a new trip across the plains, the following winter.

The intervening period was occupied in doing what he could to procure a settlement of the bills incurred in the conquest and defence of California in 1847, and in making up a report of the scientific results of his last expedition.

On the 1st of February, the military committee of the Senate, consisting of Messrs. Cass, Benton, Crittenden, Dix, Rusk and Davis, commenced an investigation in relation to the claims above referred to, amounting in all to some $700,000 for the payment of which amount a bill was afterwards introduced. The beneficiaries of this bill and its general provisions are described with sufficient minuteness in the following paragraph near the close of a speech made in its favor by Senator Benton.

"The California battalion, formed out of the American settlers on the Sacramento and the men of the topographical party (re inforced afterwards by later emigrants from the United States), finished on the Plains of Couenga the movement which had commenced at Sonoma, and in the same spirit of justice, moderation and patriotism. In conjunction with the sailors and marines, they had twice conquered California before the United States troops arrived in the country. They did it without aid from the United States—without quartermasters, commissaries, and paymasters to carry feed and pay them. The fruits of all their labors have been received by the United States, and the bill rendered is only seven hundred thousand dollars—a fraction only of the amount paid to those who arrived after the work was done. It should have been provided for in one of the public bills. It is an appropriation, and of a public nature, and of a most sacred nature. It should at least have had a place in that "Deficiency" bill of fourteen millions, which lately passed Congress, for what can be more deficient than non-payment, for almost two years for such extraordinary services? Even if this bill is passed at once and with the least possible delay from legislative forms, it will still be almost half a year before the claimants can begin to touch their pay. The bill is carefully drawn, both with a view to public and to private justice. It is intended to settle up and pay up all just claims, and to close the door forever upon all false ones. A commissioner acquainted with the subject, familiar with every transaction, is to go to California, visit every district in which claims are originated, call all before them, allow the good, reject the bad, and bar all that are not presented to them. In this way, and in this alone, can justice be done to all parties, just claimants saved from the depredations of agents and speculators; the United States saved from paying false accounts, and California prevented from becoming a mine for the production of false claims for half a century to come. The great and main facts that services have been rendered, that the United States have received the benefits of these services, and that they have not been paid for, are established by the depositions; the mode of settlement, and the detail of payment, is directed by the bill."

Senator Clarke of Rhode Island, in the course of a long and able speech upon the same subject paid the following tribute to Col. Fremont's services.

"Mr. President: The former explorations of Col. Fremont through the wilderness of the extreme West, have given him an enviable reputation in the world of science. His maturity of thought, and polished and cultivated intellect, united to a firm resolution, and a courage that never quailed—all eminently fitted him for the mission he so well and so readily undertook and performed. His energy of character qualified him for the position in which his government had placed him. If we condemn this invasion of the territory of a friendly power, I would not be understood as reflecting upon the man, who in obedience to his government, conducted that invasion and carried out those wishes to the entire subjugation of the country. I would not, sir, take a feather from his plume, nor a sprig from the garland that encircles his brow. Whatever may be the rigid rules of war, or the technicalities of the service under which this officer has suffered, his honor is untarnished—his high reputation as a soldier is unspotted—the crowning act of his eventful life is fresh in our recollection. When the commission which he bore, and which he would have yielded up only with his life, became tainted with censure, firmly he tendered it back to the executive whom he had obeyed, and to the country which he had served so faithfully. He is now a citizen amongst us, and deserves all our confidence. He is identified with the events in California, and who so fitting as he to bring these claims to a just and proper conclusion?"

In the course of the same debate, Senator Dix of New York, expressed the following opinion of Mr. Fremont and his public services.

"In the execution of these objects, the young and accomplished officer at the head of our troops, Col. Fremont, exhibited a combination of energy, promptitude, sagacity and prudence, which indicated the highest capacity for civil and military command; and, in connection with what he has done for the cause of science, it has given him a reputation at home and abroad, of which men much older and more experienced than himself might well be proud. That the country will do justice to his valuable and distinguished services, I entertain not the slightest doubt. * * * * The objects accomplished by Col. Fremont, as subsequent developments have shown, were far more important than those I have referred to. There is no doubt that his rapid and decisive movements kept California out of the hands of British subjects, and perhaps out of the hands of the British government, and it is in this point of view that I desire to present the subject to Senate. * * * * * It is in this point of view that the transaction possesses the greatest interest and importance, and that the sagacity, promptitude and decision of our youthful commander in California, at the time the disturbance broke out, have given him the strongest claims on his countrymen. Any faltering on his part—any hesitancy in acting, and acting promptly—might have cost us millions of dollars and thousands of lives; and it might also have cost us a contest of which the end is not readily foreseen."

Col. Fremont has never published any report either

of his third or subsequent expeditions. The fullest account of the third which has been made will be found in the preceding pages. On the 5th of June, the Senate ordered twenty thousand copies of a map of Oregon and California which he finished about that time. And likewise printed a Geographical Memoir of Upper California, illustrative of the map. This work gives the most compendious view of the scientific results of his explorations, and on the whole reflects most credit upon his inductive faculties and powers of statement. The want of a more complete record of his discoveries, in legislating for our Pacific possessions was seriously felt by the Senate, and they appointed a select committee to inquire into the expediency of providing for the publication of a third expedition as a National Work. Senator Breese of Illinois, the chairman of the committee, made an elaborate report in favor of the publication, in the course of which he speaks of the map and the Geographical Memoir as follows:

"This map and memoir, though hastily prepared, and as a mere preliminary to a full work, increase the reputation of their author, and give valuable information to the statesman and to the farmer, to the astronomer and the geographer, to the man of science in the walks of botany and meteorology. But they must be regarded only as a sample of the results of that expedition, from the view of which the value of the whole may be judged. As far as the exploration has been carried, everything necessary to show climate, soil, and productions, has been collected. More than one thousand specimens in botany, a great number in geology and mineralogy, with engravings of birds and animals, and remarkable scenery, and a large collection of the skins of birds with the plumage preserved, have been, as the committee are informed, brought home to enrich the stores and add to the sum of human knowledge. The botanical specimens examined by Dr. Torrey are deemed by him of great value and worthy of the expense of European engraving, if not done by our own government.*

The botanical stores referred to by the Senatorial Committee were deposited with Professor Torrey, who prepared a memoir in relation to them for the Smithsonian Institute, by whom they were beautifully engraved, and published in 1850.† A more precise idea of their value may be gathered from the following passage with which Torrey commences his memoir.

DESCRIPTIONS OF SOME NEW PLANTS COLLECTED BY COLONEL J. C. FREMONT IN CALIFORNIA.

"The important services rendered to science by that distinguished traveller, Colonel Fremont, are known to all who have read the reports of his hazardous journeys, &c.

"He has not only made valuable additions to the geographical knowledge of our remote possessions, but has greatly increased our acquaintance with the geology and natural history of the regions which he explored. His first expedition was made in the year 1842, and terminated at the Rocky Mountains. He examined the celebrated South Pass, and ascended the highest mountain of the Wind River chain, now called Fremont's Peak. The party moved so rapidly (travelling from the frontier of Missouri to the mountains, and returning in the short space of four months) that much time could not be given to botany. Never-

* For the full report see Appendix A.

† *Plantæ Fremontianæ*, or descriptions of plants collected by Colonel J. C. Fremont in California, by John Torrey, F.L.S.—*Smithsonian Contributions to Knowledge.*

theless, a collection of three hundred and fifty species of plants was made, of which I gave an account in a botanical appendix to this first report. The second expedition of Colonel Fremont was that of 1843 and 1844, embracing not only much of the ground of which he had previously explored, but extensive regions of Oregon and California. In this journey he made large collections in places never before visited by a botanist; but unfortunately, a great portion of this was lost. In the gorges of the Sierra Nevada, a mule loaded with some bales of botanical specimens, gathered in a thousand miles of travel, fell from a precipice into a deep chasm, from whence they could not be recovered. A large part of the remaining collection was destroyed, on the return of the expedition, by the flood of the Kansas River. Some of the new and more interesting plants that were rescued from destruction, were published in the Botanical Appendix to Colonel Fremont's Report of the second expedition.

"Very large collections were also made in his third expedition in 1845, and the two following years; but again, notwithstanding every precaution, some valuable packages were destroyed by the numerous and unavoidable mishaps of such a hazardous journey. Very few of the new genera and species that were saved have as yet been published, excepting several of the Compositals by Dr. Gray, in order that the priority of their discovery might be secured by Colonel Fremont. There was still another journey to California made by that zealous traveller; the disastrous one commenced late in the year 1848. Even in this he gleaned a few plants, which, with all his other botanical collections, he kindly placed at my disposal. I had hoped that arrangements would have been made by the government for the publication of a general account of the botany of California, but as there is no immediate prospect of such a work being undertaken, I have prepared the memoir on some of the more interesting new genera, discovered by Colonel Fremont. The drawings of the accompanying plates were made by Mr. Isaac

Sprague of Cambridge, Massachusetts, who ranks among the most eminent botanical draughtsmen of our day."

While alluding to the estimate placed upon the scientific results of Col. Fremont's explorations, by some of his eminent contemporaries, we may be pardoned for anticipating the tributes paid two years later to his labors by Baron Humboldt, on behalf of the King of Prussia, and by the Royal Geographical Society of London. As a minister of the Prussian government, Humboldt was charged to present Fremont with "the *great golden medal for progress in the sciences.*" He accompanied the medal with the following highly complimentary note to Fremont, in which a graceful allusion is made to that early struggle against slavery with which his political career in California commenced and closed.

"*Monsieur le Sénateur**: Il m'est bien doux, Monsieur, de vous addresser ces lignes par mon excellent ami, notre ministre

*Fremont had just been elected to the United States Senate, from California. The following is the English translation of Baron Humboldt's letter:

"*To Col. Fremont, Senator.*

"It is very agreeable to me, sir, to address you these lines by my excellent friend, our minister to the United States, M. de Gerolt. After having given you, in the new edition of my 'Aspects of Nature,' the public testimony of the admiration which is due to your gigantic labors between St. Louis, of Missouri, and the coasts of the South Sea, I feel happy to offer you, in this living token, (*dans ce petit signe de vie*) the homage of my warm acknowledgment. You have displayed a noble courage in distant expeditions, braved all the dangers of cold and famine, enriched all the branches of the natural sciences, illustrated a vast country which was almost entirely unknown to us.

"A merit so rare has been acknowledged by a sovereign warmly interested in the progress of physical geography; the king orders me to

aux États-Unis, M. de Gerolt. Après vous avoir donné dans la nouvelle édition de mes *Tableaux de la Nature* le témoignage public de l'admiration qui est due à vos gigantesques travaux entre St. Louis du Missouri et les côtes de la mer du Sud, je me sens heureux de vous offrir, dans ce petit signe de vie, l'hommage de ma vive reconnaissance. Vous avez déployé un noble courage dans des expéditions lointaines, bravé tout les dangers des frimas et du manque de nourriture, enrichi toutes les parties de sciences naturelles, illustré un vaste pays qui nous était presque entièrement inconnu. Un mérite si rare a été reconnu par un souverain vivement interessé aux progrès de la géographie physique: le roi m'ordonne de vous offrir la grande médaille d'or, destinée à ceux qui ont travaillé à des progrès scientifiques. J'espère que cette marque de la bienveillance royale vous sera agréable dans un moment, où, sur la proposition de l'illustre géographe, Charles Ritter, la Société de Géographie, residante à Berlin, vous a nommé pour membre honoraire. Quant à moi, je dois vous remercier particulièrement aussi de l'honneur que vous m'avez fait d'attacher mon nom et celui de mon collaborateur et ami intime, M. Bonpland, à des contrées voisines de celles qui ont été l'objet de nos travaux. La Californie, qui a

offer you the grand golden medal destined to those who have labored at scientific progress. I hope that this mark of the royal good will, will be agreeable to you at a time when, upon the proposition of the illustrious geographer, Chas. Ritter, the Geographical Society at Berlin has named you an honorary member. For myself, I must thank you particularly also for the houor which you have done in attaching my name, and that of my fellow-laborer and intimate friend, Mr. Bonpland, to countries neighboring to those which have been the object of our labors. *California, which has so nobly resisted the introduction of slavery, will be worthily represented by a friend of liberty and of the progress of intelligence.*

"Accept, I pray you, sir, the expression of my high and affectionate consideration.

"Your most humble and most obedient servant,

"A. v. HUMBOLDT.

"SANS SOUCI, October 7, 1850."

noblement résisté à l'introduction de l'esclavage, sera dignement représentée par un ami de la liberté et des progrès de l'intelligence.

"Agréez, je vous prie, Monsieur le Sénateur, l'expression de ma haute et affectueuse considération.

"Votre très humble et très obéissant serviteur,

"A. v. HUMBOLDT.

"A SANS SOUCI, le 7 Octobre, 1850."

On the envelope thus addressed:

"À Monsieur le Colonel Frémont, Senateur,
"Avec la grande médaille d'or,*
"Pour les progrès dans les sciences.
"BARON HUMBOLDT."

From the Royal Geographical Society Col. Fremont received the Founder's medal. It was transmitted to him through Abbot Lawrence, then our minister to England, and John M. Clayton, Secretary of State, who accompanied it with the following letter and its enclosure.

LETTER FROM THE SECRETARY OF STATE TO COLONEL FREMONT.†

DEPARTMENT OF STATE, WASHINGTON, *June 15th*, 1850.

"MY DEAR SIR: I have the honor to enclose herewith, an extract from a dispatch received at this Department yesterday, from the Hon. Abbott Lawrence, our Minister in London, from which you will perceive that the Royal Geographical Society

* The medal is of fine gold, massive, more than double the size of the American double eagle, and of exquisite workmanship. On the face is the medallion head of the king, Frederic William the Fourth, surrounded by figures emblematical of Religion, Jurisprudence, Medicine and the Arts. On the reverse, Apollo, in the chariot of the sun, drawn by four high mettled plunging horses, traversing the zodiac, and darting rays of light from his head.

† *National Intelligencer*, June 8th, 1850.

has awarded you the "Founder's Medal," for the distinguished services which you have rendered to geographical science.

"The messenger who bears you this letter, will also deliver you the medal. It affords me pleasure to be the immediate instrument in conveying to you this high tribute of respect, so well earned by the valuable and distinguished services which you have rendered, not only to your own country, but to the whole scientific world.

"I am, sir, very sincerely and truly yours,

"J. M. CLAYTON."

'Hon. J. C. FREMONT."

LETTER FROM THE UNITED STATES MINISTER AT LONDON, TO COLONEL FREMONT.

"LONDON, *May* 31*st*, 1850.

"DEAR SIR: On the 27th inst., I had the honor to receive from the President of the Royal Geographical Society the Founder's Medal, which was awarded to you by the council of that society, for your preëminent services in promoting the cause of geographical science. The meeting was public, and the reasons for according the medal to you were set forth with ability by the President. It became my duty to reply on your behalf, which I did very briefly. The proceedings of the meeting will be published at an early day, when I shall transmit a copy to you. I assure you that I feel a proud satisfaction in having the opportunity of being present at the Annual Meeting of the Society, and receiving this complimentary testimonial of merit to a citizen of the United States, who has done so much not only in the cause of science, but in every department of duty to which he has been called to promote the honor of his country.

"It is my fervent hope that your life may be long spared to enjoy your well earned fame in science, and that your success in your new and high position may be commensurate with the name and fame acquired by arduous labor in your brief but brilliant career.

"I am dear sir most faithfully,

"Your obedient servant,

"ABBOTT LAWRENCE."

"To Col. JOHN CHARLES FREMONT, &c.,

"Washington, D. C."

REPLY OF THE UNITED STATES MINISTER TO THE ADDRESS OF THE SOCIETY IN PRESENTING THE MEDAL.

"MR. PRESIDENT: It is with great pride and satisfaction that I am here to receive from your hands the medal awarded by the Council of the Royal Geographical Society to Col. Fremont. In his behalf I thank you, and the gentlemen of the Council and the Society, for an honor which I am sure he will appreciate as one of the most distinguished that has been conferred upon him in his brilliant career.

"The testimonial could not have been given to a more deserving individual. Col. Fremont possesses, in an eminent degree, the elements of a just success. He has ability, perseverance, cultivation and industry, and above all, he is endowed with high moral attributes which have won for him the esteem of those more immediately connected with him, and the confidence of his fellow citizens in the country at large, who will see with pleasure this day's evidence of your correct appreciation of his services to science.

"But I look upon this award of your Council as something more than a tribute to individual worth. I esteem it as a national honor; and, as the representative of the United States, I offer you their and my grateful thanks. It is not the least of the charms of science that it is not bounded by the limits of nations. Its influence is as wide as the world, and new discoveries, whether in the field of geographical or other science, are the common property of mankind. Scientific men form a common brotherhood throughout all nations, and the harmony of feeling between them has done much, and is destined to do yet more towards establishing and maintaining the peace of the world.

"The New has incurred a great debt to the Old World, and particularly to Great Britain, for scientific knowledge. This they hope to repay in some measure at no very distant day. We have made rapid strides in the Union within a few years, and confidently hope soon to contribute our quota to the common stock. Our desire, Mr. President and gentlemen, is persever ingly to maintain with you a friendly competition, having for its object the advancement of civilization, and the elevation of the condition of man throughout the world. And we fervently hope that nothing will recur to prevent this, either by the disturbance of the peace now happily existing between the nations of Europe, or the cessation of the very friendly feeling between this country and the United States of America."

LETTER FROM COL. FREMONT TO THE PRESIDENT OF THE ROYAL GEOGRAPHICAL SOCIETY.

WASHINGTON CITY, *June 22d*, 1850.

"SIR: I have had the gratification to receive, through the hands of the American minister and the Secretary of State, the honorable medal with which the Geographical Society has distinguished me.

"In making my acknowledgments for this high testimonial of approbation, I feel it a particular pleasure that they are rendered to a society which I am happy to recognize as my *alma mater*, to the notice of whose eminent members I am already indebted for much gratification, and in whose occasional approval I have found a reason and a stimulus for continued exertion. I deem myself highly honored in having been considered a subject for the exercise of a national courtesy, and in being made one of the thousand links among the associations and cordial sympathies which unite our kindred nations.

"With feelings of high respect and regard for yourself,

"I am, sir, very respectfully,

"Your obedient servant,

"J. C. FREMONT."

"To Sir RODERICK MURCHISON,

"President of the Royal Geographical Society,

"London."

CHAPTER XII.

CORRESPONDENCE BETWEEN COL. FREMONT AND CAPTAIN CHARLES WILKES.

While preparing his map and Geographical Memoir for publication, and a few days before its completion, Col. Fremont became accidentally involved in a public discussion with Capt. Wilkes, of the navy, which possesses an interest now quite independent of the little incident out of which it originated. That incident is stated in the following note addressed to the Editors of the *National Intelligencer*:

LETTER FROM COL. BENTON.*

"C Street, *May* 14, 1848.

"Gentlemen: We read in the *National Intelligencer* for May 9, as follows:

"'The United States sloop of war Portsmouth, Commander Montgomery, arrived in Boston, on Friday, from the Pacific Ocean.

"'Commander Montgomery states that the British frigate Herald, and the brig Pandora, are engaged in making a new survey of the gulf and coast of California.

"'The whale-ship Hope, of Providence (R. I.), was recently lost on the coast in consequence of an error in the charts now in general use, which locate the coast and islands from Monterey to

* See "National Intelligencer," May 15, 1848.

Cape San Lucas, from fifteen to forty miles too far to the eastward.'

"On reading this notice in your paper, I have to say that the error in question has already been detected by Mr. Fremont and corrected in his map of Oregon and Upper California, now in course of preparation, and nearly ready to be laid before the Senate, by whom its construction was ordered. In his last expedition, Mr. Fremont made a series of astronomical observations across the continent, terminating at Santa Cruz, near Anno Nuevo, the northwestern point of the Bay of Monterey. It was found, on laying down these positions on his map, that the west end of the line went beyond the coast, as given in Vancouver's charts (the basis of all in use), and that it projected two miles into the sea. His own map was immediately corrected accordingly, placing the coast and islands of Upper California ten miles further west.

"Mr. Fremont's observations were made in the winter and spring of 1845 and 1846. They were calculated by Professor Hubbard, of the Washington City Observatory, during the past winter; and were laid down on the map by Mr. Chas. Preuss, in February last.

"This map, with a memoir to illustrate it, and the calculations of Prof. Hubbard, will be laid before the Senate in a few days.

"Respectfully, gentlemen, your obedient servant,

"THOMAS H. BENTON.

To this note there shortly appeared the following reply:

LETTER FROM CAPTAIN WILKES.*

"MESSRS. GALES & SEATON: On my return to the city after a few weeks' absence, your paper of the 15th of May, containing some remarks on the errors existing in the charts of the northwest coast of California, by Col. *Benton*, was brought to my notice. Although I have no desire to detract from any one,

* "National Intelligencer," June 8, 1848.

yet I think it due to others, as well as to the United States Exploring Expedition, to place the following facts before the public respecting the errors which *did exist* in the longitude of this coast, the '*discovery*' of which is now claimed to have been first made, and the errors corrected, by Col. Fremont, through a series of astronomical observations across the continent.

"Shortly after the publication of Vancouver's charts in 1798, errors were suspected to exist in them (his points were determined by lunar observations, and several chronometers, which latter performed but indifferently; and from these his results were obtained), from a difference which was found between him and the Spanish surveying vessels, employed at the same time on the coast of California. The amount of error was not, however, truly ascertained until some years after this, when Captain Beechey, of H. B. M. ship, the Blossom, visited this coast in 1826. His observations were confirmed by Captain Sir Edward Belcher, in H. B. M. surveying ship, the Sulphur, in 1835; and it was again confirmed by the United States Exploring Expedition in 1841.

"These corrections were all made on the general charts published by order of Congress in 1844, from the surveys and examinations of the Exploring Expedition, and have been in possession of our ships navigating the Pacific Ocean since that time.

"By comparing dates, it will be perceived that these 'discoveries' were known long since, and that the actual amount of error was ascertained some twenty years ago by both the English and French expeditions, and were published by our own government in the results of the Exploring Expedition, a year prior to the earliest date claimed by Col. Benton, as the time when the observations of Lieut. Col. Fremont were made.

"With great respect, I am, yours, &c.,

"CHARLES WILKES.

"*Washington, June 6th*, 1848." *

* This letter was accompanied with the following editorial note:

"In a matter purely scientific, difference of opinion cannot be any

This letter brought Col. Fremont into the field, who conducted the remainder of the correspondence with Capt. Wilkes to its close.

LETTER FROM COL. FREMONT TO THE EDITORS.*

WASHINGTON, *June 8th*, 1848.

"MESSRS. GALES AND SEATON: In the absence of Col. Benton, and as the matter relates specially to myself, I desire to take some notice of the publication made in your paper of to-day by Captain Wilkes of the navy, concerning the rectification of an error on our western coast.

"Capt. Wilkes could not have examined with much care the note of Col. Benton, which he undertakes to criticise, or he would have perceived that it is not against anything stated by Col. Benton, or claimed for the observations made by myself, that his strictures apply: but that his sole dispute, if he has any, is with the reports brought in by the sloop of war Portsmouth, Commander Montgomery, and only quoted in the note of Col. Benton. He must also have perceived, with a little more attention, that the word 'discovery,' which he has introduced as a quotation italicized, does not exist in Col. Benton's note: and hence that his use of the word, as if copied from Col. Benton's note, is, in both instances unwarranted.

"The plain facts in the matter in question are these: in my map published in 1845, accompanying the report of the first and second expeditions under my command, the line of the Pacific

cause of quarrel, nor even of unkind feeling. We publish Capt. Wilkes's note as we did Mr. Benton's, without requiring any other authority than the name of the writer.

"We cannot however, repress the obvious remark, that, as Col. Fremont was not in possession of the corrected charts spoken of by Captain Wilkes, he is still entitled to the merit of having, by means of his astronomical observations, discovered the error, though others also had discovered the same error."

* "National Intelligencer," June 10th, 1848.

coast was laid down (and so stated) according to the survey of Vancouver. It was introduced merely to give a necessary completeness to the map of my reconnoissance, and without any attempt at a rectification of errors, which I supposed to come properly within the province of the naval exploring expedition which had recently surveyed the coast.

"In a recent expedition, having reference particularly to the geography on the Pacific coast, I was enabled to make 'a series of observations' in that country, depending on two main positions in the Sacramento valley, established by lunar culminations. These observations were made in 1845 and 1846; they were calculated during the last winter by Professor Hubbard of the Washington Observatory. On laying down the positions thus ascertained on the map, they were found not to correspond with the coast line, as before projected. I was aware that there had been various surveys of the coast, and discrepancies between the observations of the different navigators there. My observations agreed nearly with those of Capt. Beechey, and I immediately wrote to the city of New York, to procure, if any such had been published, a chart of the coast, founded on the surveys of either Beechey or Belcher; but was informed that there was nothing of the kind known there.

"This being the case, I caused the line to be erased, and projected further west, in conformity with my own observations. The fact of this alteration was confined to myself and to Mr. Preuss, who was engaged in drafting the map, and was not intended to be brought to the public notice in any more prominent way than by the publication of the map and observations to go for what they are worth, whether by themselves or in comparison. In the beginning of May, however, the arrival of the sloop of war Portsmouth, Commander Montgomery, from the Pacific Ocean, was announced, with the information, brought by her, that the whale-ship Hope had lately been lost on that coast in consequence of this same error *still existing* 'on the charts in common use.' In connection with this, it was also stated that two British naval vessels were engaged in a new survey of the coast. The correction made in my map (then nearly completed, and since laid before the Senate) was then mentioned, and it was thought proper, for public information, to make a statement of the fact of the correction, which was accordingly done in the note of Colonel Benton, certainly without the intent to detract from the labors of Captain Wilkes, or any one else, or to offer a remark that could have that effect. I had had the good fortune to find my observations in the Sacramento valley agree with those made in the same valley by Captain Belcher, but they differed with Captain Wilkes by about a third of a degree of longitude. These recurring discrepancies presented an additional reason, as I judged, at a moment, when a new survey by foreign authority was going on, for a public notice being made of my observations, which I conceived I had a right to give with the rest, to be taken at their value.

"The purpose of Captain Wilkes's note, as I understand it, is to show that the error in the geography of the coast was known years ago, and is corrected on the charts published in 1844, by the exploration expedition under his command, and 'in the possession of our ships navigating the Pacific Ocean since that time.' This being admitted, it only brings Captain Wilkes in conflict with the information given to the press by the officer of the sloop Portsmouth, as this was the whole authority on which it was supposed that the 'charts in common use' were erroneously projected, and that a note of correction of the error might be of interest and importance.

"It does not appear, however, why Captain Wilkes should have felt called upon to open a controversy on this matter in any shape. Certainly, whatever merit the exploring expedition which he commanded may have entitled itself to in the *publication* of corrections, it cannot claim any share in the *making* of them upon the coast in question (that of Upper California). In his card of to-day, Captain Wilkes refers to and professes to have agreed with the observations of Sir Edward Belcher. But in point of fact, the discrepancy between the positions of Captain Belcher and of Captain Wilkes is so great, as to have left the true geography of the coast more unsettled than before. Capt. Belcher's observations, like those of Capt. Wilkes, were extended into the Sacramento valley. Point Victoria, at the junction of Feather River with the Sacramento, is placed by Capt. Belcher in longitude 121° 35′ 35″ (Belcher, vol. 1, p. 121) ; as laid down by Captain Wilkes in his map, the same spot is about 30′ or half a degree further west; so that Captain Wilkes must say either that he is himself wrong by half a degree, or that Capt. Belcher is. This is a large error to make in the position of a navigable river, within two degrees of the coast parallel to it, affecting the position of the whole valley, five hundred miles in length, at the foot of the Sierra Nevada; and necessarily impairs confidence in the position of the coast itself, with which it is connected.

"Previous to the publication of my map in 1845, Capt. Wilkes was good enough to furnish me with the position established by himself at New Helvetia, as is acknowledged in my report of that date, and laid down upon the map then published. The results of my own observations, made during a recent journey to California, compelled me materially to change this position, removing it twenty miles to the eastward. The observations connected with these at this point, extended through the Sacramento and San Joaquim valleys, which, with the dependent country, are accordingly placed upon the present map twenty miles further east. As already said, these positions agreed with Capt. Belcher, and, being thus supported by his authority, and aware that my observations did not agree with those of Capt. Wilkes, I did not further consult his maps or charts. I find to-day, however, by his map of Upper California, accompanying the fifth volume of his Narrative, that he has laid down the whole extent of the Sacramento River more westerly than the longitude in which he had placed New Helvetia, and differing consequently, by half of a degree from Capt. Belcher, whom he professes to concur with and corroborate.

"It is true that the line of the coast appears to have been laid down by Capt. Wilkes in the positions which the observations of Capt. Beechey and Capt. Belcher would assign to it. But it is very strange that, if he agreed with those officers so exactly on the coast, he should, in the extension of his surveys through the short space of a degree, differ with them by half a degree of longitude. Had Capt. Wilkes referred the coast, by the true difference in longitude, to his observations in the Sacramento valley, it would have been thrown as much too far west as Vancouver had placed it too far east. It would seem, then, that Capt. Wilkes's observations do not form a connected 'series' which depend on each other, and that they do not corroborate or confirm previous surveys, except insomuch as they copy them.

"I infer from Capt. Wilkes's card, that neither Capt. Beechey nor Capt. Belcher's surveys caused the proper corrections to be made in the charts of the coasts, and that *his* publications of 1844 were the first to give the benefit of those older surveys to the seamen of the Pacific. In that case the cause must have been that the true position of the coast was considered still uncertain at the hydrographic office in London: and this is the more probable from the fact that a new survey was being made last November. That Capt. Wilkes added anything he does not pretend, and that our seamen need something more accurate than they have, is shown by the recent fate of the ship Hope, and the report of her loss brought in by a naval vessel, whose officers may be supposed to know what are the charts most in use and most authentic.

"In conclusion, I would state, that the observations which I have made, and on which the positions I have adopted depend, will be *published*, in connection with a geographical memoir of California, laid before the Senate a few days ago; and since Capt. Wilkes has thought proper to raise a controversy with me, I hope he will see the propriety of also publishing the observations, which, with his large equipment of instruments, he was so well prepared to make with accuracy. I have not learned that any such have been published, and I have had not the leisure to read through his work.

"J. C. FREMONT."

LETTER FROM CAPTAIN WILKES TO THE EDITORS.*

"GENTLEMEN: With much pleasure I avail myself of the call of Lieut. Col. Fremont to give the public the required information in relation to the observations made by the Exploration Expedition on the coast of California. It has been my constant desire to publish the astronomical and hydrographical results ever since the return of the Exploration Expedition, but from circumstances beyond my control the publication has been and will be delayed for some time.

"As Lieut. Col. Fremont wishes the public to know why I controverted the first detection of the error in the longitude of the coast of California, I will state that it arose from my desire to do justice to others and ourselves on an interesting point of geographical history, deemed of such high importance by Col. Benton as to cause him to claim, through the columns of your journal, that the merit of its detection was due to the labors of Col. Fremont, and also from a sense of duty to the public to state what I knew had been previously done by others and ourselves. I am well satisfied the public will deem me justified in doing so, without impugning my motives.

"With reference to the longitudes on the northwest coast determined by the Exploring Expedition, the limits of your whole paper would not more than suffice to give the details, I shall therefore content myself with giving a general outline of the manner in which the duty was performed, so as to be intelligible to every one, and refer to the actual results when they are published.

"Two observations were established, one at Nisqually, in

* *National Intelligencer*, June 14th, 1848.

Puget Sound, Oregon Territory, in latitude 47°, and the other at Sausalito, on the north side of the entrance in the bay of San Francisco, California, in 37° 51′ 00″. At these positions scenes of moon-culminating stars, with both limbs of the moon, were taken, and the longitude deduced from intervals observed by Wm. Cranch Bond, Esq., at the Observatory, Cambridge, Massachusetts; by Lieut. Gillis, of the Navy, at Washington; and from those also at Greenwich, both calculated in the Nautical Almanac and observed. The first position, Nisqually, was by 46 moon-culminating stars, and the second, Sausalito, by 68. These two points thus astronomically determined, were also connected by meridian distances through our chronometers, and found to correspond satisfactorily. All the intermediate points between these two latitudes have been referred to one or the other, and most to both, through the agency of our chronometers. The longitude resulting from the mean of the 68 moon-culminating stars at Sausalito places it in 122° 26′ 06″ 221‴.

"The survey of the river Sacramento was intrusted to able officers, and seven boats, including the launch, with provisions, were employed on this duty. To the untiring exertions and zeal of the party we are indebted for the accurate survey of the river, from its mouth at San Pablo, to the head of navigation for boats.

"The survey was made by triangulation until the river become too narrow to work by that method; above that it was accomplished by azimuths, and distances by sound. Four stations were occupied for longtitude and latitude, the former being determined by chronometers through equal altitudes of the sun, and the latter by circum-meridian observations and by polaris. These positions have been compared with the surveys and proved satisfactory. The chronometer used was No. 972, Arnold and Dent, an excellent instrument. It was compared with the standard time at the Observatory before leaving, and after their return, a period of eighteen days; and its rate (which was small) determined during that interval by the Observatory time. The four positions I refer to above were Karguines Straits, Capt. Sutter's Landing, Feather River, and the Fish weir at the head of navigation for canoes, and the resulting longitudes from applying the meridian distances to that of Sausalito Observatory, were as follows: Karguine's camp, 122° 10′ 58″ 95‴; Capt. Sutter's landing, 121° 22′ 23″ 55‴; Feather river, 121° 29′ 02″ 60‴; Fish weir, 121° 48′ 38″ 25‴.

"The original chart of the river was plotted during the progress of the survey on a large scale, and is 27 feet in length. This I had the pleasure of showing to Col. Benton, Capt. Fremont (just after his return from his second trip), and two or three other gentlemen, who called at my house to see it. This chart has been reduced, and is now engraved on a sufficiently large scale to show all the windings of the river.

"In February, 1845, Capt. Fremont wrote me a letter requesting I would give him the positions I had assigned Fort Vancouver, and Capt. Sutter's Fort. The letter was forwarded to me at Philadelphia, where I was then engaged reading the proofs of my Narrative. The longitude of Fort Vancouver was 122° 39′ 34″ 6‴W., and Capt. Sutter's Fort 121° 40′ 05″—the same as given in the Narrative, and which was then believed to be correct. Subsequent calculations proved it to be erroneous. When this was discovered, one of the officers (St. Eld), who was on very intimate terms with Capt. Fremont, asked me if he was at liberty to communicate to Col. Fremont, and explain to him how it had occurred. To this I of course assented, and have since presumed it had been done, though I have no further knowledge of the fact.

"The above longitude of Feather River differs from that given by Belcher, some five or six minutes, and not as stated by Col. Fremont, some thirty minutes. In respect to the observations made on the Sacramento, by the able officers intrusted with that duty, I am satisfied that every confidence is to be placed in them, both for longitude and latitude.

"I must here take exception to Col. Fremont's comparing and

measuring our longitudes from a small map eleven inches by eight, covering seventeen degrees of longitude.

"Exception is also to be taken to his treating the minor points of our surveys as though they were principal ones, and governed our coast line; this cannot be permitted; he must well know that all points of longitude in a survey are derived from and referred to that occupied as an observatory, and that there is no other true course, and none other can with fairness be adopted in comparing the longitude of different surveys.

"Capt. Beechey gives his longitude of Yerba Buena Cove from the result of twenty-two moon-culminating stars, as 122° 27′ 23″ west. (See his Appendix, page 667, quarto, London). It will be seen that this differs from ours, and with all due deference to so able an observer, I have not the slightest doubt but that Capt. Beechey himself would, in weighing the testimony of the two, decide that the preference was to be given to our longitude, the result of sixty-eight culminations. Although we do not agree with Capt. Beechey, yet I consider we confirm his longitudes.

"An inference may be drawn from a part of the remarks of Col. Fremont that the Exploration Expedition had depended for its results upon others. I have to inform him as well as others (to make use of a common expression), that the Expedition, wherever it did go, went on its *own hook*.

"Having thus considered the operations of this Exploring Expedition, let us return to the point at *issue* before the public. Capt. Beechey established his observatory in November, 1827, near the fort at Monterey, from which can be seen *Santa Cruz*, near *Anno Nuevo*, the northwestern point of the bay of Monterey, where Col. Benton claims that Lieut. Col. Fremont made the observations which detected the error in the coast-line of California. Capt. Beechey has given the longitude as 122° 51′ 46″, obtained from seven moon-culminating stars. (See Appendix, page 668). Lieut. Col. Fremont admits that he agrees with Capt. Beechey in his longitudes, and it is, therefore, to be presumed that it is with the longitude of Monterey, or that of Yerba Buena Cove, which have been connected by Beechy, and found to correspond. If he had a knowledge of these observations, the public must be satisfied that Col. Benton was not authorized to claim the detection of an error for Lieut. Col. Fremont in the longitude of the coast of California that had been previously known to him. The surveys reported to be in prosecution by Commander Montgomery, of the Portsmouth, relate no doubt to the Gulf of California and its coast, and not to the Pacific coast of California, between Monterey and Cape St. Lucas.

"This part of the coast is well known, and there are ample materials for its delineation in the possession of the British Admiralty. It is usual to account for the loss of a ship by imputing errors to charts. No vessel ought to encounter wreck on a coast, except through stress of weather; it might happen on an insulated reef, rock, or islet; but on a coast, in fair weather, it must result either from ignorance or culpable neglect.

"As you, Messrs. Editors, truly observe, 'this discussion is a matter purely scientific; difference of opinion cannot be any cause of quarrel, not even of unkind feeling.' I therefore trust, having felt none myself, I have been successful in avoiding giving cause for any to others.

"I am, very respectfully your obedient servant,

"CHARLES WILKES.

"WASHINGTON, *June* 12, 1849."

LETTER FROM COLONEL FREMONT TO THE EDITORS.*

"MESSRS. GALES AND SEATON: I should not deem it necessary to trouble you or your readers with any further remarks on the subject on which Captain Wilkes has thought proper to invite a controversy with me, were it not for the very extraordinary position taken in his letter this morning, and which goes to the extent, in effect, of imputing unfairness in my references

* *National Intelligencer*, June 16, 1848.

to his observations, because I tested them by the map and books which he has published, and not to the results of certain 'subsequent calculations,' which are now for the first time made public.

"Not long after Captain Wilkes had been polite enough to furnish me, as stated in my former letter, with the position he had established for New Helvetia, I left the country on my third expedition; and neither before my departure nor at any time until now, in the 'Intelligencer' of this morning, did I ever learn that Captain Wilkes had discovered the erroneousness of that position, nor do I now find that there are any errata or other memoranda in his book by which the correction is indicated; and I had not the power of clairvoyance to discover those 'subsequent calculations' that seem to have been meantime secure in his bureau. Captain Wilkes knew the use I was to make of the position with which he furnished me, and if, in fact, he made the discovery he now announces at the time he states, while I was still here, and my report and map open to correction, the indifference which, according to his own showing, he manifested, was neither more nor less than willfully to permit (or rather cause) the further propagation of error on his authority. I had applied to Captain Wilkes, in a written communication, for positions which would enable me to connect my reconnoissance across the country with his surveys. His reply and the positions he furnished me came in the same shape I received them and gave them to the public in full confidence; and I must confess my surprise—not to use a stronger term—now to learn that, on discovering that he had led me into so important an error, he had not at once given me the proper correction in the most authentic form.

"Undoubtedly the positions *now* set down by Captain Wilkes for the Sacramento valley agree closely with the fact; but he gives them now for the first time, and it is most unwarrantable, his assertion that it was with reference to these *new positions* that I had said he differed half a degree of longitude from

Captain Belcher. I had never heard of these new positions, and could not have spoken of them. It was with reference to Captain Wilkes's *published works*, which have now been before the public uncorrected for the space of *three years*, that I said and repeat that his positions differ half a degree from those of Captain Belcher, whom he assumes, in his letter of Thursday last, to agree with and corroborate.

"I wish it to be borne in mind that it was not in an invidious spirit, or for any purpose of attack, that I pointed out this remarkable discrepancy. Captain Wilkes claimed in his note to have published a correct delineation of the western coast prior to any observations which I had made there; and my only object was to show why, if such were the fact, I was not aware of it. The reason was this, that on comparing the position he had given me in the Sacramento valley with my own observations, I perceived that there was the wide difference of twenty miles of longitude between us, and I supposed that his observations would agree with each other, and of course the same disagreement between his positions and mine would exist on the coast. I did not know that he had published maps or charts on other surveys than his own, and hence did not further consult his labors. When, however, he raised this controversy, and referred in his note to Captain Belcher's observations as being in agreement with his, I found it proper to consult his published works, and to show, in self defence, that in the discrepancy between us he was not thus supported by Captain Belcher, but differed widely from him.

"If Captain Wilkes intends, by taking exception to my reference to his map, published with the fifth volume of his Narrative, to say that his map is incorrect and of no authority, then I admit it would be improper to use it against him hereafter. But this disavowal comes too late to affect anything that has gone before; and, moreover, if the map is to be thus discarded, and also the positions given in the text, now, after a lapse of three years, to be erased and different ones substituted, in what part of the eight magnificent volumes can we be certain that 'subsequent calculations' have not detected inaccuracies hereafter to be exhibited? It is idle to intimate that in a map, on the scale of that given in the narrative of Captain Wilkes (volume 5, beginning of chapter 5), and executed with so much precision and neatness, with the meridians and parallels of latitude drawn at distances of single degrees, discrepancies in position of such an extent as twenty to thirty minutes, cannot properly be examined. For what purpose are the lines of longitude and latitude drawn upon the map at all, if the position of places and objects given are not to be measured and ascertained by them? If the difference in question were slight, no notice would have been taken of it; but this broad discrepancy of half a degree is as palpable and as open to criticism as if the map which shows it were twenty times its actual scale; and this more especially when it relates to a section which was the object of a particular, extended, and careful survey, as Captain Wilkes informs us was the case with the river Sacramento, and embraces not an isolated point but the whole of that section.

"But Captain Wilkes further takes exception, and 'cannot permit' that I shall 'treat the minor points of his survey as principal ones.' Nor have I done so; but surely there ought to be some degree of accordance between the minor points and the principal ones, and if a large error be found in the minor a corresponding one will be found in the principal. Besides this is not the error of a single 'minor point,' but a series of errors running through the observations made in some hundreds of miles. And, furthermore, Captain Wilkes informs us in his narrative, that a prominent point in the Sacramento valley—the Prairie *Buttes* (isolated mountains)—formed 'one of the connecting links' between two surveying parties of his expedition, one coming from the north, the other from the south, and 'served to verifiy their respective observations.' Surely it was fair to conclude that the observations thus 'connected' and 'verified,' whether made at minor points or principal ones, were intended to be taken for correct, and the positions laid down accordingly. Again, these *Buttes*, 'particularly described' in the narrative, and thus forming a 'connecting link' and point of 'verification' for the surveys of the expedition, are conspicuously laid down by Captain Wilkes on his map, with the meridian of 122° passing through them. Now, does Captain Wilkes wish us to believe that all this stands for nothing? Does he mean to intimate that positions thus noted by him, and conspicuously brought forward in the book and on the map, are not to be criticised because they are minor, not principal parts in the surveys?

"Considered with relation to the position assigned to the Sacramento River, the *Buttes* are rightly placed on the map; but 'connecting link' and point of 'verification' as they are, they require, along with the whole extent of the river, to be removed many miles (in no part less than twenty) further east, in order to correspond with their true longitude. The errors, therefore, cannot be laid to the execution of the map, which is thus shown to be drawn with care, and to agree with itself. It will also be noted that, as two surveys were here 'connected' and 'verified'—if, in fact, the errors which run through the line, were the result, as we are now informed, of wrong 'calculations,' instead of wrong observation, they involved a most remarkable series of blunders, embracing the surveys of the parties both from the north and south.

"I will copy here the longitude given by Captain Wilkes in his book, contrasted with those he now, for the first time, offers as from 'subsequent calculations.' In his book (quarto edition), he places New Helvetia in longitude 121° 40′ 05″; in his letter of to-day he gives 121° 22′ 23″ 55‴ as the longitude of a point, (Sutter's landing) near two miles west of New Helvetia. The 'Fish River, at the head of navigation' he gives in his book at 122° 12′ 17″, his present correction brings it 121° 48′ 38″ 25‴. The mouth of Feather River I do not find noted in his book; in his new correction he assigns it 121° 29′ 02″ 60‴—on his map it is placed *some minutes west* of 122°. A relative position given to the coast, I repeat, would have thrown it as much too far west as Vancouver has placed it too far east.

"I will not, however, here question Captain Wilkes's observations on the coast, or further inquire whether they ought to be said to copy or corroborate those of Captain Beechey; neither will I question that the longitude *now* given by Captain Wilkes for his positions in the Sacramento valley are the true results of his observations there, corrected by "subsequent calculations;" but I will say that, after suppressing the discovery of the errors he now announces for a space of three years, he has lost any right to plead them for any purpose; least of all, for the purpose of finding fault with those who have innocently taken his book and map for authentic records. I must, moreover, be allowed to inquire what degree of credit can further attach to a work which, got ready with four year's preparation, its author, three years subsequent to its publication, thus comes forward to discredit?

"J. C. FREMONT.

"WASHINGTON, *June 14th*, 1848."

LETTER FROM CAPTAIN WILKES TO THE EDITORS.*

"GENTLEMEN: It is not my intention to trespass upon your columns, or to weary the patience of your readers; but I feel constrained to offer a few words in reply to Lieut. Col. Fremont's article in your paper of this morning.

"As the object which was *at issue* before the public is not touched upon in Lieut. Col. Fremont's last article, I consider it therefore as ended, and that the testimony that I have adduced of Capt. Beechey's observations at Monterey and Yerba Buena are entirely satisfactory to show that Col. Benton was not authorized to claim for Lieut. Col. Fremont the detection of the error in the longitude of the coast of California.

* *National Intelligencer*, June 19th, 1848.

"Lieut. Col. Fremont's absence from the country on arduous duty may perhaps be a sufficient apology for his being uninformed of what has been done or published during the time, but I do not think he can be held justified for making against me so sweeping a charge as he has done, of withholding and suppressing corrections from the public, when a slight examination or some little inquiry, would have satisfied him he was in error especially as it was a fact that the desire to meet his inquiries and oblige was in part the cause of the errors of the longitude he makes mention of on a small map, the corrections of which errors were made a short time afterwards, and I fully believed had been furnished by Lieut. Col. Fremont by Lieut. Eld, as tated in my last communication.

"Respectfully, yours, &c.,

"CHARLES WILKES.

"*June 16th*, 1848."

LETTER FROM COL. FREMONT TO THE EDITORS.*

"MESSRS. GALES & SEATON: I must confess my inability to understand what Capt. Wilkes intends to signify, in his letter of yesterday, by stating that his desire to oblige me was one cause of the errors in the map of California. I do not perceive what connection I had with those mistakes, other than to have been grossly misled by placing confidence in the positions which he furnished me.

"Apart from those I never saw any observations or calculations of Capt. Wilkes, and I never saw his publications till since the beginning of the present correspondence.

"If he means that in his haste to furnish me with the positions I had requested, the erroneous calculations were made, to which he now attributes his mistaken longitudes, I answer that his expedition had then been nearly four years returned, his publications were nearly through the press, and it is extraordinary if his

* *National Intelligencer*, June 20th, 1848.

calculations had not been made, and even the identical map (which he would thus seem disposed to hold me responsible for the blunders of) both drawn and engraved. Moreover, I had understood from Capt. Wilkes's first letter that his charts had been published the year previous to my application to him, and it would seem that his positions ought to have been calculated previous to the making of his charts. The truth is Capt. Wilkes led me into error. According to his present showing, he discovered very soon after that he had done so. I must be permitted to believe that had his desire to oblige me been so strong as is now intimated, he would have taken the trouble to apprise me of his mistake, which he never did. I discovered the error of the position he had given me in the Sacramento valley from observations made during my late tour. I did not suspect, and had no reason to suspect, that he had made any subsequent rectification, and hence I was led into the second error (if it be an error) of supposing the coast was still erroneously laid down. I ascertained, as far as I was able to make inquiry, that no chart of the coast had been issued by Beechey or Belcher; I knew that Capt. Wilkes was the last surveyor there; I knew that my observations differed from what he had furnished me as his by about twenty miles, in the Sacramento valley, and took it for granted that forty miles further west the same disagreement would exist; and so corrected the outline of my map according to my own observations. The report shortly after brought in by one of our public vessels of the wreck of a ship on the coast in consequence of error in the charts in common use, it was considered good reason for making known that a different projection of the coast would appear on the forthcoming map. If, then, there was any error in this, or in the manner of its announcement, it is attributable entirely to the wrong information given me by Capt. Wilkes, and his failure to inform me of the fact, if he afterwards discovered the error he had led me into, and which I had published on his authority; for I could not be expected to look to his publications for a correct delineation of the coast, when I knew that forty miles off he had made so large an error.

"But it is clear that, if Captain Wilkes informs us, he has made a publication of charts which give the necessary correction of the coast, he must have *abandoned his own survey* for the purpose, and *proceeded entirely by the observations of others*. He published his charts, according to his note of the 6th instant, inviting this controversy, 'in 1844.' Now, it was in the winter of 1844–5, that he furnished me the positions which, according to his own showing, are so erroneous; and, still later, his own books contain the same and many corresponding errors. His positions, Capt. Wilkes informs us, were determined by the establishment of two observations—one at Nisqually, in Puget's Sound (the longitude of which, nevertheless, he does not furnish us with), and the other Sausalito, at the north side of the entrance to the Bay of San Francisco—and the reference of all the intermediate points to *one or the other*, and most of them to both of these main positions. Now, I will venture to say that all these 'intermediate points,' thus 'referred,' and as appears by the narrative, 'connected' and 'verified,' *could not* contain a common error, as they do, both in the map and text of Captain Wilkes's book, without a like error in the main positions. Hence if Capt. Wilkes published a correction of the coast, in chart, 1844, he must have done it on the labors of others; for he does not pretend to have discovered the erroneousness of his own calculations till after the issuing of his book in 1845.

"I apprehend, Messrs. Editors, that, notwithstanding the charts by Capt. Wilkes, and the labors of the British officers, whom he quotes and seems to have copied, when the whole truth comes to be investigated, it will be found that the proper position of the coast is not much better ascertained now than it was near sixty years ago. My occupation has been that of reconnoissance and survey *inland*, and my attention had not been directed to the state of the surveys on the coast beyond the very narrow inquiry—when I found my observations to be at variance with those of Vancouver, and still more so with those of Capt. Wilkes—whether Beechey or Belcher had published a corrected chart. Since the commencement of this correspondence, however, I have given the subject some more examination. The Spanish navigator, Malaspina, to the merits of whom Humboldt bears such honorable testimony, and whose subsequent misfortunes and political persecution gave a peculiar interest to such portion of his labors as they did not destroy, made a survey of this coast in 1791. His longitudes, as far as I have been able to examine them, were nearly correct. Vancouver followed immediately after, and his surveys, disagreed with Malaspina's, threw the coast from a third to a half degree too far east; subsequent surveys, as far as they have made any change, are but little more than restoring the positions of Malaspina.

"As for Capt. Wilkes's renewed objection to having his 'small map,' taken for a test, I have to remark, that corresponding errors with those in his 'small map,' appear *in his larger map of Oregon, and in the text of his narrative*, and I am not acquainted with any other publications he has made. If he objects to having it said that he has suppressed or withheld his corrections, surely he ought to point where and when he has made them public.

"I wish again to make the remark that this controversy is not of my seeking. When I discovered the great erroneousness of the positions Capt. Wilkes had given me, I contented myself by quietly making the corrections on my map; I had received them in good faith as the result of his observations, and supposed them to be given the same way, and should have studiously avoided, therefore any mention of the descrepancy. Had I known, however, what he now informs us of, that he had shortly afterwards found those positions to be incorrect, and yet left me in ignorance of the rectification, to make an erroneous publication, I should not have been so silent.

"I stated in my first letter that I did not see why Captain Wilkes had thought himself called on to provoke this controversy, since whatever his merits in *the publication* of corrections on the coast of California, he could not claim any share in *the making* them. I am now still more at a loss to know why he felt concerned in the matter, for it has become still more plain that he could not have supposed himself in any way wronged. His surveys not only do not make any corrections on the coast of California, but I feel warranted in saying that his entire surveys in Oregon and California, as far as they follow his own observations, are erroneously laid down in his published works.

"J. C. FREMONT

"WASHINGTON, *June* 20*th*, 1848."

CHAPTER XIII.

FOURTH EXPEDITION—ENCAMPED IN KANSAS—TERRIBLE JOURNEY THROUGH THE MOUNTAINS—FRIGHTFUL SNOW STORM—ONE HUNDRED AND TWENTY MULES FROZEN TO DEATH IN ONE NIGHT—STARVATION OF HIS COMRADES—MEETS AN UNEXPECTED FRIEND—REACHES THE RANCHE OF KIT CARSON—THRILLING LETTER TO HIS WIFE—ADVENTURE WITH NAVAHOES INDIANS.

In October, 1848, Fremont sat out upon his fourth expedition. But he went now at his own expense and not at the expense of the government; as an emigrant in quest of a home in the new State which he had emancipated, and not as an officer under orders. He went to prepare for the reception of his family, who were to join him in the spring, and he chose the winter for the journey as the season best adapted to make him acquainted with several of the most serious difficulties to be encountered in the construction of a highway to the Pacific, an enterprise of which he never lost sight in any of his plans for the future. He sat out on the 19th of October, and determined to make the line of his route along the head of the Rio Grande; first, because that route had never yet been explored, and secondly, because he had been informed by the mountaineers that there was a very practicable pass through the Mountains at the head of that river. This route took him through the country of the Utahs, Apaches, Navahoes, Camanches, Kioways, and other savage tribes of Indians, then all at war with the United States. To contend with the enemies and physical dangers of the inhospitable region through which he was to pass, he had selected thirty-three of his old companions, all provided with good rifles, and one hundred and twenty of the best mules he could find. These, with an experience in the kind of life to which they were to be exposed, without a parallel, and with a courage never surpassed, constituted his outfit and his security. Their preparations for this expedition were mostly made at a small government post just over the borders of Missouri in Kansas. Mrs. Fremont attended him as far as this point, and remained with him for the five or six weeks that he was occupied with his preparations; spending her days at his camp and her nights at the more comfortable quarters hospitably assigned to her and her husband by Major Cummins, a venerable Indian agent who had lived upon the frontier for twenty or thirty years. Here, in the depths of this vast wilderness, far beyond even the shadows of advancing civilization, Col. Fremont and his little party made their first acquaintance with a country which only seven years afterwards became the theatre of events destined to change the whole plan of his life;—to call him, like Washington, from his surveying, to become the national champion of freedom and civilization.

Of the progress and results of this expedition, fortunate as well as disastrous, Col. Fremont has as yet published no complete report. A sufficiently minute account of it, however, for our present purpose may be gathered from his private correspondence during the journey, and from the sketch just published by Colonel Benton.

The following letter dated from Bent's Fort shows what he had accomplished up to that point.

LETTER FROM COL. FREMONT TO COL. BENTON.

"CAMP AT BENT'S FORT, *Nov.* 17, 1848.

"MY DEAR SIR: We have met with very reasonable success and some good results this first long step upon our journey. In order to avoid the chance of snow-storms upon the more exposed Arkansas road, I followed up the line of the Southern Kansas (the true Kansas River) and so far added something to geography. For a distance of 400 miles our route led through a country affording abundant timber, game, and excellent grass. We find that the Valley of the Kansas affords by far the most eligible approach to the Mountains. The whole valley soil is of very superior quality, well timbered, abundant grasses, and the route very direct. This line would afford continuous and good settlements certainly for 400 miles, and is therefore worthy of consideration in any plan of approach to the Mountains. We found our friend, Major Fitzpatrick, in the full exercise of his functions at a point about thirty miles below this, in what is called the 'Big Timber,' and surrounded by about 600 lodges of different nations, Apaches, Camanches, Kioways, and Arapahoes. He is a most admirable agent, entirely educated for such a post, and possessing the ability and courage necessary to make his education available. He has succeeded in drawing out from among the Camanches the whole Kioway nation, with the exception of six lodges, and brought over among them a considerable number of lodges of the Apaches and Camanches. When we arrived he was holding a talk with them, making a feast and giving them a few presents. We found them all on their good behavior, and were treated in the most friendly manner; were neither annoyed by them, nor had anything stolen from us. I hope you will be able to give him some support. He will be able to save lives and money for the government, and knowing how difficult this Indian question may become, I am particular in bringing Fitzpatrick's operations to your notice. In a few years he might have them all farming here on the Arkansas.

"Both Indians and whites here report the snow to be deeper in the mountains than has for a long time been known so early in the season, and they predict a severe winter. This morning for the first time, the mountains showed themselves, covered with snow, as well as the country around us, for it snowed steadily the greater part of yesterday and the night before. Still, I am in nowise discouraged by the prospect, and believe that we shall succeed in forcing our way across. We will ascend the Del Norte to its head, descend on to the Colorado, and so across the Wahsatch mountains and the basin country somewhere near the 37th parallel, reaching the settled parts of California, near Monterey. There is, I think, a pass in the Sierra Nevada between the 37th and 38th, which I wish to examine. The party is in good spirits and good health; we have a small store of provisions for hard times, and our instruments, *barometer* included, all in good order. We are always up an hour or two before light, and the breakfasts are all over, and the camp preparing to move, before sunrise. This breakfasting before day light, with the thermometer ranging from 12° to 18°, is a somewhat startling change from the pleasant breakfast-table in your stove-warmed house. I think that I shall never cross the continent again, except at Panama. I do not feel the pleasure that I used to have in those labors, as they remain inseparably connected with painful circumstances, due mostly to them. It needs strong incitements to undergo the hardships and self-denial of this kind of life, and as I find I have these no longer, I will drop into a quiet life. Should we have reasonable success, we shall be in California early in January, say about the 8th, where I shall expect to hear from all by the steamer. Referring you for other details to Jessie, to whom I have written at length,

"I remain, most affectionately yours,

"J. C. FREMONT."

"Arrived at Pueblos on the Upper Arkansas, the last of November," says Col. Benton,* "at the base of the first sierra to be crossed, luminous with snow, and stern in their dominating look, he dismounted, his whole company took to their feet, and wading waist deep in the vast unbroken snow-field, arrived on the other side in the beautiful valley of San Luis; but still on the eastern side of the great mountain chain which divide the waters which ran east and west to the rising and setting sun. At the head of that valley was the Pass, described to him by the old hunters. With his glasses he could see the depression in the mountain which marked its place. He had taken a local guide from the Pueblo San Carlos to lead him to that Pass. But this precaution for safety was the passport to disaster. He was behind, with his faithful draughtsman, Preuss, when he saw his guide leading the company towards a mass of mountains to the left; he rode up and stopped them, remonstrated with the guide for two hours, and then yielded to his positive assertion that the pass was there. The company entered a tortuous gorge, following a valley through which ran a head stream of the great river Del Norte. Finally they came to where the ascent was to begin, and the summit range crossed. The snow was deep, the cold intense, the acclivity steep, and the huge rocks projecting. The ascent was commenced in the morning, struggled with during the day, an elevation reached at which vegetation (wood) ceased, and the summit in view, when, buried in snow, exhausted with fatigue, freezing with cold, and incapable of further exertion, the order was given to fall back to the line of vegetation, were wood would afford a fire and shelter them for the night. With great care the animals were saved from freezing, and at the first

* Thirty Years View, vol. ii. p. 719.

dawn of day the camp, after a daybreak breakfast, were in motion for the ascent. Precautions had been taken to make it more practicable. Mauls, prepared during the night, were carried by the foremost division to beat down a road in the snow. Men went forward by relieves. Mauls and baggage followed in long single file, in the tract made in the snow. The mountain was scaled—the region of perpetual congelation, was entered. It was the winter solstice, and a place where the summer solstice brought no life to vegetation—no thaw to congelation. The summit of the sierra was bare of everything but snow, ice and rocks. It was no place to halt. Pushing down the side of the mountain to reach the wood, three miles distant, a new and awful danger presented itself: a snow storm raging, the freezing winds beating upon the exposed caravan, the snow became too deep for the mules to move in, and the cold beyond the endurance of animal life. The one hundred and twenty mules, huddling together from an instinct of self-preservation from each other's heat and shelter, froze stiff as they stood, and fell over like blocks, to become hillocks of snow. Leaving all behind, and the men's lives to be saved, the discomfited and freezing party scrambled back, recrossing the summit, and finding under the lee of the mountain some shelter from the driving storm, and in the wood that was reached, the means of making fires.

"The men's lives were now saved, but they were destitute of everything, only a remnant of provisions, and not even the resource of the dead mules, which were on the other side of the summit; and the distance computed at ten days' travel to the nearest New Mexican settlement. The guide and three picked men were dispatched thither for some supplies, and twenty days fixed for their return. When they had gone sixteen days, Fremont, preyed upon by anxiety and misgiving, set off after them on foot, snow to the waist, blankets and some morsels of food on the back: the brave Godey, his draughtsman, Preuss, and a faithful servant, his only company. When out six days, he came upon the camp of his guide, stationary and apparently without pain or object, and the men, wild and emaciated. Not seeing King, the principal one of the company, and on whom he relied, he asked for him. They pointed to an older camp, a little way off. Going there he found the man dead, and horribly devoured. He had died of exhaustion, of fatigue, and his comrades fed upon him. Gathering up these three survivors, Fremont resumed his journey, and had not gone far before he fell on signs of Indians—two lodges, implying fifteen or twenty men, and some forty or fifty horses—all recently passed along. At another time this would have been an alarm, one of his fears being that of falling in with a war party. He knew not what Indians they were, but all were hostile in that quarter, and evasion was the only security against them. To avoid their course was his obvious resource: on the contrary he followed it; for such was the desperation of his situation that even a chance of danger had an attraction. Pursuing the trail down the Del Norte, then frozen solid over, and near the place where Pike had encamped in the winter of 1807–8, they saw an Indian behind his party, stopped to get water from an air hole. He was cautiously approached, circumvented, and taken. Fremont told him his name: the young man, for he was quite young, started, and asked him if he was the Fremont that exchanged presents with the chief of the Utahs, at Les Veges de Santa Clara, three years before? He was answered, 'Yes.'

"'Then,' said the young man, 'we are friends: that chief is my father, and I remember you.'

"The incident was romantic; but it did not stop here. Though on a war inroad upon the frontiers of New Mexico, the young chief became his guide, let him have four horses, conducted him to the neighborhood of the settlements, and then took his leave to resume his scheme of depredation on the frontier.

"Fremont's party reached Taos, was sheltered in the house of his old friend Carson—obtaining the supplies needed—sent them back by the brave Godey, who was in time to save two-thirds of the party, finding the other third dead upon the road, scattered at intervals as each had sunk exhausted and frozen, or half burned in the fire which had been kindled for them to die by. The survivors were brought in by Godey, some crippled with frozen feet. Fremont found himself in a situation which tries the soul—which makes the issue between despair and heroism—and leaves no alternative but to sink under fate, or to rise above it. His whole outfit was gone: his valiant mountain men were one third dead, many crippled: he was penniless, and in a strange place. He resolved to go forward, *nulla vestigia retrorsum:* to raise another outfit, and turn the mountains by the Gila. In a few days it was done—men, horses, arms, provisions, all acquired: and the expedition resumed.

"But it was no longer the tried band of mountain men on whose vigilance, skill and courage he could rely to make their way through hostile tribes. They were new men, and to avoid danger, not to overcome it, was his resource. The Navahoes and Apaches had to be passed and eluded, a thing difficult to be done, as his party of thirty men and double as many horses would make a trail easy to be followed in the snow, though not deep. He took an unfrequented course, and relied upon the secrecy and celerity of his movements. The fourth night on the dangerous ground, the horses, picketed without the camp, gave signs of alarm. They were brought within the square of fires, and the men put on the alert. Daybreak came without visible danger. The camp moved off; a man lagged a little behind, contrary to injunctions, the crack of some rifles sent him running up. It was then clear that they were discovered, and a party hovering round them. Two Indians were seen ahead; they might be a decoy, or a watch, to keep the party in view until the neighboring warriors could come in. Evasion was no longer possible; fighting was out of the question, for the whole hostile country was ahead, and narrow defiles to be passed in the mountains. All depended upon the address of their commander. Relying upon his ascendency over the savage mind, Fremont took his interpreter, and went to the two Indians. Godey said he should not go alone, and followed. Approaching them, a deep ravine was seen between. The Indians beckoned him to go round by the head of the ravine, evidently to place that obstacle between him and his men. Symptoms of fear or distrust would mar his scheme, so he went boldly round, accosted them confidentially, and told his name. They had never heard it. He told them they ought to be ashamed not to know their best friend; enquiring for their tribe, which he wished to see: and took the whole air of confidence and friendship. He saw they were staggered. He then invited them to go to his camp, where the men had halted, and take breakfast with him. They said that might be dangerous, that they had shot at one of his men that morning, and might have killed him, and now be punished for it. He ridiculed the idea of their hurting his men, charmed them into the camp, where they ate, and smoked, and told their secret, and became messengers to lead their tribe in one direction, while Fremont and his men escaped by another, and the whole expedition went through without loss, and without molestation."

Immediately upon his arrival at Taos and while sharing the hospitality of his faithful friend Carson, he addressed the following letter to his wife, and for its length, we scarcely know a more thrilling record of personal adventure in our language:

LETTER FROM COL. FREMONT TO HIS WIFE.

"TAOS, NEW MEXICO, *Jan.* 27, 1849.

"MY VERY DEAR WIFE! I write to you from the house of our good friend Carson. This morning a cup of chocolate was brought to me, while yet in bed. To an overworn, overworked, much fatigued, and starving traveller, these little luxuries of the world offer an interest which in your comfortable home it is not possible for you to conceive. While in the enjoyment of this luxury, then, I pleased myself in imagining how gratified you would be in picturing me here in Kit's care, whom you will fancy constantly occupied and constantly uneasy in endeavoring to make me comfortable. How little could you have dreamed of this while he was enjoying the pleasant hospitality of your father's house! The furthest thing then from your mind was that he would ever repay it to me here.

"But I have now the unpleasant task of telling you how I came here. I had much rather write you some rambling letters in unison with the repose in which I feel inclined to indulge, and talk to you about the future with which I am already busily occupied; about my arrangements for getting speedily down into the more pleasant climate of the lower Del Norte and rapidly through into California; and my plans when I get there. I have an almost invincible repugnance to going back among scenes where I have endured much suffering, and for all the incidents and circumstances of which I feel a strong aversion. But as clear information is absolutely necessary to you, and to your father more particularly still, I will give you the story now instead of waiting to tell it to you in California. But I write in the great hope that you will not receive this letter. When it reaches Washington you may be on your way to California.

"Former letters have made you acquainted with our journey so far as Bent's Fort, and from report you will have heard the circumstances of our departure from the Upper Pueblo of the Arkansas. We left that place about the 25th of November, with upwards of a hundred good mules and one hundred and thirty bushels of shelled corn, intended to support our animals across the snow of the high mountains, and down to the lower parts of the Grand River tributaries, where usually the snow forms no obstacle to winter travelling. At the Pueblo, I had engaged as a guide an old trapper well known as 'Bill Williams,' and who had spent some twenty-five years of his life in trapping various parts of the Rocky Mountains. The error of our journey was committed in engaging this man. He proved never to have in the least known, or entirely to have forgotten, the whole region of country through which we were to pass. We occupied more than half a month in making the journey of a few days, blundering a tortuous way through deep snow which already began to choke up the passes, for which we were obliged to waste time in searching. About the 11th December we found ourselves at the North of the Del Norte Cañon, where that river issues from the St. John's Mountain, one of the highest, most rugged and impracticable of all the Rocky Mountain ranges, inaccessible to trappers and hunters even in the summer time. Across the point of this elevated range our guide conducted us, and having still great confidence in his knowledge, we pressed onwards with fatal resolution. Even along the river bottoms the snow was already belly deep for the mules, frequently snowing in the valley and almost constantly in the mountains. The cold was extraordinary; at the warmest hours of the day (between one and two) the thermometer (Fahrenheit) standing in the shade of only a tree trunk at zero; the day sunshiny, with a moderate breeze. We pressed up towards the summit, the snow deepening; and in four or five days reached the naked ridges which lie above the timbered country, and which form the dividing grounds between the waters of the Atlantic and Pacific oceans. Along these naked ridges, it storms nearly all winter, and the winds sweep across them with remorseless fury. On our first attempt to cross we encountered a *pouderié* (dry snow driven thick through the air by violent wind, and in which objects are visible only at a short distance), and were driven back, having some 10 or 12 men variously frozen, face, hands, or feet. The guide became nigh being frozen to death here, and dead mules were already lying about the fires. Meantime, it snowed steadily. The next day we made mauls, and beating a road or trench through the snow crossed the crest in defiance of the *pouderié*, and encamped immediately below in the edge of the timber. The trail showed as if a defeated party had passed by; pack-saddles and packs, scattered articles of clothing, and dead mules strewed along. A continuance of stormy weather paralyzed all movement. We were encamped somewhere about 12,000 feet above the sea. Westward, the country was buried in deep snow. It was impossible to advance, and to turn back was equally impracticable. We were overtaken by sudden and inevitable ruin. It so happened that the only places where any grass could be had were the extreme summit of the ridges, where the sweeping winds kept the rocky ground bare and the snow could not lie. Below these, animals could not get about, the snow being deep enough to bury them. Here, therefore, in the full violence of the storms we were obliged to keep our animals. They could not be moved either way. It was instantly apparent that we should lose every animal.

"I determined to recross the mountain more towards the open country, and haul or pack the baggage (by men) down to the Del Norte. With great labor the baggage was transported across the crest to the head springs of a little stream leading to the main river. A few days were sufficient to destroy our fine band of mules. They generally kept huddled together, and as they froze, one would be seen to tumble down and the snow would cover him; sometimes they would break off and rush down towards the timber until they were stopped by the deep snow, where they were soon hidden by the *pouderié*. The courage of the men failed fast; in fact, I have never seen men so soon discouraged by misfortune as we were on this occasion; but, as you know, the party was not constituted like the former ones. But among those who deserve to be honorably mentioned and who behaved like what they were—men of the old exploring party,—were Godey, King, and Taplin; and first of all Godey. In this situation, I determined to send in a party to the Spanish settlements of New Mexico for provisions and mules to transport

TERRIFIC SNOW STORM ON THE ROCKY MOUNTAINS—COL. FREMONT KEEPS CHRISTMAS READING BLACKSTONE—PAGE 369.

our baggage to Taos. With economy, and after we should leave the mules, we had not two weeks' provisions in the camp. These consisted of a store which I had reserved for a hard day, macaroni and bacon. From among the volunteers I choose King, Brackenridge, Creutzfeldt, and the guide Williams; the party under the command of King. In case of the least delay at the settlements, he was to send me an express. In the meantime, we were to occupy ourselves in removing the baggage and equipage down to the Del Norte, which we reached with our baggage in a few days after their departure (which was the day after Christmas). Like many a Christmas for years back, mine was spent on the summit of a wintry mountain, my heart filled with gloomy and anxious thoughts, with none of the merry faces and pleasant luxuries that belong to that happy time. You may be sure we contrasted much this with the last at Washington, and speculated much on your doings, and made many warm wishes for your happiness. Could you have looked into Agrippa's glass for a few moments only! You remember the volumes of Blackstone which I took from your father's library when we were overlooking it at our friend Brant's? They made my Christmas amusements. I read them to pass the heavy time and forget what was around me. Certainly you may suppose that my first law lessons will be well remembered. Day after day passed by and no news from our express party. Snow continued to fall almost incessantly on the mountain. The spirits of the camp grew lower. Prone laid down in the trail and froze to death. In a sunshiny day, and having with him means to make a fire, he threw his blankets down in the trail and laid there till he froze to death. After sixteen days had elapsed from King's departure, I became so uneasy at the delay that I decided to wait no longer. I was aware that our troops had been engaged in hostilities with the Spanish Utahs and Apaches, who range in the North River valley, and became fearful that they (King's party) had been cut off by these Indians; I could imagine no other accident. Leaving the camp employed with the baggage and in charge of Mr. Vincenthaler, I started down the river with a small party consisting of Godey, (with his young nephew), Mr. Preuss and Saunders. We carried our arms and provision for two or three days. In the camp the messes had provisions for two or three meals, more or less; and about five pounds of sugar to each man. Failing to meet King, my intention was to make the Red River settlement about twenty-five miles north of Taos, and send back the speediest relief possible. My instructions to the camp were, that if they did not hear from me within a stated time, they were to follow down the Del Norte.

"On the second day after leaving camp we came upon a fresh trail of Indians—two lodges, with a considerable number of animals. This did not lessen our uneasiness for our people. As their trail when we met it turned and went down the river, we followed it. On the fifth day we surprised an Indian on the ice of the river. He proved to be an Utah, son of a Grand River chief we had formerly known, and behaved to us in a friendly manner. We encamped near them at night. By a present of a rifle, my two blankets, and other promised rewards when we should get in, I prevailed upon this Indian to go with us as a guide to the Red River settlement, and take with him four of his horses, principally to carry our little baggage. These were wretchedly poor, and could get along only in a very slow walk. On that day (the sixth) we left the lodges late, and travelled only some six or seven miles. About sunset we discovered a little smoke, in a grove of timber off from the river, and thinking perhaps it might be our express party on its return, we went to see. This was the twenty-second day since they had left us, and the sixth since we had left the camp. We found them—three of them—Creutzfeldt, Brackenridge, and Williams—the most miserable objects I have ever seen. I did not recognize Creutzfeldt's features when Brackenridge brought him up to me and mentioned his name. They had been starving. King had starved to death a few days before. His remains were some six or eight miles above, near the river. By aid of the horses, we carried these three men with us to Red River settlement, which we reached (Jan. 20), on the tenth evening after leaving our camp in the mountains, having travelled through snow and on foot one hundred and sixty miles. I look upon the anxiety which induced me to set out from the camp as an inspiration. Had I remained there waiting the party which had been sent in, every man of us would probably have perished.

"The morning after reaching the Red River town, Godey and myself rode on to the Rio Hondo and Taos, in search of animals and supplies, and on the second evening after that on which we had reached Red River, Godey had returned to that place with about thirty animals, provisions, and four Mexicans, with which he set out for the camp on the following morning. On the road he received eight or ten others, which were turned over to him by the orders of Major Beale, the commanding officer of this northern district of New Mexico. I expect that Godey will reach this place with the party on Wednesday evening, the 31st. From Major Beale I received the offer of every aid in his power, and such actual assistance as he was able to render. Some horses which he had just recovered from the Utahs were loaned to me, and he supplied me from the commissary's department with provisions which I could have had nowhere else. I find myself in the midst of friends. With Carson is living Owens, and Maxwell is at his father-in-law's, doing a very prosperous business as a merchant and contractor for the troops.

"*Evening.* Mr. St. Vrain and Aubrey, who have just arrived from Santa Fé, called to see me. I had the pleasure to learn that Mr. St. Vrain sets out from Santa Fé on the 15th of February, for St. Louis, so that by him I have an early and certain opportunity of sending you my letters. Beale left Santa Fé on his journey to California on the 9th of this month. He probably carried on with him any letters which might have been at Santa Fé for me. I shall probably reach California with him or shortly after him. Say to your father that these are my plans for the future.

"At the beginning of February (about Saturday) I shall set out for California, taking the southern route, by the *Rio Abajo* the Paso del Norte, and the south side of the *Gila*, entering California at the *Agua Caliente*, thence to Los Angeles and immediately north. I shall break up my party here and take with me only a few men. The survey has been uninterrupted up to this point, and I shall carry it on consecutively. As soon as possible after reaching California I will go on with the survey of the coast and coast country. Your father knows that this is an object of great desire with me, and I trust it is not too much to hope that he may obtain the countenance and aid of the President (whoever he may be) in carrying it on effectually and rapidly to completion. For this I hope earnestly. I shall then be enabled to draw up a map and report on the whole country, agreeably to our previous anticipations. *All my other plans remain entirely unaltered.* I shall take immediate steps to make ourselves a good home in California, and to have a place ready for your reception, which I anticipate for April. My hopes and wishes are more strongly than ever turned that way.

"*Monday*, 29. My letter now assumes a journal form. No news yet from the party,—a great deal of falling weather; rain and sleet here, and snow in the mountains. This is to be considered a poor country; mountainous, with severe winters and but little arable land. To the United States it seems to me to offer little other value than the right of way. It is throughout infested with Indians, with whom in the course of the present year the United States will be at war, as well as in the Oregon Territory. To hold this country will occasion the government great expense, and, certainly, one can see no source of profit or advantage in it. An additional regiment will be required for special service here.

"Mr. St. Vrain dined with us to-day. Owens goes to Missouri in April to get married, and thence by water to California. Carson is very anxious to go there with me now, and afterwards remove his family thither, but he cannot decide to break off from Maxwell and family connections.

"I am anxiously waiting to hear from my party, in much uncertainty as to their fate. My presence kept them together and quiet, my absence may have had a bad effect. When we overtook King's starving party, Brackenridge said that he 'would rather have seen me than his father.' He felt himself safe.

"TAOS, NEW MEXICO, *February* 6, 1849.

"After a long delay, which had wearied me to a point of resolving to set out again myself, tidings have at last reached me from my ill-fated party. Mr. Haler came in last night, having the night before reached Red River settlement, with some three or four others. Including Mr. King and Proue, we have lost eleven of our party. Occurrences after I left them, are briefly these, so for as they are within Haler's knowledge. I say briefly, my dear Jessie, because now I am unwilling to force myself to dwell upon particulars. I wish for a time to shut out these things from my mind, to leave this country, and all thoughts and all things connected with recent events, which have been so signally disastrous as absolutely to astonish me with a persistence of misfortune, which no precaution has been adequate on my part to avert.

"You will remember that I had left the camp with occupation sufficient to employ them for three or four days, after which they were to follow me down the river. Within that time I had expected the relief from King, if it was to come at all.

"They remained where I had left them seven days, and then started down the river. Manuel—you will remember Manuel, the Cosumne Indian—gave way to a feeling of despair after they had travelled about two miles, begged Haler to shoot him, and then turned and made his way back to the camp; intending to die there, as he doubtless soon did. They followed our trail down the river—twenty-two men they were in all. About ten miles below the camp, Wise gave out, threw away his gun and blanket, and a few hundred yards further fell over into the snow and died. Two Indian boys, young men, countrymen of Manuel were behind. They rolled up Wise in his blanket, and buried him in the snow on the river bank. No more died that day—none the next. Carver raved during the night, his imagination wholly occupied with images of many things which he fancied himself eating. In the morning, he wandered off from the party, and probably soon died. They did not see him again. Sorel on this day gave out, and laid down to die. They built him a fire, and Morin, who was in a dying condition, and snow-blind, remained. These two did not probably last till the next morning. That evening, I think, Hubbard killed a deer. They travelled on, getting here and there a grouse, but probably nothing else, the snow having frightened off the game. Things were desperate, and brought Haler to the determination of breaking up the party, in order to prevent them from living upon each other. He told them 'that he had done all he could for them, that they had no other hope remaining than the expected relief, and that their best plan was to scatter and make the best of their way in small parties down the river. That, for his part, if he was to be eaten, he would, at all events, be found travelling when he did die.' They accordingly separated. With Mr. Haler continued five others and the two Indian boys. Rohrer now became very despondent; Haler encouraged him by recalling to mind his family, and urged him to hold out a little longer. On this day he fell behind, but promised to overtake them at evening. Haler, Scott, Hubbard, and Martin agreed that if any one of them should give out, the others were not to wait for him to die, but build a fire for him, and push on. At night, Kern's mess encamped a few hundred yards from Haler's, with the intention, according to Taplin, to remain where they were until the relief should come, and in the meantime to live upon those who had died, and upon the weaker ones as they should die. With the three Kerns were Cathcart, Andrews, McKie, Stepperfeldt, and Taplin.

"Ferguson and Beadle had remained together behind. In the evening, Rohrer came up and remained with Kern's mess. Mr. Haler learned afterwards from that mess that Rohrer and Andrews wandered off the next day and died. They say they saw their bodies. In the morning Haler's party continued on. After a few hours, Hubbard gave out. They built him a fire, gathered him some wood, and left him, without, as Haler says, turning their heads to look at him as they went off. About two miles further, Scott—you remember Scott—who used to shoot birds for you at the frontier—gave out. They did the same for him as for Hubbard, and continued on. In the afternoon, the Indian boys went ahead, and before nightfall met Godey with the relief. Haler heard and knew the guns which he fired for him at night, and starting early in the morning, soon met him. I hear that they all cried together like children. Haler turned back with Godey, and went with him to where they had left Scott. He was still alive, and was saved. Hubbard was dead—still warm. From Kern's mess they learned the death of Andrews and Rohrer, and a little above, met Ferguson, who told them that Beadle had died the night before.

"Godey continued on with a few New Mexicans and pack mules to bring down the baggage from the camp. Haler, with Martin and Bacon, on foot, and bringing Scott on horseback, have first arrived at the Red River settlement. Provisions and horses for them to ride were left with the others, who preferred to rest on the river until Godey came back. At the latest, they they should all have reached Red River settlement last night, and ought all to be here this evening. When Godey arrives, I shall know from him all the circumstances sufficiently in detail to enable me to understand clearly everything. But it will not be necessary to tell you anything further. It has been sufficient pain for you to read what I have already written.

"As I told you, I shall break up my party here. I have engaged a Spaniard to furnish mules to take my little party with our baggage, as far down the Del Norte as Albuquerque. To-morrow a friend sets out to purchase me a few mules, with which he is to meet me at Albuquerque, and thence I continue the journey on my own animals. My road will take me down the Del Norte, about 160 miles below Albuquerque and then passes between this river and the heads of the Gila, to a little Mexican town called, I think, Tusson. Thence to the mouth of the Gila and across the Colorado, direct to Agua Caliente, into California. I intend to make the journey rapidly, and about the middle of March; hope for the great pleasure of hearing from home. I look for a large supply of newspapers and documents, more perhaps because these things have a home look about them than on their own account. When I think of you all, I feel a warm glow at my heart, which renovates it like a good medicine, and I forget painful feelings in strong hope for the future. We shall yet, dearest wife, enjoy quiet and happiness together—these are nearly one and the same to me now. I make frequently pleasant pictures of the happy home we are to have, and oftenest and among the pleasantest of all I see, our library with its bright fire in the rainy stormy days, and the large windows looking out upon the sea in the bright weather. I have it all planned in my own mind. It is getting late now, La Harpe says that there are two gods which are very dear to us, Hope and Sleep. My homage shall be equally divided between them; both make the time pass lightly until I see you. So I go now to pay a willing tribute to one with my heart full of the other."

On arriving at Sicorro, he addressed the following letter to Colonel Benton:

LETTER FROM COL. FREMONT TO COL. BENTON.

SOCORRO, RIO DEL NORTE, *February* 24, 1849.

MY DEAR SIR: I write a line from this place in the hope that by way of Chihuahua and Vera Cruz, it will reach you sooner than letters by the direct mail from Santa Fé, and so be in advance of exaggerated reports of the events which have delayed my journey, and turned me in this direction. Letters which I have forwarded by Mr. St. Vrain, will inform you that we were overtaken and surrounded by deep and impracticable snows in the Rocky Mountains at the head of the Del Norte. We lost all our animals and ten men, the mules frozen, and the men starved to death, Proue only excepted. He was frozen. The miscarriage of an express party, sent in under Mr. King, was a secondary cause of our greatest calamity in the loss of our men. In six days after leaving my camp in the mountains, I overtook his party, they having been out twenty-two days, and King having been starved to death. In four days afterwards I reached the settlements, in time to save many, but too late to rescue all the men. Relief was immediately sent back, but did not meet them in time to save all. An attempt, made with fresh animals, to get our baggage out of the snow, failed entirely, resulting only in the loss of ten or twelve animals more. On the main river bottoms at the foot of the mountains, the snow was five feet deep, and in the mountains impassable. Camp furniture of all descriptions, saddles, pack-saddles, &c., clothes, money, &c., all lost. I had the good fortune to recover one of my baggage trunks, which Jessie will remember to have packed for me, and so saved some clothes, &c. My instruments, which I always carry with me, were in greater part saved.

"The officers of the army stationed in the country have been uniformly prompt and liberal in their attentions to me, offering me all the assistance in their power. In this country, where supplies are scarce and extravagantly high, this assistance was of great value to me in prosecuting my journey. Among those whom I ought particularly to mention is Major Beale, who is in command of the Northern District, Capt. Judd, Lieut. Thomas, Dr. Webb, and Capt. Buford. I mention their names particularly, knowing that you will take pleasure in reciprocating it to them. Colonel Washington desired me to call on him without reserve for anything at his command. He invited me to dine with him one out of the two days I spent at Sante Fé, and dined with me at the officers' quarters on the other. Major Weightman (of Washington, son-in-law of Mr. Cox) was very friendly in his attentions to me, and Capt. Brent, of the quartermaster's deputy, gave me some most effective aid in my equipment. Among the citizens who have treated me with some attention, I make it a duty to recommend to your attention, when you may meet him, our fellow-citizen of St. Louis, Mr. F. X. Aubry. You will remember him as having lately made an extraordinary ride from Sante Fé to Independence. We have been travelling together from Santa Fé to this place. Among other acts of kindness, I received from him a loan of $1000, to purchase animals for my journey to California.

"I reached this town at half-past eight o'clock this morning, by appointment to breakfast. Capt. Buford, who commands here, received me with much kindness, and I am staying with him. This is a military post, and with the exception of a little village or two, a few miles below, the last settlement we see until reaching Tusson, even should we pass by that route. We go on this afternoon, and perhaps reach California in twenty-five days. The weather here is warm, and the people engaged in opening the ground for sowing. I will write a brief note to Jessie, and conclude this, as I shall be much pressed to get through the business set apart for this day.

"Very affectionately,

"J. C. FREMONT.

"Hon. THOMAS H. BENTON, Washington City."

CHAPTER XIV.

FREMONT SETTLES IN MARIPOSAS—CAUSE OF INDIAN HOSTILITIES—TITLE TO MARIPOSAS—ORIGINAL DEED OF THE ESTATE—TITLE QUESTIONED AND RESISTED BY CALEB CUSHING—CONFIRMED BY THE U. S. SUPREME COURT—OPINION OF CHIEF JUSTICE TANEY—RECEIVES THE APPOINTMENT OF MEXICAN BOUNDARY COMMISSIONER—HIS MAGNANIMITY TO COL. WELLER—FIRST POLITICAL LETTER—ELECTED TO THE UNITED STATES SENATE.

COL. FREMONT had arrived in California with the intention of making it his future home. By a judicious investment of about $3,000 in 1847, he had become the proprietor of one of the most valuable tracts of land, for its size, in the world, the Mariposas, and it was his fixed intention to devote all his energies to the development of its mineral and agricultural resources.

The Mariposas Estate lies about two hundred and twenty-five miles north of San Francisco, in a basin of the mountain on the north flank of the Sierra Nevada. It covers an area of about seventy square miles. Through it run the two main gold bearing ledges of California, and it is watered by two fine streams through its entire length, the Agua Fria and the Mariposas, both of which have their rise in Mount Bullion, thus very appropriately named, out of compliment to Col. Benton. The mountains in the rear, of granite, run up into lofty peaks which are covered with eternal snow, and about twenty miles from the borders of the estate is a waterfall 2300 feet high, the highest we believe in the world. The valley of the Mariposas was the favorite hunting ground of one of the bravest and most warlike tribes of Indians on the Pacific coast, the Chauchiles, and when Col. Fremont first passed through it on his third expedition, our readers will remember that he had an alarm from them, and six men belonging to another party encamped in the neighborhood, were killed the same night. Since then they have given a great deal of trouble to the whites who have visited the estate, whom as a race they look upon with justifiable suspicion. In 1851 a regiment under the command of Col. Johnson, was sent up into the Mariposa to punish this tribe for some murders which they had committed, and the colonel is reported to have said that he never knew an Indian war that was not occasioned by the brutality of the whites, and attributed the one in which he was engaged to the same cause. The editor of the *California Courier*, who was with him, confirmed the colonel's impressions by the following story:

"Four Creeks, a long way up in the Mariposa mountains, is an excellent farming and grazing country. There the waters are as bright as moonbeams, and come down from the mountain springs as cool as the sheeted snow. Pine trees, six or eight feet through, run up as straight as an arrow, two hundred to the sky, and the wide-spreading oak will shelter a whole tribe under its branches. Although the hills are covered with heavy snows, the temperature of the valleys is as mild as those of Switzerland, the streams are full of salmon, and the crimson clover fills the whole air with a sweet perfume. It is the Indian's Paradise in California, and the Mexican population have never molested them in it. At Four Creeks, was a magnificent oak—the king oak of the mountain. It was a sacred tree to the Indians. Under its branches they held their councils, and worshipped the Great Spirit. Here, also, they buried their chiefs and wise men. It had always been respected by the immigrants, until some two months since when a cattle dealer drove a large number of oxen up from Walker's Pass to the Indian village. He was treated with the greatest kindness by the natives, and they offered to assist him to '*corral*' his beasts. But the old man took a fancy to build his '*corral*' around the old oak. He was told its sacred character, and remonstrated with, but to no purpose. He had made up his mind that his cattle should sleep in the Indian church, and he 'would be d—d if they shouldn't.' Well, the red men got out their arrows, and at night killed the old man and his herdsmen, and drove off his cattle. Who can blame them? This wanton act has already caused the death of scores of Americans, and God only knows how many more victims must fall, before their rage can be satiated."

Col. Fremont purchased this property under a Mexican title, after California became a territory of the United States, and as his rights thus acquired have been the subject of a long and expensive litigation, only brought to a final close within the last year, and as the magnitude and singularity of the estate have given it already an historical importance, we may venture to give a brief history of his title, and of the struggles he has had to maintain it.

In 1844, Manuel Micheltorrena, then governor and commandant general, issued a grant of what is now known as the Mariposas property, to Juan Alvarado, pur porting to be founded upon the patriotic services of Alvarado, who had been conspicuous in the commotions in California which resulted from the centralizing policy of Mexico, out of which grew the Texas revolution, and was afterwards appointed governor by the provincial deputation. In 1837, he repelled the effort of Cavallo who had been appointed governor by Mexico, to take possession of the government, and was afterwards confirmed as governor of California by the constitutional authorities of Mexico. He continued in that office until Micheltorrena was appointed to succeed him, and he was appointed first counsellor of the departmental junta with a salary of $1,500. For these services the following grant was made:

"Whereas, Don Juan B. Alvarado, colonel of the auxiliary militia of this department, is worthy for his patriotic services, to be preferred in his pretension for his personal benefit and that of his family, for the tract of land known by the name of the Mariposas, to the extent of ten square leagues (sitior de ganado mayor), within the limits of the Snow Mountain (Sierra Nevada) and the rivers known by the names of the Chauchilles, of the Mereed, and the San Joaquin, the necessary requirements, according to the provisions of the laws and regulations, having been previously complied with, by virtue of the authority in me vested, in the name of the Mexican nation, I have granted to him the aforesaid tract, declaring the same by these presents his property in fee, subject to the approbation of the Most Excellent the Departmental Assembly, and to the following conditions:

"'1. He shall not sell, alienate, or mortgage the same, nor subject it to taxes, entail, or any other incumbrance.

"'2. He may inclose it without obstructing the crossings, the roads, or the right of way; he shall enjoy the same freely and without hindrance, destining it to such use or cultivation as may most suit him, but he shall build a house within a year, and it shall be inhabited.

"'3. He shall solicit, from the proper magistrate, the judicial possession of the same, by virtue of this patent, by whom the boundaries shall be marked out, on the limits of which he (the grantee) shall place the proper landmarks.

"'4. The track of land granted is ten sitios de ganado mayor, (ten square leagues), as before mentioned. The magistrate who may give the possession shall cause the same to be surveyed according to the ordinance, the surplus remaining to the nation for the proper uses.

"'5. Should he violate the conditions, he will lose his right to the land, and it will be subject to being denounced by another.

"'Therefore, I command that these presents being firm and binding, that the same be registered in the proper book, and delivered to the party interested, for his security and other purposes.

"'Given in Monterey, this 20th day of the month of February, in the year of 1844.

"'MANUEL MICHELTORRENA.

"'MANUEL TIMENO, *Secretary*.'"

On the 10th of February, 1847, Alvarado executed a deed of the property as described in his own grant to Colonel Fremont, with a general warranty of title. The consideration stated in the conveyance was $3,000. On the 21st of January, 1852, he filed his claim before the commissioners appointed to ascertain and settle the private land claims in the State of California, and in December, 1852, the grant was confirmed. On the 20th of September, 1853, there was filed in the office of the commissioners, a notice from Mr. Attorney-General

Cushing, that an appeal from the decision of the Commissioners to the District Court of the United States would be prosecuted, and in consequence of that appeal the decision of the commissioners was reversed on the 7th of January, 1854. An appeal was taken from that decision by Col. Fremont to the Supreme Court of the United States. The case was argued on the part of Col. Fremont by Wm. Carey Jones, Mr. Bibb and Mr. Crittenden; on the part of the government by Caleb Cushing, Attorney-General. The grounds taken against the title by the government were as follows:

"1. That Fremont's claim is on a gratuitous colonization grant by the Mexican governor of California to one Alvarado, of which there had been no surveys, no plan, no occupation, no site even, no confirmation by the proper public authority, no performance of any of the conditions precedent or subsequent annexed to the grant.

"2. That the concession to Alvarado was null for uncertainty of description and incapability of definite location.

"3. That the concession was not confirmed by the departmental Assembly, and was not therefore entitled to confirmation by the United States Courts.

"4. That the grant was void because the conditions annexed had never been performed.

"5. That until the governor-general confirmed the concession the title remained in the crown.

"6. That none of the excuses for non-performance alleged in Alvarado's behalf possessed legal force.

"7. That the grant to Alvarado was a gratuitous one except in so far as the performance of the conditions would relate back to constitute a consideration.

"8. That the original petition, the provisional grant and the decree of the Commissioners, each assumed a floating claim not as a grant of an identical tract of land by metes and bounds.

The Supreme Court took a different view of the case from Mr. Cushing; reversed the decision of the District Court of California, and confirmed Col. Fremont's title in every particular. Chief Justice Taney delivered the opinion of the Court, in the course of which, while speaking of the provision against alienation attached to Alvarado's grant, and which, he said, was void, as being in violation of a decree of the Mexican Congress, he observes :*

"But if this condition was valid by the laws of Mexico, and if any conveyance made by Alvarado would have forfeited the land under the Mexican government as a breach of this condition, or if it would have been forfeited by a conveyance to an alien, it does not by any means follow that the same penalty would have been incurred by the conveyance to Fremont.

"California was at that time in possession of the American forces, and held by the United States as a conquered country, subject to the authority of the American government. The Mexican municipal laws, which were then administered, were administered under the authority of the United States, and might be repealed or abrogated at their pleasure; and any Mexican law inconsistent with the rights of the United States, or its public policy, or with the rights of its citizens, were annulled by the conquest. Now, there is no principle of public law which prohibits the citizen of a conquering country from purchasing property, real or personal, in the territory thus acquired and held, nor is there anything in the principles of our government, in its policy or in its laws, which forfeits it. The Mexican government, if it had regained the power, and it had been its policy to prevent the alienation of real estate, might have treated the sale by Alvarado as a violation of its laws; but it becomes a very different question when the Ame-

* Howard's United States Supreme Court Reports, vol. xvii., pp. 564–5.

rican government is called on to execute the Mexican law. And it can hardly be maintained that an American citizen, who makes a contract or purchases property under such circumstances, can be punished in a court of the United States with the penalty of forfeiture, when there is no law of Congress to inflict it. The purchase was perfectly consistent with the rights and duties of Colonel Fremont, as an American officer and an American citizen; and the country in which he made the purchase was, at the time, subject to the authority and dominion of the United States. * * * * * *

"Upon the whole, it is the opinion of the court that the claim of the petitioner is valid, and ought to be confirmed. The decree of the district court must, therefore, be reversed, and the case remanded, with directions to the district court to enter a decree conformably to this opinion."

Mariposas abounds in gold, and when Col. Fremont first passed over it, he and his party picked up large quantities lying upon the surface of the soil. It is also said to be the easiest placer to work in all California, with resources which cannot be exhausted in centuries. Guided by the information which he had acquired from personal inspection, and from the letters of his agents, he brought with him when he reached California this year—1849—a company of Spaniards, some twenty-eight in number, who joined him in Sonora, and with whom he contracted for the digging of gold on his estate upon shares. He was to provision them, and they were to divide the gold they found equally with him. This arrangement proved entirely satisfactory and very profitable. The Sonoranians were all respectable Spaniards—many of them already wealthy—and in their transactions with him, strictly honorable. He readily fulfilled his part of the contract by occasionally sending men into the south for cattle, which they drove on to the estate, and pastured there until they were wanted.

It was while thus agreeably and profitably employed in developing the resources of his magnificent estate, and rapidly providing for himself and family a pecuniary independence, that he received from President Taylor the appointment of commissioner to run the boundary line between the United States and Mexico, in place of John B. Weller, of Ohio, who had then but recently been appointed to that office by President Polk.

Col. Fremont determined to accept the office without hesitation, for he had reason to look upon it as a very friendly and unequivocal expression of General Taylor's disapproval of the verdict of the court-martial which had dismissed him from the army a few months previously. He had the less hesitation in accepting it, because he had been politically identified with the party which had opposed General Taylor's election to the presidency, a fact which, while it heightened the compliment on the one hand, on the other increased in a corresponding degree the difficulty of declining it without appearing insensible to the generous motives of its author. He promptly waited upon Mr. Weller, when he was in Monterey trying to borrow some money for the uses of the commission; informed him of what had occurred, and signified his intention to accept the place, (it being well understood by both that whether he accepted or not, Mr. Weller would not be retained) and wished to know when it would be most agreeable to Mr. W. to be relieved. Mr. Weller informed him that the affairs of the commission were in great confusion for want of funds, and that he would prefer to wait until he could get the funds he was in quest of, and return to San Diego, where he would arrange his affairs as soon as possible. Col. Fremont begged him to take his own time. Afterwards, Col. Weller having entirely failed in all his plans for raising the money that he required, Col. Fremont endorsed his drafts for him, and got them cashed, a kindness afterwards very ill-requited. We are thus particular in mentioning these details, because Col. Fremont's acceptance was subsequently used to prejudice him with the people of California, who had already determined to send him to Washington as one of their first senators. Without attempting the ungracious task of tracing the calumnious reports in regard to this appointment to their fountain, it is enough for our present purpose to say that they reached the ears of Col. Fremont's friends, who promptly took the proper means of ascertaining and exposing their falsity.

The following correspondence was the result. Mr. Snyder's letter was answered the night it was received, and Col. Fremont's reply was the first political letter he had ever written. It was in every respect worthy of the pen of an experienced statesman.

LETTER FROM JACOB R. SNYDER TO COL. FREMONT.

SAN FRANCISCO, *Dec.* 11*th*, 1849.

DEAR SIR: Your name has been long before the people of California as a candidate for the U. S. Senate. As an old resident of California, and a personal friend of long standing, I feel the deepest interest in your election, and take the liberty of asking of you information on certain points which I discover to be much agitated by some who are not your friends. Are you a believer in the distinctive tenets of the democratic party? What are your views in relation to an overland communication by railroad or otherwise, from the Pacific to the Atlantic and through the territory of the United States? What is the true history and real nature of your title to a certain tract of land which you are said to claim on the Mariposa River? What have you done, and what do you propose to do, to establish that claim?

"What has been your course in reference to a commission which you are said to have received to run the boundary line called for by the late treaty with Mexico? Was that appointment solicited by yourself or your friends, and have you accepted it? and if not, how long did you hold it under consideration?

What was the real nature of the transaction with D. Eulogio de Celis, concerning which, certain publications were sometime since made in the newspapers of this place and of some of the Eastern States? On all of these matters I would respectfully submit that as full an answer as this short notice will allow, is due to your friends and supporters, and tha' in regard to your political principles, a declaration would come from you with peculiar fitness, seeing that your occupations, honorable as they have been, and serviceable to your country, have not been of a character to call for an expression of your opinions on matters of government, and that your friends, though well persuaded themselves of your soundness, are yet daily met with the question, 'how do you know that Mr. Fremont is a democrat, and how long has he been one?' "Yours, &c.,

"JACOB R. SNYDER.

"J. C. FREMONT, ESQ."

REPLY OF COL. FREMONT.

"SAN FRANCISCO, *Dec.* 11*th*, 1849.

"MY DEAR SIR: I have the pleasure to acknowledge the receipt of your letter to-day, and to make you my kind thanks for the gratification I find in being called to make some reply to the vague accusations in circulation against me. I presume that it will be a sufficient answer to your first question, simply to state, that by association, feeling, principle and education, I am thoroughly a democrat; and without entering into any discussion of the question at issue between the two great parties, I have only further to say, that I adhere to the great principles of the democratic party as they are understood on this and the other side of the continent. I am strongly in favor of a central, national railroad from the Mississippi River to the Pacific Ocean. Recent events have converted the vague desire for that work into an organized movement throughout the great body of our fellow. citizens in the United States, and in common with them, I am warmly in favor of its immediate location and speediest possible construction. Its stupendous magnitude—the immense benefit which it will confer upon our whole country—the changes which it will operate throughout the Pacific Ocean and eastern Asia—commingling together the European, American, and Asiatic races—spreading indefinitely religious, social and political improvement—characterize it as the greatest enterprise of the age, and a great question proposed for the solution of the American people. There never has been presented an enterprise so calculated to draw together in its support all classes of society; and the perpetual and always increasing benefits which it will confer upon the human race in addition to the weighty national considerations, military, political, and commercial, which more immediately concerns us, call upon us for immediate and efficient action. Ardently in favor of the work, it follows of course that I am entirely satisfied of its practicability and believe fully in its ultimate and speedy construction. Many years of labor and exploration of the interior of our continent, and along a great part of the way the road will necessarily pass, have conclusively satisfied me not only of its entire practicability, but of extraordinary advantages offered for its construction. A late journey across the continent from the frontier of Missouri was solely directed to an examination of the country in reference to the railroad communication, and was undertaken in the season of winter in order that all the obstacles which could exist to the construction of the road might be known and fully determined. The result was entirely satisfactory. It convinced me that neither the snow of winter nor the mountain ranges were obstacles in the way of the road, and furnished me with a far better line than any I had previously known. From the frontier of Missouri along the line of the Kansas River, 400 miles of rich wooded country, well adapted to settlement—by the upper waters of the Arkansas into and through the rugged mountains in which they rise, to the valley which lies around the head waters of the great Del Norte—the profile of the route presents a regularly ascending plain, without a perceptible inequality to break the uniformity of its surface. Lying between the 28th and 29th parallels of latitude, commencing on the frontier of Missouri at the 39th and ending in the Del Norte valley at the 38th—the route presents a comparatively straight line, running for a greater part of the way through a country capable of settlement, and cultivation, and passing through the Arkansas chain (one of the most rugged in all the Rocky Mountain ranges), by a pass of imperceptible grade, and in every respect one of the best with which we are acquainted in those difficult mountains. Beyond the Del Norte that region yet remains to be explored, well known from reliable information to afford through the mountains which separate the valley of the Del Norte and Colorado, an excellent pass, travelled by the Mexicans at all seasons of the year, which gives every reason for believing that the character of the country is equally favorable. Its further progress would carry it by the southern extremity of the country now occupied by the people of Deseret, and thence by the line of the Humboldt River around into the head of the lower Sacramento valley, by a pass in the Sierra Nevada, but little above the general level of the great basin. Such a location would be entirely central, passing by the northern edge of the Mexican settlements, going through the southern part of Mormon—and branching into Oregon from the confines of California.

"Some months since, in conversation with Gen. Smith, I had the honor to propose this plan for the location of the road, I further indicated to him the existence of this favorable way and pass from the Humboldt River into the head of the lower Sacramento valley. Gen. Smith decided immediately to send an exploring party to examine the route, and requested me to send him a letter recapitulating the information, in order, as he had the kindness to say, that any credit which might hereafter belong to the origin of the line, should inure to me. The expedition was immediately sent, and although it terminated in the death of the gallant officer who commanded it, I am informed that his journal and sketches fully establish, so far as he went, the practicability of the road. You are aware that among the indefinite objections which have been raised against me, are some of a sectional character. Such objections I think may be fairly met with the statement above.

"The 'Mariposa claim' is a tract of land ten leagues in extent lying upon a creek of the same name in the San Joaquín valley. It was purchased for me by Mr. Larkin in the beginning of 1847, and during my absence with the battalion in the south, from D. Juan B. Alvarado, to whom it had been granted in consideration of his public services. Mr. Larkin paid for it $3,000. I have never seen the place, and know nothing of its character or value. The purchase was made before California was ceded to the United States, and long before any gold had been discovered. I had always intended to make my home in the country if possible, and for this purpose desired a foothold in it. On my return to the country in the present year I visited the place in company with Dr. Corrie, Mr. Reid, and several other gentlemen, and for the first time saw the land. Two-thirds are adapted only to farming; on the other third gold was discovered, and we went to work to dig it out. So soon as it was known that we were there, hundreds—soon becoming thousands

—crowded to the same place, and to this day from two to three thousand persons have been regularly employed. They have worked them freely; no one has ever offered them the slightest impediment, nor have I myself, ever expresed to any one or entertained an intention of interfering with the free working of the mines at that place. I regard the claim to the Mariposa in the same light as any other vested right. It was a purchase fairly made, and I have always supposed that at some future time the validity of the claim would be settled by the proper courts. I am satisfied to await that decision, whether it be favorable or otherwise, and in the meantime to leave the gold, as it is now, free to all who have the industry to collect it.

"I was at San José, when I had the honor to receive from President Taylor, by the hands of Dr. Beale, the commission to run the boundary line with Mexico. I regarded that commission as a disavowal on the part of the President of the proceedings recently held against me. Respect to the President, together with a full appreciation of the consideration which had induced him to make the appointment, did not, in my judgment, permit me to decline, and I accordingly accepted the commission, with the intention which I *then expressed* to Mr. Beale and others shortly afterwards to resign. I immediately went to San Francisco, where I had been informed Col. Weller had arrived. He had left that place and I shortly afterwards joined him at Monterey. The Secretary of State had made me the bearer of the letter which superseded Col. Weller. To present it was a disagreeable office, and from motives of delicacy I did not immediately present him the letter, but waited until I was about to leave the town. I then called upon Col. Weller, in order to ascertain from him, at what time and place it would be most agreeable to him, that I should relieve him. I learnt that the object of his journey to San Francisco had been to procure funds with which to discharge the liabilities of the government to his party; and that it would best suit his purposes to obtain the necessary sum, return to San Diego, and be relieved by me at that place. I then informed him that my instructions left me at liberty to relieve when I should be ready to do so, and that accordingly he might proceed to San Francisco, and it was agreed, that if Col. Weller did not succeed in obtaining money from Gen. Riley, to whom he intended to apply, an express should be forwarded to me, and the money obtained at San Francisco and brought down by me in the steamer.

"On the eve of leaving San Francisco and too late to negotiate drafts, I received an express informing me that Gen. Riley had declined furnishing the money. When the steamer reached Monterey, I found Col. Weller on the landing, ready to embark for San Diego, and fully expecting to receive the money; understanding the embarrassment of his situation, I offered, if he determined to go on to San Diego, that I would return to San Francisco, to procure the money and bring or send it to him.

"I had, in the mean time, resigned my appointment, informing the secretary that I should withhold the letter relieving Mr. Weller, and leave the department at liberty to make its own arrangements.

"It had become unnecessary for me to go to San Diego in the public service, and the management of my private affairs did not otherwise leave me the necessary time. I suppose that Col. Weller was not detained at San Diego, as he returned to this place as soon as could be expected after the receipt of the money. This is a brief statement of the course I have pursued. It was dictated altogether by a disposition to promote the interests of Col. Weller, and to make my concern in his removal as little unpleasant as possible. The office was never sought after by me, never expected by me, and never sought or expected by any of my friends for me.

"In reply to your inquiry for information regarding the "real nature of the transaction with D. Eulogio de Celis,' I have to state, that, at a time when the troops under my command were destitute of provisions, and we were able to procure them only in small and desultory supplies, on a precarious credit, Major

Samuel Hensley, then commissary for the battalion, called upon me with an offer from Mr. Celis, which I was glad to accept immediately. The offer was to furnish me with 600 head of cattle, at ten dollars per head, and a loan of $2,500, payable all in six months, with the usual interest, if not paid at that time, we were to return him the hides as the cattle were killed, and the difference in price of the cattle ($8 being the cash price then), being a *bonus* for the loan and for the relief afforded by the provisions. D. Andres Pico was charged to bring the cattle from San Louis Obispo to Los Angeles. In the interval of his absence, General Kearney issued his proclamation, taking out of my hands the partial direction of affairs which I had retained, and destroying the confidence which the people of the South had been disposed to place in me. Desirous to know for the satisfaction of those to whom I was indebted, how far Gen. Kearney designed to fulfill my contracts previously made, I *immediately* visited him for that purpose at Monterey. As I have already asserted, on my trial before the court martial at Washington, he refused to assume any responsibility or to fulfill any contract. I immediately returned to Los Angeles, and made known his reply to Mr. Celis, Mr. Cot, D. Andres Pico, and other gentlemen then at that place. D. Andres Pico had, in the meantime, brought a portion of the cattle (between 400 and 500 I believe), to the mission of San Fernando, near Los Angeles, where they were waiting to be delivered—what disposition should be made of the cattle was for some days a subject of discussion between Mr. Celis, D. Andres Pico, Major Hensley, and myself. It was at first proposed to leave the cattle with D. Andres; but agreeably to the suggestion of Major Hensley, it was decided to place them with Mr. Stearns, as a security both to Celis and to the government, until we should be able to know what course would be pursued by the government. They were to be kept by Mr. Stearns on the terms usually allowed for keeping cattle, viz.: one half the increase, and they were not placed in his hand for any fixed time, but only to await the action of the government.

"It had been made a matter of charge against me, that I gave to Mr. Celis a full receipt for the delivery of *all* the cattle, when I had received only a part. I had the right to do so. I had the right to complete my own contracts, when others, whose duty it was to resume them, endeavored rather to invalidate them. As Mr. Celis had had sufficient confidence in me to advance me money, and I was under order to leave the country immediately, I chose to have sufficient confidence in him to give him a receipt for all the cattle, and to bind the government to him, so far as I possibly could. These cattle were all delivered as soon as they could be brought to Los Angeles.

"Since my return to this country I have received a number of affidavits to all the occurrences of the forgoing transaction, from Mr. Wilson, Mr. Temple, and other gentlemen, citizens of Los Angeles. These, with some other papers, were designed for another occasion, and are now at Monterey, but they shall be published as soon as I can conveniently do so. Mr. Celis is now in this city. I have thus, my dear sir, briefly and hurriedly answered your several inquiries; I should have been better satisfied if there had been time sufficient to give to each particular point a well-digested reply, but I trust that they may answer the present purpose of removing some erroneous impressions; and in any event, I beg you to receive my thanks for the kindness of the motive which dictated your letter, and which, in every way is consistent with the same friendly spirit which has always influenced your conduct to me.

"With respect and regard, I am yours truly,

"J. C. FREMONT.

"J. R. SNYDER, Esq."

This letter put an end to any further talk about Mr. Weller's commissionership, and at once placed him in the front rank of the candidates for the United States Senate from California, under the new constitution which had just been adopted by her people. Ten days after the date of his letter the new legislature assembled at San José the seat of government, and immediately after the inauguration of the new governor, Burnett, proceeded to an election of United States senators. Fremont was elected on the first ballot by seven majority.*

This election, so flattering to a young man not yet thirty-seven years of age, and presenting such alluring prospects of political distinction, he felt it his duty to accept, although fully aware that it was certain to derange, perhaps for ever, the acceptable scheme of life he had marked out for himself. In yielding, however, he was influenced more by the solicitations of friends and a desire to testify his gratitude for their kindness, than by any personal conviction of the wisdom or prudence of his course.

* The following was the result of the first ballot.

John C. Fremont,	29	Wm. W. Gwin,	22
H. W. Walleck,	14	T. Butler King,	10
Geary,	5	Semple,	8
Henley,	9		

Gwin was also elected on the third ballot by a majority of two votes.

CHAPTER XV.

SAILS FOR WASHINGTON AS UNITED STATES SENATOR—TAKES THE CHAGRES FEVER—LETTER TO THE PHILADELPHIA PACIFIC RAILROAD CONVENTION.

The prompt action of the legislature of California in choosing their senators, resulted mainly from a desire to have the benefit of their services as early as possible in Washington, where the question upon the admission of California into the Union as a State, was under consideration. No time was lost, therefore, by Colonel Fremont in repairing to his new post of duty. He sailed from San Francisco with his family, in the steamer that bore the news of his election, to the Atlantic States, in order that the country which he had explored, conquered, and adopted for his home, and which had rewarded him by an election to the highest office in its gift, should come as soon as possible into the enjoyment of all the political rights of a sovereign State of the Republic. He was detained on the Isthmus of Panama a few weeks by the dangerous illness of Mrs. Fremont, and while there, his own system became charged with the malaria of the climate, which soon developed itself in the most malignant form of Chagres fever. It was the first and only serious illness he ever had, though it clung to him for several years, and is only worthy of particular mention here as it prevented his attendance at Washington during the second year of his senatorial term.

Soon after his arrival at the seat of government, Colonel Fremont was invited to attend a convention which was to assemble at Philadelphia on the 1st of April, for the purpose of promoting the construction of a national road to the Pacific Ocean, through the territories of the United States. As he had not yet laid the results of his last tour of exploration before the public, and as it had been undertaken avowedly for the purpose of throwing light upon the great problem of a highway across the continent, his views were looked for with great interest. His answer to the committee, which we give entire, was one of the most explicit and instructive documents which, up to that time, had appeared upon the subject, from any quarter.

LETTER FROM COLONEL FREMONT TO MESSRS. B. GERHARD AND OTHERS, COMMITTEE, &C.

"GENTLEMEN: It would have given me great pleasure to have been able to accept your kind invitation, and to have met the interesting Mississippi and Pacific Railroad Convention on Monday, but the remains of a Chagres fever confine me to my room, and leave me no other mode of showing my sense of your attention, and manifesting the interest I take in the great object which assembles this convention, than to contribute, so far as I can, to the mass of the information which will be laid before it. In doing this, I regret that the state of my health does not permit even the labor necessary to give the distances and barometrical elevations along the route which I shall offer for your consideration; but I have caused a skeleton map, rudely sketched, to be prepared to accompany this communication, and which in exhibiting the prominent features of the country, and general direction of the line, will be found sufficiently full and accurate to illustrate what I have to say.

"Many lines of explorations through the wilderness country, from our inhabited frontier to the Pacific Ocean, have conclusively satisfied me that the region or belt of country, lying between the 38th and 39th parallels of latitude, offer singular facilities and extraordinary comparative advantages for the construction of the proposed road.

"I propose, therefore, to occupy your attention solely with this line; for the clearer understanding of which, it will aid to keep under the eye the accompanying map, upon which the unbroken red lines are intended to show that the regions which they traverse have been already explored, while the broken red lines what is known only from reliable information.

"The country to be traversed by the proposed road exhibits but two great features—the prairies reaching to about the 105th degree of longtitude; and the mountains, with which it is bristling from that point to the shores of the Pacific ocean. Some years of travel among these mountains, during which I was occupied principally in searching for convenient passes and good lines of communication, gradually led me to comprehend their structure, and to understand that among this extended mass of mountains there is nowhere to be found a great continuous range having an unbroken crest, where passes are only to be found in the comparatively small depressions of the summit line. Throughout this great extent of country stretching in each way about 17 degrees, all these apparently continuous ranges are composed of lengthened blocks of mountains, separate and detached of greater or less length, according to the magnitude of the chain which they compose—each one possessing its separate, noted, and prominent peaks, and lying parallel to each other, though not usually so to the general direction of the range, but in many cases lying diagonally across it. Springing suddenly up from the general level of the country, sometimes rising into bare and rocky summits, of great height, they leave openings through the range but little above the general level, and by which they can be passed without climbing a mountain. Generally these openings are wooded valleys, where the mountain springs from either side collect together, forming often the main branches of some mighty stream. Aggregated together in this way, they go to form the great chain of the Rocky Mountains and Sierra Nevadas as well as the smaller and secondary ranges which occupy the intervening space. With the gradual discovery of this system, I became satisfied, not only of the entire practicability, but of the easy construction of a railroad across this rugged region. As this peculiarity forms the basis of my information, I desire to state it clearly at the outset, in order that I may be more readily understood in proceeding to show that this continent can be crossed from the Mississippi to the Pacific, without climbing a mountain, and on the very line which every national consideration would require to connect the great valley of the West with the Pacific Ocean.

"In describing the belt of country through which the road should pass, it will be found convenient to divide the entire line into three parts—the Eastern, reaching from the mouth of the Kansas to the head of the Del Norte; the Middle, from the head of the Del Norte to the river of the Great Basin; and the Western, from the [illegible]n of the Great Basin to the ocean. Beginning near the 39th parallel of latitude, at the mouth of the Kansas, the road would extend along the valley of that river some three or four hundred miles, traversing a beautiful and wooded country of great fertility, well adapted to settlement and cultivation. From the upper waters of the Kansas, falling easily over into the valley of Arkansas, the road strikes that river about a hundred miles below the foot of the mountains, continuing up it only to the mouth of the Huerfano River. From this point the prairie plains sweep directly up to the mountains, which dominate them as highlands to the ocean.

"The Huerfano is one of the upper branches of the Arkansas and following the lines of this stream the road would here enter into a country magnificently beautiful—timbered, having many bays or valleys of great fertility; having a mild and beautiful climate; having throughout the valley country short winters, which spend their force in the elevated regions of the mountains. The range of mountains in which this stream finds its head springs is distinguished by having its summits almost constantly enveloped in clouds of rain or snow, from which it obtains its name of Sierra Mojada, or Wet Mountain. This chain is remarkable among the Rocky Mountain ranges for the singular grandeur of its winter scenery, which has been characterized by travellers who have seen both as unsurpassed either in the Alps or the Himalayas. Their naked rocky summits are grouped into numerous peaks, which rise from the midst of black piny forests, whence issue many small streams to the valley below.

"Following by an open wagon way the valley of the Huerfano, the road reaches the immediate foot of the mountain at the entrance of a remarkable pass, almost everywhere surrounded by bold rocky mountain masses. From one foot of the mountain to the other, the pass is about five miles long; a level valley from two to four hundred yards wide, the Mountains rising abruptly on either side. With scarcely a distinguishable rise from the river plains, the road here passes directly through or between the mountains, emerging in the open valley of Del Norte, here some forty or fifty miles broad or more properly a continuation northward of the valley in which the Del Norte runs. Crossing the flat country, or opening between the mountains, and encountering no water course in its way, the road would reach the entrance of a pass in the Colorado Mountains, familiarly known to the New Mexicans and Indian traders, who are accustomed to traverse it at all seasons of the year, and who represent it as conducting to the waters of the Colorada River through a handsome rolling grass-covered country, affording practical wagon routes.

"Of this section of the route, so far as the entrance of this pass, covering twelve degrees of longtitude, I am able to speak from actual exploration, and to say that the line described is not only practicable, but affords many singular facilities for the construction of a railway, and offers many advantages in the fertile and wooded country through which it lies in the greater part of its course.

"In the whole distance there is not an elevation worthy of the name, to be surmounted; and a level of about 8,000 feet is gained almost without perceptible ascent. Upon the Kansas and Huerfano River valleys, the country is wooded and watered: the valley of the Del Norte is open, but wood is abundant in the neighboring mountains, and land fit for cultivation is found almost continuously along the water courses, from the mouth of the Kansas to the head of the valley of the Del Norte.

"A journey undertaken in the winter of 1848–49 (and interrupted here by entering more to the southward the rugged mountains of St. John's, one of the most impracticable on the continent), was intended to make a correct examination of this pass and the country beyond to the rim of the Great Basin. The failure of this expedition leaves only for this middle position of our line such knowledge as we have been able to obtain from trappers and Indian traders. The information thus obtained had led me to attempt its exploration, as all accounts concurred in representing it practicable for a road, and these accounts were considered sufficiently reliable.

"According to this information, the same structure of the country to which I have called your attention above, as forming a system among the mountains, holds good here; and I accordingly found no difficulty in believing that the road would readily avoid any obstacles which might be presented in the shape of mountain ranges, and easily reach the basin. In pronouncing upon the practicability of a road through this section, I proceed therefore upon my general knowledge of the face of the country, upon information received from hunters and residents in New Mexico, and upon the established fact that it has not only been travelled, but at all seasons of the year, and is one of the travelling routes from New Mexico to California.

"The third section of the map is from the Wahsatch Mountain to the Sierra Nevada, and thence to the Bay of San Francisco. This route traverses the Great Basin, presenting three different lines, which you will find indicated on the map. Repeated journeys have given me more or less knowledge of the country along these lines, and I consider all of them practicable, although the question of preference remains to be settled. The northern line is that of the Humboldt River, which although deflecting from the direct course of the bay, commands in its approach to the mountains several practicable passes, the lowest of which is 4,500 feet above the sea. The southern line, which in crossing the Basin has not the same freedom from obstruction enjoyed by the open river line of the North, is still entirely practicable, and possesses the advantage of crossing the Sierra Nevada at a remarkably low depression, called Walker's Pass, more commonly known as the *Point of the Mountains*, and being in fact, a termination of one of the mountains which go to form that chain.

"This pass is near the 35th degree of latitude, and near the head of the beautiful and fertile valley San Joaquin, which the road thence would follow down to its junction with the Sacramento, or to some point on the bay. This route deflects to the south about as much as the other does to the north, but secures a good way, and finds no obstacle from the Sierra, turning that mountain where is has sunk down nearly to the level of the country. Among the recent proceedings of the California legislature, resolutions were introduced in favor of beginning in the railway at that pass.

"The third line, which is the middle and direct line, and that to which I give a decided preference, is less known to me than either of the others: but I believe fully in its practicability, and only see the principal obstacle to be overcome is the Great Sierra itself, which it would strike near its centre. That obstacle is not considered insurmountable, nor in the present state of railway science, sufficient to turn us from the direct route. A pass is known as indicated by the line upon the map, which labor would render practicable. Other passes are also known to the north and south, and if tunneling became necessary, the structure of the mountains is such as to allow tunnels to be used with the greatest advantage. Narrow places are presented where opposite gorges approach each other, and a wall of some two or three thousand feet often separates points which may not be more than a quarter of a mile apart at its base. It will also be remembered that the Great Basin east of the Sierra Nevada, has a general elevation of over 4,000 feet, so that the mountains would be approached on the east at that elevation ; on the west the slope is wide, though descending too near the level of the tide water.

" The foregoing remarks embody all the general information I am now able to give upon this line. The first section of it, from the Missouri frontier to the head of the Del Norte is explored, and needs no further reconnoissances. It is ready for the location of the road by a practical engineer. The second and third sections require further explorations, to determine, not upon practicability, but upon the preference due to one over the others.

" A party of 300 men, skillfully directed, with the assistance of three or four practical road engineers, would be sufficient to lay out the whole routes, and clear and open a common road in the course of next spring and summer, so as to be passable for wagons and carriages, and as rapidly traversed as any of the common roads in the United States.

" The obstacles I have not mentioned are the winter impediments of snows, and the temporary one from the hostility of the Indians. The latter can be surmounted by military stations sending out military patrols to clear and scout the line. The snows are less formidable than would be supposed, from the great elevation of the central part of the route. They are dry, and therefore more readily passed through; are thin in the valleys, and remain only during a very brief winter. The winter of my last expedition was one of unprecedentedly deep and early snows, yet in the valley of the Kansas and Arkansas it was thin; in the valley of Huerfano, none; and in the vall ey of Del Norte the snow was only three feet deep; the thermometer at zero near midday.

"The weather in these high mountains and deep valleys is of a character adapted to such localities—extremely cold on the mountains, while temperate in the valleys. I have seen it storming for days together on the mountains in a way to be destructive to all animal life exposed to it, while in the valley, there would be a pleasant sunshine, and the animals feeding on nutritious grass. Beyond the Rocky Mountains, the cold is less, and the snows become a less and more transient obstacle. These are my views of a route for the road or roads (a common one is first wanted), from the Mississippi to the Pacific. It fulfills, in my opinion, all the conditions for a route for a national thoroughfare.

"1st. It is direct. The course is almost a straight line. St. Louis is between 38, 39; San Francisco is about the same; the route is between these parallels, or nearly between them, the whole way.

"2nd. It is central to territory. It is through the territorial centre west of the Mississippi, and its prolongation to the Atlantic ocean would be central to the States east of that river. It is also central to business and population, and unites the greatest commercial point in the valley of the Mississippi with the greatest commercial point on the coast of the Pacific.

"3rd. It combines the advantages for making and preserving the road, wood, water, and soil, for inhabitation and cultivation.

"4th. It is a healthy route. No diseases of any kind upon it; and the valetudinarian might travel it in his own vehicle, on horse, or even on foot, for the mere restoration of health and recovery of spirits.

"It not only fulfills all the conditions of a national route, but it is preferable to any other. It is preferable to the South Pass from being nearly four degrees further south, more free from open plains, and from the crossing of great rivers. Its course is parallel with the rivers, there being but one (the Upper Colorado), directly crossing its line. There are passes at the head of Arkansas, in the Three Parks, and north of them, but none equal to this by the Rio del Norte. There is no route north of it that is comparable to it; I believe there is no practicable route south of it in the United States. The disaster which turned me south from the head of the Del Norte and sent me down that river, and to the mountains around to the Upper Gila, enabled me to satisfy myself on that point.

"I went a middle route—a new way—between the Gila River and the wagon-road through the Mexican province of Sonora, and am satisfied that no route for a road can be had on that line, except going through Mexico, then crossing the Great Colorado of the West, near the mouth of the Gila, to cross the desert to arrive at San Diego, and still be six hundred miles by land, and three or four hundred by water, from the Bay of San Francisco, which now is and forever must be, the great centre of commerce, wealth and power on the American coast of the Pacific Ocean.

"In conclusion, I have to say that I believe in the practicability of this work, and that every national consideration requires it to be done, and to be done at once, and as a national work by the United States.

"Your obliged fellow-citizen,

"J. C. Fremont."

CHAPTER XVI.

FREMONT'S CAREER AS UNITED STATES SENATOR—SPEECH ON THE INDIAN AGENCY BILL—SPEECH ON THE BILL MAKING TEMPORARY PROVISIONS FOR WORKING THE MINES OF CALIFORNIA—CHALLENGES SENATOR FOOTE—FOOTE'S RETRACTION—FREMONT'S LETTER ABOUT THE AFFAIR.

THE long and anxious struggle which resulted in the admission of California into the Union, as an independent State, with a constitutional provision against slavery, is familiar to the country. The legislation upon the subject was consummated on the 9th of September, 1850. On the following day, the Californian senators presented themselves for admission to their seats. Colonel Fremont's credentials were submitted by Senator Barnwell of South Carolina, who remarked in doing so, that "it was well known he entertained the strongest constitutional objections to the admission of California into the Union, but Congress having passed an act for her admission, Mr. Fremont's admission could not be otherwise than very acceptable." Jefferson Davis, a senator from Mississippi, moved a reference of the credentials to a committee, on the ground "that the constitutional provisions for the election of senators could not have been complied with." Senators Mason of Virginia, Butler of South Carolina, and Turney of Tennessee, also favored the reference. Senators Clay of Kentucky, and Foote of Mississippi opposed the reference, which was defeated by a vote of 36 to 12.

The new senators were then sworn in, and immediately after, the Senate proceeded to ascertain by lot the class or length of senatorial term of the respective candidates. The shortest term, expiring on the 3d day of March, 1851, was drawn by Colonel Fremont. But three weeks remained of the session within which to accomplish anything for California. No time was to be lost, therefore, in doing what had to be done. On the day after he became entitled to his seat, he offered a resolution instructing the post-office committee to inquire into and report upon the expediency of establishing seventeen post routes in California, each described in the resolution, which was considered by unanimous consent, and agreed to. He, at the same time, gave notice of his intention on the following or some subsequent day, to ask leave to introduce a series of bills, designed to complete the political organization of California. The titles of those bills show their scope, and the statesmanlike views he took of the political needs of the young and as yet governmentless State which he represented.*

*"1. A bill to provide for the recording of land titles in California.

"2. A bill to provide for the survey of the public lands of California.

"3. A bill to provide for the erection of land offices in California.

"4. A bill to provide for the settlement of private land claims in California.

"5. A bill to grant donations of land to settlers before the cession of the country to the United States, and pre-emption rights to all subsequent settlers.

On the 14th of September he had leave to introduce a bill to make temporary provisions for the working and discovery of gold mines and placers in California, and for preserving order in the gold mine district. The bill, he stated, had been drawn up with great care; he had reviewed the Spanish laws, extending over a space of three hundred years, and had endeavored to embody in the bill all that he considered applicable to our age and institutions.

On the same day, the bill authorizing the President to appoint Indian agents in California being under consideration, Senator Atchison, from the Committee on Indian Affairs, stated that he was entirely unable to communicate to the Senate the information that they would probably require. The committee, he said, did not know the number of tribes of Indians, nor the num-

"6. A bill to regulate the working of mines in California.

"7. A bill to extend the laws and judicial system of the United States to the State of California.

"8. A bill to refund to said State duties collected at San Francisco and other ports, before the custom-house laws were extended to it.

"9. A bill to grant said State public lands for purposes of education.

"10. A bill to grant six townships for a university.

"11. A bill to grant land to aid in constructing public buildings.

"12. A bill to grant land for asylums for the deaf and dumb, for the blind and insane.

"13. A bill to relinquish to the city of San Francisco certain public grounds no longer needed for public purposes.

"14. A bill to grant to the State of California twelve salt springs, with a section of ground around each.

"15. A bill to grant to the city of Monterey the old government house and its grounds.

"16. A bill to provide for opening a road across the continent.

"17. A bill to grant land for internal improvement.

"18. A bill to preserve peace among the Indian tribes, by providing for the extinction of their titles to the gold districts."

ber of Indians within the State of California, nor the kind of title by which they held their lands; he therefore referred the Senate for further information, to the senators from California.

Whereupon Col.. Fremont proceeded to state his reasons for introducing the bill, as follows:

SPEECH OF COL. FREMONT IN THE UNITED STATES SENATE, ON THE INDIAN AGENT BILL.

"The general policy of Spain in her Indian relations, was the same as that which was afterwards adopted by all Europe, and recognized by the United States. The Indian right of occupation was respected, but the ultimate dominion remained in the Crown. Wherever the policy of Spain differed from that of the other European nations, it was always in favor of Indians. Grants of land were always made subject to their rights of occupancy, reserving to them the right to resume it, even in cases where it had been abandoned at the time of the grant. But the Indian right to the lands in property, under the Spanish laws, consisted not merely in possession, but extended even to that of alienation; a right recognized and affirmed in the decisions of the Supreme Court of the United States. A claim to lands in East Florida, under a title derived from grants by the Creek and Seminole Indians, and ratified by the local authorities of Spain before the cession of Florida to the United States, was confirmed.

"I have here in my hand a volume of Spanish laws, published in the city of Mexico in 1849, and purporting to contain all the legislation on this subject, which was in force in Mexico up to that date. These laws extend from 1533, some twelve years after the conquest of Mexico by Cortez, to 1817. The policy of Spain in regard to the Indians differed somewhat from that of the United States, and particularly in this: that, instead of removing the Indians from amidst the Spanish population, it kept them there and protected them in the possession of their lands among their civilized neighbors; having always in view the leading object of converting them to the Christian religion. To this end the power of the government was alwaysdirected; it was a national object, and in great part was a governing principle in the laws of which they were the subject. I will not occupy the time of the Senate by reading at length the several laws, but will merely make a few statements of such particular parts as bear directly upon the rights in question.

"A royal order of Charles V. (a supreme law in Spain), of the year 1533, decreed that the woods, pasture lands, and water contained in any grants of seigniories, which had been or should be made in the Indies, should be common to Spaniards and Indians. Another royal order of 1687 (confirming and extending an ordinance of the viceroy, Count Saint Stephen, of the year 1567) commanded that in all the villages of the Indians throughout all New Spain, who needed land to live upon and sow, there should be given to them a space of 500 yards, and as much more as they had any need of for cultivation around their village, measuring from the furthest outside house, and if the village happened to be a large one an unlimited quantity should be allowed, and that thereafter no grant of pasture ground or land should be given to any one within eleven hundred yards of the most outside house of the population.

"A law of Philip III. of 1618, ordained that no pasture grounds of black cattle should be situated within a league and a half of any village converted in old times of the Christian religion, and not within three leagues of any villages of newly converted Indians, upon pain of forfeiting the pasture ground and half the cattle which there should be upon it, and the Indians had the right to kill any cattle which should be so found trespassing upon their lands, and were subject to no penalty whatsoever from them.

"A decree of Philip IV. ordained that the sale, improvement and location of lands, should be made with such attention to the Indians, that they should be left with a superfluity beyond all the lands which might belong to them, as well individually as in communities, together with waters and water privileges, and the lands upon which they might have made canals for irrigation, or any other improvements, should be reserved to them in the first place, and in no case were they to be sold or alienated from them.

"The Spanish law likewise recognizes the Indian right to alienate, and prescribed the terms and mode in which such alienation shall be legal. A decree of Philip II. of 1571, commanded that the Indians should have the right to alienate their landed property as well as their personal effects, prescribing only that proclamation should be made during a specified time, and at a place of public sale. We have here a circular of the royal audience of Guadalajara of 1817, reviving for information, and to correct abuses, a decree of one of the superior tribunals of Mexico, which annulled a sale of the rancho of *Tena Banca*, made by the Indians of Colchis, for a failure to comply with the forms prescribed by law. In California we have both classes of Indians—the Christian or converted Indians, collected together at the missions and in large villages at the sea-coast and the interior, and the wild Indians of the mountains who never were reduced to subjection.

"The statements I have given, Mr. President, are sufficient to show that the Spanish law clearly and absolutely secured to Indians fixed rights of property in the lands they occupy, beyond what is admitted by this government in its relations with its own domestic tribes, and that some particular provision will be necessary in order to divest them of these rights. In California we are at this moment invading these rights. We lived there by the strong hand alone. The Indians dispute our rights to be there, and they extend the privilege which the law secured them of killing the cattle to that of killing the owner whenever they find an occasion. Our occupation is in conflict with them, and it is to render this occupation legal and equitable, and to preserve the peace, that I have introduced this bill. It recommends itself to the favorable consideration of the Senate by its obvious necessity, and because it is right in itself, because it is politic, and because it is conformable to the established custom of this government.

At the end of the debate the bill was reported to the Senate, and ordered to be engrossed for a third reading.

On the 25th, the bill making temporary provision for working the California mines, being under consideration, Senator Felch of Michigan, moved a substitute as an amendment to the whole bill, and made a long speech in its favor.

Mr. Fremont answered him in the longest speech that he delivered during the session, and judged by its results one of the most effective, for it disposed of all opposition, and the bill passed the Senate unanimously. We give the speech entire:

"The very advanced period of the session when we obtained our seats and were able to bring forward the California business, induced me to take a course in relation to our bills which I thought most agreeable to the Senate and best suited to secure for them a favorable consideration. This was not to use the indulgence of the Senate for making speeches, but to confine myself to a brief exposition of the nature and principles of a bill when it should be called up, and then to answer, as well as I could, the inquiries and objections of senators either to principles or details. But I find such a course difficult on this bill, which introduces a new subject, and one which, from its novelty and importance, excites, and ought to excite, much interest, and requires close examination. The principles of this bill, as I have already stated them, are to exclude all idea of making a national revenue out of those mines, to prevent the possibility of monopolies by moneyed capitalists, and to give to NATURAL CAPITAL, that is to say, LABOR and INDUSTRY, a fair chance to work, and the secure enjoyment of what they find. To carry out these principles to their just results, all the details of the bill are carefully directed.

"The senator from Michigan (Mr. Felch) who has made the motion to strike out the whole bill, and to insert a substitute, does not object to the principles, but on the contrary, supports them, and objects only to details. Adopting the principles of the bill and its leading provisions, he objects to the machinery as we may call it, of executing the system; objects to the agents, to the permits, and of course to the small sum which is to be paid for the permit. He would seem to leave the law to execute itself; that is to say, leave every man to act for himself under the law. If the honorable senator were as familiar with the workings of things in California as we who have drawn up the bill, for which he proposes his substitute, I believe he would never have introduced such a proposition. It would never work well anywhere, but would throw everything into disorder and confusion, and make every man judge and jury in his own case. Laws must have officers to execute them, and I think none could be more cheap, convenient, and suitable to the people than such as this bill provides. In the first place, there are agents, who are to reside each in a gold-mine district, grant the permits to applicants, visit the mines, and with a jury of six disinterested men, settle all disputes equitably and promptly, and without the delay and expense of a resort to a court of justice for every little question which grows up among the miners. To see that the agents are faithful and attentive, a superintendent of gold-mines is created, whose business it is to superintend all the agents, examine their books and accounts, hear complaints against them, take appeals from their decisions, and suspend them and appoint others in case of misconduct. The superintendent is thus armed with strong power, not over the miners, but over the agents, and for the benefit of the miners. It was considered necessary to have this strong, controlling power present with the agents and the miners, that all possible attention should be paid for the faithful execution of the act, and the immediate redress of all wrongs. The superintendent is necessary to give regularity to the operation of the agents, to hold them all accountable and to be the head of the system. To accomplish these purposes, an authority upon the spot is indispensable. The gorges of the Sierra Nevada are too remote from the metropolitan government—the President is too far off to observe the conduct of agents, to hear complaints, redress wrongs, or dismiss the unfaithful. It would be equivalent to no redress for injuries, if a miner who is wronged is obliged to send his complaint to Washington City, and prove it up at that distance from the scene of his complaint.

"The quantity allowed to each person is ample considering the privilege he has of changing his location as often as he pleases, and selling his lot when he is offered a good price. Thirty feet square is to be the size of a lot, to be worked by manual labor, in a placer; two hundred and ten feet, or about one acre, is to be the size of a lot in a mine to be worked by machinery, in the rock.

"A placer lot, accordingly, contains nine hundred superficial feet, with a depth to the centre of the earth. A cube of these dimensions would be twenty-seven thousand solid feet; and if a placer of tolerable richness is found, an industrious man might say his fortune is made. Sooner or later every industrious man may expect to find a good lot, and whether he sells it or works it, his reward will be ample.

"If he sells, he may take another permit, and work on until he makes another good discovery, and either sells that or exhausts it; and so on, until he is satisfied, or the mining is exhausted. Wherever he may plant his stake, exclusive possession is guaranteed to the miner, so long as he works his mining lot, or to his assignee, if sold, or to his legal representatives, in the event of his death. All that he finds is to be his own—there is no tax to be paid; no per centum—no fifth, or tenth or twentieth to the government; no officer to stand over the miner and require him to give an account of all he finds, and surrender up a part to the federal government—all is his own that he has the industry to collect; and for these multiplied advantages, with the protection of law and the security of order, the citizen pays only one dollar a month for as many months as he may choose, not exceeding twelve, with a pre-emptive right to continue his own lot. This nominal sum of one dollar a month is all that the bill proposes for him to pay; and while it will be sufficient to indemnify the government for all expenses, and to yield a respectable sum besides, it will be no burden on the miner; he will not feel it, but will pay it cheerfully in return for the advantages which the permit secures him.

"Under this system every industrious man—every one who has courage to persevere, to try in new places until fortune favors him—will feel assured that his fortune is in his own hands. For the more extended and regular operations by machinery, the dimensions of the parcel of mining ground fixed by this bill, are 210 feet square, or about one acre. In a mineral country, reputed to be of such extraordinary richness, their dimensions were considered abundantly large for the mine itself, and sufficiently so to afford room for temporary buildings in the beginning of operations. Hereafter, when the mineral district shall be better known, and the locality of the lodes or veins precisely marked out, larger contiguous spaces may be granted to miners for the construction of the buildings absolutely necessary for extensive works. In the meantime, it should be remembered that these veins will occur in tracts of ground rich in loose gold, and that all the advantages attending a permit to work a *placer*, apply to the permit to work a mine, of which the superficial contents are about 44,000 feet, and thirty feet depth, of which would be one million three hundred and twenty thousand solid feet. The dimensions of a lot of mining ground are therefore about fifty times greater than those of a placer's lot. For these great advantages we propose that the government should ask only twenty-five dollars a month, one dollar a month being the sum fixed for a placer permit, and the permit for a mine is therefore only half that for a placer, fifty to one being the proportion between them.

"The bill contains beneficial provisions in favor of first discoverers: they are to have double quantity, without the payment of any fee, and with the privilege of a pre-emptive right. These privileges have been recognized as just and politic under the laws of every mining nation. Under the regulations of the new code, Spain granted to a discoverer as many mining lots as he chose to stake out upon the vein, and under the mining ordinances of New Spain several such lots were granted to the discoverer, and upon as many veins as he might discover in an entirely new mineral ridge. It is only a proper reward to an industrious discoverer, and an inducement to prosecute researches which result in great benefit to the country. The discoverer of a new placer, or of a new mine, therefore, will have a full reward for his enterprise, and his expenditure in time and money.

"Five per centum of the proceeds from the sale of the permits is to go to the State of California for the purposes of internal improvement. This is upon the principle of the sale of the public lands. When sold by the United States, five per centum is paid to the State for that purpose. In this case the mines are to be worked out before the land is sold, and a considerable amount received, even at the low rates proposed. A hundred thousand permits would bring above a million and a quarter per annum. Five per centum upon one million would be $50,000 per annum to the State—a sum which could be beneficially expended in opening communications through the country.

"The system is temporary, and is to continue only until superseded by a better. I am doubtful if a better one will be found, and think rather that it will continue until the *placers* are exhausted; when the gold region can very properly be sold as other lands. The mode of taking effect of this system is equitable and proper, going into effect, when the agent arrives into a district and promulgates the law. In the meantime there is no prohibition to work, but every man works on, and holds a preëmptive right to the lot which he occupies. In this way the law would go into effect, without any interruption to the work which is going on, or without any shock to existing operations, and without retroactive operations upon anything that has been done. In fact all the details of the bill are carefully calculated to carry out its great leading principle—that of giving to LABOR and INDUSTRY a fair chance, and to save the mines from becoming a monopoly either in the hands of the government to make revenue, or in the hands of moneyed capitalists to amass princely fortunes. I am glad to find that the Senate evinces no disposition to create revenue by having taxes on the gold mines of our State, and that the liberal principles of this bill, from the votes already taken, are likely to prevail in this chamber.

"I think that this government should look for increase of revenues, to the expanded commerce which the discovery of these gold mines has created in the Pacific Ocean.

"Oppressive taxes on the precious metals are well suited to a government like that of Spain, which derived one of its chief supports from its mines in New Spain, which constituted its mint; which used the labor of the people only to create revenue; which demanded from them the first fruits of the earth, and taxed everything which it did not monopolize, and everything in the same proportion—agricultural products as well as mines—a tenth of the whole and all to support the extravagant expenditures of its arbitrary monarchs. In consequence of these oppressive exactions, ninety-nine were ruined out of a hundred, who engaged in gold mining operations in her dependencies. But we have adopted a wiser course. Reason and experience teach us the folly as well as the injustice of attempting such exactions from the people. We have seen their failure on a small scale on our own lead-mine leasing, and we have before us the result of their operation under the elaborate system and arbitrary power of Spain, which, with all their extravagant taxes, yielded—in those years of which I have any account, and at a flourishing period of the mines—a revenue of only about $60,000 per annum from the gold mines of New Spain. Mexico found out the folly of this course and immediately after her independence in 1831 abolished these multiplied taxes, and substituted for them all a simple duty of three per cent. Heavy taxes had almost destroyed this branch of her revenues, and liberal provisions were made to resuscitate it. The quicksilver mines were given to all who would work them, free of all tax and all kind of duty. Rewards of $25,000 each were decreed to the first four operators who should extract a certain quantity of the metal—the miners were exempted from all personal contributions and all military service—and all to restore what taxation had ruined. We cannot, certainly go back from what Mexico has done, and take up the abandoned system of old Spain; and I trust that, while we repudiate taxation, we shall also avoid anarchy and disorder, and give to the country some such brief and simple code of regulations, as will secure to every man the peaceable exercise of his industry, and the possession and enjoyment of what he gains."

"In conclusion, I trust that the substitute will be rejected and that the principles of the bill will remain as now fixed."

During the brief period that the Senate remained in session after his admission to its deliberations, Colonel Fremont confined himself almost exclusively to California business and to measures which, though of the greatest concern at that time to California have now lost much if not all of their public interest.* His speeches

*During the brief period of Col. Fremont's attendance in the Senate, he gave two or three votes on questions relating to slavery which have far more interest now than when they were given.

On the 12th of September, the second day after taking his seat, the bill to suppress the slave-trade in the District of Columbia being under consideration, Senator Seward, moved to strike out the whole bill from its enacting clause, and insert a provision for the abolition of Slavery in the District altogether. The amendment was rejected, as it was expected to be, the vote standing Yeas 5, Nays 45. Among the Nays with Col. Fremont were such Northern men as Roger S. Baldwin of Connecticut, John Davis of Massachusetts, Thomas Ewing of Ohio, H. Hamlin of Maine, Truman Smith of Connecticut, and R. C. Winthrop of Massachusetts. They all thought, doubtless, that course was best adopted to secure the practical result at which they aimed, the breaking up of the slave

though numerous were always brief and in their structure almost exclusively expository. He was looked to as the final authority upon all questions of fact in relation to the legislation required for California, and never rose without having something to say, and always sat down when he had said it. He displayed great clearness and precision of statement in the few forensic efforts which are reported, and established a character for modesty, good sense and integrity among his associates in the Senate which has survived all the political disruptions and alienations which have since overtaken the party with which he was acting.

But one incident occurred to mar the entire harmony of his intercourse with his brother senators, and that

pens and the slave auctions in the national capital—and on the 16th of September the bill passed, Fremont and Dayton voting with all the Northern Senators in its favor—Atchison, Jeff. Davis, Butler, and their partisans in the negative. During the pendency of the bill for the suppression of the District slave-trade, several votes were taken which proved plainly enough Col. Fremont's deep and constant sympathy with the cause of freedom. On the 14th of September, an amendment was pending providing that if a free person should entice or induce a slave to run away, or should harbor any such, he should be immured in the District Penitentiary five years. The vote was a close one—Yeas 22, Nays 26. Fremont voted No. Among the Yeas were Barnwell and Butler of S. C., Dawson and Berrien of Ga. (the State in which Fremont was born), Jeff. Davis, Soulé, Foote, Hunter and Mason of Va., W. R. King, Rusk and others. Among the Noes were Fremont and Dayton, Baldwin, Chase, John Davis, Ewing, Hale, Hamlin, Seward, Winthrop and others. On another amendment to authorize the Corporations of the District to prohibit free negroes within their limits, under penalty of imprisonment and fine; which also failed by Ayes 20, to Nays 28; Atchison, Butler, Soulé, Jeff. Davis and others in the affirmative; Fremont and Dayton, Hale, Chase and Seward were in the negative.

Sept. 28, when Mason of Va. moved to strike out the clause in the Navy bill which abolished flogging in the navy, Col. Fremont was found voting No, with Hale, Seward, Chase and other Northern men.

only served to increase the respect already entertained for his manly sensibilities. On the last night of the session, Senator Foote, of Mississippi, who came into the Senate somewhat excited, in the course of some remarks on the Naval Appropriation bill—it afterwards appeared as if he had not known precisely what bill he was speaking to—said in substance, or was understood to say, that the republic would be dishonored if a portion of the legislation which had been urged upon the Senate for California were consummated. Upon hearing these words, Col. Fremont left the Senate-chamber, and sent a messenger to say to Senator Foote, that he wished to speak with him. As soon as Foote had finished his speech, the message was delivered to him, and he stepped out to Col. Fremont, who then told him that he had sent for him to say that he had just used language in the Senate in reference to himself, which a gentleman in his position could not use, and which was unworthy of a senator. Foote immediately struck at him with his fist, just grazing his face. On the instant, both parties were seized by the door-keepers and senators who had noticed Foote's departure from the Senate and suspected its cause, and thus a serious issue to the affair was postponed, and, as it happened, prevented. On the following day, Col. Fremont sent Foote a note by the hand of Governor Price, of New Jersey, demanding a retraction of his offensive imputations. Governor Price brought back a note from Foote, in which he stated that in what he had said in the Senate, he had said nothing denunciatory of the bill supposed to have been referred to by him, or of those who introduced it.

Mr. Fremont's friends esteemed this equivalent to a

retraction of the offensive words, and on Monday following—the note to Foote and his reply were delivered on Saturday—the following card appeared in the *National Intelligencer*.

A CARD.

WASHINGTON, *Sept.* 28, 1850.

The undersigned are authorized to state that the difficulty between the Hon. H. S. Foote, and the Hon. J. C. Fremont—growing out of certain expressions used by the former in relation to the California land-bill, in the Senate, last evening, has been adjusted satisfactorily and honorably to both those gentlemen.

A. C. DODGE,
WM. M. GWIN,
HENRY H. SIBLEY,
RODMAN M. PRICE.

It was the custom of certain senators at Washington then, as it is still, we believe, to keep one or two letter-writers to say what they did not like to say themselves—and at the time of which we are speaking, a correspondent of the *Baltimore Sun* stood in that relation with Senator Foote. In the fulfillment of his vocation, he took it upon himself to state in a letter written the very day the affair was adjusted, that Foote had made no retraction, and to censure Col. Fremont for attempting to prevent a free discussion of California measures. As Foote's letter of retraction had not been published, and the terms of the adjustment which had been pronounced honorable and satisfactory to both gentlemen were confidential, of course the *Sun's* version would be presumed, by the uninformed reader, to be correct, in the absence of any contradiction. Col. Fremont knew that this version of the settlement originated with Foote, and immediately addressed the following letter to the editor of the *Baltimore Sun*.

SIR: Your paper of this morning (Monday, Sept. 30th) contains a paragraph in a letter from this place, which it is obligatory on me to notice and in such clear language as I believe the circumstances justify me in using. It appears under the well-known signature X, and I believe it to have been written by Mr. Grund; but the paragraph which concerns me, I consider as the work of Mr. Foote himself, and shall accordingly treat him as the author.

The following is the paragraph:

"'The difficulty between Senators Foote and Fremont has been amicably arranged, as you will have seen by the card of those gentlemen's friends in to-day's *Union*. This is as it should be. Mr. Fremont was wrong to attack Mr. Foote for words spoken in debate, which, as he (Foote) distinctly avowed at the time in the Senate, were not spoken with a view to wound the personal feelings of any senator present, but merely to protect the country against *ex parte* decisions of the California Board of Commissioners for the adjustment of land titles. All that Gen. Foote had observed was, that without Ewing's amendment, granting an appeal to the Supreme Court of the United States from the decision of the Board, he considered that the bill would disgrace the Republic, and that however inclined he was to support the bill *with* the amendment, he should assuredly vote against it without the amendment. Mr. Foote retracted nothing; but distinctly avowed that he did not intend any personal disrespect for those who were against the amendment. Col. Fremont could not be satisfied with this explanation. As a sensible man, and a man of honor, he must have seen his mistake in attempting to gag senators in regard to all legislative acts relating to California, and in constituting himself the heir apparent of a family feud which, for the benefit of the whole country, had better be buried than renewed.'

"This paragraph is false in many particulars, as I will endeavor briefly to show, but will first make a few remarks as to the authorship. When the friend whom I had sent to Mr. Foote on Saturday morning brought back his letter, and joined with other friends in saying it was sufficient, and that I ought to be satisfied with it, and with the statement which had been agreed to be published, myself and others replied that this arrangement was not satisfactory, because the affair would not rest there, but that Mr. Foote was in communication with a letter writer, who wrote for him in the *Baltimore Sun* and *Philadelphia Ledger*, and that these two papers would soon contain untrue accounts of the affair to my prejudice, and which would compel me to take further notice of it. This was repeatedly and emphatically told to the gentleman; but it was finally concluded to receive Mr. Foote's letter as satisfactory, and to watch for the letters in the *Sun* and *Ledger*. Accordingly, Monday morning's *Sun* brought the expected letter, which, as I have said above, I fully believe to be the work of Mr. Foote through Mr. Grund. The letter opens with saying, that the difficulties between Mr. Foote and Mr. Fremont have been very '*amicably*' arranged. This word '*amicably*' is false, as was well known to the writer. I merely received Mr. Foote's letter as satisfaction, and no tokens of amity were interchanged between us, not even speaking to each other. He comes then to the cause of the difficulty, all of which is falsely stated, and is so proved to be by the record. The letter says, 'Mr. Fremont was wrong to attack Mr. Foote for words spoken in debate, which as he (Foote) distinctly avowed at the time, were not spoken with a view to wound the feelings of any senator present, but merely to protect the country against *ex parte* decisions of the California Board of Commissioners.'

"This is untrue. The bill for the California land titles was not under consideration at the time, and had been previously laid upon the table, with my approbation, till the next session, with a view to give it the full consideration, for which there was now no time. Other measures had been taken up, and the naval appropriation bill was then under discussion; and it was on this bill—on the pretext of a motion from Mr. Gwin, having no relation to the land titles—that the words were spoken. It was not, therefore, to 'protect' the country against any action under that bill that the injurious words were spoken, for the bill was not before the Senate, and had been laid over until the next session.

"The letter says Mr. Foote retracted nothing. This is untrue, as will be seen by the copy of Mr. Foote's remarks, as furnished to me by the reporter for the *Intelligencer*, contrasted with his own letter to me; both of which are herewith given in their order. And to avow no retraction, is to re-affirm the orginal insult, by an insidious implication. I make no account of difference between *retraction* and *denial* in this case.

"The letter says, 'Mr. Fremont must have seen his error in attempting to gag senators in regard to all legislative measures in relation to California.' This is absurdly false—absurd in the idea that I should attempt to gag senators, and false in the fact. Much as the circumstances of the country required the bill to be passed to prevent violence and bloodshed in California, yet, when it was kept off until the afternoon of Friday, I gave it up for the session—said so, before the evening recess, to Messrs. Ewing and Benton, the two principal speakers on it—agreed to have it laid upon the table—and, satisfied that this would be done, did not return to the Senate until after the evening session had commenced, and until after the bill had been laid upon the table; and when I did come in, I was surprised to find Mr. Foote referring to the California land title bill, the naval appropriation bill being the one under consideration. It is, therefore, false, as well as ridiculous, to say that I attempted to gag senators; I laid it over to the next session expressly to admit the fullest discussion, which is exactly the reverse of gagging.'

"The Baltimore letter says, 'Mr. Foote did not intend to wound the feelings of any senator—but distinctly avowed at the time in the Senate, that he did not intend any personal disrespect for those who were against the amendment.' This is false again, and is proved to be so by all the circumstances of the case, and by the words themselves. This is the report of them, as furnished me by one of the *National Intelligencer* reporters:

"'We had some little admonition this morning at to the danger of hasty legislation in regard to California matters. Nevertheless, I say deliberately, I say it with due consideration of the matter and of the consequences of the declaration, that if the views which have been expressed in certain quarters this morning in regard to a portion of the legislation which is urged upon us for California, should be adopted in the same hasty manner in which it is now proposed to us to give our sanction to the present proposition, the admission of California into the Union would be productive of more detriment to the republic, and, in my opinion, be fraught with more real dishonor to the nation, than any event that has ever occurred in the historic annals of the country. Sir, we must be cautious about this California business. Not only is California a State of this Union, but she is a great State. Her resources are large. Her interests are vast. They are of vast importance to herself and to the country at large. In dealing with them we must act cautiously, circumspectly, vigilantly, and permit no man, or set of men, to urge us hastily and indiscreetly into the adoption of any legislation for which, hereafter, we may have reason to repent in sackcloth and in ashes.'

"Now, take this language, and see if there was not a design to be personal and insulting in it, and that upon a plan previously resolved upon. He avows deliberation—due consideration—disregard of consequences. What does this mean, but a pre-determined design to give both insult and defiance? And in that light it would doubtless have been represented, if I had not called him to account. Then the terrible consequences of passing the bill, the dishonor to the nation, the corruption, the repentance in sackcloth and ashes: what did all this refer to, but the bill which I had brought in? And why refer to it at all, when it was not before the Senate, not under consideration—actually laid upon the table, to lie there until the next session? Why not wait till the next session, if he only wanted to speak against the bill? Why refer to it at all, under such circumstances, unless for a purpose unconnected with the bill? and in such language, except for insult? It is useless to pretend the contrary; and, therefore, the Baltimore letter is false in saying that

Mr. Foote had no design to wound feelings—no intent to be disrespectful. The contrary was understood by every senator at the time, and is proved by the words themselves, and the circumstances under which they were spoken, and there is no disavowal, distinct or indistinct, of personal disrespect to anybody.

"The Baltimore letter admonishes me not to make myself '*heir*' to a family feud. The admonition would be unnecessary, even if it came from a source entitled to respect; but, found where it is, it is both false and impertinent. I make myself '*heir*' to no one's feuds. I begin none of my own. I prefer to live in peace with the world. But everybody will see from the remarks of Mr. Foote in the Senate, in relation to the bill I brought in, and his letter to the *Baltimore Sun*, that it is intended to make me '*heir*' to his feelings towards Col. Benton.

"I conclude this notice with giving Mr. Foote's letter to me, in answer to the note which I sent him by a friend:

"'SENATE CHAMBER, *Sept.* 28, 1850.

"'SIR: I do not feel that I should be doing justice to myself, did I not, in writing, (as I thought I did very explicitly last night, *orally*), deny that I said anything denunciatory of the bill to which you refer, or of those who introduced it. I was in favor of Mr. Ewing's amendment, and in favor of the bill itself, provided his amendment could be incorporated with it. This your colleague well knows. I said that certain views had been expressed in the course of debate upon that bill, and in support of it, that if sanctioned by Congress would disgrace the republic. What I meant was, that the establishment of a Board of Commissioners in California for the adjustment of land titles, *without the privilege* of appeal to the Supreme Court of the United States, would, in my opinion, result in scenes of corruption, and acts of injustice, which would be seriously derogatory to the national character. So I think yet, and so I shall always think and say.

"'If, after this statement, you persevere in the demand contained in your note, I shall certainly gratify you, though I shall, from certain prudential considerations, defer a formal *acceptance* of your proposition until I can leave the District of Columbia.

"'Your obedient servant,

"'H. S. FOOTE.

"'Hon. J. C. FREMONT.'

"This was the letter received. It contradicts the speech, denies the denunciation and insult which the speech contains, and is itself contradicted both by the actual words spoken in the Senate, and by the letter to the *Baltimore Sun;* and, although both of these are themselves untrue, yet it is not for Mr. Foote to say so, or to impeach their competency to invalidate the other. All three of these documents are given, and those who please may compare them, and see how entirely they convict each other. The letter to me, and the statement published by friends, would have been a *quietus* to the affair with me, if it had not been for the Baltimore letter. The letter to me, to be sure was untrue; but that was not my affair, provided nothing more was written. But I expected more—expected letters injurious to me in the *Baltimore Sun* and the *Philadelphia Ledger*, and so said at the time, and so the event has verified—and that has forced me to make this brief exposition of the threefold falsehoods of the premeditated attack upon me in the Senate, its denial in a letter to me, and its insidious implied repetition in the *Baltimore Sun*, by asserting that he retracted nothing.

"To put the whole case into three words, it is this; Mr. Foote went out of his way when the subject was not before the Senate, to deliver a deliberately considered insult and defiance to me—then denied the insult and defiance, and disclaimed all disrespect, in a letter to me—then re-affirmed, by inevitable implication, the same insult and defiance in a letter to the *Baltimore Sun*, denying all retraction.

"With this summing up of the case and the precedent proofs, I leave the affair to the judgment of the public.

(Signed) J. C. FREMONT.

"*September* 30, 1850."

Senator Foote has never publicly, nor so far as we know, privately, denied his complicity with the author of the letter to the *Sun*, nor did he ever in any way attempt to alter the position of the case as it was left by Col. Fremont's letter to the Baltimore journal. In a moment of undue excitement he had done a wrong for which he was ashamed publicly to apologize. Then to get credit for a triumph which he was not entitled to, he gets another person to write what he knew was not true. When convicted of both offences, he doubtless came to the conclusion that the most prudent course he could pursue towards Col. Fremont for the future, was to let him alone.*

* The *Albany Atlas*, of that date, commenting upon this affair says:—

"Senator Foote, of Mississippi, spent the closing hours of the late session of Congress in penning a retraction to Senator Fremont for gratuitous insult rendered in debate.

"It seems that he chose to attribute to corrupt private motives, the solicitude of Mr. Fremont to secure the passage of the California Mining Regulation bills. Called to account for such language, and stigmatized for its use, he resorted to a blow. Challenged, he had recourse to a letter of explanation and retraction.

"This seems to be the tactics of the man—to give insult in public, and to make apologies for it in private. He threatened Mr. Hale, on his accession to the Senate, that if he should be caught in his State, he would be strung up to the first tree without law, and that he would assist in the execution; but he apologized to the New Hampshire senator in private. He insulted Mr. Seward, if not as grossly, at least with as much malignancy; but he deprecated the ill opinion of the New York senator, and privately cultivated a better acquaintance, as his guest, at frequent tea parties. He insulted Borland, of Arkansas, was knocked down in the street by him for it, and apologized—privately. He 'flared up' at Clay and Calhoun in the Senate, to fawn upon them servilely afterwards. Mr. Benton was the only man upon whom he could not play this double game. He had eulogized him, in this city, as the superior of Cicero and of Burke, and as the greatest of statesmen. He maligned him afterwards, in the Senate like a common drab. Afraid to come near the great Missourian to apologize for insult, he kept himself privately armed, and once drew a pistol on his adversary in the Senate, but retreated before the mere frown of an unarmed man. He ends where he began—in insult and retraction.

"He doubtless expects that the fame of his public ruffianism will reach his State, and that the story of his pliancy will remain secret. This accounts for these alternations of bullying, hazarded in public, with mean compliances in private.

"Possibly the retracting senator of the repudiating State, in this course but represents his constituency; but we wish, for the sake of the national decency, that Mississippi would carry her peculiar system of ethics a little further and retract or repudiate him."

CHAPTER XVII.

RETURN TO CALIFORNIA—ILLNESS—CANDIDATE FOR RE-ELECTION TO THE UNITED STATES SENATE—GOES TO EUROPE—PROJECTS HIS FIFTH AND LAST EXPLORING TOUR—HIS HARDSHIPS AND TRIUMPH—LETTER FROM PARAWAN—PRAIRIES ON FIRE—A CARELESS SENTINEL—HUERFANO BUTTE—A CHEERLESS NIGHT—FALL OF MULES DOWN THE MOUNTAINS—THREATENED BY INDIANS—HOW THEY WERE REPELLED—REDUCED TO EAT HORSE MEAT—THEY SWEAR NOT TO EAT EACH OTHER—FREEZING, DEATH, AND BURIAL OF FULLER—DECLINES A PUBLIC DINNER IN SAN FRANCISCO—RETURNS TO WASHINGTON.

Col. Fremont left again for California by the steamer which sailed first after the adjournment of Congress. Upon leaving Panama he had another return of the Chagres fever, which was so obstinate and enfeebling that he was prevented from returning to Washington the following winter. Meantime the Pro-Slavery party, strengthened by all the influence of the Federal Administration, had acquired such a controlling influence in California, that at the fall elections of 1851, the party which had advocated the proviso against Slavery in the State constitution, and with which Fremont was identified, was no longer in the majority, and a combination was successfully made to prevent his re-election. The legislature went into an election of his successor in February, and after one hundred and forty-two ballotings, the convention adjourned until the 1st of January following, without making a choice. The candidates were Fremont, T. Butler King, Heydenfelt, Geary, Weller and Collier.

The next two years Col. Fremont devoted mainly to his private affairs. He took the preliminary steps necessary to perfect his title to the Mariposas tract, which he also surveyed and mapped; resumed his old business of cattle-drover, and in these pursuits gradually repaired a portion of the losses which his private interests had sustained while attending to public duties.

The negotiations to which his proprietorship of the Mariposas property gave rise took him to Europe in the spring of 1852, where he spent a year with his family, mostly in Paris, and where he had the satisfaction of observing that his fame had preceded him, and prepared for him an extremely flattering reception from several of the most eminent men of science and letters then living.

At the close of the session of Congress in March, 1852, through the good management of Senator Chase, an appropriation was made for the survey of three routes to the Pacific ocean with the view of getting some further information as a basis of legislation for a national highway between the Mississippi valley and the Pacific Ocean. When Col. Fremont heard of this, he determined to return, fit out an expedition on his own account, and complete the survey of the route which he had taken on his last expedition, from the point where he was led astray by his guide, and which he believed he could prove to be quite the best, if not the only practicable route for a national road. For this purpose he left Paris for the United States, in June, and in August, 1853, set out upon his fifth and last trans-continental expedition.

Among the colonel's companions on this trip was S. N. Carvalho, Esq., of Baltimore, who went as the artist of the expedition.

We have been permitted to inspect his journal and correspondence, in which he has preserved graphic memoranda of the most striking incidents of this most perilous and eventful journey. The following extracts are quoted from these records:

EXTRACTS FROM THE JOURNAL AND LETTERS OF S. N. CARVALHO.

"*Westport, Kansas, Sept.* 15*th*, 1853.—To-day Col. Fremont, Mr. Eglostein, Mr. Fuller and myself arrived at Westport from St. Louis. We found the rest of the expedition here with the baggage and provisions—Col. Fremont immediately selected a camp ground in a wood near town, and had all the material conveyed there.

"20*th*.—All hands slept in camp last night, and a storm of rain drenched us, giving the uninitiated an inkling of what they had to expect. During the day, different lots of mules and horses have been brought in, from which Col. Fremont selected those he required. Holders of animals took advantage of our necessities and charged two prices, to which extortion we were obliged to submit.

"The men have all been armed with rifles, Colt's six-shooters, sheath-knives, &c.; and the baggage arranged ready for packing to-morrow, when we are to have a trial start. Col. Fremont to-day engaged ten Delaware Braves, to accompany the expedition, under charge of Captain Wolf, 'a *big Indian*.'

"They are to meet us on the Kansas River near a Potawatomie village.

"21*st*.—Branding the animals with Col. Fremont's mark having been completed, we packed our animals, mounted our men, and started in high spirits. We proceeded about four miles to the Methodist Mission, and camped. Finding several things more required we sent back to Westport for them. My daguerreotype apparatus was unpacked, and views of the Mission were made; all the arrangements I had made for taking pictures in the open air were perfectly successful.

"22*d*.—We made an early start this morning, our camp equipage being in complete order. Col. Fremont intends to accomplish the journey as speedily as possible across the continent on a proposed line of 38. He supplied the expedition with the necessary provisions as well as luxuries, which the nature of the journey demanded, besides this seventy-two barrels of 'Alden's preserved milk, cream, cocoa, Java coffee,' and &c., were supplied by the manufacturer for testing the nutritive qualities and value during our voyage, from N. Y. I brought them into camp under my charge. These preparations alone were sufficient to sustain the lives of seventy men for a month. An extra mule was purchased on purpose to convey them.

"We camped at Shawnee Mission, some twelve or fifteen miles from our last camp. Colonel Fremont complains to-night of being indisposed.

"23*d*.—The illness of Fremont increasing, he has found it necessary to return to Westport for advice. He left orders for the party to proceed and join the Delawares who were awaiting us, at the distance of three days' journey—when he expected to rejoin us.

"To-day we met our brave Delawares, all armed and mounted; more noble specimens of men in their natural state, do not exist anywhere. Our party proceeded and camped near the Potawatomies, where we remained several days.

"*Oct.* 1*st*.—A messenger arrived with a letter from Colonel Fremont, informing us that his increasing illness forced him to return to St. Louis for advice. He counselled us to proceed as far as Smoky Hills and encamp, where there was plenty of buffalo, and to send back 'Solomon,' the Indian chief, who had accompanied him in a former voyage to Westport, to conduct him to camp. He thought he would be with us in a fortnight. This letter was addressed to Mr. W. H. Palmer, requesting him to take the direction of superintending the expedition during '*their encampment*.' We accordingly proceeded on the journey, under the guidance of Capt. Wolf and his Delawares, on the 6th October. We saw and killed our first buffaloes on the 7th. We encamped on the Saline fork of the Kansas River, better known as 'Salt Creek,' where there was abundance of grass for our animals.

"10*th*.— * * * * Our Delawares brought into camp this evenan abundant supply of buffalo and antelope. The gentleman in charge of the commissariat finds great difficulty in preventing the muleteers and those whose duty it is to perform the manual labor of the camp, from consuming unnecessary quantities of it.

"The result is, that the stores which were intended to sustain us on our journey are being wantonly and shamefully destroyed.

* * * * * * * *

Oct. 30th. During the day, the sun was completely obscured by low, dark clouds. The atmosphere was filled with a most disagreeable and suffocating smoke, which rolled over our heads. We were still encamped on the Saline fork of the Kansas River, impatiently awaiting the arrival of Col. Fremont, who had not yet returned from St. Louis. His continued absence alarmed us for his safety, and the circumstance that the prairies had been on fire for several days past in the direction through which he must pass to reach us, added to our anxiety. Night came on, and the dark clouds, which overhung us like an immense pall, now assumed a horrible lurid glare all along the horizon. As far as the eye could reach, a belt of fire was visible. We were on the prairie, between Kansas River on one side, Solomon's Fork on another, and Salt Creek on the third, and a large belt of woods about four miles from camp on the fourth. We were thus completely hemmed and incomparatively secure from danger. Our animals were grazing near this belt of woods the day before, and when they had been driven into camp at night, one of the mules was missing. At daylight a number of Indians, the Topographical Engineer (Mr. Eglostein), and myself, sallied out in search of it. After looking through the woods for an hour, we discovered our mule lying dead, with his lariat drawn close around his neck. It had become loose, and trailing along the ground had become entangled with the branches of an old tree, and in his endeavors to extricate himself he was strangled. We were attracted to the spot by the howling of wolves, and we found that he had been partially devoured by them. Our engineer, who wanted a wolf-skin for a saddle-cloth, determined to remain to kill one of them.

I assisted him to ascend a high tree immediately over the body of the mule, untied the lariat, and attaching his rifle to one end of it, he pulled it up to him. The rest of the party returned to camp. About four o'clock in the afternoon, he being still out, I roasted some buffalo meat and went to seek him. I found him still in the tree, quietly awaiting an opportunity to kill his wolf. He declined to come down. I told him to what danger he was exposing himself, and entreated him to return to camp. Finding him determined to remain, I sent him up his supper and returned to camp, expecting him to be in at sundown. The prairies were now on fire just beyond the belt of woods, and through which Col. Fremont had to pass. Becoming alarmed for Mr. Eglostein, several of us went to bring him in. We found him half way to camp, dragging by the lariat the dead body of an immense wolf, which he

PRAIRIE ON FIRE.—TO OUR GREAT JOY, WE SAW COL. FREMONT, FOLLOWED BY AN IMMENSE MAN, WHO PROVED TO BE THE DOCTOR, ON AN IMMENSE MULE, AND THE INDIAN CHIEF AND HIS SERVANT, GALLOPING THROUGH THE BLAZING ELEMENT IN THE DIRECTION OF OUR CAMP—PAGE 433.

had shot. We assisted him on with his booty as well as well as we could. My "guard" came on at two o'clock. I lay down to take a three hours' rest; when I went on duty, the scene that presented itself was sublime. A breeze had sprung up which dissipated the smoke to windward. The full moon was shining brightly, and the piles of clouds which surrounded her presented magnificent studies of light and shadow which Claude Lorraine so loved to paint. The fire had reached the belt of woods, and had already burned part of the tree our friend had been seated on all day. The fire on the north side had burned up to the water's edge, and had there stopped. The whole horizon now seemed bounded by fire; our Delawares by this time had picketed all the animals near the creek we were camped on, and all the baggage of the camp safely carried down the banks near the water. When day dawned, the magnificent woods which had sheltered our animals now appeared a forest of black scathed trunks. When the fire gradually increased around us, we dared not change our ground: first, because we saw no point where there was not more danger than where we were: second, if we moved away, the Indian chief, Solomon, who, after conducting us to the camp-ground we now occupied, had returned to guide Col. Fremont, would not know exactly where to find us again. Just after breakfast, one of the Delawares gave a loud whoop, and pointed to the burning prairie before us, where, to our great joy, we saw Col. Fremont, followed by an immense man, who proved to be the doctor, on an immense mule, and the Indian chief and his servant, galloping through the blazing element in the direction of our camp. Instantly, with one accord, all the men discharged their rifles in a volley; our tents were struck, and we wanted to make a signal for their guidance. We all reloaded, and when they were very near, we fired a salute. Our men and Indians immediately surrounded Col. Fremont, with kind inquiries after his health. No father who had been absent from his children could have been received with more enthusiasm and real joy. To reach us, he had to travel over nearly fifty miles of country which had been on fire; the Indian trail which led to our camp from Solomon's fork being obliterated, it was most difficult and arduous to follow it; but the keen sense of the Indian directed him under all difficulties, directly to the spot where he had left us.

"During the balance of the day we put the camp in travelling order. With the arrival of the colonel our provisions had received considerable additions, more in fact, than he had any good reason to suppose we had consumed during his absence. During the night the fire crossed the Kansas River, and was directly approaching our camp. At day-light our animals were all packed—the camp raised, and all the men in their saddles. Our only escape was through the blazing grass,—we dashed into it, Col. Fremont at the head, his officers following, while the rest of the party were driving up the baggage animals. The distance we rode through the blazing fire could not have been more than one hundred feet—the grass which quickly ignites, as quickly consumes, leaving only black ashes in the rear. We passsed through the fiery ordeal unscathed; made that day over the burnt prairie about fifteen miles, and camped for the night on the dry bed of a creek, beyond the reach of the devouring element. * * * * * * *

"*Walnut Creek Camp.*—The weather is very cold and disagreeable. One of the officers on guard left the animals and came into camp to warm himself,—Col. Fremont saw him at the fire and asked if he had been relieved; he said, 'no.' Col. F. told him that he expected him to travel on foot during the next day's journey.

"From being unaccustomed to a life among the Indians, I thought the punishment very severe; but the sequel vindicated the justice of it. When the animals were driven to camp in the morning, five horses and mules were missing; half the day was spent in an unsuccessful search for them. Our Delawares reported Cheyenne moccasin tracks in the vicinity, which led Col. Fremont to follow them, they being also on the line of our travel; he soon discovered the marks of horse shoes, which proved that we were on the track of the robbers. (The Indian horses are never shod.) We crossed the divide, to the Arkansas, and followed up that river a considerable distance to "Big Tombee" where there was a Cheyenne Indian village. Here we found the animals as well as the thieves. On examination they confessed that they had watched our camp until the man left his guard to warm himself by the camp fire, during which time they took the opportunity to run off five animals, and if they had been unguarded a half hour longer, they would have stolen the whole of them.

"Thus the lives of the whole party were jeopardized by the inconsiderate conduct of this sentinel. We were about four hundred miles from the frontiers, at the commencement of a most inclement winter. Had we lost our animals, we must have perished, exposed as we were on those vast prairies to bands of Pawnee, Camanche, and other hostile Indians.

"The party proceeded to Mr. Bent's House, a few miles further, where we camped. Col. Fremont intended to procure fresh supplies of provisions at Bent's Fort; but the Indians had destroyed and sacked it. Mr. Bent had saved some sugar and coffee with which he kindly supplied us. Here all the men were provided with fresh animals preparatory to ascending the immense mountains now in sight. An Indian lodge sufficient to shelter our whole party, with a small one for Col. Fremont, together with a buffalo robe for each man, and buffalo robe overshoes, moccasins, &c., were also provided by Mr. Bent.

"We remained here several days, which gave me an opportunity to daguerreotype and sketch interesting scenes at the Cheyenne Village. About the 26th November we started for the mountains.

"After crossing the Huarfano River, we saw the immense pile of granite rock which rises perpendicularly to the height of four or five hundred feet from a perfectly level valley; it appeared like a mammoth sugar-loaf, (called the Huarfano Butte). Col. Fremont expressed a desire to have several views of it from different distances; the main party proceeded on the journey, leaving under my charge the mules which carried our apparatus, and also the blankets and buffalo robes of the whole camp, it being necessary, in order to equalize their weight, to distribute the different boxes on three or four animals. Mr. Eglostein, Mr. Fuller, and two Delawares remained with me. To make a daguerreotype view generally occupied from one to two hours—the principal part of that time, however, was occupied in opening the apparatus, and repacking and reloading the mules. When we came up to the Butte, Mr. Fuller made barometrical observations at its base, and also ascended to the top to make observations, in order to ascertain its exact height. This took considerable time, and when we had completed our work, we found that we were four hours behind camp, which was equal to twelve miles. We followed the trail of our party, through the immense fields of artimesia, until night overtook us. We travelled until we could no longer distinguish the trail.

"We discharged our arms as a signal to our camp—they answered us by firing off their rifles, but the wind being then high, we could not determine their exact distance or position. When taking counsel together we determined to encamp for the night on the side of a mountain covered with pines near by. We soon had a large fire burning, for the weather was intensely cold and disagreeable; but upon unloading our animals we found that we had with us all the blankets and buffalo robes of the camp, but nothing to eat or drink, the night was so dark that although not more than half a mile from a creek, we preferred to suffer from thirst rather than incur fresh danger which might lurk about it. I had with me three tin boxes containing preserved eggs and milk, but I preferred to go supperless to bed rather than touch the small supply which I had, unknown to the rest, carefully hid away in my boxes to be used on some more pressing occasion. Our absence was most keenly felt by the camp for they had to remain up around their fire all night, not having anything to sleep on. We also watched all night fearful lest our animals should stray away or that we should be attacked by Indians. At day-dawn we reloaded our animals, found our lost trail, and we soon met some of our party whom Col. Fremont had sent out to find us; when we got to the camp they were all ready for a start awaiting us. A delicious breakfast of venison and buffalo, pot-pourri had been prepared, and we discussed its merits with an appetite sharpened by a twenty-four hours fast.

"We entered the San Luis valley through the Sand Hill Pass, which was admirably adapted for railroad purposes. We continued through the valley of the Rio Grande over the Sarawatch mountains into the Sarawatch valley, through the Cochatope Pass, on the summit of which we found but little snow. Our road lay through a forest of trees still in foliage, with immensely high mountains of snow on either side of the pass.

"From the top of the highest I made daguerreotype panorama of the continuous ranges of mountains which slumbered at my feet covered with their everlasting mantle of snow in which we were destined to suffer so many privations.

"Several days after we came down from the pass, it became necessary to ascend a steep mountain covered with from two to three feet of snow. When we were about half way up, the foremost baggage mule lost his balance and fell down, carrying with him nearly all the party, who might have been seen tumbling head over heels down the mountain, a distance of several hundred feet. I was thrown from my horse, and remained up to my head in the snow, but my horse was rolled over to the very bottom, where I found him unharmed. One horse and one mule were killed on the spot.

* * * * * * * *

"After descending a very steep mountain on the deep snows of which we passed the coldest night I experienced during our journey—thermometer at daylight, being near 30°. We camped on a creek fringed with willows, and interspersed with cottonwood; the country indicating that there might be game about, our Delawares sallied out in quest of some. We at this time were on rations of meat, biscuit, and had killed our first horse for food; towards night our hunters returned and brought with them the choice parts of a fine fat young horse, that they had killed. He was one of three or four wild ones which they discovered grazing some four miles from camp. Our men, in consequence, received a considerable addition to their stock of provision, which when cooked proved much more palatable than our broken down horses.

"The Delawares also discovered recent foot-prints of Utah Indians. This information caused Col. Fremont to double the guard and examine the arms of the whole party, who hitherto had been warned by him of the necessity there was for keeping them in perfect order. Suddenly it occurred to me that my double barrelled gun might be out of order; I had used it as a 'walking stick,' in descending the mountain; that day the snow was so deep that I was obliged to resort to that course, to ascend myself. I quietly went to the place where I had laid it down, and attempted to fire it off—both caps snapped; the quick ear of Col. Fremont, heard the cap explode. He approached me very solemnly and gave me a lecture, setting forth the consequences which might have resulted from a sudden attack of the Indians, on our camp. 'Under present circumstances, Mr. Carvalho,' he said, 'I should have to fight for you.' His rebuke was merited, and had its effect throughout the camp, for all the men were most particular afterwards in keeping their arms in perfect order. We travelled that day nearly twenty miles, and encamped in an Utah Indian village, containing a large number of lodges and probably several hundred persons. The men were mostly armed with rifles, powder-horns, and also with their Indian implements of warfare. On our mules was packed the balance of our 'fat horse' of the night before. These Indians received us very kindly, and during the evening we exposed our wares, viz.:—Blankets, knives, &c., which we brought along to conciliate the Indians, and also to trade with them for horses and venison. We made several purchases, &c.—About 9 o'clock after placing double guard round our animals, and while we were regaling on fat deer meat, loud noises were heard approaching the camp. We soon distinguished the voices of women in bitter bewailment. I thought it was a religious ceremony of burial, or something of the kind. Col. Fremont, requested me to see from what it proceeded; I found the procession of the whole Indian camp; the warriors all armed, headed by a half-breed who had been some time in Mexico, and had acquired a smattering of the Spanish language, who acted as interpreter—understanding Spanish, gleaned from him that the horse our Delawares had killed, the evening before, some 20 miles away, belonged to one of the squaws, who valued it very highly, and demanded payment. On informing Col. Fremont, who had denied himself to the Indians, he remarked to the women we had no right to kill it without remunerating her for it, and he deputed the person in charge of the baggage, to give them what was right. Having seen our assortment, they wanted a part of everything we had, including a keg of gunpowder. To this demand, Col. Fremont gave an absolute refusal, and at the same time, expressed his desire that the men should not sell, barter, or give away a single grain of gunpowder, on pain of his severest displeasure. The Indians then threatened to attack us. Col. Fremont defied them. After considerable patience, we succeeded in pacifying them and sending them off. It was now daylight. We repacked our animals and raised camp. At the end of our day's journey, we found ourselves on the Grand River, thirty miles from our last camp. While at supper, the guard on the look-out gave the alarm that Indians were approaching. The word was given to arm and prepare to receive them.

About fifty or sixty mounted Utah Indian warriors all armed with rifles and bows and arrows, displaying their powder-horns and cartouch-boxes most conspicuously, their horses full of mettle and gaily caparisoned, came galloping and tearing into camp. They also had come to be compensated for the horse which had been paid for the night before. They insisted that the horse did not belong to the woman, but to one of the Indians then present, and threatened if we did not pay them "a great deal of red cloth and blankets, knives, powder," &c., they would fall upon us and massacre the whole party. On these occasions, Col. Fremont never showed himself, which caused the Indians to have considerable more respect for the Great Captain, as they usually called him; nor did he ever communicate directly with them, which gave him time to deliberate, and lent a mysterious importance to his messages.

Very much alarmed, I entered Col. Fremont's lodge, and told him their errand and their threats. He at once expressed his determination not to submit to such imposition, and at the same time laughed at their threats. I could not comprehend his calmness. I deemed our position most alarming, surrounded as we were by armed savages, and I evidently betrayed my alarm in my countenance. Col. Fremont, without apparently noticing my nervous state, remarked that he knew the Indian character perfectly, and he did not hesitate to state that there was not sufficient powder to load a single rifle in the possession of the whole tribe of Utahs. "If," continued he, "they had had any ammunition, they would have surrounded and massacred us, and stolen what they now demand and are parleying for." I at once saw that it was a most sensible deduction, and gathered fresh courage; the general aspect of the enemy was at once changed; and I listened to his directions in a very different frame of mind than when I entered. He tore a leaf from his journal, and handing it to me, said: "Here, take this, and place it against a tree, and, a distance near enough to hit it every time. Discharge your Colt's navy six shooters—fire at intervals of ten to fifteen seconds—and call the attention of the Indians to the fact that it is not necessary for white men to load their arms. I did so. After the first shot, they pointed to their own rifles, as much as to say they could do the same (if they had happened to have the powder.) I, without lowering my arm, fired a second shot; this startled them. I discharged it a third time; their curiosity and amazement was increased; the fourth time I placed the pistol in the hands of the chief, and told him to discharge it, which he did, hitting the paper and making another impression of the bullet. The fifth and sixth times two other Indians exploded it; having discharged the six, it was time to replace it in my belt. I had another one ready loaded, which I dexterously substituted, and scared them into the acknowledgment that they were all at our mercy, for we could kill them as fast as we liked, if we were so disposed. After this exhibition, they forgot their first demand, but proposed to exchange some of their horses for blankets. We effected a trade for three or four apparently sound strong animals—which in a few days proved utterly worthless, having gone so lame that we had to kill them for food. The Indians asked to remain in camp as it was then near dark, and they had ridden thirty miles. Col. Fremont assented, but on this occasion, eleven men were on guard at one time, all armed. The Indians, who no doubt waited in our camp to run our horses off during the night, were much disappointed in not having an opportunity. They quietly departed next morning, while our whole camp listened to the energetic exclamation of Col. Fremont, that the 'Price of safety is eternal vigilance.'

* * * * * * * *

"At last we are drawn to the necessity of killing our brave horses for food. To-day the first sacrifice was made. It was with us all a solemn event, rendered far more solemn however by the impressive scene which followed. Col. Fremont came out to us, and after referring to the dreadful necessities to which his men had been reduced on a previous expedition, of eating each other, he begged us to swear that in no extremity of hunger would any of his men lift his hand against or attempt to prey upon a comrade; sooner let him die with them than live upon them. They all promptly took the oath, and threatened to shoot the first one that hinted or proposed such a thing.

"It was a most impressive scene, to witness twenty-two men on a snowy mountain, with bare heads, and hands and eyes upraised to Heaven, uttering the solemn vow 'So help me God!'—and the valley echoed, 'So help me God!' I never, until that moment, realized the awful situation in which I was placed. I remembered the words of the Psalmist, and felt perfectly assured of my final safety. They *wandered in the wilderness* in *a solitary way;* they found *no city to dwell in. Hungry and thirsty their soul fainteth within them, and they cried unto the Lord in their trouble and he delivered them out of their distresses.*'

* * * * * * * *

"When an animal gave out, he was shot down by the Indians, who immediately cut his throat, and saved all the blood in our camp kettle. This animal was divided into twenty-two parts. Two parts for Col. Fremont and his cook, ten parts for the white camp, and ten parts for the Indians. Col. Fremont hitherto messed with his officers; at this time he requested that they would excuse him, as it gave him pain, and called tc mind the horrible scenes which had been enacted during his last expedition—he could not see his officers obliged to partake of such disgusting food.

"The rule he adopted was that one animal should serve for six meals for the whole party. If one gave out in the meantime, of course it was an exception; but otherwise, on no consideration was an animal to be slaughtered, for, every one that was killed, placed a man on foot, and limited our chances of escape from our present situation. If the men chose to eat up their six meals all in one day, they would have to go without until the time arrived for killing another. It frequently happened that the white camp was without food from twenty-four to thirty-six hours, while Col. Fremont and the Delawares always had a meal. The latter religiously abstained from encroaching on the portion allotted for another meal, while many men of our camp, I may say all of them, not content with their portion, would, to satisfy the cravings of hunger, surreptitiously purloin from their pile of meat, at different times, sundry pieces, thus depriving themselves of each other's allowance. My own sense of right was so subdued by the sufferings I endured by hunger, and walking almost barefooted through the snow, that while going to guard one night, I stole a piece of frozen horse liver, ate it raw, and thought it, at the time, the most delicious morsel I ever tasted.

"The entrails of the horse were 'well shaken' (for we had no water to wash them in) and boiled with snow, producing a highly flavored soup, which the men considered so valuable and delicious that they forbade the cook to skim the pot for fear any portion of it might be lost. The hide was divided into equal portions, and with the bones roasted and burnt to a crisp. This we munched on the road; but the men not being satisfied with the division of the meat by the cook, made him turn his back, while another took up each share separately, and inquired who should have it. When the snows admitted it we collected the thick leaves of a species of cactus which we also put in the fire to burn off the prickles, and ate. It then resembled in taste and nourishment an Irish potato peeling. We lived in this way for nearly fifty days, travelling from Grand River across the divide to Green River, and over the first range of the Wahsach Mountains, on foot, Col. Fremont at our head, tramping a pathway for his men tofollow. He, as well as the rest of the party, towards the last were entirely barefoot—some of them had a piece of raw hide on their feet, which, however, becoming hard and stiff by the frost, made them more uncomfortable than walking without any.

"About the end of January we crossed the Green River, and entered upon a country—barren and sterile to a degree, over which we travelled until we got to the base of the Wahsach mountains.

"*February* 1*st.* Yesterday Mr. Oliver Fuller, of St Louis, who had been on foot for some weeks, suddenly gave out. Our engineers and myself were with him. He found himself unable to proceed—the snow was very deep, and his feet were badly frozen. He insisted that we should leave him, and hasten to camp for relief; not being able to render him any assistance by remaining, we wrapped his blankets around him and left him on the trail. In vain we searched for material to build him a fire—nothing was visible but a wild waste of snow; we were also badly crippled, and we did not arrive in camp until ten o'clock at night at which time it began snowing furiously. We told Col. Fremont of Mr. Fuller's situation, when he sent a Mexican named Frank, with the two best animals and cooked horsemeat, to bring Mr. Fuller in. There was not a dry eye in the whole camp that night—the men sat up anxiously awaiting the return of our companions. At daylight they being still out, Col. Fremont sent three Delawares mounted, to look for them—about ten o'clock one of them returned with the Mexican and two mules. Frank was badly frozen, he had lost the track, and bewildered and cold, he sank down holding on to the animals, where he was found by the Delaware during the afternoon. The two Delawares supporting Mr. Fuller were seen approaching. He was found awake but almost dead from the cold and faintness. Col. Fremont personally rendered him all the assistance in his power. So did all of us—for he was beloved and respected by the whole camp for his gentlemanly behavior and his many virtues. Col. Fremont remained at this dreary place near three days to allow poor Fuller time to recruit—and afterwards assigned to him the best mule to carry him, while two of the men walked on either side to support him, A portion of our scanty food was appropriated at every meal from each man's portion to make Mr. Fuller's larger, as he required sustenance more than they did. On the 7th February, almost in sight of succor, the Almighty took him to himself: he died on horseback—his two companions wrapped him in his India rubber blanket and laid him across the trail. We arrived next day at Parawan. After the men had rested a little, we went in company with three or four of the inhabitants of Parawan, to bury our deceased friend. His remains had not been disturbed during our absence.

"When we arrived at Parawan the Mormons treated us very kindly, and several of them told me if they had known of our situation they would have hastened to our assistance. My illness prevented my accompanying Col. Fremont on the 21st of February; I followed about three months after, on his trail of 1844 and arrived at Los Angeles in June, thence by steamboat to San Francisco where I again met our late leader."

Col. Benton, speaking of this last expedition of Col. Fremont, says, "He went straight to the spot where the guide had gone astray—followed the course described by the mountain men and found safe and easy passes all the way to California, through a good country, and upon the straight line of 38 and 39 degrees."

Though the result of this expedition, was so satisfactory, the processes by which it was reached were anything but satisfactory. Nothing was heard of the party in the United States until three months after their departure. That came through Col. Babbitt, the Secretary of Utah Territory. On the 8th of February, 1854, four days' journey from Great Salt Lake, on his way to Washington with the United States mail, an Indian came to his camp and said that he had just met a party of Americans who were "very hungry." Babbitt soon overtook the party, and found it consisted of Col. Fremont and his companions. They had lived fifty days on horse-flesh, and for the last forty-eight hours had been without food of any kind.

Col. Babbitt, who was then on his way to San Francisco, wished Fremont to go directly there with him, but he refused, notwithstanding the enfeebled condition of his party, because he had not yet completed his surveys, and he was determined never to return without them. He therefore held on his course the next day, having first written the following letter, which he requested Col. Babbitt to hand to Col. Benton as soon as possible.

"PARAWAN, IRON COUNTY,*
"UTAH TERRITORY, *Feb.* 9, 1854.

"DEAR SIR: I have had the good fortune to meet here our friend, Mr. Babbitt, the Secretary of the Territory, who is on his way to Washington, in charge of the mail and other very interesting dispatches, the importance of which is urging him forward with extreme rapidity. He passes directly on this morning, and I have barely a few moments to give you intelligence of our safe arrival and of our general good health and reasonable success in the object of our expedition.

"This winter has happened to be one of extreme and unusual cold. Here, the citizens inform me, it has been altogether the severest since the settlement of this valley. Consequently, so far as the snows are concerned, the main condition of our exploration has been fulfilled. We entered the mountain regions on the Huerfano River on the 3rd of December, and issued from it here on the 7th of this month, arriving here yesterday afternoon. We went through the Cochatope Pass on the 14th December, with four inches—not feet, take notice, but inches—of snow on the level, among the pines and in the shade on the summit of the Pass.

"This decides what you consider the great question, and fulfills the leading condition of my explorations; and therefore I go no further into details in this letter.

"I congratulate you on this verification of your judgment, and the good prospect it holds out of final success in carrying the road by this central line. Nature has been bountiful to this region, in accumulating here, within a few miles of where I am writing, vast deposits of iron, and coal, and timber, all of the most excellent quality; and a great and powerful interior State will spring up immediately in the steps of the Congressional action which should decide to carry the road through this region. In making my expedition to this point I save nearly a parallel of latitude, shortening the usual distance from Green River to this point by over a hundred miles. In crossing to the Sierra Nevada I shall go direct by an unexplored route, aiming to strike directly the Tejon Passes at the head of the San Joaquin valley, through which in 1850, I drove from two to three thousand head of cattle that I delivered

*Valley of the Parawan, about 60 miles east of the meadows of Santa Clara, between 37 and 38 degrees of north latitude, and between 113 and 114 degrees of west longitude: elevation above the sea about 5,000 feet.

to the Indian Commissioners. I shall make what speed I possibly can, going light, and abandoning the more elaborated survey of my previous line, to gain speed.

"Until within about a hundred miles of this place we had daguerreotyped the country over which we passed, but were forced to abandon all our heavy baggage to save the men, and I shall not stop to send back for it. The Delawares all came in sound, but the whites of my party were all exhausted and broken up, and more or less frost-bitten. I lost one, Mr. Fuller, of St. Louis, Missouri, who died on entering this valley. He died like a man, on horseback, in his saddle, and will be buried like a soldier on the spot where he fell.*

"I hope soon to see you in Washington. Mr. Babbitt expects to see you before the end of March. Among other documents which he carries with him are the maps and report of Captain Gunnison's party.

"Sincerely and affectionately,

"JOHN C. FREMONT.

"Col. BENTON, Washington.

"P. S.—This is the Little Salt Lake settlement, and was commenced three years since. Population now four hundred, and one death by sickness since the settlement was made. We have been most hospitably received. Mr. Babbitt has been particularly kind, and has rendered me very valuable assistance."

Col. Babbitt reported in San Francisco that the chances were against the party ever coming through, they were so enfeebled. In this, however, he had miscalculated the energy and resources of the man who conducted it, though he did not exaggerate the difficulties which were to be met and overcome. Col. Fremont did arrive about the first of May, worn and enfeebled it is true, by his journey, but with the evidences for which he had encountered all its perils in his hand.

Col. Fremont was tendered a public dinner by the citizens of San Francisco soon after his arrival; he declined the compliment however, as he did every engagement having a tendency to delay his departure

* See journal of Mr. Carvalho.

for Washington, whither he desired to carry the results of his explorations with all practicable dispatch, in order that Congress, then occupied with the subject of a trans-continental road, might have the benefit of his observations.

No official report of this expedition has yet been prepared, but immediately upon reaching Washington he summed out its results and the conclusions to which it had brought him, in a very instructive and interesting letter communicated to a Washington paper.*

* See Appendix.

CHAPTER XVIII.

COL. FREMONT COMES TO RESIDE IN NEW YORK—IS TALKED OF FOR THE PRESIDENCY—LETTER TO GOV. ROBINSON OF KANSAS—LETTER TO A PUBLIC MEETING IN NEW YORK UPON THE SUBJECT OF TROUBLES IN KANSAS—IS NOMINATED FOR THE PRESIDENCY BY THE NATIONAL REPUBLICAN CONVENTION—LETTER OF ACCEPTANCE—LETTER ACCEPTING THE NOMINATION OF THE "NATIONAL AMERICANS."

In the spring of 1855, Col. Fremont, with his family, took up his residence in the city of New York for a few months, that he might avail himself of the facilities which that metropolis would afford him in bringing out an elaborate report of his last expedition. While thus employed and living in the most absolute seclusion, his name began to be discussed in political circles as a suitable candidate of the parties opposed to extending slavery and slave representation in the country, for the next Presidency. Wherever the suggestion was made it was favorably received, and before the meeting of Congress, in December, the feeling of the Northern States was ascertained to be not unfriendly to his nomination, though his name, up to that time, we believe had not been mentioned in connection with the Presidency by a single leading journal.

The election to the speakership of the thirty-fourth Congress, of N. P. Banks, of Massachusetts, who had been one of the first to discern the fitness and expediency of nominating Col. Fremont for the Presidency, and the publication of a friendly letter from an old California friend, Governor Charles Robinson, who had then recently become involved in a perilous struggle for freedom in Kansas, removed whatever doubts had existed among Col. Fremont's friends about the propriety of publicly presenting his name. Gov. Robinson had shared with Col. Fremont some of the penalties of too great devotion to the cause of freedom when they were together in California, and the letter to which we have referred, was written to give the governor assurance of his cordial sympathy with him in the important contest which he was waging so bravely against fearful odds in Kansas. It ran as follows:

LETTER FROM COL. FREMONT TO GOV. ROBINSON.

NEW YORK, *March* 17, 1856.

"MY DEAR SIR: Your letter of February reached me in Washington some time since. I read it with much satisfaction. It was a great pleasure to find you retained so lively a recollection of our intercourse in California. But my own experience is, that permanent and valuable friendships are most often formed in contests and struggles. If a man has good points, then they become salient, and we know each other suddenly.

"I had both been thinking and speaking of you latterly. The Banks balloting in the House, and your movements in Kansas, have naturally carried my mind back to our hundred odd ballots in California and your letter came seasonably and fitly to complete the connection. We were defeated then; but that contest was only an incident in a great struggle, and the victory was deferred, not lost. You have carried to another field the same principle, with courage and ability to maintain it; and I make you my sincere congratulations on your success—incomplete so far, but destined in the end to triumph absolutely. I had been waiting to see what shape the Kansas question would take in Congress, that I might be enabled to give you some views in relation to the probable result. Nothing yet has been accomplished. But I am satisfied that in the end Congress will take efficient measures to lay before the American people the exact truth concerning your affairs. Neither you nor I can have any doubt what verdict the people will pronounce upon a truthful exposition.

"It is to be feared, from the proclamation of the President, that he intends to recognize the usurpation in Kansas as the legitimate government, and that its sedition law, the test oath, and the means to be taken to expel its people as aliens, will all, directly or indirectly, be supported by the army of the United States. Your position will undoubtedly be difficult; but you know I have great confidence in your firmness and prudence. When the critical moment arrives, you must act for yourself—no man can give you counsel. A true man will always find his best counsel in that inspiration which a good cause never fails to give him at the instant of trial. All history teaches us that great results are ruled by a wise Providence, and we are but units in the great plan. Your actions will be determined by events, as they present themselves; and at this distance I can only say that I sympathize cordially with you, and that, as you stood by me firmly and generously, when we were defeated by the nullifiers in California, I have every disposition to stand by you in the same way in your battle with them in Kansas.

"You see what I have been saying is more a reply to the suggestions which your condition makes to me, than any answer to your letter, which more particularly regards myself. The notices which you have seen of me, in connection with the Presidency, came from the partial disposition of friends who think of me more flatteringly than I do of myself, and do not, therefore call for any action from us. Repeating that I am really and sincerely gratified in the renewal of our friendship, or rather in the expressions of it, which I hope will not hereafter have so long an interval,

"I am yours, very truly,

"J. C. Fremont.

Gov. Charles Robinson, Lawrence, Kansas."

In April, 1856, he was invited to attend a large meeting in New York, called for the purpose of obtaining a full expression of opinion from the commercial metropolis of the country, against the policy which President Pierce was pursuing in Kansas. The following was his brief but highly acceptable reply:

"NEW YORK, *April* 29, '56.

"GENTLEMEN: I have to thank you for the honor of an invitation to a meeting this evening, at the Broadway Tabernacle, and regret that other engagements have interfered to prevent my being present.

"I heartily concur in all movements which have for their object 'to repair the mischiefs arising from the violation of good faith in the repeal of the Missouri Compromise.' I am opposed to slavery in the abstract and upon principle, sustained and made habitual by long settled convictions.

"While I feel inflexible in the belief that it ought not to be interfered with where it exists, under the shield of State sovereignty, I am as inflexibly opposed to its extension on this continent beyond its present limits.

"With the assurance of regard for yourselves, I am very respectfully yours,

"J. C. FREMONT."

Some months previous to this, Millard Fillmore of New York, and Andrew Jackson Donelson of Tennessee, had been nominated for the presidency and vice-presidency in Philadelphia, by the pro-slavery segment of a convention of Know-nothings—a name chosen by the Native-American party for themselves. In June following, James Buchanan of Pennsylvania, and John C. Breckinridge of Kentucky, were nominated by the administration party at Cincinnati, for the same offices. Both these sets of candidates were identified with the slave interest of the country, and both were the choice of the southern States of the Union more particularly. It was apprehended, and with good reason, that the effect of electing either would be to nationalize slavery in the United States, or indefinitely extend and aggravate the disorder and anarchy which prevailed on our western frontier. To avoid either of these disastrous results, a convention was called, of three delegates from each congressional district of the United States, and a proportionate number of senatorial delegates, to meet in Philadelphia on the 17th of June, for the purpose of nominating candidates for the presidency and vice-presidency, who would properly reflect the views of those who were prepared to make freedom in the territories the paramount issue in the approaching presidential canvass.

On the day appointed, the convention met at Musical Fund Hall in that city, where the Declaration of the Independence of these United States was first read and promulgated. Over a thousand delegates were in attendance, and among them a larger number of prominent and influential public men than ever before assembled, probably, in a national convention. Robert Emmet of New York was selected for temporary chairman, and Colonel Henry S. Lane of Indiana, for president of the convention. Representatives were in attendance from all the free States, from the territories of Kansas, Nebraska, and Minnesota, and from the following slave States and territories, viz., Virginia, Maryland, Kentucky, Delaware, and the District of Columbia.

The convention, numerous as it was, and composed of men of every variety of political sentiment, seemed animated by the single desire to select the candidate who should seem best calculated to unite all the sincere friends of freedom throughout the Union, in his support, and though there were several candidates who had many warm friends in the convention, the judgment of the great majority settled down very early in favor of Fremont, as combining in himself most of the requisites for a candidate of the republican party in the existing condition of the country. On an informal ballot he received 359 votes, more than two-thirds of the whole convention, and was afterwards, nominated unanimously.*

The Hon. William L. Dayton, for many years a distinguished member of the United States Senate, and

* The following was the result of the informal ballot:

	FREMONT.	Mc LEAN.
Maine,	13	11
New Hampshire,	15	—
Vermont,	15	—
Massachusetts,	39	—
Rhode Island,	12	—
Connecticut,	18	—
New York,	93	3
New Jersey,	7	14
Pennsylvania,	10	71
Delaware,	—	3
Maryland,	4	3
Virginia,	Declined voting.	
Kentucky,	5	—
Ohio,	30	39
Indiana,	18	21
Illinois,	14	19
Michigan,	18	—
Iowa,	12	—
Wisconsin,	15	—
California,	12	—
Kansas,	9	—
District of Columbia,	Declined to vote.	
Minnesota,	—	3
Nebraska,	—	3
Total,	359	196

New York cast two votes for Charles Sumner, one for N. P. Banks, and one for Wm. H. Seward.

always a faithful friend of freedom, was then nominated for the vice-presidency. His vote on the first informal ballot was not quite a majority,* but his nomination was made unanimous on the first formal ballot.

The following declaration of principles was also unanimously adopted by the convention:

THE PLATFORM.

"This Convention of Delegates, assembled in pursuance of a call, addressed to the people of the United States, without regard to past political differences or divisions, who are opposed to the repeal of the Missouri Compromise; to the policy of the present administration and to the extension of slavery into free territory; who are in favor of the admission of Kansas as a free State; of

* INFORMAL BALLOT.

STATES.	Dayton, N. J.	Lincoln, Ill.	Wilmot, Penn.	King, N. Y.	Sumner, Mass.	Ford. Ohio.	Clay, Kentucky.	Collamer, Vt.	Johnston, Penn.	Banks, Mass.	Wilson, Mass.	Pennington, N. J.	Carey, N. J.	Pomeroy, Kan.	Giddings, Ohio.
Maine,	20	1	..	..	1	1	1	..	..	..	..	..	..	..	..
New Hampshire,	7	8	..	..	..	..	..	..	..	..	..	..	..	..	..
Vermont,	..	....	..	..	..	..	..	15	..	..	..	..	..	..	..
Massachusetts,	25	7	2	..	1	..	..	..	2	1	..	..	..	..	2
Rhode Island,	8	2	..	..	1	..	..	..	..	1	..	..	..	..	..
Connecticut,	1	....	..	..	..	..	..	..	..	17	..	..	..	..	..
New York,	15	3	1	9	30	6	1	..	..	24	3	1	..	..	..
New Jersey,	21	....	..	..	..	..	..	..	..	..	..	..	..	..	..
Pennsylvania,	28	11	31	..	2	..	..	..	..	..	4	..	3	..	..
Delaware,	9	....	..	..	..	..	..	..	..	..	..	..	..	..	..
Maryland,	6	....	..	..	..	..	..	..	..	..	..	..	..	..	..
Virginia,	....	....	3	..	..	..	..	..	..	..	..	..	..	..	..
Kentucky,	..	....	5	..	..	..	..	..	..	..	..	..	..	..	..
Ohio,	65	2	1	..	..	..	1	..	..	..	..	..	..	..	..
Indiana,	13	26	..	..	..	..	..	..	..	..	..	..	..	..	..
Illinois,	..	33	..	..	..	..	..	..	..	..	..	..	..	..	..
Michigan,	13	5	..	..	..	..	..	..	..	..	..	..	..	..	..
Iowa,	7	....	..	..	1	..	..	..	..	4	..	..	..	..	..
Wisconsin,	15	....	..	..	..	..	..	..	..	..	..	..	..	..	..
California,	....	12	..	..	..	..	..	..	..	..	..	..	..	..	..
Kansas,	....	..	..	..	..	..	..	..	..	..	..	..	..	8	..
Minnesota,	3	....	..	..	..	..	..	..	..	..	..	..	..	..	..
District of Columbia,	3	..	..	..	..	..	..	..	..	..	..	..	..	..	..
Total,	259	110	43	9	36	7	3	15	2	46	7	1	3	8	2

restoring the action of the Federal Government to the principles of Washington and Jefferson; and who purpose to unite in presenting candidates for the offices of President and Vice-President, do

"1. *Resolve*, That the maintenance of the principles promulgated in the Declaration of Independence and embodied in the Federal Constitution, is essential to the preservation of our republican institutions; and that the Federal Constitution, the rights of the States, and the Union of the States, shall be preserved.

"2. *Resolved*, That with our republican fathers we hold it to be a self-evident truth that all men are endowed with inalienable rights to life, liberty and the pursuit of happiness, and that the primary object and ulterior design of our Federal Government were to secure those rights to all persons within its exclusive jurisdiction; that, as our republican fathers, when they had abolished slavery in all our national territory, ordained that no person should be deprived of life, liberty, or property, without due process of law, it becomes our duty to maintain this provision of the Constitution against all attempts to violate, for the purpose of establishing slavery in any territory of the United States, by positive legislation prohibiting its existence or extension therein; and we deny the authority of Congress, of a territorial legislature, of any individual or any association of individuals, to give legal existence to slavery in any territory of the United States, while the present Constitution shall be maintained.

"3. *Resolved*, That the Constitution confers upon Congress sovereign power over the territories of the United States for their government, and that in the exercise of this power it is both the right and duty of Congress to prohibit in the territories, those twin relics of barbarism—polygamy and slavery.

"4. *Resolved*, That while the Constitution of the United States was ordained and established by the people in order to 'form a more perfect Union, establish justice, insure domestic tranquillity, provide for the common defence, and secure the blessings of Liberty,' and contains ample provisions for the protection of the life, liberty and property of every citizen, the dearest constitutional rights of the people of Kansas have been fraudulently and violently taken from them;

"Their territory has been invaded by an armed force;

"Spurious and pretended legislative, judicial and executive officers have been set over them, by whose usurped authority, sustained by the military power of the government, tyrannical and unconstitutional laws have been enacted and enforced;

'The rights of the people to keep and bear arms have been infringed;

"Test oaths, of an extraordinary and entangling nature, have been imposed as a condition of exercising the right of suffrage and holding office;

"The right of an accused person to a speedy and public trial by an impartial jury has been denied;

"The right of the people to be secure in their persons, houses, papers, and effects against unreasonable searches and seizures, has been violated;

"They have been deprived of life, liberty and property without due process of law;

"The freedom of speech and of the press has been abridged;

"The right to choose their representatives has been made of no effect;

"Murders, robberies, and arsons have been instigated and encouraged, and the offenders have been allowed to go unpunished;

"That all these things have been done with the knowledge, sanction, and procurement of the present administration, and that for this high crime against the Constitution, and the Union, and humanity, we arraign that administration, the President, his advisers, agents, supporters, apologists, and accessories either before or after the facts—before the country and before the world; and that it is our fixed purpose to bring the actual perpetrators of these atrocious outrages and their accomplices, to a sure and condign punishment.

"5. *Resolved*, That Kansas should be immediately admitted as a State of the Union, with her present free Constitution, as at once the most effectual way of securing to her citizens the enjoyment of the rights and privileges to which they are entitled and of ending the civil strife now raging in her territory.

"6. *Resolved*, That the highwayman's plea that 'might makes right,' embodied in the Ostend Circular, was in every respect unworthy of American diplomacy, and would bring shame and dishonor upon any government and people that should give it sanction.

"7. *Resolved*, That a railroad to the Pacific Ocean, by the most central and practicable route, is imperatively demanded by the interests of the whole country, and that the Federal Government ought to render immediate and efficient aid to its construction, and as an auxiliary thereto, promote the immediate construction of an emigrant route on the line of the railroad.

"8. *Resolved*, That appropriations by Congress for the improvement of rivers and harbors of a national character, required for the accommodation and security of our existing commerce, are authorized by the Constitution, and justified by the obligation of the government to protect the lives and property of its citizens.

"9. *Resolved*, That we invite the affiliation and co-operation of men of all parties, however differing from us in other respects, in support of the principles herein declared; and believing that the spirit of our institutions, as well as the Constitution of our country, guarantees liberty of conscience, and equality of rights among citizens, oppose all legislation impairing their security." *

—The result of the deliberations of the Convention was communicated to Col. Fremont by a committee of the Convention appointed for that purpose, in a letter which, with its reply, ran as follows:

LETTER FROM THE COMMITTEE APPOINTED TO APPRISE COL. FREMONT OF HIS NOMINATION FOR THE PRESIDENCY BY THE REPUBLICAN NATIONAL CONVENTION.

"PHILADELPHIA, *June* 19, 1856.

"SIR: A convention of Delegates assembled at Philadelphia on the 17th, 18th and 19th days of *June*, 1856, under a call addressed

* The following gentlemen composed the Committee on Resolutions:

Maine—Henry Carter.
New Hampshire—D. Clark.
Massachusetts—E. Rockwood Hoar.
Connecticut—Hon. G. Wells.
Rhode Island—Hon. Thos. Davis.
Vermont—E. Kirkland.
New York—Hon. Preston King.
New Jersey—E. W. Whelpley.
Delaware—E. G. Bradford.
Maryland—Hon. F. P. Blair.
Virginia—John C. Underwood.
Pennsylvania—Hon. D. Wilmot.
Ohio—Hon. J. R. Giddings.
Michigan—Hon. Isaac Chesterey.
Wisconsin—John F. Potter.
Indiana—John P. Durfee.
Illinois—George S. Brown.
Iowa—James B. Holland.
California—Hon. John A. Wills.
Kansas—John L. Winchell.
Dist. of Columbia—Jacob Bigelow
Kentucky—Geo. D. Blakeley.
Minnesota—Hon. Alex. Ramsey.

to the people of the United States, without regard to past political differences or divisions, who are opposed to the repeal of the Missouri Compromise, to the policy of the present Administration, to the extension of slavery into free territory, in favor of the admission of Kansas as a free State, and of restoring the action of the federal government to the principles of Washington and Jefferson, adopted a declaration of principles and purposes for which they are united in political action—a copy of which we have the honor to inclose—and unanimously nominated you as their candidate for the office of President of the United States at the approaching election, as the chosen representative of those principles in this important political contest, and with the assured conviction that you would give them full practical operation, should the suffrages of the people of the Union place you at the head of the national government.

The undersigned were directed by the Convention to communicate to you the fact of your nomination, and to request you in their name, and as they believe, in the name of a large majority of the people of the country, to accept it.

"Offering you the assurance of our high personal respect, we are your fellow-citizens,

"H. S. LANE,
"*President of the Convention.*

"James M. Ashley, Anthony J. Bleecker, Joseph C. Hornblower, E. R. Hoar, Thaddeus Stevens, Kingsley S. Bingham, John A. Wills, C. F. Cleveland, Cyrus Aldrich.

"To JOHN C. FREMONT, of California."

COL. FREMONT'S REPLY.

"NEW YORK, *July* 8, 1856.

"GENTLEMEN: You call me to a high responsibility by placing me in the van of a great movement of the people of the United States, who, without regard to past differences, are uniting in a common effort to bring back the action of the federal government to the principles of Washington and Jefferson. Comprehending the magnitude of the trust which they have declared themselves willing to place in my hands, and deeply sensible of the honor which their unreserved confidence, in this threatening position of the public affairs, implies, I feel that I cannot better respond than by a sincere declaration that, in the event of my election to the Presidency, I

COL. FREMONT CAME OUT TO US, AND AFTER REFERRING TO THE DREADFUL NECESSITIES TO WHICH HIS MEN HAD BEEN REDUCED ON A PREVIOUS EXPEDITION, OF EATING EACH OTHER, HE BEGGED US TO SWEAR THAT IN NO EXTREMITY OF HUNGER WOULD ANY OF HIS MEN LIFT HIS HAND AGAINST OR ATTEMPT TO PREY UPON A COMRADE; SOONER LET HIM DIE WITH THEM THAN LIVE UPON THEM—PAGE 439.

should enter upon the execution of its duties with a single-hearted determination to promote the good of the whole country, and to direct solely to this end all the power of the government, irrespective of party issues and regardless of sectional strifes. The declaration of principles embodied in the resolves of your Convention expresses the sentiments in which I have been educated, and which have been ripened into convictions by personal observation and experience. With this declaration and avowal, I think it necessary to revert to only two of the subjects embraced in the resolutions, and to those only because events have surrounded them with grave and critical circumstances, and given to them especial importance.

"I concur in the views of the Convention deprecating the foreign policy to which it adverts. The assumption that we have the right to take from another nation its domains because we want them, is an abandonment of the honest character which our country has acquired. To provoke hostilities by unjust assumptions would be to sacrifice the peace and character of the country, when all its interests might be more certainly secured and its objects attained by just and healing counsels, involving no loss of reputation.

"International embarrassments are mainly the results of a secret diplomacy, which aims to keep from the knowledge of the people the operations of the government. This system is inconsistent with the character of our institutions, and is itself yielding gradually to a more enlightened public opinion, and to the power of a free press, which, by its broad dissemination of political intelligence, secures in advance to the side of justice, the judgment of the civilized world. An honest, firm and open policy in our foreign relations would command the united support of the nation, whose deliberate opinions it would necessarily reflect.

"Nothing is clearer in the history of our institutions than the design of the nation in asserting its own independence and freedom, to avoid giving countenance to the extension of slavery. The influence of the small but compact and powerful class of men interested in slavery, who command one section of the country, and wield a vast political control as a consequence in the other, is now directed to turn this impulse of the Revolution and reverse its principles. The extension of slavery across the continent is the object of the power which now rules the government; and from this spirit has sprung those kindred wrongs in Kansas so truly portrayed in one of your resolutions, which prove that the elements of the most arbitrary governments have not been vanquished by the just theory of our own

"It would be out of place here to pledge myself to any particular policy that may be suggested to terminate the sectional controversy engendered by political animosities, operating on a powerful class, banded together by a common interest. A practical remedy is the admission of Kansas into the Union as a free State. The South should, in my judgment, earnestly desire such consummation. It would vindicate the good faith—it would correct the mistake of the repeal; and the North, having practically the benefit of the agreement between the two sections, would be satisfied, and good feeling be restored. The measure is perfectly consistent with the honor of the South, and vital to its interests.

"That fatal act which gave birth to this purely sectional strife, originating in the scheme to take from free labor the country secured to it by a solemn covenant cannot be too soon disarmed of its pernicious force. The only genial region of the middle latitudes left to the emigrants of the northern States for homes, cannot be conquered from the free laborers, who have long considered it as set apart for them in our inheritance, without provoking a desperate struggle. Whatever may be the persistence of the particular class which seems ready to hazard everything for the success of the unjust scheme it has partially effected, I firmly believe that the great heart of the nation, which throbs with the patriotism of the freemen of both sections, will have power to overcome it. They will look to the rights secured to them by the Constitution of the Union as their best safeguard from the oppression of the class, which, by a monopoly of the soil and of slave-labor to till it, might in time reduce them to the extremity of laboring upon the same terms with the slaves. The great body of non-slaveholding freemen, including those of the South, upon whose welfare slavery is an oppression, will discover that the power of the general government over the public lands may be beneficially exerted to advance their interests and secure their independence. Knowing this, their suffrages will not be wanting to maintain that authority in the Union which is absolutely essential to the maintenance of their own liberties, and which has more than once indicated the purpose of disposing of the public lands in such a way as would make every settler upon them a freeholder.

"If the people intrust to me the administration of the government, the laws of Congress in relation to the territories will be faithfully executed. All its authority will be exerted in aid of the national will to re-establish the peace of the country on the just principles which have heretofore received the sanction of the federal government, of the States, and of the people of both sections. Such a policy would leave no aliment to that sectional party which seeks its aggrandizement by appropriating the new territories to capital in the form of slavery, but would inevitably result in the triumph of free labor—the natural capital which constitutes the real wealth of this great country, and creates that intelligent power in the masses alone to be relied on as the bulwark of free institutions.

Trusting that I have a heart capable of comprehending our whole country, with its varied interests, and confident that patriotism exists in all parts of the Union, I accept the nomination of your Convention, in the hope that I may be enabled to serve usefully its cause, which I consider the cause of constitutional freedom.

"Very respectfully, your obedient servant,

"J. C. FREMONT.

"To Messrs. H. S. Lane, President of the Convention; James M Ashley, Anthony J. Bleecker, Joseph C. Hornblower, E. R Hoar, Thaddeus Stevens, Kingsley S. Bingham, John A. Wills, C. F. Cleveland, Cyrus Aldrich, Committee, &c."

Soon after the nominations were made in Philadelphia, a "National American" convention, then in session in New York, tendered the support of that party also to Colonel Fremont, who acknowledged the letter announcing their determination in the following terms:

"NEW YORK, *June* 30, 1856.

"GENTLEMEN: I received with deep sensibility your communication, informing me that a convention of my fellow-citizens, recently assembled in this city, have nominated me their candidate for the highest office in the gift of the American People; and I desire, through you, to offer to the members of that body, and to their respective constituencies, my grateful acknowledgment for this distinguished expression of confidence. In common with all who are interested in the welfare of the country, I had been strongly impressed by the generous spirit of conciliation which influenced the action of your assembly and characterizes your note. A disposition to avoid all special questions tending to defeat unanimity in the great cause, for the sake of which it was conceded that differences of opinion on less eventful questions should be held in abeyance, was evinced alike in the proceedings of your convention in reference to me, and in the manner by which you have communicated the result. In this course, no sacrifice of opinion on any side becomes necessary.

"I shall, in a few days, be able to transmit you a paper,* designed for all parties engaged in our cause, in which I present to the country my views of the leading subjects which are now put in issue in the contest for the presidency. My confidence in the success of our cause is greatly strengthened by the belief that these views will meet the approbation of your constituents.

"Trusting that the national and patriotic feelings evinced by the tender of your co-operation in the work of regenerating the government, may increase the glow of enthusiasm which pervades the country, and harmonize all elements in our truly great and common cause, I accept the nomination with which you have honored me, and am, gentlemen, very respectfully,

"Your fellow-citizen,

"J. C. Fremont."

Messrs. Thomas H. Ford, Ambrose Stephens, W. A. Howard, Stephen M. Allen, Simon P. Kase, Thomas Shankland, J. E. Dunham, M. C. Geer—a Committee of the National American party.

Since his nomination, more than half of the political journals of the free States have advocated his election, and public meetings throughout the country indicate a degree of enthusiasm in his support which, taking all the circumstances into consideration, is without a parallel in the history of American politics. His friends confidently predict his election by a nearly unanimous vote of the free States, and the developments of each succeeding day render them more and more sanguine.

* Letter of July 8, p. 456 *et seq.*

CHAPTER XIX.

CONCLUSION.

Col. Fremont is now but forty-three years of age. Though in the prime of life, he is already eminent. Before he was thirty he had enrolled his name among the most eminent explorers and geographers, and had given it to the rivers and the mountains and the productions of the soil, which he was the first to explore. Before he was thirty-five, he had emancipated an empire from Mexican tyranny, and was unanimously elected its governor by those whom he had delivered. When but thirty-seven, he was elected to the highest legislative dignity in the American republic; and within the last year, his earlier distinctions have been thrown into comparative obscurity by his selection as the national champion of freedom and civilization in the approaching Presidential election. His nomination at Philadelphia on the 19th of June, gave symmetry and completeness to a career which is more commended by its results to the American people than that of any man, at his years, whom the country has produced.

Col. Fremont is about five feet nine inches high, slight and sinewy in his structure, but gracefully proportioned and eminently prepossessing in his personal appearance. His eyes are blue and very large, his nose aquiline, his forehead, over which his brown curling hair is parted at the centre, is high and capacious. He never shaves, but wears his beard neatly trimmed.

His head as well as person are strikingly symmetrical, and indicate the compact strength and symmetry of character which he has displayed through life. The height of his head above the ears also reveals the elevation of his sentiments and the general benevolence and purity of his nature.

Scarcely any trait of his character will impress a stranger sooner than his modesty. He never dwells upon his own achievements, and rarely alludes to them except when specially invited. Even in his reports, his own personality is as much concealed as it could be without making them unintelligible. He has a soft, clear and gentle voice, and in conversation speaks deliberately, but with the utmost precision and clearness. He always knows exactly what he means to say when he begins a sentence, and rarely if ever changes or repeats a word in the enunciation of it. His mind is eminently orderly and logical, and though without any propensity for metaphysical speculations, his faculties of induction are very superior. Like Washington, whom he resembles in many other respects, he generalizes with rapidity, but always for practical results, and rarely or never to test hypotheses.

His accomplishments are manifold. Of course he understands surveying and engineering; his reports display a familiarity with the sciences of Astronomy, Botany, Mineralogy and Geology. He was distinguished at school, Dr. Roberton tells us, for his knowledge of the Latin and Greek languages, besides which he speaks French and Spanish as fluently as English. It is not too much to say that we have had no President since the time of Jefferson who could appear to equal advantage, or fill so exalted a seat, in the literary or scientific circles of his generation.

In his manners he is eminently well bred and refined, and always prepossesses a new acquaintance in his favor. He is sensitive to anything affecting his character, but slow to take offence, or to suspect the motives of men. He has twice in his life appealed to what is termed the code of honor, but never for the redress of merely personal wrongs. In both instances, the particulars of which are recorded in the foregoing pages, he was the victim of a combination formed to break down a party and principles of which he happened to occupy the position of a protector. In the affair with Senator Foote, he represented the party of freedom in California, and as the son-in-law of Col. Benton, was a very suitable target for the archery of that class of politicians who had felt that the best, if not the only way of securing an immunity for their own mischievous designs, was to drive that fearless statesman from the Senate, and if possible, from public life. Had Col. Fremont tolerated the first insult, it would have been repeated with aggravations in twenty-four hours. He saw that his usefulness as a senator, and his influence as a public man depended upon his putting an end at once to the impression, if it existed in any quarter, that his character could be trifled with by any one. For such a purpose he was willing to risk his life.

In the case of Mason, he thought he saw a disposition to sacrifice him for having presumed to win sudden distinction in the army by unusual services, without the aid of a diploma from West Point. In five years he had risen to the rank of lieutenant-colonel in the army, over the heads of hundreds of officers who had enjoyed better opportunities than he of doing what he had done, but who lacked the necessary ability, or ambition.

When Col. Fremont detected this jealousy, and felt the indignities which were the fruit of it, he suddenly found himself the representative and champion of the small but valuable class of men who, by extraordinary devotion to their profession, provoke the envy of the larger and meaner class who are unwilling to make similar exertions or sacrifices. If he had submitted to Mason's insolence, patiently, he would have proved recreant to the class of which he was the exponent, and have forsaken the high position he had secured, and which, by the course he pursued, he not only maintained, but entrenched impregnably. Had he yielded, he would never have received the compliment soon afterwards paid him by President Taylor, and which he properly interpreted as a deliberate justification of his conduct, from the highest military as well as civil authority in the country. Except in cases where the rights and interests of others were, to some extent, in his keeping, Col. Fremont has never appealed to the code of honor for the redress of personal wrongs.

His domestic tastes are very decided, and he has a rooted aversion to the ordinary metropolitan gaieties. He is extremely temperate in his habits, though he makes no merit of it, and does not use tobacco in any form, nor profane language; three peculiarities which distinguish him honorably from most of our public men.

In all the manifold relations of father, husband, friend and neighbor, his character is unimpeached and unimpeachable. He was confirmed as a member of the Protestant Episcopal church in Charleston, when he was sixteen years of age, and at a time when he was under very profound religious convictions. He became so much absorbed by the subject of religion at this time, as to inspire his friends with a general expectation that he would devote himself to the ministry. He used to study and commit chapter after chapter of the Bible to memory—sometimes as many as three hundred verses a day—and fatigued his instructors with the length of his biblical recitations. Upon leaving Charleston and embarking in the career which has occupied his adult life, he has rarely enjoyed the privilege of worshipping in a Christian country. He has had all his children, however, baptized in the Episcopal church, and since his return to the United States, has been in the habit of attending the churches of that denomination.

As a candidate for the presidency, Col. Fremont enjoys some rare advantages over any competitor for that honor, for he is not identified with any old political controversies, except the one which constitutes the controlling issue in the present canvass. Though a democrat from principle, and by political association, he has never been a partisan, and though always opposed to the extension of slavery, his name has never been associated with any of the lateral issues to which that institution has given rise. Though never a politician, and with but little experience as a statesman, no man of his age was so universally, and, at the same time, so favorably known to the whole country, when his name was suggested as the leader of the party of freedom. His adventures and discoveries had been the theme of conversation and of inexhaustible wonder in every village and hamlet throughout the Union, and "none named him but to praise." He was not therefore, an unknown man in any part of his country, though he had probably never attended a political caucus in his life.

But he has other qualities which specially commend him to his countrymen at the present time; a courage which renders him insensible to any form of intimidation, and a coolness and caution which are equally important guaranties against impetuosity and indiscretion. If he is elected, no one supposes that he will be afraid to act according to his inclinations or convictions, and every one feels that we have long stood much in need of such a President. The country is rapidly approaching a crisis when the civilization of half a century will be staked upon the firmness, wisdom and justice of our chief magistrate. Fremont is looked upon by the great body of his countrymen in the free States, as the fittest exponent of the highest and best interests of civilization that has been named in connection with the presidency for many years. He is identified in their minds with the great struggle for freedom on this continent, and upon his success or failure, the hopes of many, for the future of this republic, are suspended.

APPENDIX.

[A]

REPORT OF SENATOR BREESE, OF ILLINOIS.

UNITED STATES SENATE, AUGUST 1, 1848.

The Select Committee, to whom was referred the resolution of the Senate to inquire into the expediency of providing for the publication of the result of the late Exploring Expedition of John. C. Fremont to California and Oregon, to be published as a national work, free from copyright, and subject to the disposition of Congress; and also to inquire into the expediency of providing for the continuation and completion of the Surveys and Explorations of the said John C. Fremont, with a view to develope the geographical character of the country, and the practicability of establishing railroads or other communications between the Valley of the Mississippi and the Pacific Ocean, the result of said farther Surveys and Explorations to be also published as a national work, free from copyright, and subject to the disposition of Congress respectfully ask leave to report:

That it is a matter of great public interest, the committee believe, for the government and for the people of the United States to become accurately acquainted with the value of the large possessions, now belonging to the United States, beyond the Rocky Mountains, and also with the means of communicating with those possessions and with the Pacific Ocean, on which they border, by railroads or other modes of travel and conveyance; and the committee believe, from the knowledge they have of the inclination of Mr. Fremont's mind, his habits and pursuits, and his already great acquaintance with the countries in question, acquired through extraordinary perseverance, to be peculiarly well fitted to give to the government and to the people the information it is so desirable for them to possess in relation to the value of California and Oregon, and the means of communicating with them.

From the early age of seventeen, as the committee are informed, Mr. Fremont has been almost constantly engaged in astronomical and geographical pursuits, and nearly the whole time in the open field, and the last six years in the country beyond the Mississippi and the Rocky Mountains. He has made three expeditions to those remote and interesting regions. The results of the two first were published by order of Congress, and commanded general applause both in this country and in Europe. The celebrated Baron Humboldt, and the President of the Royal Geological and Royal Geographical Societies, London, have spoken of them in most favorable terms, and eminent scientific men and journals of our own country have yielded equal commendation. (See appendix to this report.) An assistant of the celebrated Nicollet who was a distinguished member of the French National Institute, he has reached a most commanding position as a scientific explorer, and achieved for himself the designation of the American Humboldt.

The first question with the committee was to inquire into the expediency of publishing, as a national work free of copyright, and subject to the disposition of Congress, the results of this last or third expedition of Mr. Fremont; and, although favorably impressed with the value of these results, from the previous labors and character of the author, it was deemed proper to inquire into the real character of the proposed publication, means for forming some judgment on this point being already at hand in the manuscript map of Oregon and California, (now in the hands of the lithographer, and which several of the committee have examined), and also in the geographical memoir to illustrate that map, published by order of the Senate, and which, it is presumed, all have read. This map and memoir, in the judgment of the committee, not only sustain the previous reputation of the author, but enhance it, as might well be expected from a more ripened intellect, from a more experienced explorer and from a spirit ardent in the pursuit of science, and excited by applause to higher exertions. This map and memoir, though hastily prepared, and as a mere preliminary to a full work, increase the reputation of their author, and give valuable information to the statesman and the farmer, to the astronomer and geographer, to the man of science in the walks of botany and meteorology. But they must be regarded only as a sample of the results of that expedition, from the view of which the value of the whole may be judged. As far as the exploration has been carried, everything necessary to show climate, soil, and productions, has been collected. More than one thousand specimens in botany, a great number in geology and mineralogy, with drawings of birds and animals, and remarkable scenery, and a large collection of the skins of birds, with the plumage preserved, have been, as the committee are informed, brought home, to enrich the stores and add to the sum of human knowledge. The botanical specimens, examined by Dr. Torrey, are deemed by him of great value, and worthy of the expense of European engraving, if not done by our own government.

The committee upon this view of the results of the last expedition of Mr. Fremont, deem them of great national importance, giving just ideas of Oregon and California, and such as ought to be published in the manner suggested in the resolution under consideration. The continuation of the surveys and explorations by Mr. Fremont, with a view to complete our knowledge of the great country between the Mississippi and the Pacific ocean, is the remaining inquiry referred to this committee; and of the expediency of providing for such continuation they entertain no doubt. It is, in their judgment, but carrying out the plain suggestion of reason, and the plan of Mr. Jefferson, when he sent Lewis and Clark to th Pacific ocean.

The committee think they do not err when they assume it as an indisputable position, that the public interest and the wishes of the people require further examinations into the character of the soil, climate and productions; the geology, botany, and mineralogy of Oregon and California; and also into the practicability of railroad and other communications between those countries and the valley of the Mississippi, to which the public attention has been lately, and is now, so much excited, and they do not hesitate to say, that Mr. Fremont is one of the most, if not the most, suitable person to make these examinations, and a publication of the results, under the direction of Congress, and without copyright, as the most judicious and advantageous mode of publication. Mr. Fremont has spent six years of his life in explorations to these distant regions, and in that time has crossed the Rocky Mountains, as the committee are informed, at seven different points; has traversed the country from the Mississippi on several different lines, and has made about twenty thousand miles of exploration in wilderness countries, and understands thoroughly, there is no doubt, the general structure and configuration of the country, and knows where to go and what to do to complete his examinations. He has shown himself to be possessed of all the qualifications for such an enterprise, with resources to supply wants, to conquer difficulties, and to command success—and talent to execute his task to the satisfaction and admiration of his own countrymen, and of the first men in Europe.

The committee learn with pleasure that it is Mr. Fremont's own desire to finish up the great work in which he was so unexpectedly interrupted in the course of the last year. No other person probably could, for the reasons stated, do the work so well, or in so short a time, or at so small an expense. No other person could be employed in the work without appropriating to himself the fruits of his long and arduous labors, and building upon foundations which he has laid, and taking the credit of operations which only want the finishing hand of their author to erect a monument of honor to himself and of utility to his country. It therefore seems but an act of justice to this individual that he should be continued in a work which he commenced, and has thus far so successfully prosecuted.

In his geographical memoir, printed by order of the Senate, Mr. Fremont proposes to continue and complete his explorations in Oregon and California, and to publish the results under the direction of Congress, as a national work, and without copyright. It is the mode in which the results of his previous expeditions have been published, and with great advantage to the public, as all will acknowledge, his journals and maps being reprinted, and multiplied in cheap editions, as well in Europe as in this country, and thus all his discoveries, and all the information he acquired, passing at once into the mass of general knowledge. It is deemed by the committee, the proper mode of disseminating useful information obtained at the expense of the government, and which should be diffused at once without the impediment of copyrights, and the author, where deserving it, compensated in some other form for any extraordinary service which he has rendered. * * * *

The committee, therefore, feeling all the reasons in favor of such explorations, to be greatly increased by the recent acquisition of California, and the exclusive possession of Oregon, and where so much has been done towards exploring Oregon and California, ascertaining practicable routes for a railroad or other communications between the Valley of the Mississippi and the Pacific Ocean, and for publishing the results as a national work under the direction of Congress, and without a copyright; they have with one accord directed their chairman to move the necessary appropriation, to wit, $30,000, being the amount usually appropriated for topographical surveys beyond the Mississippi.

EXTRACT OF A LETTER FROM THE HON. EDWARD EVERETT.

CAMBRIDGE, MASS., *March* 20, 1846.

"DEAR SIR: A short time since, I sent two copies of the Congressional documents, containing Captain Fremont's two reports, to London, one to Doctor Holland (who spoke of you with great kindness on his return to Boston,) and one to Sir R. I. Murchison, late president both of the Geological and Geographical societies, and one of the most eminent British geologists. In a letter received from the last named gentleman, by the steamer of the 4th March, he speaks in the following terms of Captain Fremont's report:

"'The work of Captain Fremont so much interested me, (it is really the most romantic, as well as instructive survey,) that I wrote out a little analysis of it, for the president of our geological society, Mr. Horner,* and if he has not space enough to do it justice in his anniversary discourse, I will take care that the excellent services of your countryman, are duly noticed in the speech of Lord Colchester, my successor as President of the Royal Geographical Society. Knowing your connection with Captain Fremont, I have thought it might be some satisfaction to you to learn that his labors were appreciated by good judges abroad. I should long since have made him my personal acknowledgments for the gratification and instruction which I have derived from his reports, had I had the honor of his acquaintance. I should have sent more copies to England could I have procured them.'"

[B.]

EXTRACT FROM A LETTER FROM THE UNITED STATES CONSUL, WARREN, TRIESTE.

"I travelled, not as I first intended, over Hamburgh and Berlin to this city, but took a passage to Leghorn, from which place I

*Mr. Lyell's father-in-law.

proceeded to Trieste. I availed myself of a favorable opportunity to forward the books which you intrusted to my care, to Baron von Humboldt. During the month I obtained a short leave of absence from my post, and proceeded to the north of Germany. Whilst at Berlin, I had an interview with Baron von Humboldt. He bade me thank you for the present with which you had so favored him. He had already in his possession 'Fremont's reports,' but not Nicollet's work. He put some questions to me in relation to yourself, your political career, your age, and so forth, to which I gave full replies. He then inquired in relation to Col. Fremont, whose work he said had been read by him with great interest as the work of a man of talent, courage, industry, and enterprise. These were the words literally used by Mr. von Humboldt.

"Extracts from the reports which have made their appearance in many of the German papers, and the scientific world (through the republication of the work by Wiley & Putnam in London), has become generally acquainted with it; and I can say truly, from the conversation I have had on the subject with many men entitled to a judgment, it is appreciated as a very able work."

[C.]

PACIFIC RAILROAD.

LETTER FROM COLONEL FREMONT GIVING THE RESULTS OF HIS FIFTH EXPEDITION IN 1854—5, WITH SPECIAL REFERENCE TO THE MOST PRACTICABLE ROUTE FOR A RAILWAY TO THE PACIFIC.

To the Editors of the National Intelligencer:

GENTLEMEN: While the proceedings in Congress are occupying public attention, more particularly with the subject of a Pacific Railway, I desire to offer to your paper, for publication, some general results of a recent winter expedition across the Rocky Mountains, confining myself to mere results, in anticipation of a fuller report, with maps and illustrations, which will necessarily require some months to prepare.

The country examined was for about three-fourths of the distance—from the Missouri frontier, at the mouth of the Kansas river, to the valley of Parawan, at the foot of the Wahsatch Mountains, within the rim of the Great Basin, at its southeastern bend—along and between the 38th and 39th parallels of latitude; and the whole line divides itself naturally into three sections, which may be conveniently followed in description.

The *first* or eastern section consists of the great prairie slope, spreading from the base of the *Sierra Blanca* to the Missouri frontier, about 700 miles; the *second* or middle section, comprehends the various Rocky Mountain ranges and interlying valleys, between the termination of the Great Plains at the foot of the *Sierra Blanca*, and the Great Basin of the Parawan Valley and Wahsatch Mountains, where the first Mormon settlement is found, about 450 miles; the *third* or western section comprehends the mountainous plateau lying between the Wahsatch Mountains and the *Sierra Nevada*, a distance of about 400 miles.

The country examined was upon a very direct line, the travelled route being about 1,550 miles over an air-line distance of about 1,300 miles.

The First Section.—Four separate expeditions across this section, made before the present one, and which carried me over various lines at different seasons of the year, enable me to speak of it with the confidence of intimate knowledge. It is a plain of easy inclination, sweeping directly up to the foot of the mountains which dominate it as highlands do the ocean. Its character is open prairie, over which summer travelling is made in every direction.

For a railway or a winter-travelling road, the route would be, in consideration of wood, coal, building-stone, water, and fertile land, about two hundred miles up the immediate valley of Kansas (which might be made one rich continuous cornfield), and afterwards along the immediate valley of the Upper Arkansas, of which about two hundred miles, as you approach the mountains, is continuously well adapted to settlements as well as to roads. Numerous well watered and fertile valleys—broad and level—open up among the mountains, which present themselves in detached blocks—outliers—gradually closing in around the heads of the streams, but leaving open approaches to the central ridges. The whole of the inter-mountain region is abundant in grasses, wood, coal, and fertile soil. The *Pueblos* above Bent's Fort, prove it to be well adapted to the grains and vegetables common to the latitude, including Indian corn, which ripens well, and to the support of healthy stock, which increase well and take care of themselves summer and winter.

The climate is mild and the winters short, the autumn usually having its full length of bright open weather, without snow, which in winter falls rarely and passes off quickly. In this belt of country lying along the mountains, the snow falls more early and much more thinly than in the open plains to the eastward; the storms congregate about the high mountains and leave the valleys free. In the beginning of December we found yet no snow on the *Huerfano* River, and were informed by an old resident, then engaged in establishing a farm at the mouth of this stream, that snow seldom or never falls there, and that cattle were left in the range all the winter through.

This character of country continued to the foot of the dividing crest, and to this point our journey resulted in showing a very easy grade for a road, over a country unobstructed either by snow or other impediments, and having all the elements necessary to the prosperity of an agricultural population, in fertility of soil, abundance of food for stock, wood and coal for fuel, and timber for necessary constructions.

Our examinations around the southern headwaters of the Arkansas, have made us acquainted with many passes, grouped together in a small space of country, conducting by short and practicable valleys from the waters of the Arkansas just described, to the valleys of the *Del Norte* and East Colorado. The *Sierra Blanca*, through which these passes lie, is high and rugged, presenting a very broken appearance, but rises abruptly from the open country on either side, narrowed at the points through which the passes are cut, leaving them only six or eight miles in length from valley to valley, and entirely unobstructed by outlying ranges or broken country. To the best of these passes the ascent is along the open valley of watercourses, uniform and very gradual in ascent. Standing immediately at the mouth of the *Sand Hill Pass*—one of the most practicable in the *Sierra Blanca*, and above those usually travelled—at one of the remotest headsprings of the *Huerfano* River, the eye of the traveller follows down without obstruction or abrupt descent along the gradual slope of the valley to the great plains which reach the Missouri. The straight river and the open valley form, with the plains beyond, one great slope, without a hill to break the line of sight or obstruct the course of the road. On either side of this line hills slope easily to the river, with lines of timber and yellow autumnal grass, and the water, which flows smoothly between, is not interrupted by a fall in its course to the ocean. The surrounding country is wooded with pines and covered with luxuriant grasses, up to the very crags of the central summits. On the 8th of December we found this whole country free from snow and Daguerre views taken at this time show the grass entirely uncovered in the passes.

Along all this line the elevation was carefully determined by frequent barometrical observations, and its character exhibited by a series of daguerreotype views, comprehending the face of the country almost continuously, or at least sufficiently so, to give a thoroughly correct impression of the whole.

Two tunnel-like passes pierce the mountains here, almost in juxtaposition, connecting the plain country on either side by short passages five to eight miles long. The mountains which they perforate constitute the only obstruction, and are the only break in the plane or valley line of road from the frontier of Missouri to the summit hills of the Rocky Mountains, a distance of about 850 miles, or more than half way to the San Joaquin valley. Entering one of these passes from the eastern plain, a distance of about one mile upon a wagon road, already travelled by wagons, commands an open view of the broad valley of *San Luis* and the great range of *San Juan* beyond on its western side. I here connected the line of the present expedition with one explored in 1848–'49 from the mouth of the Kansas to this point, and the results of both will be embodied in a full report.

At this place the line entered the middle section, and continued its western course over an open valley country, admirably adapted for settlement, across the *San Luis* valley, and up the flat bottom lands of the Sah-watch to the heights of the central ridge of the Rocky Mountains. Across those wooded heights—wooded and grass-covered up to and over their rounded summits—to the Coocha-to-pe pass, the line followed an open easy wagon-way, such as is usual to a rolling country. On the high summit lands were forests of coniferous trees, and the snow in the pass was four inches deep. This was on the 14th of December. A day earlier our horses' feet would not have touched snow in the crossing. Up to this point we had enjoyed clear and dry pleasant weather. Our journey had been all along on dry ground; and travelling slowly along waiting for the winter, there had been abundant leisure for becoming acquainted with the country. The open character of the country, joined to good information, indicated the existence of other passes about the head of the Sah-watch. This it was desirable to verify, and especially to examine a neighboring and lower pass connecting more directly with the Arkansas valley, known as the Poow-che.

But the winter had now set in over all the mountain regions, and the country was so constantly enveloped and hidden in clouds which rested upon it, and the air so darkened by falling snow, that exploring became difficult and dangerous, precisely where we felt most interested in making a thorough examination. We were moving in fogs and clouds, through a region wholly unknown to us, and without guides, and were therefore obliged to content ourselves with the examination of a single line, and the ascertainment of the winter condition of the country over which it passed; which was in fact the main object of our expedition.

Our progress in this mountainous region was necessarily slow, and during ten days which it occupied us to pass through about one hundred miles of the mountainous country bordering the eastern side of the Upper Colorado valley, the greatest depth of snow was, among the pines and aspens, on the ridges about two and a half feet, and in the valleys about six inches. The atmosphere is too cold and dry for much snow, and the valleys, protected by the mountains, are comparatively free from it, and warm. We here found villages of Utah Indians in their wintering ground, in little valleys along the foot of the highest mountains and bordering the more open country of the Colorado valley. Snow was here (December 25) only a few inches deep—the grass generally appearing above it, and there being none under trees and on southern hill-sides.

The horses of the *Utahs* were living on the range, and notwithstanding that they were used in hunting, were in excellent condition. One which we had occasion to kill for food had on it about two inches of fat, being in as good order as any buffalo we had killed in November on the eastern plains. Over this valley country—about 150 miles across—the Indians informed us that snow falls only a few inches in depth, such as we saw it at the time.

The immediate valley of the Upper Colorada for about 100 miles in breath, and from the 7th to the 22d of January, was entirely bare of snow, and the weather resembled that of autumn in this country. The line here entered the body of mountains known as the *Wa-satch* and *Chu-ter-ria* ranges, which are practicable at several places in this part of their course; but the falling snow and destitute condition of my party again interfered to impede examinations. They lie between the Colorado valley and the Great Basin, and at their western base are established the Mormon settlements of Parawan and Cedar City. They are what are called fertile mountains, abundant in water, wood, and grass, and fertile valleys, offering inducements to settlement and facilities for making a road. These mountains are a great store-house of materials—timber, iron, coal—which would be of indispensable use in the construction and maintenance of the road, and are solid foundations to build up the future prosperity of the rapidly-increasing Utah State.

Salt is abundant on the eastern border mountains, as the *Sierra de Sal*, being named from it. In the ranges lying behind the Mormon settlements, among the mountains through which the line passes, are accumulated a great wealth of iron and coal, and extensive forests of heavy timber. These forests are the largest I am acquainted with in the Rocky Mountains, being in some places twenty miles in depth of continuous forest; the general growth lofty and large, frequently over three feet in diameter, and sometimes reaching five feet, the red spruce and yellow pine predominating. At the actual southern extremity of the Mormon settlements, consisting of the two enclosed towns of Parawan and Cedar City, near to which our line passed, a coal mine has been opened for about eighty yards, and iron works already established. Iron here occurs in extraordinary masses, in some parts accumulated into mountains, which come out in crests of solid iron thirty feet thick and a hundred yards long.

In passing through this bed of mountains about fourteen days had been occupied, from January 24th to February 7th, the deepest snow we here encountered being about up to the saddle-skirts, or four feet; this occurring only in occasional drifts in the passes on northern exposures, and in the small mountain flats hemmed in by woods and hills. In the valley it was sometimes a few inches deep, and as often none at all. On our arrival at the Mormon settlements, February 8th, we found it a few inches deep, and were there informed that the winter had been unusually long-continued and severe, the thermometer having been as low as 17° below zero, and more snow having fallen than in all the previous winters together since the establishment of this colony.

At this season their farmers had usually been occupied with their ploughs, preparing the land for grain.

At this point the line of exploration entered the *third* or western section, comprehending the mountainous *plateau* between the Wahsatch Mountains and the Sierra Nevada of California. Two routes have suggested themselves to me for examination, one directly across the *plateau*, between the 37th and 38th parallels; the other keeping to the south of the mountains and following for about 200 miles down a valley of the *Rio Virgen*—Virgin River—thence direct to the Tejon Pass, at the head of the San Joaquin valley. This route down the Virgin River had been examined the year before with a view to settlement this summer by a Mormon exploring party under the command of Major Steele of Parawan, who (and others of the party) informed me that they found fertile valleys inhabited by Indians who cultivated corn and melons, and the rich ground in many places matted over with grape vines. The Tejon Passes are two, one of them (from the abundance of vines at its lower end) called *Caxon de las Uvas*. They were of long use, and were examined by me and their practicability ascertained in my expedition of 1848–'49, and in 1851 I again passed through them both, bringing three thousand head of cattle through one of them.

Knowing the practicability of these passes, and confiding in the report of Major Steele as to the intermediate country, I determined to take the other (between the 37th and 38th parallels), it recommending itself to me as being more direct towards San Francisco, and preferable on that account for a road, if suitable ground could be found; and also as being unknown. The Mormons informed me, that various attempts had been made to explore it, and all failed for want of water. Although biased in favor of the Virgin River route, I determined to examine this one in the interest of geography, and accordingly set out for this purpose from the settlement about the 20th of February, travelling directly westward from Cedar City (eighteen miles west of Parawan). We found the country a high table land, bristling with mountains, often in short isolated blocks, and sometimes accumulated into considerable ranges, with numerous open and low passes.

We were thus always in a valley and always surrounded by mountains more or less closely, which apparently altered in shape and position as we advanced. The valleys are dry and naked, without water or wood; but the mountains are generally covered with grass and well wooded with pines; springs are very rare, and occasionally small streams are at remote distances. Not a human being was encountered between the Santa Clara road, near the Mormon Settlements and the *Sierra Nevada*, over a distance of more than 300 miles. The solitary character of this uninhabited region, the naked valleys without watercourses, among mountains with fertile soil and grass and woods abundant, give it the appearance of an unfinished country.

Commencing on the 38th, we struck the Sierra Nevada on or about the 37th parallel about the 15th March.

On our route across we had for the greater part of the time pleasant and rather warm weather; the valley grounds and low ridges uncovered, but snow over the upper parts of the higher mountains. Between the 20th of February and 17th of March we had several snow-storms, sometimes accompanied with hail and heavy thunder; but the snow remained on the valley ground only a few hours after the storm was over. It forms not the least impediment at any time of the winter. I was prepared to find the Sierra here broad, rugged, and blocked up with snow, and was not disappointed in my expectation. The first range we attempted to cross carried us to an elevation of 8,000 or 9,000 feet and into impassable snow, which was further increased on the 16th by a considerable fall.

There was no object in forcing a passage, and I accordingly turned at once some sixty or eighty miles to the southward, making a wide sweep to strike the *Point of the California Mountain* where the Sierra Nevada suddenly breaks off and declines into a lower country. Information obtained years before from the Indians led me to believe, that the low mountains were broken into many passes, and at all events I had the certainty of an easy passage through either of Walker's passes.

When the Point was reached I found the Indian information fully verified; the mountain suddenly terminated and broke down into lower grounds barely above the level of the country, and making numerous openings into the valley of the San Joaquin. I entered into the first which offered (taking no time to search, as we were entirely out of provisions and living upon horses), which led us by an open and almost level hollow thirteen miles long to an upland not steep enough to be called a hill, over into the valley of a small affluent to Kern River; the hollow and the valley making together a way where a wagon would not find any obstruction for forty miles.

The country around the passes in which the Sierra Nevada here terminates, declines considerably below its more northern elevations. There was no snow to be seen at all on its eastern face, and none in the pass; but we were in the midst of opening spring, flowers blooming in fields on both sides of the Sierra.

Between the point of the mountains and the head of the valley at the Tejon the passes generally are free from snow throughout the year, and the descent from them to the ocean is distributed over a long slope of more than 200 miles. The low dry country and the long slope, in contradistinction to the high country and short sudden descent and heavy snows of the passes behind the bay of San Francisco, are among the considerations which suggest themselves in favor of the route by the head of the San Joaquin.

The above results embody general impressions made upon my mind during this journey. It is clearly established, that the winter condition of the country constitutes no impediment, and from what has been said, the entire practicability of the line will be as clearly inferred. A fuller account hereafter will comprehend detailed descriptions of the country, with their absolute and relative elevations, and show the ground upon which the conclusions were based. They are contributed at this time as an element to aid the public in forming an opinion on the subject of the projected railway, and in gratification of my great desire to do something for its advancement. It seems a treason against mankind and the spirit of progress which marks the age, to refuse to put this one completing link to our national prosperity and the civilization of the world. Europe still lies between Asia and America: build this railroad and things will have revolved about: America will lie between Asia and Europe—the golden vein which runs through the history of the world will follow the iron track to San Fransisco, and the Asiatic trade will finally fall into its last and permanent road, when the new and the modern Chryse throw open their gates to the thoroughfare of the world.

I am, gentlemen, with much regard, respectfully yours,

J. C. FREMONT.

WASHINGTON, *June* 18.

FINIS.

www.ingramcontent.com/pod-product-compliance
Lightning Source LLC
LaVergne TN
LVHW020915110826
845150LV00004B/684

9781425555955